Linguistic Inquiries into Donald Trump's Language

Also available from Bloomsbury

More Wordcrime, John Olsson
Political Metaphor Analysis, by Andreas Musolff
The Art of Political Storytelling, by Philip Seargeant
The Language of Brexit, by Steve Buckledee

Linguistic Inquiries into Donald Trump's Language

From 'Fake News' to 'Tremendous Success'

Edited by
Ulrike Schneider and Matthias Eitelmann

BLOOMSBURY ACADEMIC
LONDON • NEW YORK • OXFORD • NEW DELHI • SYDNEY

BLOOMSBURY ACADEMIC
Bloomsbury Publishing Plc
50 Bedford Square, London, WC1B 3DP, UK
1385 Broadway, New York, NY 10018, USA
29 Earlsfort Terrace, Dublin 2, Ireland

BLOOMSBURY, BLOOMSBURY ACADEMIC and the Diana logo are trademarks of
Bloomsbury Publishing Plc

First published in Great Britain 2020
This paperback edition published in 2022

Copyright © Ulrike Schneider, Matthias Eitelmann and Contributors, 2020
Ulrike Schneider and Matthias Eitelmann have asserted their right under the Copyright, Designs and Patents Act, 1988, to be identified as Editors of this work.

For legal purposes the Acknowledgments on p. x constitute an extension of this copyright page.

Cover design by Ben Anslow

All rights reserved. No part of this publication may be reproduced or transmitted in any form or by any means, electronic or mechanical, including photocopying, recording, or any information storage or retrieval system, without prior permission in writing from the publishers.

Bloomsbury Publishing Plc does not have any control over, or responsibility for, any third-party websites referred to or in this book. All internet addresses given in this book were correct at the time of going to press. The author and publisher regret any inconvenience caused if addresses have changed or sites have ceased to exist, but can accept no responsibility for any such changes.

A catalogue record for this book is available from the British Library.

Library of Congress Cataloging-in-Publication Data
Names: Schneider, Ulrike, 1982- editor. | Eitelmann, Matthias, editor.
Title: Linguistic inquiries into Donald Trump's language: from 'fake news' to 'tremendous success' / edited by Ulrike Schneider and Matthias Eitelmann.
Description: London; New York: Bloomsbury Academic, 2020. | Includes bibliographical references and index.
Identifiers: LCCN 2020026395 (print) | LCCN 2020026396 (ebook) | ISBN 9781350115514 (hardback) | ISBN 9781350115521 (ebook) | ISBN 9781350115538 (epub)
Subjects: LCSH: Trump, Donald, 1946—Language. | Trump, Donald, 1946—Oratory. | Communication in politics–United States–History–21st century. | Rhetoric–Political aspects–United States. | Discourse analysis–Political aspects–United States. | Social media–Political aspects–United States. | United States–Politics and government–2009-2017. | United States–Politics and government–2017-
Classification: LCC E913.3 .L56 2020 (print) | LCC E913.3 (ebook) | DDC 973.933092—dc23
LC record available at https://lccn.loc.gov/2020026395
LC ebook record available at https://lccn.loc.gov/2020026396

ISBN: HB: 978-1-3501-1551-4
PB: 978-1-3501-8630-9
ePDF: 978-1-3501-1552-1
eBook: 978-1-3501-1553-8

Typeset by Deanta Global Publishing Services, Chennai, India

To find out more about our authors and books visit www.bloomsbury.com and sign up for our newsletters.

Contents

List of Illustrations — vii
Acknowledgments — x

1 From *Fake News* to *Tremendous Success*: Introduction
   Matthias Eitelmann and Ulrike Schneider — 1

Part I Rhetoric and Repetition

2 *It's Just Words, Folks. It's Just Words*: Donald Trump's Distinctive Linguistic Style
   Jesse Egbert and Douglas Biber — 17
3 *I Know Words, I Have the Best Words*: Repetitions, Parallelisms, and Matters of (In)Coherence
   Kristina Nilsson Björkenstam and Gintarė Grigonytė — 41
4 *A Man who Was Just an Incredible Man, an Incredible Man*: Age Factors and Coherence in Donald Trump's Spontaneous Speech
   Patricia Ronan and Gerold Schneider — 62

Part II Evaluation and Emotion

5 *Very Emotional, Totally Conservative,* and *Somewhat All over the Place*: An Analysis of Intensifiers in Donald Trump's Speech
   Ulrike Stange — 87
6 *Crooked Hillary, Lyin' Ted*, and *Failing* New York Times: Nicknames in Donald Trump's Tweets
   Jukka Tyrkkö and Irina Frisk — 109
7 *I'm Doing Great with the Hispanics. Nobody Knows It*: The Distancing Effect of Donald Trump's *the*-Plurals
   Ulrike Schneider and Kristene K. McClure — 130

Part III Discourse and Metaphor

8 *Either We WIN this Election, or We Are Going to LOSE this Country!*: Trump's WARLIKE COMPETITION Metaphor
   Anthony Koth — 155

9   Silence and Denial: Trump's Discourse on the Environment
    Marta Degani and Alexander Onysko   173
10 Donald Trump's "Fake News" Agenda: A Pragmatic Account of
    Rhetorical Delegitimization
    Christoph Schubert   196
11 *Sorry Not Sorry*: Political Apology in the Age of Trump
    Jan David Hauck and Teruko Vida Mitsuhara   215

Part IV Conclusion

12 *Great Movement* versus *Crooked Opponents*: Is Donald Trump's
    Language Populist?
    Ulrike Schneider and Matthias Eitelmann   235

Notes on Contributors   251
Index   254

Illustrations

Figures

2.1	Key lexico-grammatical features of Donald Trump's discourse (exceeding threshold of > +/−0.8)	31
3.1	A comparison of the vocabulary used in the Clinton–Trump presidential debates	50
3.2	Proportion of utterances containing repetitions in the transcripts of the three presidential debates	51
3.3	Proportion of utterances containing repetitions in transcripts of speaking events during the Clinton and Trump presidential campaigns	52
3.4	A comparison of the total number of words (tokens) in the teleprompter scripts and the corresponding transcripts of the Trump campaign rallies in Bedford, New Hampshire (NH), West Palm Beach, Florida (FL), and Phoenix, Arizona (AZ)	53
3.5	Proportion of utterances containing repetitions in the teleprompter scripts and the corresponding transcripts of the Trump campaign rallies in Bedford, New Hampshire (NH), West Palm Beach, Florida (FL), and Phoenix, Arizona (AZ)	54
4.1	Use of vague semantic expressions in Donald Trump's language	70
4.2	Type–token ratios of presidential debates compared to Trump and Obama data	72
4.3	Average sentence length (mean) in political debates	73
4.4	Average sentence length (mean) in Donald Trump's spontaneous speech	74
4.5	Distribution of personal pronouns (PRP), nouns (N) and verbs (V) in Donald Trump's speech from the 1980s and 2010s and in Barack Obama's 2017 speech	76
4.6	Repetitions per 1,000 words	78
4.7	False starts in unscripted speech	78
4.8	Numbers of incoherencies and irrelevance per sentence	79
5.1	Frequency of selected intensifiers in tweets and in spoken language	94
5.2	Frequency of selected intensifiers in remarks and in spoken language	95
5.3	Collocational behavior of *totally* in Trump's tweets (frequency threshold: three occurrences)	98
5.4	Frequency of *truly* and *highly*	100
5.5	Intensification rates with *very*|*really*|*so*	100
5.6	Frequency of intensifier–adjective|adverb bigrams	101
5.7	Top five downtoners in Trump's tweets	103

5.8	Top five downtoners in COCA Spoken 2010–17	103
5.9	Frequency of intensifiers	105
6.1	Schematic diagram of the three dimensions of nicknaming	111
6.2	Trump's nicknames by category and referent	118
6.3	Breakdown of nicknames by referent and moral dimension	122
6.4	Multiple correspondence analysis of nickname features	124
6.5	Nicknames tweeted between January 2015 and December 2017	126
7.1	Graphical representation of Acton's (2019: 42) results	132
7.2	Percentage of *Democrats* and *Republicans* preceded by a definite article in tweets sent from Donald Trump's account	137
7.3	Rate of *the*-plurals in spoken references to *Latinos* and *Hispanics* over time	144
7.4	Rate of *the*-plurals of *Latinos* and *Hispanics* by semantic category	145
10.1	Trump's allegations of misrepresentation in primary election debates	203

Tables

2.1	Composition of the Presidential Debates Corpus	19
2.2	Lexico-Grammatical Features Included in the Key Feature Analysis	21
2.3	Keywords for Donald Trump, Divided into Semantic and Functional Categories	24
2.4	Positive Key Features	31
2.5	Negative Key Features	35
3.1	Excerpt from a Speech Trump Held in Phoenix, Arizona, on October 29, 2016	42
3.2	Selection of Trump Campaign Speaking Events 2016	47
3.3	Selection of Clinton Campaign Speaking Events 2016	47
3.4	Televised Debates between Presidential Candidates Clinton and Trump 2016	48
3.5	Excerpt from a Speech Trump Held in New Hampshire on September 29, 2016	49
3.6	Excerpt from a Speech Trump Held in Florida on October 13, 2016	55
3.7	Excerpt from a Speech Trump Held in New Hampshire on September 29, 2016	56
3.8	Excerpt from a Speech Trump Held in Florida on October 13, 2016	56
4.1	Data Sources	68
4.2	Mean Segmental Type–Token Ratio of Spontaneous Speech	71
4.3	Percentages of Subordinated versus Coordinated Clauses in Spontaneous Speech by Donald Trump	75
4.4	Sources	82
5.1	Dataset	92
5.2	Top Five Collocates of *Very*	96
5.3	Top Five Collocates of *So*	97

5.4	Top Five Collocates of *Totally*	98
5.5	Frequencies per 10,000 Words	101
5.6	Number of Relevant Hits for *Very|Really|So|Too|Totally* plus ADJ|ADV	106
5.7	Number of Relevant Hits for *Truly* and *Highly* plus ADJ|ADV	106
5.8	Number of Relevant Hits for Top Five Downtoners plus ADJ|ADV	106
7.1	Plural References to Demographic Groups in Trump's Tweets	139
7.2	Distribution of *Latinos* and *Hispanics* in the Factba.se Data	141
7.3	Contexts in which *Latinos* and *Hispanics* Are Used	142
8.1	IDEAS ARE FOOD	157
8.2	Conceptual Elements of the COMPETITION Source Domain	159
8.3	Trump's COMPETITION Word Choice	163
9.1	Details of Trump's Remarks on Energy and Environment	180
9.2	Metaphors Defining the Paris Accord	191
10.1	Republican Debates in the Dataset	202

Acknowledgments

We are grateful to all those engaged in the realization of this volume. First and foremost, we would like to thank our contributors without whom this volume would not be as multifaceted as it is. Special thanks go to Andrew Wardell and Becky Holland from Bloomsbury Academic, who supported this project from the start. We are especially grateful to our student assistants Pascal Peifer and Victoria Fox, who were an excellent help editing the manuscript. We would also like to thank Britta Mondorf, Chair of English Linguistics at the University of Mainz, for her support as well as our colleague Anke Lensch, who conducted the first inquiries into Donald Trump's language with us. Further thanks go to our students from various courses on political discourse and the language of Donald Trump, particularly to Julia Schilling for a continuous stream of the latest literature on Donald Trump's language and politics. Moreover, we are grateful to the audiences of our presentations on Donald Trump's Twitter voice given at the universities of Brighton and Augsburg, at ICAME 39 in Tampere and LAUD 2018 in Landau for the feedback and productive conversations—never did we have a better small talk topic than Donald Trump's language.

1

From *Fake News* to *Tremendous Success*

Introduction

Matthias Eitelmann and Ulrike Schneider

1.1 The Celebrity President

When Donald Trump announced his ambition to run for president in 2015—starting what would be an unprecedented campaign—he had already firmly established himself as a media personality known to the American public (and beyond).

First and foremost, people had come to know him as a businessman who heavily promoted the Trump brand as manifested in, for example, the New York Trump Tower or various Trump International Hotels in different US states. His public appearances as a businessman consistently strived to evoke an impression of 'tremendous success', which is underlined in several books with catchy titles such as *The Art of the Deal* (1987), *Think like a Billionaire: Everything You Need to Know About Success, Real Estate, and Life* (2004), or *Think Big and Kick Ass in Business and Life* (2007). In addition, Trump had become widely known as an entertainer: he had cameo appearances in movies (most famously *Home Alone 2: Lost in New York*, 1992) or TV series (e.g., *The Nanny*, 1996; *Sex and the City*, 1999) and was executive producer in the Miss USA and Miss Universe beauty pageants (2001–15). Of course, it was his role as host of *The Apprentice* (seven seasons, 2004–10) and *The Celebrity Apprentice* (seven seasons, 2008–15) that cemented his status as a TV icon, reinforcing the impression of business as competition in which only the best can excel while losers are dismissed once and for all (the decisive sentence being Trump's catchphrase "You're fired!"). Moreover, Trump had shown serious aspirations of a political career as early as 2000, then running for president as a candidate for the Reform Party, but he decided to end his campaign seeing that chances were slim (Pomper et al. 2001; Sides et al. 2012).[1]

Donald Trump's development from millionaire businessman and TV personality to American president has provoked extensive commentary on striking features of his language use particularly as Trump's language repertoire ranges from the boastful talk of "tremendous success" to the inflammatory, spiteful discourse on "fake news"—to name but two extremes. The fact that laypeople, journalists, and language experts all show a deep interest in how Trump speaks is due to the significant role that language plays in politics. As the prime instrument of persuasion in politics (Partington and Taylor 2018), language serves to appeal to the electorate, influence opinions to achieve positive results in polls, win over the majority of the electorate to prove successful at the ballot, and—once elected—promote agendas and policies. In this respect, *how* the political message is conveyed is just as important as *what* the politician's message actually is (even though in recent times, especially with the rise of populist parties and politicians all across the globe, content seems to play a minor role at times).

1.2 The Extraordinary President

Against this backdrop, it does not come as a surprise that the media abound with all kinds of claims about Donald Trump's language, which has been argued to be crucially different from that of his predecessors, political rivals, and other contemporary politicians. Some of these claims—each represented by one exemplary source here—concern perceptions of Trump's speaking style as non-presidential in various respects:

(i)   Trump only uses simple language. (Burleigh 2018)
(ii) Trump is incapable of forming coherent sentences. (Leith 2017)
(iii) Trump predominantly uses negative language. (Blake 2016)
(iv) Trump uses rude language, as evidenced by his extensive use of nicknames for his political opponents. (Flegenheimer 2018)
(v)   Trump speaks in extremes. (Pruden 2017)
(vi) Trump only thinks in black and white, adhering to a discourse of dualities. (Cofman Wittes and Goldenberg 2017)
(vii) Trump's body language is unique in its flamboyancy. (Van Edwards 2017)

Other claims aim at criticizing Trump more heavily, thus questioning his ability as US president more explicitly than by means of the previous claims:

(viii) Trump's language displays racist traits. (Holloway 2016)
(ix)   Trump's speech does not show signs of normal aging, but rather contains features characteristic of dementia. (Gartner 2019)
(x)   Trump has a narcissistic personality, which shows itself in an overuse of certain linguistic elements such as first-person pronouns. (Senior 2019)
(xi)   Trump uses typical salesmen's tactics, adopting the rhetoric of advertisers. (Acuna 2018)
(xii) Trump lies excessively (Dale 2019).

Claims such as these lean on language features in order to make inferences about Trump's political persona—at times, along the lines of 'if you don't like the content, ridicule the vessel.'[2] Some of these assessments, however, do not entirely hold water, and thus they offer an easy target for dismantlement.

A case in point concerns the first claim about Trump's allegedly simple speech style, which has been repeatedly commented upon in various press articles. In order to relay to the public how simple Trump's language is, his speech style is variously characterized as that of a third-, fourth-, fifth-, or sixth-grader (Shafer 2015; Smith 2016; Schumacher and Eskenazi 2016; Spice 2016; Burleigh 2018) or, in Shugerman's (2017) sensationalist terms, he is speaking "at the level of an 8-year-old." The message that authors attempt to drive home is that Trump talks like a (pre-)pubescent schoolchild—unable to produce anything more elaborate. Case closed.

Yet, we need to take a step back and look at the studies underlying these reports. Most of them are based on the so-called Flesch-Kincaid test (Kincaid et al. 1975), a tool to measure *reading* comprehensibility. The test estimates the complexity of *written* texts based on sentence length and numbers of syllables per word (the assumption being that multisyllabic words are part of a more formal, sophisticated vocabulary). It then estimates at which grade level students should be able to read and comprehend the text.

When applied to Trump's *spoken* language, the Flesch-Kincaid test renders spectacular results—with the special bonus that they now seem to be empirically validated. At second glance, however, this method is highly problematic, since speech and writing are two different modes of communication (Ong 1982): we do not speak the way we write—let alone use syntax and vocabulary similar to the most complex sentences we can read. Spoken language will therefore generally receive a lower score than writing, even if produced by the same speaker (see also Liberman 2015).

Another confounding factor is that the word count of a sentence is heavily dependent on transcription and punctuation—consider the difference between "I came. I saw. I conquered." (three two-word sentences) and "I came, I saw, I conquered." (one six-word sentence). In other words, the length of a sentence depends on the transcriber's choice of commas and full stops. In the case of Burleigh's (2018) study, which relies on transcripts made by different persons over a span of eighty years, we cannot be sure to what extent punctuation practices have changed.

1.3 The Ordinary President

One fact that does show up across the Flesch-Kincaid tests is that Trump uses simpler language than other politicians. His way of communicating might be "a deliberate projection of the 'normal guy' ethos" (Partington and Taylor 2018: 190) and thus form part of his communicative strategy to appeal to 'the people.' As Thoemmes and Conway (2007: 215) argue, with reference to Tetlock (1981), "successful candidates are aware that lower complexity increases their likelihood of winning—so they make their rhetoric simpler on purpose with that strategic goal in mind." In this respect, the use of simpler sentences and a less varied vocabulary does not indicate lower cognitive skills, but rather shows political chutzpah—Trump simply seems to go to greater lengths to appear like the ordinary guy next door. Thus, the alleged simplicity of Trump's language becomes a feature of rhetoric or communicative style. To explore this, we would want to know just how varied his vocabulary is compared to that of other speakers, how many distinct words he uses, and to what extent a political purpose might be behind what we observe as a less distinct, less enriched vocabulary.

In order to shed light on any such particularities, more fine-grained linguistic analyses are needed that take larger amounts of data into account. To be sure, there are already a number of previous studies that take a closer look at Donald Trump's language from a linguistic perspective. Of particular interest has been Trump's allegedly distinct speech style (Degani 2016; Hunston 2017; Ahmadian, Azarshahi and Paulhus 2017; Donadio 2017; Casañ-Pitarch 2018), with a particular focus on linguistic traits such as discourse markers, for example, *believe me*[3] (Lakoff 2016a; Sclafani 2018) or his "rhetorical signature" (Jamieson and Taussig 2017). Other studies use sentiment analysis, investigating to what extent emotions evoked in Trump's speech are particularly negative (Jordan and Pennebaker 2016; Jordan and Pennebacker 2017; Hoffmann 2018). Another strand of research has focused on metaphorical expressions contributing to a discourse of dualities (Lakoff 2016b; Lakoff 2017; Nguyen 2018; Pilyarchuk and Onysko 2018; McCallum-Bayliss 2019).

1.4 The Twenty-First-Century President

Trump's communication style is also symptomatic of a general twentieth-century style shift, which has also had ramifications on political discourse. As Lakoff (1982: 242, 256) observes, a shift in writing style has taken place so that now (with "now" referring to then, 1982) the ideal written text emulates "the oral mode of discourse." This is part of more general sociolinguistic processes of language change that took place during the twentieth century: colloquialization (i.e., the increasing use of spoken features in written texts, such as contracted verb forms), democratization (i.e., the tendency to avoid expressions that indicate hierarchical relationships between speakers, thus aiming for a democratic state of equality), and informalization (i.e., the observation that formal registers such as academic writing or journalistic texts display informal, colloquial features—for more details see Farrelly and Seoane 2012).

This had an impact on political language: successful political speeches in the United States were increasingly carried out in a conversational manner, which—in distinction to formal writing—conveys "warmth, closeness, and vividness" (Lakoff 1982: 242). This is particularly evident in Ronald Reagan's speeches during his presidency in the 1980s. As a former movie actor, he changed the form of political communication toward what Atkinson (1984 167) calls a "low-key television performing style." In his inaugural speech, Reagan was—as Jamieson (1988: 165) points out—the first president ever to use contractions (*it's*, *we're*) and informal transitions (*now*, *well*, *and*, *but*). In a time when speeches had to sound like written texts, he thus produced a "type of oral prose [that] is not meant to be read, but to be listened to" (Kowal and O' Connell 1993: 178). Furthermore, inaugural addresses after Reagan continued the process of informalization, as observable in George H. W. Bush's inaugural address, which means that American political communication is becoming ever more conversational (Kowal and O'Connell 1993: 182).

As it seems, the 'Age of Television' had taken over—the former 'Age of Typography' had given way. The question is whether the Age of Television is itself now in the process of being ousted by the 'Age of Twitter' or generally the 'Age of Social Media,' as Ott (2017: 59) claims. He sees a "fundamental shift in the dominant mode of communication," with Twitter's key features determining the way messages are encoded—basically following Marshall McLuhan's (1964) well-known dictum of "the medium is the message." More specifically, Twitter's character limitation allegedly results in simplicity and a lack of complexity and moreover (as Ott sees it) fosters impulsivity and incivility: since Twitter is so informal and tweeting requires little forethought or reflection, it is claimed to encourage uncivil discourse.

As for Trump, he took to Twitter early on, joining the platform in March 2009, and tweeted his opinion on practically everything, for example, correcting the public perception of his persona, as in (1) and (2).[4]

(1) I know some of you may think I'm tough and harsh but actually I'm a very compassionate person (with a very high IQ) with strong common sense (@realDonaldTrump, April 21, 2013)

(2) As everybody knows, but the haters & losers refuse to acknowledge, I do not wear a "wig." My hair may not be perfect but it's mine. (@realDonaldTrump, April 24, 2013)

However, beyond such tweets on his character and looks, during the presidential election he posted far more excessively. Surely, it is no exaggeration to say that Twitter played a central role in his presidential campaign—definitely more so than with other candidates. For example, he tweeted his announcement to run for president and his agenda-setting campaign slogan:

(3) I am officially running for President of the United States. #MakeAmericaGreatAgain (@realDonaldTrump, June 16, 2015)

He disparaged his opponents via nicknames:

(4) Wow, Lyin' Ted Cruz really went wacko today. Made all sorts of crazy charges. Can't function under pressure – not very presidential. Sad! (@realDonaldTrump, May 4, 2016)

Trump also voiced his opinion on issues of political significance such as global warming:

(5) This very expensive GLOBAL WARMING bullshit has got to stop. Our planet is freezing, record low temps, and our GW scientists are stuck in ice (@realDonaldTrump, January 2, 2014)

He often shot volatile accusations against Hillary Clinton (here concerning the revelation that classified mails had been sent from her private mail account):

(6) Crooked Hillary Clinton deleted 33,000 e-mails AFTER they were subpoenaed by the United States Congress. Guilty – cannot run. Rigged system! (@realDonaldTrump, November 2, 2016)

And he dealt with scandal, like the *Access Hollywood* tape, which momentarily threw his campaign into turmoil right before the second presidential debate.

(7) I'm not proud of my locker room talk. But this world has serious problems. We need serious leaders. #debate #BigLeagueTruth (@realDonaldTrump, October 9, 2016)

Once elected, Trump still continued using Twitter, defending political decisions such as the US withdrawal from the Paris Climate Agreement, see (8), or commenting on diplomatic relations with foreign countries, see (9).

(8) The badly flawed Paris Climate Agreement protects the polluters, hurts Americans, and cost a fortune. NOT ON MY WATCH! (@realDonaldTrump, September 4, 2019)
(9) The United States is asking Britain, France, Germany and other European allies to take back over 800 ISIS fighters that we captured in Syria and put them on trial. The Caliphate is ready to fall. The alternative is not a good one in that we will be forced to release them........ (@realDonaldTrump, February 16, 2019)

Most recently, his tweets covered the impeachment process, from first reactions as the controversy over his phone call with the Ukrainian president broke out (10), over his framing of the trial as a "hoax" (11) to his first retort once the Senate acquitted him, which was expected in light of the Republican majority in the upper chamber of the Congress (12).

(10) If that perfect phone call with the President of Ukraine Isn't considered appropriate, then no future President can EVER again speak to another foreign leader! (@realDonaldTrump, September 27, 2019)
(11) The only crimes in the Impeachment Hoax were committed by Shifty Adam Schiff, when he totally made up my phone conversation with the Ukrainian President and read it to Congress, together with numerous others on Shifty's side. Schiff should be Impeached, and worse! (@realDonaldTrump, October 28, 2019)
(12) I will be making a public statement tomorrow at 12:00pm from the @WhiteHouse to discuss our Country's VICTORY on the Impeachment Hoax! (@realDonaldTrump, February 5, 2020)

Truly, Trump is a representative of the 'Age of Twitter,' and we can rightfully call him the first 'Social Media President' (see also Wodak 2018: xx). Because of Trump's unprecedented use of Twitter as a medium to voice his political and personal opinions, quite a lot of studies have dealt with his language use as witnessed in his tweets (see, for example, Kreis 2017; Oborne and Roberts 2017; Ott 2017; Clarke and Grieve 2019).

1.5 The Trump Brand

Trump's language as evidenced in tweets, but also in other kinds of texts, gives rise to the claims listed at the beginning. The question is to what extent features found in his language are characteristic and exclusive to his individual speech style—in linguistic terms, his idiolectal language use, which in the sense of Coulthard and Johnson (2007: 161–3) manifests itself through distinctive and idiosyncratic choices in texts, both in terms of actual items that are more or less unique to one's language and in the form of preferences for selecting certain items rather than others. Of course, such 'linguistic fingerprinting' is difficult—not only for the reason that we most often lack samples exhaustive enough for the conclusive identification of genuinely individual features, but also because an individual's language use varies all the time depending on the speech situation or the mode of communication, and is also prone to change over the course of time.

An additional confounding factor is that most political discourse is mediated; that is, what we are seeing or hearing is not necessarily the politician's own language, but rather the language scripted by spokespeople, who produce a voice that is officially promoted as the politician's. In the early days of Trump's presidential campaign, there was a lot of discussion whether even his tweets were authored by him alone. In an analysis of tweets posted throughout 2016, Robinson (2016) found striking differences between those tweets sent from an iPhone and those sent from an Android device, which makes him assume that the Android tweets are more likely to have been authored by Trump himself, whereas the iPhone messages are said to originate from his staff. The study, however, suffers from circularities, and its finding—if at all true—only holds for 2016 (Schneider, Eitelmann, and Mondorf 2018).

Despite the influence of different script writers, Trump's language is highly recognizable. As Sclafani (2018: 23) puts it, Trump's idiolect may be described as a "publically [sic] recognizable branded individual style," with the notion of a branded speech style essentially harking back to the brand that Trump already heavily promoted as a businessman and as a TV personality back in his *Apprentice* days. It is a language variety that we could call 'Trumpish': a variety that is definitely worthwhile investigating with respect to its particular features of political rhetoric, its effect on Trump's addressees—supporters and opponents alike—and its impact on political discourse in the twenty-first century. In order to provide a fine-grained analysis of Trump's language that goes beyond what meets the eye (or rather, ear), expertise is called for that comes from the field of linguistics.

1.6 Brief Outline of this Volume

Against this backdrop, the present volume provides a multifaceted investigation of Donald Trump's language, addressing popular (mis-)conceptions about his speech style from a linguistic perspective and discussing to what extent his idiolect links to political developments of the twenty-first century. The volume shows that 'Trumpish' is more than simply a salient idiolect, but also a reflection of changing social and political norms. All contributions proceed from claims circulating in the media about Trump's language with the aim of testing whether these claims withstand vigorous linguistic testing. The chapters provide an in-depth exploration of Trump's language; all in all, they address three main aspects:

(a) What are the characteristic features of Trump's idiolect? How distinct is Trump's idiolect actually from that of other politicians?
(b) Which linguistic means does Trump use to convey emotions? How does he steer evaluations of others?
(c) What are Trump's discursive strategies to frame political issues? Do these reflect an agenda?

The volume comprises ten analyses of linguistic features, divided into three parts. Part I, "Rhetoric and Repetition," harks back to assumptions that Donald Trump's language is simple in terms of grammar and lexis, which manifests in repetitive sentence structures and a less varied vocabulary. All of the contributions in this section are comparative in that Trump's language as evidenced in various text types is contrasted to other language users. Setting the scene, Jesse Egbert and Douglas Biber provide a fine-grained, corpus-based analysis that seeks to identify characteristic style features. Their investigation of presidential debates since the 1960s reveals not only vocabulary choices characteristically different from other former presidential candidates and presidents but also subtle grammatical distinctions that are less salient. Kristina Nilsson Björkenstam and Gyntarė Grigonytė—following up on the common assumption that Trump likes to repeat himself—analyze repetitions and parallelisms as a rhetorical device. They show that a distinct preference for repetitions can indeed be detected in Trump's speech style, particularly when he deviates from his script. Patricia Ronan and Gerold Schneider pursue the claim circulating online that Trump's speech shows signs of old age; for this purpose, they consider a different type of repetition, namely hesitant repetitions, which, if used increasingly, can be taken as an indicator of aging. Their diachronic analysis contrasts interviews conducted at various stages in Trump's career, thus shedding light on the question to what extent Trump's speech behavior has changed, if at all, and to what extent it is different to other speakers.

Part II, "Evaluation and Emotion," takes a closer look at language features that contribute to evaluative assessments and convey emotions. Ulrike Stange investigates Trump's allegedly distinctive use of intensifying adverbs such as *very* or *really*, which speakers use to strengthen the emotional effect of the message. Her study contrasts the occurrence of intensifiers in Trump's language to those in other politicians' speech and a baseline of 'regular' spoken language, thus re-assessing claims about Trump as a heavy user of intensifiers. Jukka Tyrkkö and Irina Frisk analyze Trump's practice of giving nicknames to his political opponents, used to underpin his negative evaluation of the persons and institutions thus targeted and to manipulate recipients' emotional perceptions of the nicknamed entities. Their study is a large-scale analysis of the nicknames used in his tweets and zooms in on gender-related differences as well as on trajectories of change. Ulrike Schneider and Kristene McClure investigate Trump's use of the definite article *the* with minoritized ethnic groups, which has been heavily criticized as an 'othering' technique, which conveys negative evaluations of the people referred to. Based on a quantitative analysis of plural references to groups in Trump's speeches and tweets, they discuss to what extent Trump's speech shows traces of racist discourse.

Part III, "Discourse and Metaphor," zooms in on selected issues that feature prominently in Trump's discourse and investigates discursive strategies. Drawing on the cognitive-linguistic notion of conceptual metaphors, Anthony Koth reveals to what extent Trump's discourse is marked by a competition metaphor that conceptualizes politics in terms of winning and losing. He shows that the intricacies of immigration politics, in particular, are reduced to a zero-sum game in which one competitor's win necessarily entails another's loss—with problematic implications. Marta Degani and Alexander Onysko deal with Trump's discourse on environmental issues, which is characterized by discursive strategies of denying and silencing scientifically proven facts about the state of the climate. Special attention is given to Trump's withdrawal from the Paris Climate Agreement, which displays a striking use of metaphorical expressions that justify adhering to an anti-environmental stance against all odds. Christoph Schubert investigates the intricate problem of lying, which has gained an additionally complex dimension with the notion of *fake news*. While fake news may also refer to news that turn out to be false, in Trump's "fake news" agenda, the term is used to wrongfully brand news as fake, thus delegitimizing the media. Finally, Jan David Hauck and Teruko Vida Mitsuhara take a closer look at Trump's way of apologizing for his misogynistic comments in the *Access Hollywood* tape. By contrasting his (non-) apologies to those of Bill Clinton as a response to his affair with Monica Lewinsky, they show that Trump adapts the canonical format of the Christian testimonial in a way that allows him to present himself as a coherent, authentic political persona and at the same time promote his anti-establishment agenda.

The volume is wrapped up by a concluding chapter in which we raise the question to what extent Trump's speech style can be considered synonymous to populist rhetoric—after all, his strategy of 'othering' and strongly antagonizing his opponents tick boxes of a textbook definition of populism: first, an anti-elite stance against the current ruling class, the system in place, or a group in power, as evidenced in Trump's infamous tweets in which he called for "draining the swamp" in Washington; second, an anti-mainstream media stance, which can be found in Trump's calling out newspapers such as the *New York Times* for allegedly publishing fake news; and third, an anti-minority stance, most notoriously represented in Trump's promise of building a wall on the Mexican border to counteract illegal immigration. We will show to what extent the findings from the individual studies collected in the present volume do indeed corroborate the perception of Trump using populist rhetoric.

The contributions comprise quantitative and qualitative approaches to language. Quantitative analyses take large, digitized data samples into consideration and seek to arrive at deductions by quantifying linguistic features; for such studies, corpus linguistic methodologies are applied. In order to support the validity of findings, tests for statistical significance are sometimes conducted in addition to the reporting of results. Qualitative analyses, on the other hand, opt for more detailed descriptions and are able to uncover fine distinctions by way of close reading. Most often, quantitative and qualitative analyses complement each other, as is also the case in the majority of contributions collected in this volume.

Furthermore, the contributions cover a multitude of different text types representing Donald Trump's public language: tweets (Koth; Schneider and McClure; Stange; Tyrkkö and Frisk), presidential debates (Björkenstam and Grigonytė; Egbert and Biber), campaign rally speeches (Björkenstam and Grigonytė; Schneider and McClure), Republican primary debates (Koth; Schneider and McClure; Schubert), phone-ins to TV shows (Ronan and Schneider), remarks (Degani and Onysko; Stange), interviews (Ronan and Schneider; Schneider and McClure), and video statements (Hauck and Mitsuhara). It needs to be noted that the time frame covered in most contributions centers on the years 2015–18, which means that certain events currently looming large in public discussions about the Trump presidency—such as the recent impeachment trial and Trump's handling of the coronavirus outbreak—are not taken into consideration; these issues are left for future inquiries into the language of Donald Trump.

Notes

1 Trump seems to have been "flirting with candidacy" (Coombs 2013: 173) again in the 2012 presidential election but does not appear to have taken any official steps to enter the race.
2 As one of the most prominent examples, consider Trump's misspelling of *coverage* as "covfefe," which has resulted not only in wide media attention (Flegenheimer 2017) but also in a large number of internet memes.
3 A brief remark on linguistic notation conventions: Words or expressions are *italicized* whenever they are used as examples in a more general sense; for instance, when we say that Trump frequently uses the expression *believe me*, we do not refer to a particular quote of his but talk about the discourse marker *believe me* in general which comes up particularly often in his speech. In contrast, references to direct quotes are indicated by double quotation marks, as in "Believe me, it was much better" (@realDonaldTrump, January 8, 2014).
4 It is a convention in linguistics to number examples consecutively and set them off typographically.

References

Acuna, Kirsten (2018), "Barbara Corcoran Says Donald Trump Is 'a Phenomenal Salesman' and He Used that to His Advantage in the 2016 Election," *Insider*, December 4. Available online: https://www.insider.com/barbara-corcoran-says-donald-trump-used-salesman-tactics-election-2018-12 (accessed March 13, 2020).

Ahmadian, Sara, Sara Azarshahi, and Delroy L. Paulhus (2017), "Explaining Donald Trump via Communication Style: Grandiosity, Informality, and Dynamism," *Personality and Individual Differences*, 107 (1): 49–53.

Atkinson, Max (1984), *Our Masters' Voices: The Language and Body Language of Politics*, London: Routledge.

Blake, Aaron (2016), "Welcome to the Next, Most Negative Presidential Election of our Lives," *The Washington Post*, July 29. Available online: https://www.washingtonpost.com/news/the-fix/wp/2016/07/29/clinton-and-trump-accept-their-nominations-by-telling-you-what-you-should-vote-against/ (accessed March 13, 2020).

Burleigh, Nina (2018), "Trump Speaks at Fourth-Grade Level, Lowest of Last 15 U.S. Presidents, New Analysis Finds," *Newsweek*, January 8. Available online: https://www.newsweek.com/trump-fire-and-fury-smart-genius-obama-774169 (accessed March 13, 2020).

Casañ-Pitarch, Ricardo (2018), "Mr. President, Discourse Matters: A Contrastive Analysis of Donald Trump and Barack Obama's Discourse," *RUDN Journal of Language Studies, Semiotics and Semantics*, 9 (1): 173–85.

Clarke, Isobelle and Jack Grieve (2019), "Stylistic Variation on the Donald Trump Twitter Account: A Linguistic Analysis of Tweets Posted Between 2009 and 2018," *PloS one*, 14 (9): e0222062.

Cofman Wittes, Tamara and Ilan Goldenberg (2017), "How Trump's Black and White World View Met Reality in the Middle East," *Brookings*, June 15. Available online: https://www.brookings.edu/blog/markaz/2017/06/15/how-trumps-black-and-white-world-view-met-reality-in-the-middle-east/ (accessed March 3, 2020).

Coombs, Danielle Sarver (2013), *Last Man Standing: Media, Framing, and the 2012 Republican Primaries*, Lanham, MD: Rowman & Littlefield Publishers.

Coulthard, Malcolm and Alison Johnson (2007), *An Introduction to Forensic Linguistics: Language in Evidence*, London and New York: Routledge.

Dale, Daniel (2019), "A Month-by-Month Look at Donald Trump's Top Lies of 2019," *CNN Politics*, December 31. Available online: https://edition.cnn.com/2019/12/31/politics/fact-check-donald-trump-top-lies-of-2019-daniel-dale/index.html (accessed March 13, 2020).

Degani, Marta (2016), "Endangered Intellect: A Case Study of Clinton vs Trump Campaign Discourse," *Iperstoria—Testi Letterature Linguaggi*, 8: 131–45.

Donadio, Paolo (2017), "Understanding Trump: Power Back to the People," *I-LanD Journal*, 2: 84–101.

Farrelly, Michael and Elena Seoane (2012), "Democratization," in Terttu Nevalainen and Elizabeth Closs Traugott (eds.), *The Oxford Handbook of the History of English*, 392–401, New York: Oxford University Press.

Flegenheimer, Matt (2017), "What's a 'Covfefe'? Trump Tweet Unites a Bewildered Nation," *The New York Times*, May 31. Available online: https://www.nytimes.com/2017/05/31/us/politics/covfefe-trump-twitter.html (accessed February 28, 2020).

Flegenheimer, Matt (2018), "Band of the Insulted: The Nicknames of Trump's Adversaries," *New York Times*, January 5. Available online: https://www.nytimes.com/2018/01/05/us/politics/trump-nicknames.html (accessed March 13, 2020).

Gartner, John (2019), "Trump's Cognitive Deficits Seem Worse. We Need to Know If He Has Dementia: Psychologist," *USA TODAY*, December 15. Available online: https://eu.usatoday.com/story/opinion/2019/04/09/does-donald-trump-have-dementia-we-need-know-psychologist-column/3404007002/ (accessed February 28, 2020).

Hoffmann, Thomas (2018), "'Too Many Americans Are Trapped in Fear, Violence and Poverty': A Psychology-Informed Sentiment Analysis of Campaign Speeches from the 2016 US Presidential Election," *Linguistics Vanguard*, 4 (1): 1–9.

Holloway, Kali (2016), "Why Trump's Language Reveals His Racist Attitudes," *AlterNet*, October 22. Available online: https://www.alternet.org/2016/10/blacks-and-latinos-trumps-blatant-racism-visible-all-see/ (accessed November 21, 2019).

Hunston, Susan (2017), "Talking Trump: Literally Speaking," University of Birmingham. Available online: https://www.birmingham.ac.uk/research/perspective/talking-trump-literally-speaking.aspx (accessed April 16, 2018).

Jamieson, Kathleen Hall (1988), *Eloquence in an Electronic Age: The Transformation of Political Speechmaking*, New York: Oxford University Press.

Jamieson, Kathleen Hall and Doron Taussig (2017), "Disruption, Demonization, Deliverance, and Norm Destruction: The Rhetorical Signature of Donald J. Trump," *Political Science Quarterly*, 132 (4): 619–50.

Jordan, Kayla N. and James W. Pennebaker (2016), "Accepting the Nomination: A Comparison of the Speeches of Trump and Clinton," *Wordwatchers*, August 1. Available online: https://wordwatchers.wordpress.com/2016/08/01/accepting-the-nomination-a-comparison-of-the-speeches-of-trump-and-clinton/ (accessed March 13, 2020).

Jordan, Kayla N. and James W. Pennebaker (2017), "Trump's First State of the Union Address," *Wordwatchers*, March 1. Available online: https://wordwatchers.wordpress.com/2017/03/01/trumps-first-state-of-the-union-address/ (acessed March 13, 2020).

Kincaid, J. Peter, Robert P. Fishburne, Richard L. Rodgers, and Brad S. Chissom (1975), "Derivation of New Readability Formulas (Automated Readability Index, Fog Count, and Flesch Reading Ease Formula) for Navy Enlisted Personnel," Research Branch Report 8–75.

Kowal, Sabine and Daniel C. O'Connell (1993), "Television Rhetoric in an Age of Secondary Orality: Psycholinguistic Analyses of the Speaking Performance of Ronald Reagan," *Georgetown Journal of Languages and Linguisticsm*, 1 (1): 174–85.

Kreis, Ramona (2017), "The 'Tweet Politics' of President Trump," *Journal of Language and Politics*, 16 (4): 607–18.

Lakoff, George (2016a), "Understanding Trump's Use of Language," *George Lakoff*, August 19. Available online: https://georgelakoff.com/2016/08/19/understanding-trumps-use-of-language/ (accessed March 13, 2020).

Lakoff, George (2016b), "Understanding Trump," *George Lakoff*, July 23. Available online: https://georgelakoff.com/2016/07/23/understanding-trump-2/ (accessed March 13, 2020).

Lakoff, George (2017), "The President Is the Nation: The Central Metaphor Trump Lives By," *George Lakoff*, August 1. Available online: https://georgelakoff.com/2017/08/01/the-president-is-the-nation-the-central-metaphor-trump-lives-by/ (accessed March 13, 2020).

Lakoff, Robin T. (1982), "Some of My Favorite Writers Are Literate: The Mingling of Oral and Literate Strategies in Written Communication," in Deborah Tannen (ed.), *Spoken and Written Language: Exploring Orality and Literacy*, 239–60, Norwood, NJ: Ablex.

Leith, Sam (2017), "Trump's Rhetoric: A Triumph of Inarticulacy," *The Guardian*, January 13. Available online: https://www.theguardian.com/us-news/2017/jan/13/donald-trumps-rhetoric-how-being-inarticulate-is-seen-as-authentic (accessed August 6, 2018).

Liberman, Marc (2015), "More Flesch-Kincaid Grade-Level Nonsense," *Language Log*, October 23. Available online: http://languagelog.ldc.upenn.edu/nll/?p=21847 (accessed March 9, 2020).

McCallum-Bayliss, Heather (2019), "Donald Trump Is a Conqueror: How the Cognitive Analysis of Trump's Discourse Reveals His Worldview," in Encarnación Hidalgo-Tenorio, Miguel-Ángel Benítez-Castro, and Francesca De Cesare (eds.), *Populist Discourse: Critical Approaches to Contemporary Politics*, 242–58, London and New York: Routledge.

McLuhan, Marshall (1964), *Understanding Media: The Extensions of Man*, New York: McGraw-Hill.

Nguyen, Vi-Thong (2018), "A Comparative Analysis on Metaphoric Strategies in Presidential Inaugurals of Barack Obama and Donald Trump," *ResearchGate*. Available online: https://www.researchgate.net/publication/326755818_A_Comparative_Analysis_on_Metaphoric_Strategies_in_Presidential_Inaugurals_of_Barack_Obama_andDonald_Trump (accessed March 13, 2020).

Oborne, Peter and Tom Roberts (2017), *How Trump Thinks: His Tweets and the Birth of a New Political Language*, London: Head of Zeus.

Ong, Walter J. (1982), *Orality and Literacy: The Technologizing of the Word*, London and New York: Methuen.

Ott, Brian L. (2017), "The Age of Twitter: Donald J. Trump and the Politics of Debasement," *Critical Studies in Media Communication*, 34 (1): 59–68.

Partington, Alan and Charlotte Taylor (2018), *The Language of Persuasion in Politics: An Introduction*, London and New York: Routledge.

Pilyarchuk, Kateryna and Alexander Onysko (2018), "Conceptual Metaphors in Donald Trump's Political Speeches: Framing his Topics and (Self-)Constructing his Persona," *Colloquium: New Philologies*, 3 (2): 98–156.

Pomper, Gerald M., Anthony Corrado, Eugene J. Dionne Jr., Kathleen A. Frankovic, Paul S. Herrnson, Marjorie R. Hershey, William G. Mayer, Monika L. McDermott, and Wilson C. McWilliams (2001), *The Election of 2000: Reports and Interpretations*, Washington, DC: CQ Press.

Pruden, Wesley (2017), "Trumpspeak, a Language Rich in Adjectives," *The Washington Times*, February 23. Available online: https://www.washingtontimes.com/news/2017/feb/23/donald-trumps-speech-features-superlatives/ (accessed March 3, 2020).

Robinson, David (2016), "Text Analysis of Trump's Tweets Confirms He Writes Only the (Angrier) Android Half," *Variance Explained*, August 9. Available online: http://varianceexplained.org/r/trump-tweets/

Schneider, Ulrike, Matthias Eitelmann, and Britta Mondorf (2018), "Zooming in on Trumpish: A Corpus-based Analysis of Donald Trump's Idiolectal Language Use in the Social Media." Presentation held at *ICAME* 39, Tampere, May 30–June 3.

Schumacher, Elliot and Maxine Eskenazi (2016), *A Readability Analysis of Campaign Speeches from the 2016 US Presidential Campaign*, Pittsburgh, PA: Language Technologies Institute, School of Computer Science Carnegie Mellon University.

Sclafani, Jennifer (2018), *Talking Donald Trump: A Sociolinguist Study of Style, Metadiscourse, and Political Identity*, London and New York: Routledge.

Senior, Jennifer (2019), "We Are All at the Mercy of the Narcissist in Chief," *The New York Times*, October 11. Available online: https://www.nytimes.com/2019/10/11/opinion/trump-narcissism.html (accessed March 3, 2020).

Shafer, Jack (2015), "Donald Trump Talks like a Third-Grader," *Politico*, August 13. Available online: https://www.politico.com/magazine/story/2015/08/donald-trump-talks-like-a-third-grader-121340 (accessed April 12, 2018).

Shugerman, Emily (2017), "Trump Speaks at Level of 8-year-old, New Analysis Finds," *Independent*, January 9. Available online: https://www.independent.co.uk/news/world/

americas/us-politics/trump-language-level-speaking-skills-age-eight-year-old-vocabulary-analysis-a8149926.html (accessed March 13, 2020).

Sides, John, Daron Shaw, Matt Grossmann, and Keena Lipsitz (2012), *Campaigns and Elections: Rules, Reality, Strategy, Choice*, New York: W.W. Norton & Company.

Smith, Allison Jane (2016), "Donald Trump Speaks Like a Sixth-Grader: All Politicians Should," *The Washington Post*, May 3. Available online: https://www.washingtonpost.com/posteverything/wp/2016/05/03/donald-trump-speaks-like-a-sixth-grader-all-politicians-should/ (accessed March 13, 2020).

Spice, Byron (2016), "Most Presidential Candidates Speak at Grade 6–8 Level," *Carnegie Mellon University News*, March 16. Available online: https://www.cmu.edu/news/stories/archives/2016/march/speechifying.html (accessed March 13, 2020).

Tetlock, Philip E. (1981), "Cognitive Style and Political Ideology," *Journal of Personality and Social Psychology*, 41: 118–26.

Thoemmes, Felix J. and Lucian Gideon Conway III (2007), "Integrative Complexity of 41 U.S. Presidents," *Political Psychology*, 28 (2): 193–226.

Trump, Donald J. and Bill Zanker (2007), *Think Big and Kick Ass in Business and Life*, New York: Harper Business.

Trump, Donald J. and Meredith McIver (2004), *Trump: Think Like a Billionaire: Everything You Need to Know about Success, Real Estate, and Life*, New York: Random House.

Trump, Donald J. and Tony Schwartz (1987), *Trump: The Art of the Deal*, New York: Random House.

Van Edwards, Vanessa (2017), "Trump's Hands Speak—What Do They Say?," *CNN*, May 12. Available online: https://edition.cnn.com/2017/05/12/opinions/hand-gestures-matter-for-presidents-van-edwards-opinion/index.html (accessed February 28, 2020). varianceexplained.org/r/trump-tweets/ (accessed March 9, 2020).

Wodak, Ruth (2018), "Preface: From 'Hate Speech' to 'Hate Tweets,'" in Mojca Pajnik and Birgit Sauer (eds.), *Populism and the Web: Communicative Practices of Parties and Movements in Europe*, xvii–xxiii, London and New York: Routledge.

Part I

Rhetoric and Repetition

2

It's Just Words, Folks. It's Just Words
Donald Trump's Distinctive Linguistic Style

Jesse Egbert and Douglas Biber

2.1 Introduction

Many who watched the presidential debates of 2016 noticed that Donald Trump used language in dramatically different ways from previous presidential candidates. There was a great deal of media coverage about Trump's style, with many journalists making observations about Trump's language choices, particularly during the 2016 debates with Hillary Clinton. Observers commented on how frequently he interrupted his opponent (Nelson 2016), and his reliance on insults and name-calling (Diamond 2016). Some referred to his style as stream of consciousness and "word salad" (Digby Parton 2016). His use of nicknames, imperatives, and hyperbole was noted by another journalist (Mascaro 2016). Other observers also noticed particular words that Trump relied heavily on, including the pronouns *I* and *me* (Coe 2016), and particular phrases that were especially noticeable, such as his repeated use of *believe me* and *people say* (Viser 2016).

Most descriptions of Trump's language fall into the category of so-called folk linguistics: commentaries by journalists and bloggers that focus on some of the most salient characteristics of Trump's style (such as his use of the term *bigly* or his pronunciation of the word *huge* as 'yooge'). However, empirical linguistic research into Trump's language has been much more limited. Scholarly studies have investigated Trump's informal communication style (Ahmadian, Azarshahi, and Paulhus 2017), his rhetorical strategies during his campaign (Jamieson and Taussig 2017), the readability of his speeches (Wang and Liu 2017), his use of narrative and analytic language (Jordan and Pennebaker 2017), his use of hand gestures (Hall, Goldstein and Ingram 2016), and the linguistic style of his tweets (Clarke and Grieve 2019). In what is likely the most comprehensive study of Trump's use of language to date, Sclafani (2017) analyzes the style of the president from a qualitative discourse analytic perspective. She describes Trump's idiolect in terms of his use of discourse-marking devices, such as *by the way* and *believe me*, as well as his use of interactional devices, such as constructed dialogue. In a blog post, Hunston (2016) shows stark differences between the debate styles of Trump and Clinton, concluding that Trump's language is less formal and relies on longer clauses. She notes that "[i]t may be, then, that Trump's speaking style deliberately sacrifices 'intelligence' for 'matiness,' and that Clinton does the opposite. Alternatively, it could be that this is the only way he knows how to speak." In another blog post widely cited by the media, Lakoff (2016) analyzes the language of Donald Trump, ultimately concluding that while "Trump's crimes against clarity are multifarious," his "use of language is anything but" what abovementioned journalists have referred to as "'word salad.' His words and his use of grammar are carefully chosen, and put together artfully, automatically, and quickly."

These studies have been instrumental in providing insights into the distinctive linguistic characteristics of Donald Trump's language. Most of this research has been qualitative and focused on Trump's use of words, discourse strategies, rhetoric, and gesture. There is much less scholarship that takes a comparative quantitative approach to Trump's language. Additionally, there is almost no research that has investigated Trump's use of grammatical structures. One notable exception is a comparative analysis of the language of Trump and Clinton during the three presidential debates, published online by Krzywinski (2016). He compares the two candidates in their use of words, parts of speech, and syntactic complexity, ultimately showing that Trump uses shorter sentences, more high-frequency words, and more repetition of words.

In another empirical study, Vrana and Schneider (2017) investigate the use of a range of stylistic features by recent presidential candidates. They show that Trump uses shorter words (indicating simpler vocabulary), fewer complex words, and fewer words per sentence (indicating simpler syntax). Consequently, his speeches have a lower type–token ratio (indicating less variety in word choice).

In this chapter, we build on previous scholarship by using corpus linguistic analysis to compare the lexical and grammatical characteristics of Donald Trump's linguistic style to that of other presidential candidates. To accomplish this, we use a so-called corpus of transcripts from every general election since 1960. A corpus is a large sample of naturally occurring texts used by corpus linguists to investigate questions about language use, variation, and change over time. Computer programs were written to extract all the language produced by each candidate in each debate, resulting in a corpus of sixty-nine texts. Illustrated through two case studies, the chapter shows how corpus-based analysis permits a description of Trump's linguistic style that goes well beyond features that are noticeable to the casual observer.

The first case study focuses on Trump's keywords, that is, words that are strongly associated with Trump when compared with other presidential candidates. Keywords can provide insights into the topics, stylistic choices, and other language characteristics that make a language user or variety distinct from others. The second case study—focusing on key grammatical characteristics—reveals linguistic patterns that are less noticeable. The corpus-based findings in this study provide insights into the rhetorical and linguistic choices of presidential candidates as they speak to millions of potential voters. The quantitative results will be combined with qualitative investigations of excerpts from the debates and compared with prior discussion of Trump's linguistic style from scholars and the media. The results present empirical evidence to confirm casual observations about Donald Trump's language use and, more importantly, reveal other patterns in his language that are not salient or easy to identify.

2.2 Methods

2.2.1 Corpus Design and Compilation

This study is based on transcripts of every recorded presidential debate since the first official debate between Kennedy and Nixon in 1960. There were no presidential debates held in 1964, 1968, and 1972. The debates resumed in 1976, and since then between two and three debates have been held every election cycle. Table 2.1 contains a complete description of all of the debates and candidates included in this study. The complete transcripts for each of the thirty-three debates were downloaded from the American Presidency Project hosted by the University of California, Santa Barbara (Woolley and Peters 1999).

A computer program was created by the authors in the programming language Python to automatically segment each of the transcripts into speaker utterances and to store all of the utterances from each speaker into a separate file. All utterances from moderators, audience members, and other speakers were omitted from these text files. This resulted in sixty-nine text files, each containing all of the utterances from one candidate in one debate. We refer to this dataset as the Presidential Debates Corpus (PDC). The PDC contains 451,103 words. No discussion of the representativeness of the PDC is necessary because it contains the full population of recorded presidential debates since their beginning. Thus, while the PDC may be small relative to many contemporary corpora, its exhaustiveness allows us to generalize the findings in this study to all recorded presidential debates.

2.2.2 Keyword Analysis

Keyword analysis is a method for determining the 'aboutness' of one or more texts (Firth 1957; Williams 1983). Keywords have been shown to be useful for discovering the topics, themes, and discourses that make a text or a collection of texts unique

Table 2.1 Composition of the Presidential Debates Corpus

Year	Debates	Candidates
1960	4	Richard Nixon; John F. Kennedy
1976	3	Gerald Ford; Jimmy Carter
1980	1	Ronald Reagan; John B. Anderson
	1	Ronald Reagan; Jimmy Carter
1984	2	Ronald Reagan; Walter Mondale
1988	2	George H. W. Bush; Michael Dukakis
1992	3	George H. W. Bush; Bill Clinton; Ross Perot
1996	2	Bill Clinton; Bob Dole
2000	3	Al Gore; George W. Bush
2004	3	George Bush; John Kerry
2008	3	John McCain; Barack Obama
2012	3	Barack Obama; Mitt Romney
2016	3	Donald Trump; Hillary Clinton

or distinctive when compared to another text or collection. In the present analysis, we employ keyword analysis to identify the words used by Trump with statistically greater or lesser frequencies than by all other presidential candidates. Because keyword analysis, first developed by Mike Scott in the 1990s (see Scott 1997), relies on quantitative/statistical analysis, it has often identified sets of words that are not perceptually salient and therefore have not been previously noticed.

Keyword analysis is typically done by comparing the frequencies of words in a target corpus to the frequencies of the same words in a reference corpus. In this study, we treat each unlemmatized type as a separate word. This means that, for instance, *says, said,* and *saying* are treated as three different words, called three different types. For ease of replication, we used AntConc, a software program for corpus analysis, for the keyword analysis. Trump's three debate files were treated as the target corpus and the other sixty-six debate files as the reference corpus.

We extracted all of the words that achieved the Keyword Statistic Threshold.[1] We then attempted to use bottom-up, qualitative methods to classify these words into a smaller set of categories based on their semantic or functional content. This included a review of concordance lines for most of the words (i.e., all occurrences of a keyword in the corpus were inspected in their respective surrounding contexts) to further explore their meaning or function. These categories were then labeled and used to interpret the words that make Trump's debate speech lexically distinct from other presidential candidates' speeches. It is worth noting that any lexical analysis of this corpus is inherently problematic due to the extreme variation in historical context present in the corpus. Not only are words prone to change in frequency over time but they are also highly sensitive to prevalent topics and issues that are the focus of these debates. In an effort to eliminate words that are related to the 2016 election generally rather than to Trump's style specifically, we excluded any words from Trump's keyword list that also appeared on the list of keywords for Clinton's debate speech. We also make every effort to account for historical context in our interpretations in order to avoid overstating any claims about words that are key due to factors other than Trump's distinctive style.

2.2.3 Key Feature Analysis

In order to gain additional insights into the distinctive characteristics of Trump's speaking style, we investigated the grammatical and lexico-grammatical structures that Trump uses much more frequently or less frequently when compared with other presidential candidates. This was done using a new method called key feature analysis (see Biber and Egbert 2018).

Each of the sixty-nine texts in the PDC was grammatically tagged using the Biber Tagger. Grammatical tagging is an automatic process whereby every word in a text is annotated for its grammatical category, and other lexico-grammatical features are identified that span across multiple words. The Biber Tagger has been developed and revised by Douglas Biber over the past thirty years; the current version has both probabilistic and rule-based components, uses multiple large-scale dictionaries, and runs under Windows. This tagger achieves accuracy levels (i.e., the degree to which features are tagged correctly) comparable to other existing taggers (see, for example,

Gray 2011), but it analyzes a larger set of lexico-grammatical features than most other taggers, including a wide range of semantic categories for words (e.g., nouns: animate, cognitive, concrete, technical, quantity, place, group, abstract) and lexico-grammatical features (e.g., *that*-complement clauses controlled by stance nouns, such as in *The <u>claim</u> that I would even do that is ridiculous.*). After tagging, we calculated normalized rates of occurrence for more than 150 lexico-grammatical features. From this feature set, we selected sixty-six features based on their importance in previous research on interactive spoken discourse and other relevant registers (e.g., Biber 1988; Table 2.2). It is important to note here that the tagger treats contractions as two words, whereas we treated them as a single word for the purposes of the keyword analysis.

The counts for each of the sixty-six features were used to calculate means and standard deviations for (a) the three Donald Trump texts and (b) the other sixty-six debate texts. Means and standard deviations were calculated for (a) and (b), and these values were used to calculate a standardized mean difference using Cohen's *d*, a formula for calculating the difference between two means on a standard scale.[2] In this case, Cohen's *d* represents the difference between the frequency of a feature in the Trump corpus and its mean rate of occurrence in all other debates. This approach allows us to rank lexico-grammatical features from those that are used much more in the target (large positive *d* values) to those that are used much less in the target (large negative *d* values). According to Cohen (1977), any *d* value above +/−0.8 can be considered "large." Thus, we will only discuss the key features that fall above or

Table 2.2 Lexico-Grammatical Features Included in the Key Feature Analysis

Nouns	Verbs	Adjectives	Adverbs
Common nouns	All verbs (-auxiliary)	All adjectives	All adverbs
Proper nouns	Verb (simple)	Attributive adjective	Place
Nominalizations	Past tense	Color	Time
Pre-modifying nouns	Present progressive	Evaluative	Amplifier
Other abstract	Perfect aspect	Relational	Emphatic
Cognitive	All passives	Size	Hedge
Concrete	Activity	Time	Adverbial conjuncts
Group/institution	Aspectual	Topical	Stance adverbs
Animate	Causative		
Place	Communication		
Process	Existence		
Quantity	Mental		
Technical/concrete	Occurrence		

Complement clauses	Modals	Pronouns	Other
Verb + *that*	All modals	All pronouns	Contraction
That deletion	Necessity	First person	Coordinating
Verb + *that* (stance)	Possibility	Second person	Clausal conjunction
Noun + *that* (stance)	Prediction	Third person	Discourse particle
Adjective + *that* (stance)		It	Preposition
Verb + *to* (stance)			Conditional subordinator
Adjective + *to* (stance)			Type–token ratio
All *to* clauses (stance)			*Wh*-question
All *that* clauses (stance)			

below this threshold, with the positive values being interpreted as features associated with Trump's style and the negative values being more strongly associated with other presidential candidates.

2.3 Results and Discussion

2.3.1 Keywords

The keyword methods described earlier produced a list of 146 keywords for Donald Trump. There were thirteen words that overlapped between the list of Trump keywords and Clinton keywords: *really, so, ISIS, Mosul, Lester, Bernie, Sanders, Barack, Putin, African, Syria, because, that's*. These were removed from the list of Trump keywords, resulting in a list of 133 keywords. It is worth noting that using the same statistical criteria, Clinton's keyword list only contained fifty-two words (sixty-five minus thirteen overlapping), meaning that Trump used more than two and a half times more distinctive words than his opponent. A similar finding was also discovered by Vrana and Schneider (2017).

These words were manually classified into thirteen categories, and an 'Other' category, based on their meaning and function in context. These keyword categories range in size from three words to twenty-four words. The full set of keywords, organized according to category, is displayed in Table 2.3.

Three of the keyword categories are based on categories that have clear grammatical functions: pronouns, contractions, and lexical verbs. The pronouns that were used more by Trump than other presidential candidates include third-person pronouns (*she, her, they*), the second-person pronoun *you*, and the impersonal pronoun *it*.

Trump's use of *she* and *her* is not surprising; these are usually references to his opponent, Hillary Clinton, who was the first female candidate for president to run in a general election. Hence, all other presidential candidates referred to their opponents using male pronouns. Consequently, it is more interesting that Trump used *they* more than other candidates. A closer look reveals that Trump often used *they* to make vague references to unnamed sources of authority or groups of people:[3]

(1) She did call it the gold standard. And **they** actually fact checked and **they** said I was right. (Trump 2016, Debate 3)
(2) But I will tell you, I've been all over. And I've met some of the greatest people I'll ever meet within these communities. And **they** are very, very upset with what their politicians have told them and what their politicians have done. (Trump 2016, Debate 1)

Often, Trump repeats the pronoun *they* in parallel constructions, such as the following:

(3) And, Lester, **they**'re taking our jobs, **they**'re giving incentives, **they**'re doing things that, frankly, we don't do. (Trump 2016, Debate 1)
(4) And in many cases, **they**'re illegally here, illegal immigrants. And **they** have guns. And **they** shoot people. (Trump 2016, Debate 1)

This type of repetition has been noted by Lakoff (2016). These uses of *they* correspond to a narrative style that Trump often adopts and in which he recounts brief, vague anecdotes that serve to provide support for a prior claim. A similar pattern occurred with Trump's use of *it*:

(5) ... what's happened in Haiti with the Clinton Foundation is a disgrace. And you know **it** and they know **it** and everybody knows **it**. (Trump 2016, Debate 3)

Trump also used *it* to make anaphoric references to issues and topics that were previously mentioned:

(6) And **it** was continued on by Mayor Bloomberg. And **it** was terminated by current mayor. But stop-and-frisk had a tremendous impact on the safety of New York City. Tremendous beyond belief. So, when you say **it** has no impact, **it** really did. **It** had a very, very big impact. (Trump 2016, Debate 1)

These uses of *it* often occurred in rapid successions of short sentences about a preceding antecedent. Occasionally, particularly in longer utterances, Trump would remind the hearer of the antecedent, as in example (6).

Another category of grammatical keywords is contractions. Contractions function to make spoken language more fluent by reducing the effort required to articulate combinations of two or more words. Thus, contractions are strongly associated with speech, particularly with speech that is interactive and unplanned (see, for example, Biber 1988: 243). As a result of these associations, contractions are relatively infrequent in formal written registers and even in planned speeches. Trump uses certain contractions much more often than other presidential candidates, particularly contractions that include *not* (*don't, didn't, can't, hasn't*) and the previously mentioned *they* and *it* in combination with forms of *be*.

(7) **They're** on line waiting. We're going to speed up the process bigly, because **it's** very inefficient. But **they're** on line and **they're** waiting to become citizens. (Trump 2016, Debate 3)

The use of contractions such as these seems to be both a product of Trump's off-the-cuff, colloquial style and the source of the common perception that he is speaking in a stream of consciousness style. By contrast, other presidential candidates were less likely to use contractions which could be explained in part by the planned nature of their responses and an effort to be perceived as articulate and learned. We will see similar results in the lexico-grammatical analysis later, which reveal Trump's discourse style to be less formal (Hunston 2016) and apparently unscripted (Lakoff 2016).

Additionally, Trump used several lexical verbs (e.g., *allowed, formed, started, wants*) more than other presidential candidates. In most cases, these are used to describe a negative state of affairs in the United States.

(8) Because you look at some of these countries, you look at North Korea, we're **doing** nothing there. (Trump 2016, Debate 1)

Table 2.3 Keywords for Donald Trump, Divided into Semantic and Functional Categories

Pronouns	Contractions	Lexical verbs	Attacks on Clinton	Defending against attacks	Issues/ policies	Business deals/ negotiation
she	don't	Happened	emails	audit	leaving	deals
you	didn't	allowed	inner	tape	borders	trade
her	can't	formed	subpoena	audited	pouring	cash
they	hasn't	started	donors	avenue	frisk	vacuum
she's	what's	wants	cities	locker	airports	gold
it	they're	did	husband	fiction	border	
	it's	say	delete	sheet	migration	
		doing	stamina	commercials	lists	
			temperament	fame	companies	
			pictures	name		
			deleted			
			o'clock			
			releases			
			website			
			outsmarted			
			outplayed			

Stance/evaluation	Emphatics/absolutes	Accomplishments	Involvement	Vague language	Proper nouns	Other
bad	very	endorsed	look	thousands	Hillary	country
disaster	many	certificate	tell	hundreds	Russia	have
lied	nothing	admirals	okay	millions	NAFTA	at
horrible	much		wait	politicians	Sean	going
hacks	all			places	Chicago	but
horribly	lots			thing	Hannity	were
irredeemable	ever			things	Obamacare	almost
siege	nobody				BlumenthalAassad	
lie	totally				Sidney	
murders	no				Soros	
unbelievable					Pennsylvania	
depreciation					Iran	
worse					NATO	
mess					Arabia	
sad					Saudi	
defective					DNC	
hell					Macarthur	
shootings					Schultz	
stupidity					Wasserman	
rebels						
tougher						
nice						
frankly						
great						
tremendous						
massive						

(9) Not good. Our government shouldn't have **allowed** that to happen. (Trump 2016, Debate 2)

Most of these verbs are active voice, and in many cases, the agent is Clinton:

(10) She **wants** amnesty for everybody. (Trump 2016, Debate 2)
(11) ... a lot of other things Hillary Clinton as a senator **allowed** and she always **allowed** because the people that give her all this money, they want it. (Trump 2016, Debate 2)

The next two keyword categories are related to Trump's attacks on Clinton and his defense against attacks from her. These keywords capture Trump's repeated references to Clinton's emails (*emails, subpoena, delete, deleted, releases*), her *stamina* and *temperament*, her campaign funding (*donors*), her claims about *inner cities*, the 3 a.m. phone call about Benghazi (*o'clock*), *pictures* of Obama "in a certain garb" (Trump 2016, Debates 1 and 2), the plan for handling ISIS that she published on her *website*, and Clinton's foreign affairs record (*outsmarted, outplayed*). These types of attacks on his opponents have been noted by journalists, who refer to them as "insults and name-calling" (Diamond 2016) or as "personal insults" (Nelson 2016).

(12) She has been **outsmarted** by Putin and all you have to do is look at the Middle East. They've taken over. We've spent $6 trillion. They've taken over the Middle East. She has been **outsmarted** and **outplayed** worse than anybody I've ever seen in any government whatsoever. (Trump 2016, Debate 3)

Trump also defended himself in response to attacks from Clinton regarding the Access Hollywood tape (*tape, locker*) and his financial records (*audit, audited, sheet, avenue*):

(13) I have a very very great balance **sheet**. So great that when I did the old post office, on Pennsylvania **Avenue**, the United States government because of my balance **sheet**, which they actually know very well, chose me to do the old post office between the White House and Congress. They chose me to do the old post office—one of the primary things, in fact, perhaps the primary thing was balance **sheet**. (Trump 2016, Debate 2)

He also responds to claims made about him by Clinton's campaign and the media (*fiction, commercials, fame*).

The next keyword category is the only one related to substantive issues and, in some cases, proposed policies. Trump focused on issues related to stop-and-frisk (*frisk*), border security (*pouring, borders, airports, border, lists*), and businesses leaving the United States (*leaving, companies*).

(14) ... the special interests want those **companies** to leave, because in many cases, they own the **companies**. So what I'm saying is, we can stop them from **leaving**. We have to stop them from **leaving**. (Trump 2016, Debate 1)

Trump also focused more on business strategy and the importance of negotiating better deals than previous leaders had done.

(15) You have to be able to **negotiate** our **trade deals**. You have to be able to **negotiate** . . . . (Trump 2016, Debate 1)

The next category contains keywords related to Trump's stance or qualitative evaluations. The words in this category are overwhelmingly negative, with twenty of the twenty-four being clearly negative and, as it turns out, only two being positive (*great* and *unbelievable*)

(16) But when I started this campaign, I started it very strongly. It's called Make America **Great** Again. We're going to make America **great**. (Trump 2016, Debate 3)

Nice appears to be positive but was actually preceded by *not* nearly half of the time. The adjective *massive* was overwhelmingly used for negative evaluations of Clinton: *massive deductions, massive amounts of depreciation, massive tax write-offs*. The word *tremendous* was used negatively about half the time (e.g., *tremendous hate in her heart*) and positively half the time (*I have a tremendous income*). The negative evaluative words used to describe the state of affairs include adjectives and adverbs (*bad, horrible, unbelievable, worse, sad, defective, tougher, horribly*) as well as nouns and verbs (*disaster, hacks, siege, murders, depreciation, mess, hell, shootings, stupidity, rebels, lied, lie*). Often this strong negative language was used in response to questions related to scandals or other attacks from Clinton. At one point in the second debate, Trump responded to a direct question about the famous Access Hollywood tape where he made lewd remarks about his relations with women to Billy Bush, which had been released forty-eight hours prior. It is clear to see how he strategically shifts the focus of the conversation from that tape to extreme negative language about the state of affairs with ISIS. He does this twice during a single utterance, making sure to end with a focus on issues that are "much more important and bigger things" than his comments about women. For a more detailed analysis of this passage from the debates, see Hauck and Mitsuhara (this volume).

Another prominent keyword category was labeled "Emphatics/absolutes." Some have noted that Trump is prone to hyperbole (e.g., Mascaro 2016). We see evidence of this in his use of absolutes (*nothing, all, ever, nobody, totally, no*) and emphatics and amplifiers (*very, many, much, lots*; see also Stange, this volume). Other presidential candidates seem to be much more cautious about speaking in absolutes, which Trump uses when making claims about himself:

(17) I have great respect for women. **Nobody** has more respect for women than I do. (Trump 2016, Debate 2)

He also uses absolutes and emphatics/amplifiers when attacking the record of his opponent:

(18) She's got bad judgment and honestly, so bad that she should **never** be president of the United States. That I can tell you. (Trump 2016, Debate 2)

A notable pattern that emerges from a close review of Trump's hyperbole is that he often begins by making claims in the mold of what other politicians might say, immediately before proceeding to use an absolute. He begins with "I have great respect for women," "She's got bad judgment," and "She has done a terrible job," but then finishes with "Nobody has more respect for women than I do," "she should never be president," and "she does nothing." The tone in these latter statements is far less likely to be used by other presidential candidates.

As we have seen, Trump focuses a great deal on self-promotion and self-aggrandizing statements. This is not unique to Trump, by any means, but he seems to speak in more grandiose terms and to use more repetition when referring to his accomplishments. Keywords in the accomplishments category include words like *endorsed*, *certificate*, and *admirals* where Trump makes reference to groups that have endorsed him.

(19) I do want to say that I was just **endorsed**—and more are coming next week—it will be over 200 **admirals**, many of them here—**admirals** and generals endorsed me to lead this country. That just happened, and many more are coming. And I'm very proud of it. In addition, I was just **endorsed** by ICE. They've never **endorsed** anybody before on immigration. I was just **endorsed** by ICE. I was just recently **endorsed**—16,500 Border Patrol agents. (Trump 2016, Debate 1)

In line with the colloquial style we mentioned earlier, Trump uses verbs that indicate an interactive and involved style. He interacts directly with his opponent and the debate moderator:

(20) You have—**wait** a minute. **Wait** a minute, Lester. You asked me a question. Did you ask me a question? (Trump 2016, Debate 1)

He also seems to interact directly with the public viewers. During the course of four utterances in the first debate he uses the verb *look* five times, each as part of directives:

(21) And I will tell you, you **look** at the inner cities . . .
And you can go **look** it up . . .
And if you **look** at CNN this past week . . . . (Trump 2016, Debate 1)

Nearly all of the fifty instances of *tell* are part of some version of the constructions *let me tell you* or *I'll tell you*. These are highly interactive discourse constructions that are rarely used in edited writing or prepared speeches. They give Trump's discourse a highly involved, interactive tone that is likely to heighten the listeners' level of engagement.

Another distinctive feature of Trump's speech is vague language. This has been noted by both linguists, who referred to his vague, general statements (Hunston 2016), and journalists, one of whom described the "lack of precision in his use of language" (Black 2016). This is closely related to his reliance on hyperbole and extreme expressions of stance. He uses the quantifiers *hundreds*, *thousands*, and *millions*, but in almost every case these are not actually used for precise quantification. Instead, they are used to make vague references that serve to express a large number.

(22) They're going to Mexico. So many **hundreds** and **hundreds** of companies are doing this. (Trump 2016, Debate 1)
(23) She wants 550% more people than Barack Obama. And he has **thousands** and **thousands** of people. (Trump 2016, Debate 3)
(24) What she doesn't say is that President Obama has deported **millions** and **millions** of people. (Trump 2016, Debate 3)

Surprisingly, fact checks of these numbers reveal most of them to be technically accurate, albeit at times misleading. It can be seen that Trump likes to repeat these values in a "number and number" construction. When interpreted literally, "millions and millions" means that there are two million or more. In the case of Trump's reference to Obama's deportation record, as of the debate the Obama administration had seen 2.5 million deportations, just slightly over the minimum number required to make 'millions and millions' technically accurate.[4] It is likely, though, that at least some listeners were picturing many more than 2.5 million.

Other examples of Trump's vague language include general references to *politicians*, *places*, and *thing/things* without specifying who or what is being referred to.

(25) It's been defective for a long time, many years, but the **politicians** haven't done anything about it. (Trump 2016, Debate 1)
(26) Right now, it's getting tougher and tougher to defeat them, because they're in more and more **places**, more and more states, more and more nations. (Trump 2016, Debate 1)
(27) But she lied about a lot of **things**. (Trump 2016, Debate 2)

In contrast with Trump, other presidential candidates seem to be much more technically precise in their references to quantities and issues. Many fact checkers have noted that Trump's claims are often unclear or vague, leading one to note that "verifying President Trump's statements beyond reasonable doubt is more difficult than with previous Presidential-level politicians" (Chapman 2019).

The final two categories of keywords include a list of proper nouns and a set of unclassified 'other' words. The proper nouns, in most cases, are indicative of the historical and political context at the time of the election and do not offer particularly interesting insights into Trump's style. Most of the keywords in the 'other' category are function words. The most frequently used content word is *country*, which was used in a wide variety of contexts, including references to other countries and the United States, most of which were negative comments on the state of affairs in America:

(28) How stupid is our **country**? (Trump 2016, Debate 2)
(29) But that's the kind of thinking that our **country** needs. When we have a **country** that's doing so badly, that's being ripped off by every single **country** in the world, it's the kind of thinking that our **country** needs. (Trump 2016, Debate 1)

This rhetoric seems to present a backdrop of turmoil in the United States that sets the stage for Trump's "Make America Great Again":

(30) People are pouring into our **country** and they're coming in from the Middle East and other places. We're gonna make America safe again, we're gonna make America great again but we're gonna make America safe again and we're gonna make America wealthy again. Because if you don't do that, it just, it sounds harsh to say, but we have to build up the wealth of our nation. Other nations are taking our job and they're taking our wealth. (Trump 2016, Debate 2)

We now turn our attention to the distinctive characteristics of Trump's use of grammar and lexico-grammar.

2.3.2 Key Features

As mentioned earlier, the key feature analysis can provide insights into the characteristics of a language user's style. Lexico-grammatical choices are especially interesting because they are fundamental to a speaker's style, yet they are typically much less salient than keywords. At the same time, lexical choices and grammatical choices are interdependent and, as we will see repeatedly later, the lexico-grammatical results can serve as a complement to the keyword results. Of the original sixty-six lexico-grammatical features included in the key feature analysis, thirty-nine features exceeded our threshold of +/−0.8, with d values ranging between 3.98 and −2.83. For a point of reference, we can compare this with the results of the same key feature analysis of Clinton's texts, which resulted in only twenty-five features that were greater than the threshold, with a narrower range of 2.26 to −1.50. As with the keyword analysis, this confirms that when compared with previous presidential candidates, Trump's language is more distinct than Clinton's. Whereas Clinton seems to perpetuate a traditional presidential debate style, Trump stands in sharp contrast, challenging these traditions on many fronts. Figure 2.1 displays the d values for the thirty-nine features that were established as key for Trump, in order from strongest positive to strongest negative. In this section, we begin by organizing these thirty-nine features into categories based on shared functions. These categories were established in a bottom-up fashion according to the discourse functions that have been associated with these features in previous studies, particularly studies that have employed multi-dimensional analysis, a method that explicitly accounts for co-occurrence patterns among lexico-grammatical features (see, for example, Biber 1988). In that framework, co-occurrence patterns among lexico-grammatical features are interpreted according to their shared discourse functions. We follow a similar approach here.

For the purposes of this study, we manually classified the positive key features into four categories: (i) Narrative, (ii) Impersonal Stance, (iii) Subjective Commentary and Description, and (iv) Involvement/Interaction. Table 2.4 displays the key features that were assigned to each of these categories, as well as their corresponding d values.

The Narrative category contains the two quintessential narrative features, past tense verbs and third-person pronouns, as well as communication verbs and *it*. In the previous section, we observed examples of Trump's reliance on third-person pronouns,

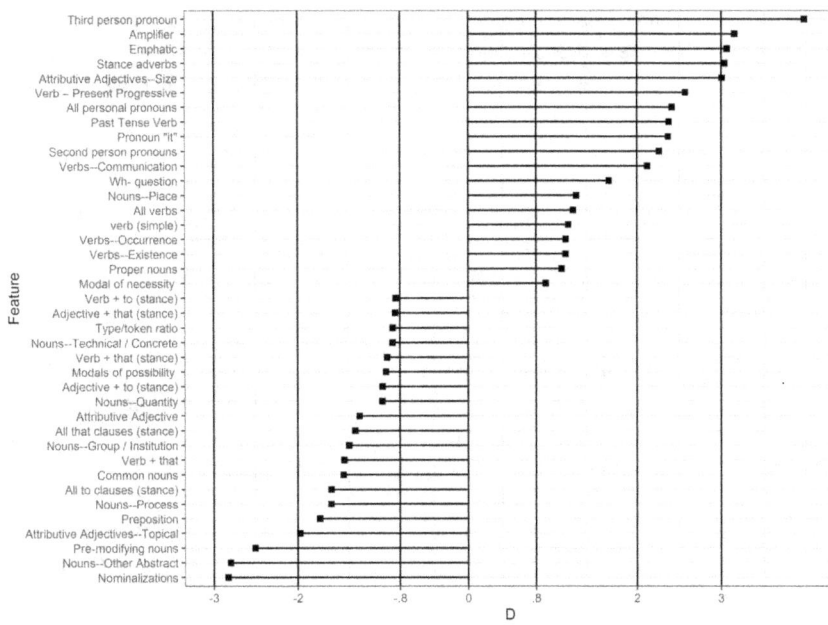

Figure 2.1 Key lexico-grammatical features of Donald Trump's discourse (exceeding threshold of > +/−0.8).

Table 2.4 Positive Key Features

	d
Narrative	
Third-person pronoun	3.98
Past tense verb	2.38
Verbs—communication	2.12
Pronoun *it*	2.37
Impersonal Stance	
Adverb/qualifier—amplifier	3.15
Adverb/qualifier—emphatic	3.07
Sum stance adverbs	3.04
Modal of necessity	0.91
Subjective Commentary and Description	
Attributive adjectives—size	3.01
Verb—present progressive	2.58
Nouns—place	1.28
Verb (-auxiliary)	1.24
Verb (simple)	1.18
Verbs—occurrence	1.15
Verbs—existence	1.15
Proper nouns	1.10
Involvement/Interaction	
Second-person pronouns	2.26
All personal pronouns	2.42
Wh-questions	1.67

especially *it* and those that referenced his opponent. We also saw examples of many verbs in the past tense and communication verbs (*say, tell*) on the keyword list. Much of his speech in the debates is devoted to recounting anecdotes that are used to support his claims.

(31) I then **spoke** to Sean Hannity, which everybody refuses to call Sean Hannity. I **had** numerous conversations with Sean Hannity at Fox. And Sean Hannity **said**—and **he called** me the other day—and I **spoke** to **him** about it—**he said** you **were** totally against the war, because **he was** for the war. (Trump 2016, Debate 1)

Expressions of stance are another important function of Trump's style. Stance is the use of language by a speaker or writer to evaluate the truth-value of their utterances (e.g., *obviously, possibly*), or to state other attitudes (e.g., *fortunately, sadly*). Trump's discourse style is interesting in that it is marked by an extremely frequent use of some stance features—especially amplifiers, emphatics, and other stance adverbs—while at the same time avoiding alternative stance features, such as verb + (*that*) complement clauses, and thus using those alternative devices considerably less often than other presidential candidates.

It turns out that there is an important functional difference associated with this stylistic choice: Verb + complement clause constructions are directly attributed to the speaker, and thus they explicitly represent the evaluation of that person. By contrast, stance adverbs are not overtly attributed to anyone, and instead they suggest that the stance evaluation is a generally accepted fact. Thus, compare the following use of stance features by Clinton and Trump. Clinton, using stance verb + complement clause, directly attributed to the speaker:

(32) Lester, **I think** implicit bias is a problem for everyone, not just police. (Clinton 2016, Debate 1)
(33) And **I believe strongly** that commonsense gun safety measures would assist us. (Clinton 2016, Debate 1)

Trump, using stance adverbs with no direct attribution:

(34) The wealthy are going to create tremendous jobs. They're going to expand their companies. They're going to do a tremendous job. I'm getting rid of the carried interest provision. And if you **really** look, it's not a tax—it's **really** not a great thing for the wealthy. (Trump 2016, Debate 1)

We refer to these stance features favored by Trump as 'Impersonal Stance.' This label reflects the use of language to establish a stance that is vague in the sense that the possessor of the stance is not explicitly identified. In fact, many of these stance devices are entirely agentless. This can be seen in the use of adverbs (e.g., *clearly, obviously*), as well as in adverbials used as amplifiers and emphatics (e.g., *really, very, extremely*). Impersonal stance devices provide a strategy for expressing a personal stance without being accountable for that stance. Trump's stance expressions tended to come in the form of persuasive statements that are high in certainty but lacking in evidentiality, that is, lacking direct references to the source of the information or the possessor of the stance. In the excerpt in (35), he expresses stance using adverbs to make reference to information that is "actual," "obvious," and "certain," and yet he does this without any evidentiality. It is not clear whether this is done because the facts are not known, or because they are known but strategically avoided, or for some other reason.

(35) Nobody's **ever** seen that before. That turned out to be wrong. It was **actually** $1.7 billion in cash, **obviously**, I guess for the hostages. It **certainly** looks that way. (Trump 2016, Debate 1)

Earlier, we noted prior claims that Trump's statements are difficult to fact-check. The use of impersonal stance devices is a grammatical device that serves related discourse functions: it is impossible to check the source of a claim or evaluation if that source is never mentioned. This is especially the case when the claim is simply evaluated as generally accepted certainty, rather than the opinion of the speaker.

In addition to the extremely frequent use of stance adverbs, Trump's discourse style is also characterized by the frequent use of necessity modals (*must, have to, got to*). This feature is also a type of impersonal stance, expressing an obligation as if it was generally accepted rather than overtly attributing the attitude to the speaker. For example, in the debates, Trump would often refer to events that *have to* take place, without any explicit reference to whose position this is or on what grounds the subject *has to* do something:

(36) They **have to** pay up. We're protecting people. They **have to** pay up. And I'm a big fan of NATO but they **have to** pay up. She comes out and says we love our allies. We think our allies are great. Well, it is **awfully** hard to get them to pay up when you have somebody saying we think how great they are. We **have to** tell Japan in a **very** nice way, we **have to** tell Germany, all of these countries, South Korea. We **have to** say, you **have to** help us out. (Trump 2016, Debate 3)

Trump uses verbs much more frequently than other presidential candidates. Not only does he rely on verbs in his narratives but he also relies on subjective commentary about the state of affairs in the world and particularly in the United States. He also frequently makes predictions about events that will or will not *happen* in the future, especially if Clinton becomes president.

(37) Nothing is going to ever **happen**. Let me tell you, if she is president of the United States, nothing's going to **happen**. It's going to be talk. (Trump 2016, Debate 2)

Generally speaking, Trump uses fewer lexico-grammatical features associated with information than other presidential candidates, as we will see later. However, when he does express information, it tends to be in the form of subjective descriptions about places, people, and magnitudes. This comes as no surprise after observing the keywords in the categories of Stance/evaluation, vague language, and proper nouns.

(38) That's when—okay, Honest **Abe** never lied. That's the good thing. That's the **big** difference between **Abraham Lincoln** and you. That's a **big**, **big** difference. We're talking about some difference. But, as far as other elements of what you were saying, I don't know **Putin**. (Trump 2016, Debate 2)

In the previous section, we discovered keywords related to Trump's involved and interactive style. We see even more evidence of that in his use of personal pronouns, especially second-person pronouns, and *Wh*-questions. Trump frequently addresses the audience and the debate moderator directly and asks direct questions, rhetorical or otherwise.

(39) And **you** know what **she** should have done? **You** know Hillary, **what you** should have done? **You** should have changed the law when **you** were a United States senator if **you** don't like it—because **your** donors and special interests are doing the same thing as I do except even more so. (Trump 2016, Debate 3)

We now turn to the negative key features, or features that are more strongly associated with other presidential candidates than with Donald Trump. The negative key features are contained in Table 2.5.

The first category of key features that are more strongly associated with the other presidential candidates is Personal Stance. This type of stance stands in sharp contrast with the Impersonal Stance devices that Trump prefers. Personal stance usually comes in the form of complement clauses that position a speaker in relation to a proposition in an explicit way. Personal stance usually requires evidentiality and accountability: the possessor of the stance is explicitly spelled out in the stance device itself. We can see examples of this type of stance in excerpts from Mitt Romney and Hillary Clinton:

(40) I'd just note that **I don't believe** that bureaucrats in Washington should tell someone whether they can use contraceptives or not. (Romney 2012, Debate 2)
(41) I **think** we can compete with high wage countries and I **believe** we should. (Clinton 2016, Debate 3)

In stark contrast with Trump's impersonal stance, which is high in certainty but low in accountability, these complement clause structures are usually lower in certainty but high in accountability. For example, among the other presidential candidates, *verb + that* complement clauses were controlled by non-factive verbs (e.g., *think*) rather than by factive verbs (e.g., *know*). Using these structures, the candidates were able to explicitly identify themselves as the possessor of a particular stance while establishing their degree of certainty.

The use of technical language was another key feature that distinguished the other presidential candidates from Trump. In contrast with the subjective commentary and

Table 2.5 Negative Key Features

	d
Personal Stance	
All *to* clauses (stance)	−1.61
Verb + *that*	−1.45
All *that* clauses (stance)	−1.32
Adjective + *to* (stance)	−1.00
Verb + *that* (stance)	−0.95
Adjective + *that* (stance)	−0.85
Verb + *to* (stance)	−0.84
Technical Description	
Nouns—other abstract	−2.80
Attributive adjectives—topical	−1.97
Nouns—process	−1.61
Nouns—group/institution	−1.40
Nouns—quantity	−1.01
Nouns—technical/concrete	−0.89
Type-token ratio	−0.88
Informational Density	
Nominalizations	−2.83
Pre-modifying nouns	−2.51
Preposition	−1.74
Common nouns	−1.46
Attributive adjective	−1.27
Possibility	
Modals of possibility	−0.96

description we saw in Trump's speech, other presidential candidates were much more likely to provide technical descriptions of the state of affairs and the policies necessary to address them. These candidates relied on specialized language to refer to details about political, geographic, economic, and social issues to make logical arguments.

(42) **Median income** is down **$4,300 a family** and 23 million Americans out of work. That's what this election is about. It's about who can get the middle class in this country a bright and prosperous future and assure our kids the kind of hope and optimism they deserve. (Romney 2012, Debate 2)

In this example, we see Romney using specialized terms such as *middle income*, as well as statistics related to income per family and unemployment numbers. In the following excerpt, we see similar statistics and specialized terminology from Ronald Reagan.

(43) In the first half of 1980, **gross national product** was down a minus 3.7 percent. The first half of 84 it's up 8 and a half percent. **Productivity** in the first half of 1980 was down a minus 2 percent. Today it is up a plus 4 percent. **Personal earnings** after taxes per capita have gone up almost $3,000 in these 4 years.

In 1980—or 1979, a person with a **fixed income** of $8,000 was $500 above the **poverty line**, and this maybe explains why there are the numbers still in poverty. By 1980 that same person was $500 below the **poverty line**. (Reagan 1984, Debate 1)

Both of the two previous excerpts use a wide range of vocabulary, which increases the type–token ratio (i.e., an indicator of vocabulary diversity), including specialized terms such as *gross national product, median income, personal earnings, fixed income, poverty line,* and *productivity*. Terms such as these were used much more frequently by other candidates than by Trump.

Related to the category of technical description is that of informational density, or the compression of information into dense linguistic structures, in particular noun phrases. Trump tended to rely on verbs and elaborated clause structures rather than dense noun phrases, a feature noted previously by Hunston (2016). This gave his speech a more colloquial, informal tone because dense information is much more likely to occur in expository writing or scripted speech than in interactive dialogue. Trump uses fewer nouns, nominalizations, pre-modifying nouns, and attributive adjectives, all of which are functionally associated with informational language, as well as prepositions that typically correspond to these other features. In the following excerpt from George W. Bush, we see examples of the nouns, adjectives, nominalizations, prepositions, and pre-modifying nouns that are so characteristic of traditional presidential debate speech.

(44) I know we can do a **better job** of **clean coal technologies**. I'm going to ask the **Congress** for $2 **billion** to make sure we have the **cleanest coal technologies in** the **world**. My **answer to** you is **in** the **short-term** we need to get after it here **in America**. We need to explore our **resources** and we need to **develop** our **reservoirs of domestic production**. We also need to have a **hemispheric energy policy** where **Canada, Mexico** and the **United States** come **together**. (George W. Bush 2000, Debate 1)

As we have seen, Trump's style runs counter to this style. In one sense, this led to the perception that he is unintelligent and unprofessional. However, it was likely this very style that played a role in his appeal to many American voters.

The final category is Possibility, containing only possibility modals. The rhetoric of presidential debates has traditionally been focused not only on criticizing one's opponent but also on offering a vision of hope for the future of America and what it can be. Possibility modals allow candidates to speculate on what might be possible if he or she becomes president.

(45) If we're lucky and we do it right, that **could** potentially happen but in the short term there's an outlay and we **may** not see that money for a while. (Barack Obama 2008, Debate 1)

Despite Trump's "Make America Great Again" slogan, he rarely offered insights into what policies he would implement if he became president. And when he did comment on the future, he typically used *will* and *going to* rather than *could*, *may*, and *might*. Possibility modals can also be used to hedge claims about the state of affairs, but hedging is not a defining characteristic of Trump's style.

2.4 Conclusion

To summarize, our findings reaffirm the value of applying quantitative corpus linguistics to questions regarding the linguistic style of particular speakers. Using these methods, we were able to reveal patterns that are not salient and therefore not noticed by other observers. The keyword results confirm that there are many words Trump used more frequently than other presidential candidates. Paradoxically, while he used many more distinctive words than his opponent, he also used fewer distinct words in general. In other words, his vocabulary was distinctive when compared with other candidates, but it was also highly repetitive. Moreover, when we classify these words into semantic and functional categories, we find that Trump's lexical choices offer meaningful insights into his style of speaking, including his colloquial style, the nature of his attacks and counterattacks, the issues he chose to focus on, his extensive use of hyperbole, and his reliance on vague language and references.

The key feature analysis showed that Trump's linguistic style is extremely distinctive when compared with other presidential candidates. He uses a large set of lexico-grammatical features with extreme frequencies when compared with other candidates. He uses more lexico-grammatical features associated with the functions of Narrative, Impersonal Stance, Subjective Commentary and Description, Involvement/Interaction, and Concrete References, and he uses fewer lexico-grammatical features associated with the functions of Personal Stance, Technical Description, Informational Density, and Possibility.

We also found that when we evaluate the results of the keyword analysis together with those from the key feature analysis, we find that many of the patterns are consistent. For example, we found evidence of Trump's narrative style in both sets of results. Likewise, his impersonal stance was revealed through his use of words and grammar. We concluded that his style is involved and interactive from both analyses. We also found that the two analyses provided non-overlapping and complementary findings. For example, Trump's avoidance of technical and informational language was much more clear in the key feature results than in the keyword results. Likewise, semantic categories such as the nature of his attacks on Clinton and his discussion of policies and negotiation were abundantly clear in the keyword results but were almost entirely absent from the key feature results. Thus, we can see the advantages of analyzing both the words and the (lexico-)grammatical structures used by Trump in order to reveal his distinctive style.

It was also meaningful to adopt a comparative approach here. This allowed us to quantify Trump's language with reference to a baseline and thus derive statistical evidence for the extent and nature of his distinctiveness. Using this approach, we were able to not only confirm that Trump is indeed distinct from other presidential candidates but also to pinpoint exactly where those differences lie. The linguistic evidence from this study can be used to address the question of whether Trump's "words and his use of grammar are carefully chosen, and put together artfully, automatically, and quickly" (Lakoff 2016), or simply that "this is the only way he knows how to speak" (Hunston 2016). The combination of semantic choices in the form of words and functional choices manifested through grammar suggests that Trump's style is a deliberate one. He relies on it because it works. It works not only in politics. His style worked for him long before he was a politician, whether it was in high stakes New York City real estate deals or as a host of *The (Celebrity) Apprentice*. However, it is unlikely that Trump's style would have been effective in earlier elections. Recent linguistic research suggests that Trump's language, while extremely distinctive, is also part of a "long-developing presidential pattern" (Jordan and Pennebaker 2017: 312). The evidence seems to suggest that Trump's distinctive language helped him to win voters through, among other things, simplified language, a colloquial tone, impersonal stance, and an involved style—and an overall extremely distinctive linguistic style. During the debates, Trump polarized voters to a greater degree than any prior presidential candidate. Regardless of which pole voters find themselves on, it is hard to deny that Trump's distinctive language played an instrumental role in his election as president. His stylistic strategies allowed him to be a disruptive innovator in a political sense as well as in a linguistic sense (cf. Bower and Christensen 1995; see also Jamieson and Taussig 2017). As a result, it is probably the case that presidential debates, presidential language, and even political discourse in the United States in general have changed forever.

Notes

1. There is a wide range of statistical methods used for keyword analysis. We used the following Keyword List settings in AntConc: Keyword Statistic = 'Log-Likelihood (4-term),' Keyword Statistic Threshold = 'p<0.05 (+Bonferroni),' and Keyword Effect Size Measure = 'Phi coefficient (Cramer's V),' and Keyword Effect Size Threshold = 'All Values.'
2. For more information, see https://www.socscistatistics.com/effectsize/default3.aspx
3. For more information on Trump's vague use of pronouns, see also the following two chapters.
4. https://www.factcheck.org/2016/11/trump-repeats-criminal-alien-claim/

References

Ahmadian, Sara, Sara Azarshahi, and Delroy L. Paulhus (2017), "Explaining Donald Trump via Communication Style: Grandiosity, Informality, and Dynamism," *Personality and Individual Differences*, 107 (1): 49–53.

Biber, Douglas (1988), *Variation across Speech and Writing*, Cambridge: Cambridge University Press.

Biber, Douglas and Jesse Egbert (2018), *Register Variation Online*, Cambridge: Cambridge University Press.

Black, Eric (2016), "Comparing the Speaking Styles of Clinton and Trump—and What It Reveals about Their Minds," *Minnesota Post*, June 23. Available online: https://www.minnpost.com/eric-black-ink/2016/06/comparing-speaking-styles-clinton-and-trump-and-what-it-reveals-about-their-m/ (accessed January 13, 2020).

Bower, Joseph L. and Clayton M. Christensen (1995), "Disruptive Technologies: Catching the Wave," *Harvard Business Review*, 73 (1): 43–53.

Chapman, Ben (2019), "I Started Fact-Checking Trump—And Realized It's Not Easy," *A Medium Corporation*, January 14. Available online: https://medium.com/spec/i-started-fact-checking-trump-and-realized-its-not-easy-a19ad52f390 (accessed January 13, 2020).

Clarke, Isobelle and Jack Grieve (2019), "Stylistic Variation on the Donald Trump Twitter Account: A Linguistic Analysis of Tweets Posted Between 2009 and 2018," *PloS one*, 14 (9): e0222062.

Coe, Chelsea (2016), "WIRED Opinion: The Way Trump Talks in Debates Is Contagious," *Wired*, October 3. Available online: https://www.wired.com/2016/03/wired-opinion-way-trump-talks-debates-contagious/ (accessed January 13, 2020).

Cohen, Jacob (1977), *Statistical Power Analysis for the Behavioral Sciences*, New York: Academic Press.

Diamond, Jeremy (2016), "Donald Trump's 6 Debate Tactics," *CNN*, September 26. Available online: https://www.cnn.com/2016/09/25/politics/presidential-debate-trump-style/index.html (accessed January 13, 2020).

Digby Parton, Heather (2016), "Trump's Incoherent Greatest Hits: His Stream-Of-Nonsense Debate Style Is Tough to Combat," *Salon*, September 26. Available online: https://www.salon.com/2016/09/26/trumps-incoherent-greatest-hits-his-stream-of-nonsense-debate-style-is-tough-to-combat/ (accessed January 13, 2020).

Firth, John R. (1957), *Papers in Linguistics 1934–1951*, London: Oxford University Press.

Gray, Bethany (2011), "Exploring Academic Writing through Corpus Linguistics: When Discipline Tells only Part of the Story," PhD diss., Northern Arizona University.

Hall, Kira, Donna M. Goldstein, and Matthew B. Ingram (2016), "The Hands of Donald Trump: Entertainment, Gesture, Spectacle," *HAU: Journal of Ethnographic Theory*, 6 (2): 71–100.

Hunston, Susan (2016), "Clinton Versus Trump: A Question of (Language) Style," *Birmingham Blogs*, October 3. Available online: https://blog.bham.ac.uk/susanhunston/2016/10/03/clinton-versus-trump-a-question-of-language-style/ (accessed January 13, 2020).

Jamieson, Kathleen Hall and Doron Taussig (2017), "Disruption, Demonization, Deliverance, and Norm Destruction: The Rhetorical Signature of Donald J. Trump," *Political Science Quarterly*, 132 (4): 619–51.

Jordan, Kayla N. and James W. Pennebaker (2017), "The Exception or the Rule: Using Words to Assess Analytic Thinking, Donald Trump, and the American Presidency," *Translational Issues in Psychological Science*, 3 (3): 312–16.

Krzywinski, Martin (2016), "Word Analysis of 2016 Presidential Debates—Clinton vs. Trump." Available online: http://mkweb.bcgsc.ca/debates2016/ (accessed January 13, 2020).

Lakoff, George (2016), "Following Trump's Use of Language," *Berkeley Blog*, 24 August. Available online: https://blogs.berkeley.edu/2016/08/24/following-trumps-use-of-language/ (accessed January 13, 2020).

Mascaro, Lisa (2016), "'Believe Me': People Say Trump's Language Is Affecting Political Discourse 'Bigly,'" *LA Times*, September 12. Available online: https://www.latimes.com/politics/la-na-pol-trump-language-20160912-snap-story.html (accessed January 13, 2020).

Nelson, Libby (2016), "A Taxonomy of Donald Trump's Most Reliable Debate Tactics," *Vox*, October 7. Available online: https://www.vox.com/2016/9/26/13036258/donald-trump-debate-win-lies-preparation (accessed January 13, 2020).

Sclafani, Jennifer (2017), *Talking Donald Trump: A Sociolinguistic Study of Style, Metadiscourse, and Political Identity*, New York: Routledge.

Scott, Mike (1997), "PC Analysis of Key Words—and Key Key Words," *System*, 25 (2): 233–45.

Viser, Matt (2016), "Donald Trump Relies on a Simple Phrase: 'Believe me,'" *Boston Globe*, May 24. Available online: https://www.bostonglobe.com/news/politics/2016/05/24/donald-trump-relies-heavily-simple-phrase-believe/0pyVI36H70AOHgXzuP1P5H/story.html (accessed January 13, 2020).

Vrana, Leo and Gerold Schneider (2017), "Saying Whatever It Takes: Creating and Analyzing Corpora from US Presidential Debate Transcripts," *Presentation given at the International Corpus Linguistics Conference*, Birmingham, UK.

Wang, Yaqin and Haitao Liu (2017), "Is Trump Always Rambling Like a Fourth-Grade Student? An Analysis of Stylistic Features of Donald Trump's Political Discourse during the 2016 Election," *Discourse and Society*, 29(3): 299–323.

Williams, Raymond (1983), *Keywords: A Vocabulary of Culture and Society*, London: Fontana.

Woolley, John T. and Gerhard Peters (1999–), "The American Presidency Project." Available online: https://www.presidency.ucsb.edu/documents/presidential-documents-archive-guidebook/presidential-candidates-debates-1960-2016 (accessed January 13, 2020).

3

I Know Words, I Have the Best Words

Repetitions, Parallelisms, and Matters of (In)Coherence

Kristina Nilsson Björkenstam and Gintarė Grigonytė

3.1 Introduction

A common observation, often remarked upon in both traditional and social media, is that Donald Trump repeats himself, and that his vocabulary is more limited and his grammar less complex than the language of other politicians (see, for example, Burleigh 2018; Smith 2016; Shafer 2015). His casual speaking style in general and frequent use of repetitions in particular are commonly attributed to efforts to persuade by means of influencing the emotions of the audience (see, for example, Goldhill 2017; Golshan 2016) and to distance himself from career politicians (Shafer 2015). Leith (2017) notes that "[s]imple (or absent) grammatical structures leave the audience with nothing so taxing as a train of thought: rather, a random collage of emotive terms, repeated for emphasis. You come away from a Trump speech with a feeling, not an argument."

A frequently cited—and often ridiculed—Trump quote originated at a campaign stop in South Carolina on December 30, 2015, when Trump made the following comment on the Obama administration's handling of the Syrian conflict (audience response in brackets).

(1) I used to call them incompetent, now I just call them stupid. I went to an Ivy League School. I'm very highly educated. I know words, I have the best words. I have the b— But there's no better word than stupid, right? [*Laughter*] There's no better, there's no better. [*Applause, laughter*]

This quote illustrates many of the characteristics and mannerisms of Trump as a public speaker: the use of simple words (*stupid* rather than *incompetent*) and short sentences, sequential utterances with related or similar meaning (e.g., "I went to an Ivy League School. I'm very highly educated."), and repetition of words or phrases (e.g., "There's no better, there's no better."). But despite—or perhaps because of—these characteristics and mannerisms, Trump is an effective communicator with a well-honed ability to connect with, entertain, and persuade his audience (McWhorter 2016).

In a study on Trump's rhetoric during the first hundred days of his presidency, Holland and Fermor (2017) mention the effectiveness of his simple, repetitive, and emotional rhetorical style. They note that "Trump, like Bush, is particularly adept at repeating the most important elements of his discourse, and therefore succeeds in driving his core identity messages home for key audiences" (Holland and Fermor 2017: 183).

Repetition of words or phrases for emphasis, or repetition of a refrain (e.g., "Lock her up!"), contributes to *parallelism*, defined by Fahnestock (2011: 225) as "a formal quality of similarity between phrases, clauses, or larger units of discourse." Beyond repetition of words or phrases, parallelism can be established through similar syntactic patterns, and prosodic and metric similarities. While Trump's frequent use of repetition has been framed as a symptom of a small vocabulary (Shafer 2015; Smith 2016; Burleigh 2018), it can also be a sign of message consistency.

As we will show, it is another characteristic feature of Trump's speeches that he frequently goes off script. In fact, as he notes himself during a speech on October 11, 2019, he likes to speak off the cuff: "I got to tell you, isn't it much better when I go off script? Isn't it better?" (Chait 2019). An example of such a switch between scripted and spontaneous speech can be seen in the comparison between the teleprompter script and the transcript of a Trump campaign rally speech in Table 3.1, where Trump adds an off-script remark on the catch phrase "drain the swamp."

This side-by-side comparison exemplifies both repetition in Trump's pre-planned script (e.g., *We Are Going To* in the first column) and his casual and conversational

Table 3.1 Excerpt from a Speech Trump Held in Phoenix, Arizona, on October 29, 2016 (Audience Response in Brackets)*

Teleprompter script	Transcript
When we win on November 8th, We Are Going To Washington DC. And We Are Going To DRAIN THE SWAMP.	When we win on November 8th, we are going to Washington, D.C., and we are going to drain the swamp. [*Applause, chanting* "Drain the swamp"]
	You know, when I first heard that term, I hated it, I said, oh that's so hokey. [*Laughter*] That is so hokey. But I said, look, let's give it a shot. I tried it, the place went crazy. Then I said, maybe we'll try it again. The place went crazy, and now I like it. [*Cheer*]
	You know, great, great singers, a lot of great artists, great singers, Frank Sinatra. So Frank Sinatra didn't like My Way when he first sang it. And then he noticed the audience liked it a lot, and then it went out, became number one like big. And all of a sudden he started to love that song My Way, right? So drain the swamp.

*The following transcription conventions are used in the examples:
Comma: clause-final intonation (indicating that there is more to come)
Question mark: rising intonation
Period: sentence-final falling intonation and/or pause
Underline: repetition

use of repetition when expanding on this script. In the off-script remarks, he repeats words (e.g., "great") as well as longer linguistic units (e.g., "That is so hokey"), and paraphrases himself by repeating the same content using different words (e.g., "give it a shot," "try it again") before ending by repeating the refrain "drain the swamp."

Importantly, political speeches differ from the kinds of speech data that linguists typically study, that is, spontaneous speech produced by individual speakers, in that both the form and the content are pre-planned, influenced, and shaped by members of staff and other political operatives in cooperation with the politician. Professional speech writers express the message in the voice of the politician. The end result of this collaborative effort, "the presidential voice" (Schlesinger 2008; Ritter and Medhurst 2004), is a performance by the politician in interaction with an audience, a hybrid of scripted and spontaneous speech in which carefully crafted policy statements are intertwined with unprepared remarks. If a politician's voice is recognizable and consistent, it contributes to the construction of a political identity.

The aim of this study is to expand on observations on the pervasiveness of repetition in Trump's speech. To that end, we first compare and contrast repetition in the three presidential debates between Trump and Clinton. Although largely unscripted, political debates do not necessarily consist of spontaneous interaction. Candidates prepare for the event by studying briefing books, learning their opening statements and answers to likely queries by heart, and practicing how to pivot from a tough question to the campaign talking points. It has been reported that during the 2008 presidential election, both the McCain and the Obama campaign held dress rehearsals in the form of mock debates with stand-ins for the opponent (see, for example, Heilemann and Halperin 2010: 390–1, 400–6). Thus, debate transcripts likely consist of a combination of prepared remarks as well as both pre-planned and spontaneous answers and rebuttals. In this study, the debates are primarily used to compare the speaking styles of the two opponents during the debates, with a focus on repetition.

Second, we explore differences and similarities between scripted and spontaneous repetition in Trump's speech by comparing teleprompter scripts provided by the Trump campaign to the corresponding transcripts of the delivered speeches. As shown in a quantitative analysis of Trump's and Clinton's speaking styles during the 2016 presidential election (Savoy 2017), there are large stylistic differences between Trump's prepared speeches and his unprepared remarks, indicating that he did not write his speeches, whereas the comparison of Clinton's speeches and unprepared remarks suggest that she was more directly involved in the speech writing process. In this study, we try to expand on these findings by contrasting Trump's presidential voice, as captured in transcripts of his speeches, to the pre-planned rhetoric in the corresponding teleprompter scripts.

A final note on the linguistic study of political speech is that any speaking event also has a non-linguistic context that influences interpretation, including the topic of the speech and the purpose of the speaking event, the setting (e.g., a local diner during lunch hour vs. a large stadium at night), and the physical aspects (e.g., the staging and other physical attributes), as well as the participants and the relationships between them (e.g., a political candidate and non-committed voters vs. dedicated supporters). In this study, we primarily focus on the linguistic context, but we take the non-linguistic context into account both in the selection of data and in the presentation of results. Further, we will not discuss concepts such as truth and lies, but we would like to point out that research in psychology shows that repeatedly hearing a statement increases the subjective impression that the statement is true (see, for example, Unkelbach 2007).

In order to expand on observations of Trump's use of repetition, we apply a novel approach to the study of repetition and parallelism in political speech in that we turn to a computational method originally developed for the analysis of repetition in child-directed speech (Wirén et al. 2016). This approach allows us to identify and extract examples of repetition for further quantitative and qualitative analysis. Our data consists of a selection of transcripts from Trump's speaking events during the 2016 presidential campaign—from the Republican National Convention in July to the election in November. The selection includes transcripts of the nomination acceptance speech, three campaign rallies, remarks at a charity event, and the victory speech. Transcripts of comparable speeches by Hillary Clinton are used for a comparison between the two presidential candidates across different types of speaking events.

The chapter is structured as follows. First, we provide some background on repetition, parallelism, and coherence from rhetorical and linguistic perspectives. Second, the selection and pre-processing of data and our method to extract repeated and parallel utterances are described. Third, we analyze Trump's use of different types of repetition and parallelism found in our data and how they contribute to what may be perceived as coherence in some cases and incoherence in other cases. Finally, we discuss how differences between speaking events and audience involvement may influence Trump's speaking style.

3.2 Repetition as a Rhetorical Device and as a Feature of Spontaneous Speech

Examples of the use of rhetorical devices based on repetition and parallelism can be found in many of the more memorable political speeches, for example, in this quote from President Reagan's speech at the Brandenburg Gate, Berlin, on June 12, 1987.

(2) General Secretary Gorbachev, if you seek peace, if you seek prosperity for the Soviet Union and Eastern Europe, if you seek liberalization: Come here to this gate. Mr. Gorbachev, open this gate. Mr. Gorbachev, tear down this wall.

In (2), we find a combination of rhetorical devices based on repetition. For instance, in his opening line, Reagan begins three clauses with "if you seek," which is referred to as an opening repetition (in rhetoric termed *anaphora*). He furthermore ends two clauses with "this gate"—a terminal repetition (also called *epistrophe/antistrophe*).

To a certain extent, Trump also makes strategic use of repetition. In a study on Trump's use of discourse markers during public speaking events, Sclafani (2018: 39) notes that repetition of short phrases such as "Believe me!" that signal certainty or doubt is a pattern in Trump's rhetoric. Sclafani refers to this pattern as "epistrophic punctuation," which can be used to cue the audience to a topic shift, as well as to invite the audience's participation.

Rhetorical devices based on lexical repetition also include immediate repetition of a word or phrase (*epizeuxis*), typically used for emphasis, for example, "O horror, horror, horror" in Shakespeare's *Macbeth*, and repetition of the same refrain (*epimone*), for example, Martin Luther King's "I have a dream," or Barack Obama's "Yes, we can." In (2), we also find the repetition of a syntactic pattern that creates a speech rhythm, namely the imperative clauses "come here to this gate," "open this gate," and "tear down this wall."

While repetition as a rhetorical device is highly valued in literature and classical oratory, the opposite is true for repetition in spontaneous speech.[1] According to Tannen (1987: 585–6), this is a consequence of viewing language merely as a means to transfer information, which results in the common view that "[a]ny use of language that does not convey information is seen as superfluous and therefore bad." However, studies show that repetition is frequent in spontaneous adult conversation (Tannen 1987; Szmrecsanyi 2005). These findings align with psycholinguistic studies on so-called production priming. Both show that speakers tend to repeat previously used or heard linguistic patterns (Pickering and Ferreira 2008). Tannen (1987: 576) argues that "repetition functions in production, comprehension, cohesion, and interaction— and that the congruence of these levels of discourse creates coherence." She thereby further expands on Halliday and Hasan's (1976: 282) finding that repetition or reiteration, for instance through a synonym or a superordinate term, is one of the means by which a speaker can link new utterances to what has been said before. Tannen (1987) further suggests that repetition can provide the speaker with re-usable patterns and aid hearer comprehension by slowing down the pace with which new information is added. Also, repetition can function as a stalling technique that gives the speaker time to plan what to say next while keeping the floor. The latter kind of repetition is part of a larger group of hesitation devices, which will be analyzed in Chapter 4 by Ronan and Schneider.

As her study concerns conversational data, Tannen (1987) distinguishes between *self-repetitions*, when a speaker repeats himself or herself, and *allo-repetitions* (or *other-repetitions*), when a speaker repeats something another speaker has said. She further categorizes repetitions based on form: a repetition can be *exact* (word for word in a similar rhythmic pattern), *partial* (with some variation), or a *paraphrase* (when similar ideas are expressed using different words). Her categories also include *patterned rhythm*, defined as repetition of a syntactic or rhythmic pattern with different words. (The observant reader will recognize the overlap with the types of rhetorical devices mentioned earlier.) Tannen (1987) further points to the timing of the repetition as a distinguishing feature: a repetition can be *immediate*, if there are no other linguistic elements between the first and second occurrence, or *delayed*.

Research on repetition often concerns first-language acquisition (see, for example, Wirén et al. 2016, for a brief overview), which, as Tannen (1987) notes, is due to the prevalence of repetition in both child speech and child-directed speech. The present study is inspired by corpus-based studies of self-repetition in child-directed speech, referred to as "variation sets" by Küntay and Slobin (1996). In variation sets, the speaker's message is repeated (i.e., the speaker intent is constant), but variation may occur in the surface form, for example, through expansion, insertion, and deletion, or word order change, as in example (3), adapted from Grigonytė and Björkenstam (2016) where "le petit chat" and "tu m'aides" are repeated and expanded upon.

(3) Le petit chat? Tu m'aides? <u>Tu m'aides</u> à chercher? Il est où là <u>le petit chat</u>?
(The small cat? Will you help me? Will you help me look? Where is the small cat?)

The variation can be semantic, for example, in cases of lexical substitution such as in example (4) from Wirén et al. (2016), where the verbs *titta*, *sett*, and *kolla* are variations of 'to look (at something).'

(4) Titta här då! Har du sett vilka tjusiga byxor? Kolla!
(Look at this! Have you seen such fancy pants? Look!)

Variation can also be prosodic in cases of exact self-repetition (see Wirén et al. 2016 for an example). Studies show that about 20 percent of utterances in child-directed speech appear within variation sets (Küntay and Slobin 1996; Waterfall 2006), and that the proportion decreases consistently as a function of children's age across languages (Wirén et al. 2016; Grigonytė and Björkenstam 2016). Variation sets have been shown to have positive effects on learning in both naturalistic and experimental settings irrespective of whether the learners are children or adults (Tal and Arnon 2018; Onnis, Waterfall, and Edelman 2008).

Naturally, political speech differs from both child-directed speech and spontaneous adult conversation, but there are also similarities in that the speaker must draw and hold the attention of the audience while conveying a message. In spontaneous speech, repetition provides the speaker with re-usable patterns and additional planning time, and helps the hearer by reducing the information load by introducing new information at a slower pace. In child-directed speech, repetition in the form of variation sets helps children learn language by providing appropriate input. In political rhetoric, repetition provides a rhythm that attracts the attention of the audience, evokes emotion, and makes the speech easier to process and remember.

In the present study, the unit of analysis is a sequence of utterances that constitute a meaningful whole and include repetition, as in example (5) from a Trump campaign rally in Arizona.

(5) And I don't know, you know, this dishonest media, the world's most dishonest people. [*Booing*] Terrible people. You can have a 100 percent homerun and they'll make it look bad. They'll make it look bad. They're bad people.

In (5), we find several instances of exact repetition of words, for example, "know," "dishonest," and "people" (each repeated twice), and "bad" (repeated three times). We also find an example of partial repetition of an utterance in "They'll make it look bad," and a combination of word-level repetition and paraphrase in "Terrible people. . . . They're bad people." We extract such sequences from transcripts of speaking events during the 2016 presidential campaign in order to quantitatively and qualitatively study repetition and parallelism.

3.3 Data and Method

From the large amount of data available from the 2016 presidential campaign, we selected a small but representative subset of debates and other public speaking events for analysis. These events span the Trump presidential campaign, from the presidential nomination acceptance speech at the Republican National Convention on July 21, 2016, to the election victory speech on the morning of November 9, 2016. The data includes formal speeches from the conventions and the election, partially scripted campaign rally speeches, and a toast at a white-tie charity event. An overview of this data is presented in Table 3.2. Transcripts of speeches by Clinton, given on or around the same dates in similar settings, are used as reference (see Table 3.3). We also added transcripts from the three televised debates between Trump and Clinton to the data selection (see Table 3.4).

Table 3.2 Selection of Trump Campaign Speaking Events 2016

Date	Setting	Type of speaking event
July 21, 2016	The Republican National Convention, Cleveland, Ohio	Presidential nomination acceptance address
September 29, 2016	New Hampshire Sportsplex in Bedford, New Hampshire	Campaign rally
October 13, 2016	South Florida Fair Expo Center in West Palm Beach, Florida	Campaign rally
October 29, 2016	Phoenix Convention Center in Phoenix, Arizona	Campaign rally
October 20, 2016	Alfred E. Smith Memorial Dinner, Waldorf-Astoria Hotel, New York, New York	White-tie charity event
November 9, 2016	The New York Hilton, New York, New York	Remarks accepting election as president

Table 3.3 Selection of Clinton Campaign Speaking Events 2016

Date	Setting	Type of speaking event
July 28, 2016	The Democratic National Convention, Philadelphia, Pennsylvania	Presidential nomination acceptance address
September 30, 2016	The Sunrise Theatre in Fort Pierce, Florida	Campaign rally
October 12, 2016	The Colorado State Fairgrounds in Pueblo, Colorado	Campaign rally
October 31, 2016	Small Riverfront Park in Cincinnati, Ohio	Campaign rally
October 20, 2016	Alfred E. Smith Memorial Dinner, Waldorf-Astoria Hotel, New York, New York	White-tie charity event
November 9, 2016	The New Yorker Hotel, New York, New York	Remarks conceding the presidential election

Table 3.4 Televised Debates between Presidential Candidates Clinton and Trump 2016

Date	Setting	Moderators (broadcaster)
September 26, 2016	Hofstra University, Hempstead, New York	Lester Holt (NBC)
October 9, 2016	Washington University, St Louis, Mississippi	Martha Raddatz (ABC News), Anderson Cooper (CNN)
October 19, 2016	University of Nevada, Las Vegas, Nevada	Chris Wallace (Fox News)

Transcripts of the formal speeches, the Clinton campaign rally speeches, and the debate transcripts are made available by the American Presidency Project (Woolley and Peters 1999–) at the University of Santa Barbara. The Trump campaign rally transcripts were downloaded from media outlets as well as from the online resource Factba.se (FactSquared 2019). These transcripts were originally produced by different outlets in order to provide a written record of what was said, which means that the transcribers did not follow a common set of transcription guidelines. Therefore, all transcripts were compared to video recordings of each event, made available on YouTube, and corrections and additional annotations to the transcripts were made manually. In all transcripts, utterances are structured in sentences, with sentence boundaries being defined by punctuation (full stop, exclamation mark, or question mark followed by a blank space).

Despite the fact that politicians own their words, both spontaneous and scripted (see, for example, Schlesinger 2008: 143–4), they rarely have literal authorship of their scripted speeches. Presidential candidates' prepared remarks are no exception. Typically, these are written by a team of professional speech writers, defined by Schlesinger (2008: 13) as "collaborators who could help [politicians] develop and elevate their own rhetorical voices" and communicate their political agenda in an effective manner. In this study, we will try to distinguish between Trump's performance of a prepared manuscript, and any spontaneous off-the-cuff remarks added during delivery. To that end, transcripts of the three selected campaign rallies (rows 3–5 in Table 3.2) are compared to teleprompter scripts for these events. The teleprompter scripts were also made available by the American Presidency Project (Woolley and Peters 1999–). On closer inspection, we found differences in punctuation, hyphenation, and segmentation between the teleprompter scripts and the transcripts. Since the transcripts are representations of spoken English, whereas the scripts are written texts, such differences are to be expected. The utterance segmentation of the transcripts captures the rhythm of delivery, including, for example, interruptions due to audience responses. In the example shown in Table 3.5, taken from a campaign rally speech held on September 29, 2016, in New Hampshire, the teleprompter script excerpt (left column) includes a list of campaign promises, mainly verb phrases separated by semicolons in the script, that Trump expanded on during delivery by repeatedly adding to each promise the construction *we're going to*, and statements on Clinton's purported actions in the parallel construction *she's going to* (right column).

In order to make the two data sources for each speaking event—the teleprompter script and the transcript—comparable for further analysis, the segmentation of each script was manually adjusted to better align with the segmentation of the corresponding

Table 3.5 Excerpt from a Speech Trump Held in New Hampshire on September 29, 2016

Teleprompter script	Transcript (off-script additions in bold)
Here is [sic] just some of the great things that will happen for your country: We are going to lower your taxes; eliminate every unnecessary regulation; repeal and replace job-killing Obamacare; make childcare more affordable; bring back our manufacturing jobs; keep Radical Islamic terrorists out of our country....	Here **are** just some of the things—**and these are great things**—that will happen for your country. We're going to lower your taxes, **she is going to raise your taxes. We're going to** eliminate every unnecessary regulation **that are** [sic] **strangling your businesses, she's going to add more regulation. We're going to** repeal and replace job killing Obamacare. [*Cheer*] **We're going to** make childcare more affordable **and available to the families and to the mothers, we need help. Childcare, something that my daughter Ivanka feels very strongly about. So do I.** [*Brief applause*] **We're going to** bring back our manufacturing jobs **which have been ripped away from us by incompetent politicians. We're going to** keep radical Islamic terrorist out of our country. [*Applause*]

transcript (e.g., clauses separated by semicolon or hyphens in the teleprompter scripts are treated as separate sentences).

Sequences of self-repetition and parallelism were extracted from these transcripts and teleprompter scripts using the open-source tool Varseta, originally developed to explore variation sets in transcripts of longitudinal child-directed speech (Wirén et al. 2016; Grigonytė and Björkenstam 2016; see also https://github.com/ginta-re/Varseta). Varseta is an implementation of a surface-based, language-independent algorithm that performs a stepwise comparison of pairs of successive utterances based on string similarity. The similarity or difference between a pair of utterances (as two strings of characters) is determined by counting the minimum number of edits (insertions, deletions, and substitutions of characters) that are required to turn one string into the other. Exact repetition results in a similarity value of one, and no overlap of words results in a value of zero. Up to two intervening utterances are allowed in a variation set, in order to cover some cases of delayed repetition. The criterion for labeling an utterance as a repetition of a preceding utterance is that the difference between them does not fall below a certain similarity threshold (for this study, the threshold was set to 0.55). Even though the tool operates strictly on the surface level, most forms of repetition can be handled, including partial repetition and repetition of syntactic patterns (captured through, for example, function words or verbs). The tool cannot handle complete paraphrases, or repetition within utterances. We did not make any modifications to the tool for this study and applied the settings that performed best during the evaluation reported in Grigonytė and Björkenstam (2016). If provided with input in the form of transcripts (or teleprompter scripts) segmented into utterances, the tool returns a list of sequences of utterances with some degree of repetition—that is, utterances that are in close proximity and that are either identical or sufficiently similar. The tool also returns information on the total number of utterances in the transcript, the number of sequences of utterances with repetition (i.e., variation sets), and the total number of utterances with repetition (i.e., utterances that occur in such sequences). This output is presented and discussed in the following sections.

3.4 Analysis and Results

3.4.1 Repetitions in the Debates

As a starting point, we will examine the size of the vocabulary used by the two opponents in the Clinton–Trump debates from 2016. Figure 3.1 shows the number of words uttered (tokens) by each candidate on the horizontal axis, and the number of unique words (types) on the vertical axis.

By looking at the total number of tokens, we find that Trump uttered a larger amount of words, about 22,500 words compared to Clinton's 19,300, even though the total speaking time was roughly equal: 2:00:54 hours for Trump, and 2:02:41 hours for Clinton, according to Hellman (2016). But if we instead compare the number of unique words (types) used by each candidate (on the vertical axis), we find that Trump used a smaller vocabulary than Clinton during the debates, or to put it another way, that he repeated words more often than Clinton. Ronan and Schneider (this volume) conduct a similar analysis and confirm that this is also true if Trump's debate contributions are compared to those that Obama and other previous presidents made in their respective debates.

Figure 3.2 illustrates the proportion of utterances containing repetitions/parallelism in the debate transcripts. In all three debates, the proportion of utterances with repetitions falls between 6 and 8 percent in Clinton's speech, whereas the proportion in Trump's speech falls between 13 and 16 percent. The format of the three debates differed, which may account for some of the intra-speaker variation: the second debate at Washington University in St. Louis had a town hall format which included questions

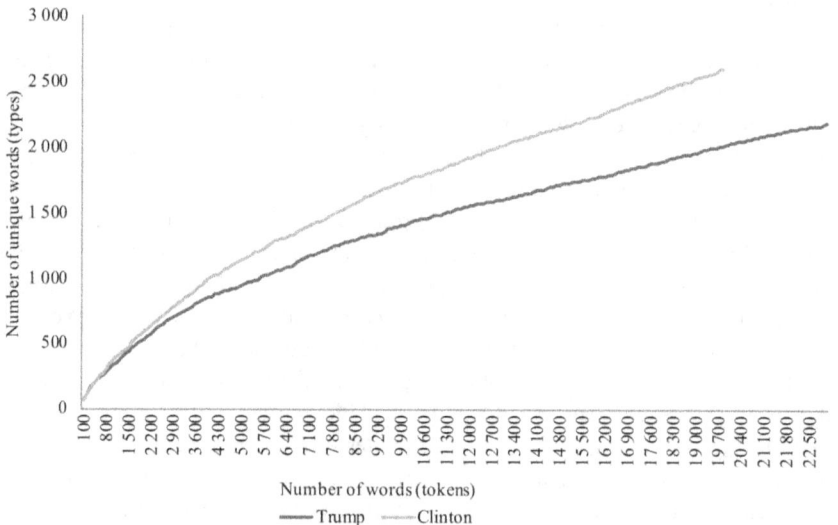

Figure 3.1 A comparison of the vocabulary used in the Clinton–Trump presidential debates.

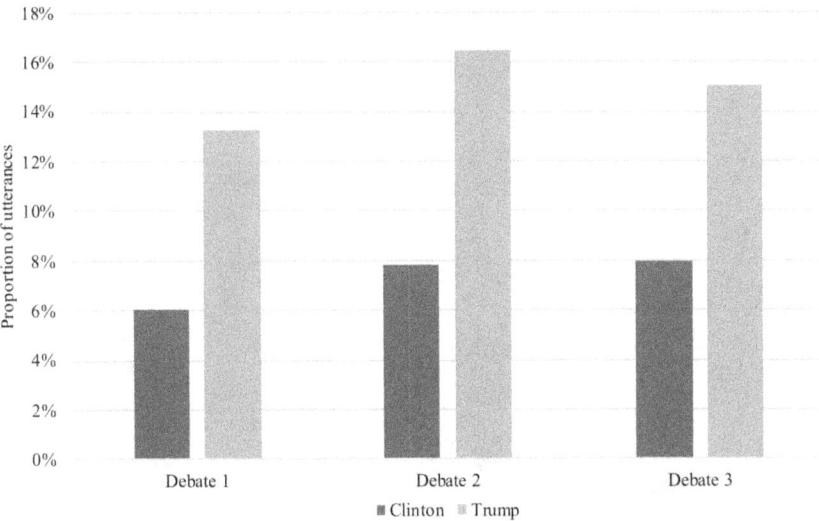

Figure 3.2 Proportion of utterances containing repetitions in the transcripts of the three presidential debates.

from the audience, whereas the first and third debate had no audience participation. This, however, does not explain the difference between Trump and Clinton across all three debates, which shows that he consistently repeated himself more often than her.

3.4.2 Repetitions in Campaign Speaking Events

Turning now to some of the scripted speaking events during the 2016 presidential election, Figure 3.3 shows the proportion of utterances with repetitions in the transcripts of the nomination acceptance speeches, campaign rallies, the toasts at the Al Smith Memorial Dinner, a charity event, as well as the concession and acceptance speeches after the election. For most of these events, larger proportions of utterances with repetitions are found in the Trump transcripts (ranging from 8 to 20 percent) than in the Clinton transcripts (ranging from 4 to 8 percent). The exception is the transcript from the charity event, where we find 7 percent of utterances with repetition in the Trump transcript, compared to 8 percent in the Clinton transcript. The largest proportion of utterances containing repetitions, just over 20 percent, is found in the transcripts of the Trump campaign rallies.

At most types of speaking events, Clinton and Trump use similar proportions of repetitions, with the exception of the campaign rallies. Our interpretation is that these results mirror the formality and setting of each event. These speaking events differ in their degree of formality, from the pomp and circumstance surrounding the nomination acceptance address to the more informal campaign rallies. The settings, locations, and audiences differ from arenas with large audiences to a charity dinner with a group of select guests. The mood of the events also differs, from the rowdy and

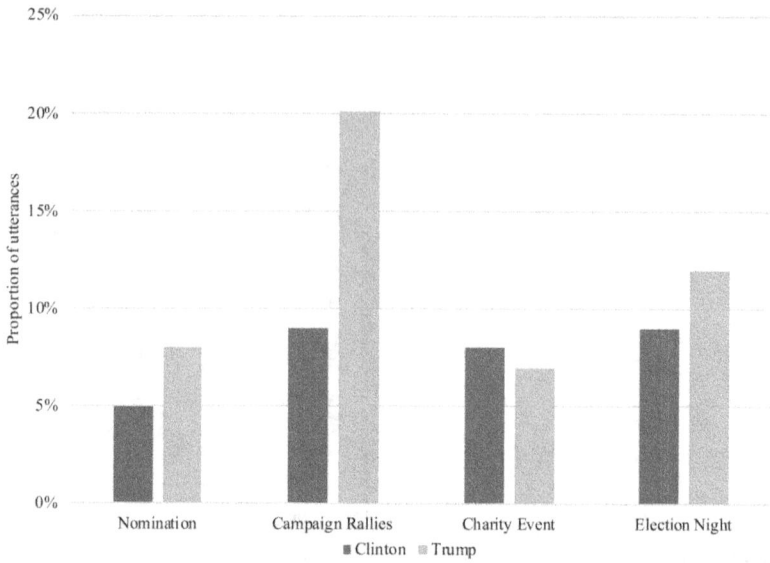

Figure 3.3 Proportion of utterances containing repetitions in transcripts of speaking events during the Clinton and Trump presidential campaigns.

loud campaign rallies to the solemn aftermath of the election. Our results show that of all the investigated speaking events, formal as well as informal, Trump repeated himself the least at the prestigious Al Smith dinner hosted by the Roman Catholic archbishop of New York, indicating that most of the speech was read from written notes he had before him on the lectern. A video of the event supports this interpretation. Interestingly enough, the *New York Times* reported that Trump "lost the room" during his speech, and that "[t]hose on the dais with him seemed to almost visibly writhe away from him at points—brows furrowing, smiles turning to grimaces" (Flegenheimer and Parker 2016). This account by the *New York Times* has little in common with reports on the mood and level of audience response at Trump's rallies (see, for example, Kragie 2018), which further suggests that the Al Smith dinner was a different type of speaking event than a typical Trump campaign rally and that Trump's performance was affected by the interaction with the audience.

3.4.3 Analysis of Scripted and Unscripted Repetition

In order to better understand Trump's performance during the campaign rallies, and why the proportion of utterances with repetitions in the rally transcripts presented in Figure 3.3 differs from the proportion of repetitions at all other speaking events, we will now compare the transcripts to the teleprompter scripts prepared for these events.

Over the course of the three rallies we have studied, Trump uttered progressively more words, due to increasing off-script segments (see Figure 3.4). During the rally in New Hampshire on September 29, 2016, Trump spoke 4,134 words—compared to

Repetitions, Parallelisms, and Matters of (In)Coherence 53

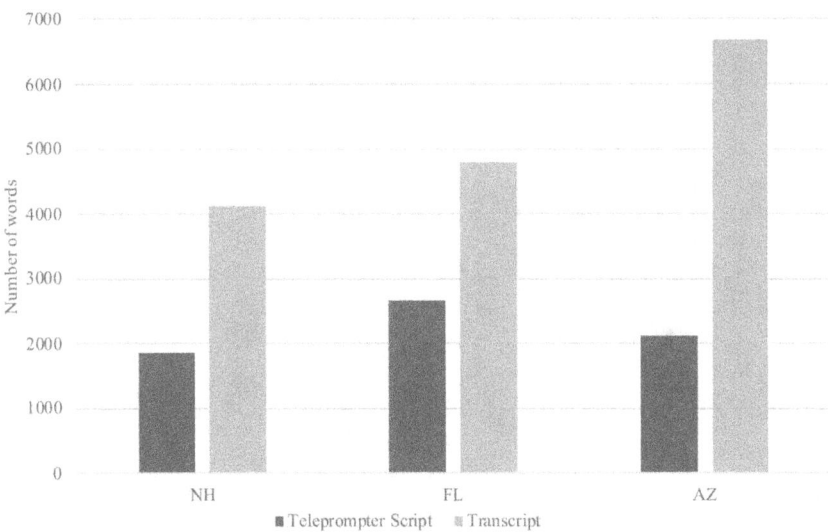

Figure 3.4 A comparison of the total number of words (tokens) in the teleprompter scripts and the corresponding transcripts of the Trump campaign rallies in Bedford, New Hampshire (NH), West Palm Beach, Florida (FL), and Phoenix, Arizona (AZ).

1,885 words in the teleprompter script, that is 119 percent more words than scripted. On October 13, in Arizona, he spoke 4,798 words—compared to 2,668 words in the teleprompter script—that is, 80 percent more words than scripted. Finally, during the rally on October 29, in Colorado, he spoke 6,719 words—compared to 2,098 words in the teleprompter script—so, 220 percent more than scripted. Between the three rallies, the proportion of utterances with repetitions varies in both teleprompter scripts and transcripts (see Figure 3.5). In both the script and the transcript of the rally in New Hampshire, the proportion of utterances with repetitions is around 20 percent, but for the other two events, there are large differences in the proportions of utterances with repetitions between the teleprompter scripts and the corresponding transcripts.

On closer inspection, we see clear differences between the types of repetition found in the scripted and in the unscripted segments of the speeches. Sequences of utterances containing repetitions in the scripted segments are typically examples of rhetorical devices such as opening and/or terminal repetition, as evident in (6) and (7).

(6) We will make America wealthy again. We will make America strong again. And we will make America great again.
(7) Their financial resources are unlimited. Their political resources are unlimited. Their media resources are unlimited.

We also found examples of repetition combined with syntactic parallelism, such as the rather long-winded segment from the teleprompter script for the New Hampshire rally in (8), where the pattern *American X will Y* is repeated seven times.

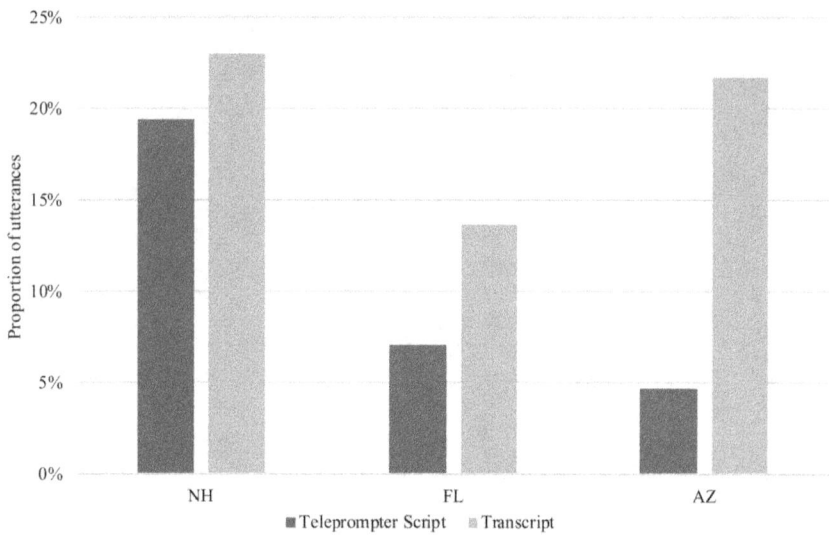

Figure 3.5 Proportion of utterances containing repetitions in the teleprompter scripts and the corresponding transcripts of the Trump campaign rallies in Bedford, New Hampshire (NH), West Palm Beach, Florida (FL), and Phoenix, Arizona (AZ).

(8) American cars will travel the roads, American planes will soar in the skies, and American ships will patrol the seas. American steel will send new skyscrapers into the clouds. American hands will rebuild this nation—and American energy, harvested from American sources, will power this nation. American workers will be hired to do the job. We will put new American steel into the spine of this country.

We found the teleprompter script for the New Hampshire speech to be quite different from the other two scripts in terms of style, mainly due to heavy use of rhetorical devices such as opening and terminal repetition, repeated syntactic patterns, and variations on refrains such as *Make America Great Again*. We speculate that this speech may have been written by a different speechwriter than the other two speeches, but we have not been able to obtain information on the identity of the speechwriters.

We found most of the shifts from scripted to spontaneous speech abrupt and therefore easy to identify in the transcripts even without consulting the corresponding teleprompter script. At first glance, the rhetorical, stylistic, and semantic differences between the scripted and unscripted segments give the impression that Trump alternates between two voices, the Candidate and the Outsider. There are several instances where he comments (in bold) on the lines in the teleprompter script that he just uttered as if he were hearing them for the first time, such as when he comments "So true" in the discourse segment from the Florida rally in Table 3.6.

While the sequences of utterances containing repetitions extracted from the teleprompter scripts (and the corresponding segments of the transcripts) can be

Repetitions, Parallelisms, and Matters of (In)Coherence　　　　55

Table 3.6 Excerpt from a Speech Trump Held in Florida on October 13, 2016

Teleprompter script	Transcript (unscripted in bold)
The Clinton Machine is at the center of this power structure. We've seen this firsthand in the WikiLeaks documents in which Hillary Clinton meets in secret with international banks to plot the destruction of US sovereignty in order to enrich these global financial powers.	The Clinton machine is at the center of this power structure. We've seen this first hand in the WikiLeaks documents, in which Hillary Clinton meets in secret with international banks to plot the destruction of US sovereignty in order to enrich these global financial powers, **her special interest friends and her donors**. [*Booing*, ca. 4 sec.] **So true**. ["Lock her up!" *chants*, ca. 15 sec.] **Honestly, she should be locked up. Should be.** [*Cheering*] **Should be locked up.**

identified as patterns built from rhetorical devices, repetitions found in the unscripted segments of the transcripts span from rhetorical devices to efforts to repair mistakes in the delivery of the speeches. While the size of our data set does not permit a quantitative analysis, we found that many of the unscripted sequences of utterances with repetitions can be categorized as rhetorical emphasis, such as example (9) from the Florida rally.

(9) The Clintons are criminals, remember that. They're criminals.

In contrast to the more rhetorical and formal scripted segments, the unscripted segments with repetitions are often casual and conversational in style. In example (10) taken from the Arizona rally, Trump adds an unscripted segment about Clinton's adviser John Podesta whose email had recently been hacked and leaked to the media. This segment follows another unscripted passage on how Trump's choice of Mike Pence as running mate shows good judgment. His comments about Clinton start with the statement that she has bad judgment that is later paraphrased as "she has bad instincts." The segment also contains several examples of repetition for emphasis.

(10) Bernie Sanders said Hillary has bad judgment. And Podesta—you know, I don't know this guy Podesta. Whoever the hell he is, I would fire him so fast. He says nothing [*Booing*]—no, no. He says nothing but bad things about crooked Hillary. That's all he says. The guy says nothing but bad things—he says nothing but bad. He has a memo, she has bad instincts. How would you—if somebody said that about me, even if it were true, I'd fire him—I'd fire him. [*Laughter*]

While repetitions in the transcripts can often be categorized as emphasis, we also found a small number of repetitions that we interpret as efforts to repair mistakes in the delivery of the speeches. In the excerpt from the New Hampshire rally in Table 3.7, the scripted line is "America is Back—Bigger and Better and Stronger than

Table 3.7 Excerpt from a Speech Trump Held in New Hampshire on September 29, 2016

Teleprompter script	Transcript (off script in bold)
On November 8th, we are going to show the whole world that America is Back—Bigger and Better and Stronger than ever before.	On November 8th, we're going to show the whole world that America is back, bigger and **bigger—oh you know that, right? You know. You know it.** America will be back, **I promise**, bigger and better and stronger than ever before. **Bigger and better and stronger.** [*Applause*]

Table 3.8 Excerpt from a Speech Trump Held in Florida on October 13, 2016

Teleprompter script	Transcript (off script in bold)
I ask a very simple question, why wasn't it part of the story that appeared twelve years ago? I was one of the biggest stars on television, and it would have been one of the biggest stories of the year.	And I asked very simple question, why wasn't it part of the story that appeared twenty, or twelve years ago? **Why wasn't it a part of the story? Why didn't they make it part of the story?** I was one of the biggest stars on television with The Apprentice and I would've been one of the biggest stories of the year.

ever before," but Trump misspeaks ("bigger and bigger"), interrupts himself, and then involves the audience by adding a conversational element ("oh you know that, right? You know. You know it.") before starting over again. This repetition can be categorized as stalling, while he plans how to repair the mistake. After re-reading the line from the teleprompter correctly, he repeats part of the line ("Bigger and better and stronger") to cue the audience to a topic shift and to once more invite them to participate by applauding.

An example of a more blatant repair can be found in the excerpt from the transcript of the Florida rally in Table 3.8. The scripted line is "why wasn't it part of the story that appeared twelve years ago?" Here, Trump mistakenly says twenty instead of twelve, and then corrects himself by adding "or twelve years ago." He then twice repeats variations of the first line, before returning to the script.

There are instances where Trump adds unscripted lines following a pattern of repetition in the speech. Such repetitive additions further increase the similarity within a segment, such as in (11), an example of juxtaposition from the New Hampshire speech where Trump's campaign promises are contrasted by statements on Clinton's purported politics (unscripted in bold).

(11) We're going to lower your taxes, **she is going to raise your taxes**. We're going to eliminate every unnecessary regulation that are [*sic*] strangling your businesses, **she's going to add more regulation.**

We also find this example interesting because the person referred to using the pronoun *she* is not mentioned by name, neither in this discourse segment, nor in the preceding segment. In this case, very little background knowledge is needed to correctly interpret the reference. However, interpretation of the segment in (12) (unscripted in bold) from the transcript of the Florida rally held on October 13, 2016, is more challenging.

(12) They control incredibly, the Department of Justice. And they even secretly meet with the Attorney General of the United States. In the back of her airplane, while on the runway—**remember he was there—he was going to play golf.** **There's the Attorney General. Let me go say hello**—plane's on the runway. **Let me go say hello** to the Attorney General. **He never got to play golf,** I understand, and it was Arizona, a place I love, but, the weather was about a hundred and some odd degrees—**he's not gonna play. He was never there to play golf**, folks, don't be foolish.

They met for thirty-nine minutes and most likely it was to discuss her re-appointment, in a Clinton administration, as the Attorney General, just prior to making a decision over whether or not to prosecute Hillary Clinton. [*Booing*]

OK? **That's** what happened, **that's** called real life and **that's** pretty sad. **They** met for thirty-nine minutes. Remember **he** said, **we talked golf**, and **we talked** about **our grandchildren**. [*Booing*]

Three minutes for **the grandchildren**, two minutes for **the golf**, then **they** sat there and **they** twiddled their thumbs. Now **I believe they** talked about her remaining in her position under a crooked Hillary Clinton administration. **That's what I believe. That's what I believe folks. That's what I believe** and I think **that's what** most people in this room **believe**. [*Applause*]

In (12), Trump discusses the so-called "tarmac meeting" between Bill Clinton and the Attorney General Loretta Lynch at an airport in Arizona (see, for example, Bump 2020). In this excerpt, he interchangeably narrates and comments on the event, and he even playacts the part of Bill Clinton when he says "Let me go say hello."

This is an interesting example of the limits of repetition as a cohesive device: superficial lexical cohesion is created by repetition of words, phrases, and clauses, but referential cohesion is lacking—because none of the participants are mentioned by name, the pronouns are so vaguely used that they are difficult to interpret despite the pervasiveness of repetition. In order to understand the message, the hearer needs knowledge of the principal actors involved in the meeting, as well as insights into how this meeting was reported on in right-wing populist media and interpreted by Trump and his supporters. While segments such as this seem incoherent to an outsider, a Trump supporter who shares his worldview may perceive this differently. The reliance on shared knowledge in such narratives may even create a sense of inclusion for his supporters, especially when followed by expressions of epistemic stance such as "That's what I believe folks. That's what I believe and I think that's what most people in this room believe." (For further discussions of Trump's vague use of pronouns, see Egbert and Biber as well as Ronan and Schneider, this volume.)

Similar discourse segments in our data (i.e., segments with a high degree of lexical cohesion through word-level repetition but lacking referential cohesion, thus requiring shared background knowledge) concern some of Trump's core narratives, for example, the alleged incompetence and corruption of Clinton and the Obama administration. There are also unscripted narratives on the sexual misconduct allegations against Trump, and—present in all of the speeches examined here—the purported dishonesty of the media.

In (12), we also find an example of Trump paraphrasing the syntactically and lexically complex scripted line "discuss her re-appointment, in a Clinton administration as the Attorney General, just prior to making a decision over whether or not to prosecute Hillary Clinton" in his own words as "talked about her remaining in her position under a crooked Hillary Clinton administration." We suggest that such spontaneous and conversational narratives add to Trump's successful "performance of the low" (Lowndes 2017: 9), that is, portraying himself as different from the establishment not only in his political views but also in the performance of these views. As part of his casual speaking style, which comes across as authentic and sincere to his supporters (McWhorter 2016), this reliance on shared knowledge might give his supporters a sense of exclusivity and inclusion.

3.5 Conclusion

As expected, our results confirm the observation that Trump repeats himself. Our study adds to this observation in that we found more repetition in speeches delivered at informal speaking events than at more formal speaking events, due to the former being characterized by long segments of unscripted speech with large proportions of utterances with repetitions. Repetitions found in the formal speeches are typically examples of rhetorical patterns. However, in less formal speeches, a wider variety of repetition is found, ranging from words repeated for rhetorical emphasis to paraphrases and repeated phrases and clauses in longer unscripted narratives.

While we interpret the majority of repetition as emphatic, we found a few instances where repetition was used in self-corrections. In the case of the campaign rally speeches, the comparison between the teleprompter scripts and the corresponding transcripts showed that Trump went off-script more often as the campaign progressed, and that these off-the-cuff segments were less coherent despite containing large proportions of utterances with repetitions.

Although repetitions add lexical cohesion, referential cohesion is often lacking and thus shared background knowledge is needed for interpretation. This reliance on shared background knowledge may give his supporters a sense of inclusion. By adding his own voice in a casual and conversational performance, Trump can distance himself from ordinary politicians and amplify his message by the use of repetition as a rhetorical device.

Note

1   The word *repetition* has a negative connotation; adjectives that typically co-occur with *repetition* are, for example, *endless*, *constant*, and *mindless* (based on a search in the *Corpus of Contemporary American English*, Davies 2008–).

References

Bump, Philip (2020), "In 2016, Trump Constantly Alleged that the Clintons Improperly Influenced the Attorney General," *Washington Post*, February 12. Available online: https://www.washingtonpost.com/politics/2020/02/12/2016-trump-constantly-alleged-that-clintons-improperly-influenced-attorney-general/ (accessed February 20, 2020).

Burleigh, Nina (2018), "Trump Speaks at Fourth-Grade Level, Lowest of Last 15 U.S. Presidents, New Analysis Finds," *Newsweek*, January 8. Available online: https://www.newsweek.com/trump-fire-and-fury-smart-genius-obama-774169 (accessed January 15, 2020).

Chait, Jonathan (2019), "Trump Bored by His Own Speech, Just Wants to Talk About TV Shows," *New York Intelligencer*, October 11. Available online: http://nymag.com/intelligencer/2019/10/trump-rally-minneapolis-speech-television-fox-news.html (accessed January 15, 2020).

FactSquared (2019), "Trump," *Factba.se* https://factba.se/trump (accessed October 1, 2019).

Fahnestock, Jeanne (2011), *Rhetorical Style: The Uses of Language in Persuasion*, Oxford: Oxford University Press.

Flegenheimer, Matt and Ashley Parker (2016), "Donald Trump Heckled by New York Elite at Charity Dinner," *New York Times*, October 20. Available online: https://www.nytimes.com/2016/10/21/us/politics/al-smith-dinner-clinton-trump.html (accessed January 15, 2020).

Goldhill, Olivia (2017), "Rhetoric Scholars Pinpoint why Trump's Inarticulate Speaking Style Is so Persuasive," *Quartz*, April 22. Available online: https://qz.com/965004/rhetoric-scholars-pinpoint-why-trumps-inarticulate-speaking-style-is-so-persuasive/ (accessed January 15, 2020).

Golshan, Tara (2016), "Donald Trump's Strange Speaking Style, as Explained by Linguists: Is Donald Trump a Throwback to Ancient Oratory—or an Undisciplined Rambler?," *Vox*, October 19. Available online: https://www.vox.com/2016/8/18/12423688/donald-trump-speech-style-explained-by-linguists (accessed January 15, 2020).

Grigonytė, Gintarė and Kristina N. Björkenstam (2016), "Language-Independent Exploration of Repetition and Variation in Longitudinal Child-Directed Speech: A Tool and Resources," *Proceedings of the Joint Workshop on NLP for Computer Assisted Language Learning and NLP for Language Acquisition at SLTC 2016*. Linköping: Linköping Electronic Conference Proceedings 130: 41–50.

Halliday, Michael A. K. and Ruqaiya Hasan (1976), *Cohesion in English*, London: Longman.

Heilemann, John and Mark Halperin (2010), *Game Change: Obama and the Clintons, McCain and Palin, and the Race of a Lifetime*, New York: Harper-Collins Publishers.

Hellman, Jessie (2016), "Clinton Surpasses Trump in Speaking Time at Final Debate," *The Hill*, October 20. Available online: https://thehill.com/blogs/ballot-box/presidential-races/301957-clinton-surpasses-trump-in-speaking-time-at-final-debate (accessed January 15, 2020).

Holland, Jack and Ben Fermor (2017), "Trump's Rhetoric at 100 Days: Contradictions within Effective Emotional Narratives", *Critical Studies on Security*, 5(2): 182–6.

Küntay, Aylin and Dan Isaac Slobin (1996), "Listening to a Turkish Mother: Some Puzzles for Acquisition," in Dan Isaac Slobin, Julie Gerhardt, Amy Kyratzis, and Jiansheng Guo (eds.), *Social Interaction, Social Context, and Language: Essays in Honor of Susan Ervin-Tripp*, 265–86. Lawrence Erlbaum.

Kragie, Andrew (2018), "Inside the Alternative Universe of the Trump Rallies," *The Atlantic*, November 6. Available online: https://www.theatlantic.com/politics/archive/2018/11/donald-trump-stokes-fear-immigrants-his-rallies/574984/ (accessed January 15, 2020).

Leith, Sam (2017), "Trump's Rhetoric: A Triumph of Inarticulacy," *The Guardian*, January 13. Available online: https://www.theguardian.com/us-news/2017/jan/13/donald-trumps-rhetoric-how-being-inarticulate-is-seen-as-authentic (accessed January 15, 2020).

Lowndes, Joseph (2017), "Populism in the United States," in Rovira Kaltwasser, Paul Taggart, Paulina Ochoa Espejo, and Pierre Ostiguy (eds.), *The Oxford Handbook of Populism*, 232–47, Oxford: Oxford University Press.

McWhorter, John (2016), "Trump Is Extremely Articulate—That's Why He's So Dangerous," *Time*, March 14. Available online: https://time.com/4245690/donald-trump-language/ (accessed January 15, 2020).

Onnis, Luca, Heidi R. Waterfall, and Shimon Edelman (2008), "Learn Locally, Act Globally: Learning Language from Variation Set Cues," *Cognition*, 109 (3): 423–30.

Pickering, Martin J. and Victor S. Ferreira (2008), "Structural Priming: A Critical Review," *Psychological Bulletin*, 134 (3): 427–59.

Ritter, Kurt W. and Martin J. Medhurst (2004), *Presidential Speechwriting: From the New Deal to the Reagan Revolution and Beyond*, College Station, TX: Texas A&M University Press.

Savoy, Jacques (2017), "Trump's and Clinton's Style and Rhetoric during the 2016 Presidential Election," *Journal of Quantitative Linguistics*, 25 (2): 168–89.

Schlesinger, Robert (2008), *White House Ghosts: Presidents and Their Speechwriters*, New York: Simon & Schuster.

Sclafani, Jennifer (2018), *Talking Donald Trump: A Sociolinguistic Study of Style, Metadiscourse, and Political Identity*, New York: Routledge.

Shafer, Jack (2015), "Donald Trump Talks Like a Third-Grader," *Politico*, August 14. Available online: https://www.politico.com/magazine/story/2015/08/donald-trump-talks-like-a-third-grader-121340 (accessed January 15, 2020).

Smith, Allison J. (2016), "Donald Trump Speaks Like a Sixth-Grader: All Politicians Should," *Washington Post*, May 3. Available online: https://www.washingtonpost.com/posteverything/wp/2016/05/03/donald-trump-speaks-like-a-sixth-grader-all-politicians-should/?utm_term=.8ac44911033f (accessed January 15, 2020).

Szmrecsanyi, Benedikt (2005), "Language Users as Creatures of Habit: A Corpus-Based Analysis of Persistence in Spoken English," *Corpus Linguistics and Linguistic Theory*, 1 (1): 113–50.

Tal, Shira and Inbal Arnon (2018), "SES Effects on the Use of Variation Sets in Child-Directed Speech," *Journal of Child Language*, 45 (6): 1423–38.

Tannen, Deborah (1987), "Repetition in Conversation: Toward a Poetics of Talk," *Language*, 63 (3): 574–605.

Unkelbach, Christian (2007), "Reversing the Truth Effect: Learning the Interpretation of Processing Fluency in Judgments of Truth," *Journal of Experimental Psychology: Learning, Memory, and Cognition*, 33 (1): 219–30.

Waterfall, Heidi R. (2006), "A Little Change Is a Good Thing: Feature Theory, Language Acquisition and Variation Sets," PhD thesis, University of Chicago.

Wirén, Mats, Kristina Nilsson Björkenstam, Gintarė Grigonytė, and Elisabet E. Cortes (2016), "Longitudinal Studies of Variation Sets in Child-Directed Speech," *The 54th Annual Meeting of the Association for Computational Linguistics: Proceedings of the 7th Workshop on Cognitive Aspects of Computational Language Learning*, 44–52, Stroudsburg, PA: Association for Computational Linguistics.

Woolley, John T. and Gerhard Peters (1999–), "The American Presidency Project." Available online: http://www.presidency.ucsb.edu/ (accessed January 15, 2020).

4

A Man who Was Just an Incredible Man, an Incredible Man

Age Factors and Coherence in Donald Trump's Spontaneous Speech

Patricia Ronan and Gerold Schneider

4.1 Introduction

Donald Trump was seventy years old when he assumed office on January 20, 2017. Considering the style of his language, we can observe that Trump uses simple, populist language in order to reach his audience. Occasionally, however, his speech is characterized by a striking incoherence—to such a degree that it has come to be repeatedly parodied (Sclafani 2018: 71–2). Some journalists wonder "Trump wasn't always so linguistically challenged. What could explain the change?" (Begley 2017). Referring to a statement that Trump had given at a press conference, Begley comments:

> When President Trump offered that response to a question at a press conference last week, it was the latest example of his tortured syntax, mid-thought changes of subject, and apparent trouble formulating complete sentences, let alone a coherent paragraph, in unscripted speech. (Begley 2017)[1]

Other authors take different views. Thus, McWhorter argues,

> the distinction between public and private speech is key here, so I am unconvinced that his current speech patterns can be analyzed as evidence of dementia. Instead, they're characteristics of casual speech as it has always existed. (McWhorter 2018)

This chapter investigates in how far Trump's language shows evidence of features typical of aging speakers and to what extent it shows linguistic incoherence. To do so, the study compares TV appearances from the 1980s with more recent ones. In order to mitigate the possible influence of speech writers preparing Trump's wording, only spontaneous speech, especially from interviews, is investigated, and we bear in mind that we are dealing with political language. This latter fact is important as politicians typically aim to transmit a clear message to voters and thus make sure that their grammar and vocabulary is simple enough to be understood (e.g., Beard 1999; Wodak 2015). To analyze Trump's language, this study uses a corpus linguistic approach, which investigates language variation and change. The questions that are asked are as follows:

- Can features of aging be detected in President Trump's language, and if so, which?
- Is there any evidence for incoherence?
- How does President Trump's language compare to other politicians'?
- Does President Trump use simple colloquial language to attract his target voter base?

In order to do this, we will first give an overview of linguistic approaches investigating written versus spoken language and spontaneous language of aging speakers.

4.2 Spoken Language and Aging

4.2.1 Spoken versus Written Language

It is important to note that spoken and written language typically show differences. In a number of respects, spoken language can be similar to written language, especially if we are dealing with texts that have been written to be read or performed, such as speeches, but there are also a number of notable differences between the written and spoken genres (Biber 1988: 36). In a study on genre features, Johnson (2017: 45–6) enumerates the following features as typical of written language in comparison to spoken language.

Typical of written language is that it is structurally more complex and has longer sentences and more nominal and fewer verbal constructions than spoken language. Written language also typically contains more complex information and is more pre-planned and organized than spoken language. As a result, it has more subordinate clauses, such as relative clauses, more passive voice constructions and more gerunds, participles, and attributive adjectives. It also uses longer words and more diverse vocabulary (resulting in a higher type–token ratio [TTR], see section 4.3) and contains more content words but fewer function words than spoken language.

By contrast, there is also a range of features that are typical of spoken language. It has more auxiliary verbs, which in turn are more likely to form contractions (e.g., *can't* or *we're* instead of *cannot* or *we are*) than in written language. Spoken language also tends to have more pronouns, particularly demonstrative pronouns, deictic pronouns, and first-person pronouns. It also has more discourse markers (such as *well* or *I think*), interjections, and negation than written language. Clauses are more likely to be linked with the subordinator *because*, and there are more questions than in written language. Finally, as most spoken language is produced 'online', that is, it is not pre-edited, we also find more repetitions and redundant information than in written or non-spontaneous spoken language, and it may contain phenomena of disfluency, such as pauses and false starts. While some pauses tell the other speaker that they are now welcome to make a contribution, in other cases, speakers want to continue speaking themselves, and signal this with the help of elements like *uhm/erm*. However, different types of texts can show various degrees of typical written or spoken features.

4.2.2 Language and Aging

Our investigation deals with spoken language of a septuagenarian politician. There are typical aging phenomena that can be observed in the language of healthy speakers (Kemper 2015; Wendelstein 2016). Thus, many studies (e.g., Cheung and Kemper 1992; Horton, Spieler and Shriberg 2010; Wendelstein 2016: 113; Luo et al. 2019) observe that, as speakers gather more and more experience with age, the number of words they know—that is, their lexicon—increases continuously. Wendelstein (2016) also reports that speakers' competence of situationally correct language use—that is, their pragmatic competence—also further increases. Finally, speakers' competence to create well-formed sentences—that is, the syntactic competence—remains high.

In addition, as Wendelstein (2016) points out, the level of education of the speaker is a crucial factor for both vocabulary richness and pragmatic competence: the better educated speakers are, the better their linguistic performance generally is. Luo et al. (2019) further notice that vocabulary richness strongly depends on the genre and the context. While their study confirms that, overall, vocabulary richness increases with age, particularly in small talk and at work, there are also genres in which there are no significant differences, or younger speakers even use richer vocabulary. Possible interpretations are that older adults may simply be more inclined to use formal language in professional settings or in small talk than young adults, while the few situations in which younger adults use a richer vocabulary, such as when doing housework, watching TV, or exercising, are dual task situations, which are known to be more challenging for older adults (Kemper et al. 2008), or where they may have different attitudes to appropriate behavior in public.

Furthermore, Kemper (2015: 59–60) observes that in older age, brain volume is lost and there is reduced activity in parts of the brain that process language, like the frontal cortex, as well as in the interaction between cells due to changes in various neurotransmitter systems. Thus, while vocabulary richness tends to increase for older speakers, their working memory decreases (e.g., Kemper 2015; Moscoso del Prado 2016). This means that older speakers often produce shorter clauses and sentences, that is, grammatically simpler constructions. Sentences can also become increasingly less informative. Similarly, noun phrases are overall becoming less complex as well. Again, additional factors complicate the picture. Moscoso del Prado (2016) reports a strong gender difference: the complexity of women's syntactic structures does not significantly decrease, while male speakers show a significant decrease. Luo et al. (2019) measure clause length and report that, counter to the general trend, at work, older adults actually use longer clauses than young adults. Possible interpretations are again that the older speakers put more effort into what they are saying at work or that, in contrast to psycholinguistic experiments, corpus-based studies measure average performance instead of maximum ability (e.g., Kemper, Herman, and Lian 2003).

Finally, Mulder and Hulstijn (2011) find that increasing age affects lexical knowledge positively, but it negatively affects lexical fluency and memory. A further issue that aging speakers typically face is that, also due to reduced working memory, access to the words stored in their mental lexicon is more often impeded. This leads to tip-of-the-tongue phenomena, where speakers just cannot think of the word they want to use at that very moment. These lexical access difficulties also lead the speakers to use more pronouns, like *he, she, it,* or *they,* instead of the nouns that are becoming more difficult to access (Hendriks et al. 2008). For Donald Trump, such a study has been carried out by Tyrkkö (2016). He points out that President Trump can be seen to make strong use of third-person plural pronouns. Repeatedly, the referents of the pronouns remain unclear. Tyrkkö provides the example of a speech delivered by Donald Trump in Hilton Head, South Carolina, on December 30, 2015, given in (1). In the speech, *they* is used to refer to Trump's own supporters (italics) and to the media (bold) side by side. Repeatedly, it remains unclear who is referred to in a given case: the media or the supporters (Tyrkkö 2016).

(1) **They** want to marginalize us, **they** want to do all of this and **they** want to make everybody look like, "Oh, gee." The level of genius—*they* fully understand. *They* know **they**'re crooked, *they* know **they**'re dishonest and *they* really—otherwise, who gets worse publicity than me? (quoted from Tyrkkö 2016)

In an apparent clash with lexical access difficulties, older speakers may provide increasing amounts of off-target verbosity, that is, statements that are not related to the topic under discussion. These digressions may, of course, be due to different self-construal of the speaker's and interlocutors' needs, or due to insufficient social contacts. However, they may also be due to a decline in executive brain functions (Kemper 2015). Executive brain functions are processes that ensure the cognitive control of our behavior, especially when it comes to selecting and monitoring the right behaviors to reach one's chosen goals. If these are impaired, the speakers' responses may lack relevance for, or coherence regarding the topic under discussion. Such speakers may also produce an extensive number of words, many repetitions, or paraphrases.

Aging speakers' cognitive slowdowns also influence interactional processes in speech production. Next to the reduction of working memory and decreasing executive brain functions, a reduction of sensory capacities, such as hearing and seeing less well, of course also impacts on speakers' interactions (Kemper 2015). In some cases, the decrease of speakers' capacities may also be pathological: Wendelstein (2016) points out that 15–28 percent of speakers older than sixty-five have Alzheimer or Lewy body dementia (Wendelstein 2016), which further impairs linguistic capacities (see section 4.2.4).

Based on these findings, we can identify various target areas to be investigated in the context of the language of aging speakers. These are as follows:

1. The pragmatic competence of speakers on the basis of the clarity of pronoun reference.
2. The level of lexical competence on the basis of how many words are used in a given piece of text by means of the TTR. A preliminary study on this has

been carried out by Vrana and Schneider (2017). Further factors that can be investigated here are indicators for problems in lexical access indicated by indefinite words such as *thing*.
3. The complexity of a speaker's syntax on the basis of average sentence length, as well as the extent of syntactic complexity as marked by coordination and subordination. Here, too, a preliminary study exists by Vrana and Schneider (2017).
4. Assessing the coherence and relevance of a contribution.

A further indication of aging in speech is that while textual density may decrease, more reflection about what is said can be observed, and this, in turn, results in slower speech rates. This, however, would need a different methodology from the corpus-based investigation employed here. Therefore, this point is not considered in this study.

4.2.3 Disfluency and Repetition

As we have seen, previous studies have found that fluency of speech decreases with age. In this section, we will therefore discuss disfluency and particularly repetitions and self-corrections in more detail. Importantly, when analyzing repetitions, we need to differentiate between several types of repetition that fulfill very different functions. On the one hand, there are rhetorical repetitions that can be used to strengthen an argument. They can be used to manipulate listeners if the repetition seems to partially correct what has been said before. Lakoff (2016) gives examples where repetitions with slight changes of wording seem to correct a previous statement, but also serve to in fact reinforce the original message, such as "Hillary wants to abolish, essentially abolish the Second Amendment." Such repetitions are predominantly considered features of written language, but can also be found in spoken language. They are means of style rather than features of performance and were discussed in Chapter 3. Emphatic repetitions, such as *very very nice*, are not considered here for the same reason (but see Stange, this volume, on Trump's conspicuous use of *very very*).

Instead, we focus on hesitant repetitions, which take place when speakers do not produce an ideally formed sentence (Clark 1996: 258). In that case, speakers return to an earlier point in their utterance to resume it from there (known as suspension and resumption, Clark 1996: 264, or as retraction, for example, Birkner et al. 2012). They can do so in several ways (Clark 1996: 264; Birkner et al. 2012: 1418):

1. By repeating a word or phrase
    with { } with bicycles (adapted from Birkner et al. 2012: 1418)
2. By substituting an item for another, which is often referred to as self-repair
    *what is { } **has** happened since then* (Clark 1996: 264)
3. By adding an item
    *one of the things that {-uh} one of the **many** things* (Clark 1996: 264)
4. By deleting an item
    I don't think they've {.} they ever in fact embodied (Clark 1996: 264)

Types 2, 3, and 4 are sometimes collectively referred to as false starts. The hiatus between the original and the resumed utterance, marked above by { }, can be a silent pause, a filler like *uh*, a discourse marker like *I mean*, an elongation (*oh*), a gesture, or a combination of these (Clark 1996: 262).

Bortfeld et al. (2001) find that disfluency rates are influenced by age, speaker relationship, topic, speaker role, and gender. They also find that middle-aged and older speakers utter more words per unit than younger speakers, and that older speakers produce slightly higher numbers of disfluencies than young or middle-aged speakers. Further, male participants produce more disfluencies and also restarts than females (Bortfeld et al. 2001: 139). Disfluency rates also increase with the complexity of the conversation topics and of the speech planning situation, such as when describing abstract entities rather than non-abstract ones (Bortfeld et al. 2001: 141–2). By contrast, relationship, that is, whether the speakers are married couples who know each other well or whether they are strangers, makes no difference to the fluency of speech (Bortfeld et al. 2001: 143).

Average numbers of disfluent repetitions in Bortfeld et al.'s (2001: 135) data vary between 1.17 and 1.77 per 100 words depending on the task; the average number of false starts lies between 1.65 and 2.22. Further counts of disfluency phenomena are provided by other authors. Maclay and Osgood (1959: 34) report on similar rates of 1.68 repetitions and 1.48 false starts per 100 words (for an overview of further studies, see Fox Tree 1995: 709 and Schneider 2014: 66).

Kemper (2015) notes that older speakers may produce increasing numbers of repetitions due to decreases in executive brain functions. And, indeed, Bortfeld et al. (2001: 138–9) find that

> [o]verall, older speakers produced higher disfluency rates (6.65, with repeats, restarts, and fillers combined) than middle-aged (5.69) and younger (5.55) speakers. . . . The important distinction was whether the speaker was in the older group (which ranged from 63 to 72 years of age); there was no difference between the younger and middle-aged groups.

These numbers boil down to older speakers uttering about 1.59 repetitions and 2.18 false starts per 100 words compared to 1.42 repetitions and 1.81 restarts used by young and middle-aged speakers.

4.2.4 Pathological Aging

While a reduction in vocabulary richness, and an increase in disfluencies and hesitations, is moderate in healthy aging situations, these are considerably more pronounced in conditions of cognitive impairment, such as Alzheimer's dementia. Thus, Gomez and White (2006) show that already in cases of very mild Alzheimer's dementia, fluency declines very early in comparison to healthy older adults.

Gayraud et al. (2011) show that Alzheimer patients use more unfilled pauses but also that the pauses occur more often outside syntactic boundaries and are followed by more frequent words. While healthy older speakers signal their planning difficulties with filled pauses, Alzheimer patients do not. The Alzheimer patients show particular difficulties in the lexical and semantic domains and replace open concepts with vague expressions such as *thing* or *stuff*.

4.3 Data and Method

The current study is a linguistic analysis on the basis of transcripts of spontaneous, non-scripted speech. This allows us to analyze data which has not been prepared by scriptwriters, and therefore represents Trump's own language. An overview of the sources that are used for our study is given in Table 4.1. The data consists of various sources predominantly from 2017 and 2018. First and foremost, these are interviews given to the *New York Times*, *Time Magazine*, and the *Wall Street Journal*.[2] This portion of the dataset comprises approximately 20,000 words. Further transcripts have been made of phone-ins into the television show *Fox & Friends* on April 26 and October 11, 2018, where President Trump is interviewed by the presenters. The transcripts are based on videos of the interviews[3] and have been double-checked by the authors of this chapter. Sentence boundaries were determined on the basis of falling intonation at the end of an utterance. In many cases, however, falling intonation was difficult to determine, especially before the conjunction *and*. In case of doubt, clauses were assumed to be coordinated rather than to constitute separate sentences. These transcripts add up to *circa* 8,500 words. The internet addresses of the sources are given in the Appendix (see Table 4.4).

This data is compared to, on the one hand, an interview by President Obama given to ABC TV in 2017[4] (length: 6,300 words) and, on the other hand, to three television interviews with Donald Trump in 1980 and 1987. Transcripts of these interviews amount to 6,000 words. They were transcribed and checked in the same manner as the more recent interviews.

The data has been analyzed automatically for TTR and sentence length. The TTR is a measure of how many different words a speaker uses. It is calculated by dividing the number of different words in a text (types) by the total number of words (tokens) in the text. If sixty-nine different words are used in a text of one hundred words, we divide sixty-nine by one hundred and see that the text has a TTR of 0.69. Generally,

Table 4.1 Data Sources

Source	Date	Words	Sentences	Length of recording
Trump 1980	1980	578	29	4:06
Trump Late Nite 1987	1986	1,728	123	13:09
Trump LarryKing Live 1987	1987	3,045	246	19:21
Trump NYT 2016	2016	9,099	709	NA
Trump WSJ 2017	2017	7,028	672	NA
Trump Time 2017	2017	2,575	229	NA
Trump Fox 04-2018	2018	4,687	235	30:01
Trump Fox 10-2018	2018	2,849	134	17:25
Obama ABC 2017	2017	6,331	292	21:09

the higher this ratio is, the more diverse the speaker's vocabulary is, and this diversity forms part of that speaker's linguistic competence.

However, the TTR depends not only on the speaker's competence but also on the length of the text. Shorter texts have a higher TTR, because the chance for a word to occur again is smaller. And very long texts have a low TTR, because after a while hardly any new word types are encountered, while the token count keeps increasing. In order to compare texts of different lengths, textual segments of, for example, 1,000 words each can be created and the TTR is calculated for each of them. We can then calculate the mean TTR of the different segments of the document. This measure is thus called Mean Segmental Type–Token Ratio (MSTTR); as we use segments of 1,000 words, we can also refer to it as MSTTR-1,000. MSTTR delivers numbers between zero and one, which some people may find difficult to interpret. Instead of a Type-per-Token ratio, one can also measure Token-per-Type, that is, 1/MSTTR, which expresses how many occurrences a type has on average. Thus, a high 1/MSTTR indicates a less diverse vocabulary. In our results, both measures are given.

The next group of investigated features pertains to sentence structure. First, the syntactic complexity of a text is measured on the basis of the average sentence length, which was determined automatically. Further, given that older speakers typically produce grammatically less complex sentences (Luo et al. 2019; Wendelstein 2016), we show how many of the sentences are long, but structurally simple in the sense that one sentence is added after the next with the help of coordinating structures. By contrast, complex sentences, which are difficult to process, can be created with subordinate clauses. This study determines the ratio of subordinate clauses to main clauses. To this end, all coordinate clauses with *and* or *but*, and all subordinate clauses, regardless of whether they had an overt subordinator or not, were counted manually in the texts.

The last group of investigated features concerns markers of sentence coherence in the texts. They are analyzed manually. We count false starts, repetitions, and features of semantic incoherence.

Finally, to allow comparison with other presidential candidates, transcriptions of presidential primary debates from 2016 are used (see also Vrana and Schneider 2017); these were sourced from the American Presidency Project (Woolley and Peters 1999–).

4.4 Results

4.4.1 Vagueness

Research has shown that, typically, older speakers increasingly use unspecific personal pronouns instead of nouns, such as saying *he* rather than *Paul Ryan* or *she* rather than *Theresa May*, as this places fewer demands on the working memory. As a result, older speakers also use more verbs compared to nouns (Wendelstein 2016; Hendriks et al. 2008). However, frequent use of pronouns is associated not only with older age but also informal registers (Pennebaker et al. 2014), and with a greater focus on one's self or one's social group (Tausczik and Pennebaker 2009).

While a large proportion of pronouns in a text does not indicate that all pronouns need to be vague, the number of vague pronouns may be higher. As we saw in Chapters 2 and 3, many of Trump's pronouns are indeed vague. Consider (2), where the reference of *they/them* is not always clear, and (3), where the reference of *it* is often unclear.

(2) We have judges that are waiting top-of-the-line people, the best people in our country and—, and by the way **they**'re going to be approved, but **they** take **them** out until the very, very end, and **they** said over nine years before **they** get approved. (Fox 04-2018)

(3) I think there's a lot of pressure on the Democrats. But the Democrats are nothing more than obstructionists. That's all they can do. That's all they seem to be good at. So they're obstructionists, so what they will do, even though **it**'s for the good of the country, they will obstruct. They can't do anything about Obamacare, and I understand that. They don't want to vote against **it**. But now, once **it**'s done—**it** was my original theory: Once **it**'s begun, now they can get together. They can do something. But they won't do that. There's too much—and this isn't with respect to me; this is years. This is years, Gerry. I mean, if you look at what's been going on over the last long period of time. I actually asked people that are political people—I could ask you people—you know, is **it** the worst you've seen **it**? (Trump WSJ 2017)

In addition to vagueness in pronoun reference, we can also observe the use of vague words such as *thing* or *things* instead of more specific nouns in the language of older speakers (e.g., Wendelstein 2016). Figure 4.1 gives an overview of the percentage of vague words in Trump's language. We have considered uses of the words *they* and

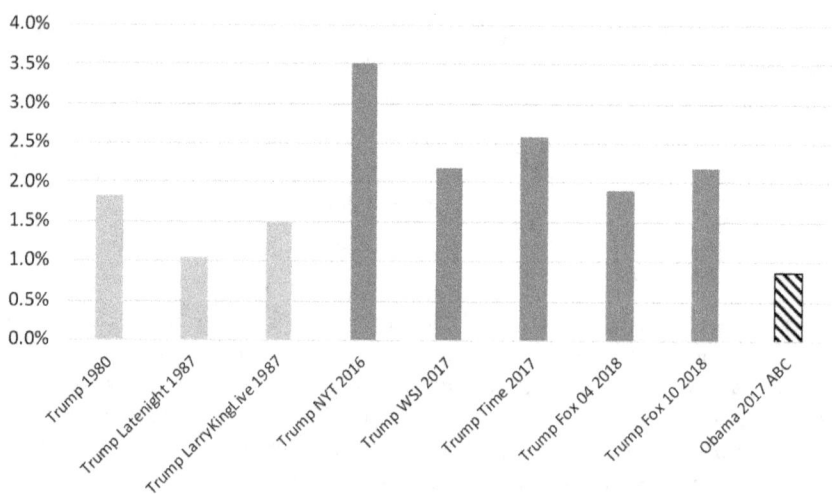

Figure 4.1 Use of vague semantic expressions in Donald Trump's language.

thing(s), as well as the compounds *something* or *everything*. For reasons of comparison, data from an interview with President Obama in 2017 is added.

Figure 4.1 shows that, in his 2017 interview, President Obama used a low rate of indefinite words like *they* and *thing/things*, *something*, or *everything*. In the interviews in 1987, Donald Trump used percentages of vague words that are more comparable to Obama in 2017. Other than that, all the investigated interviews show consistently higher uses of vague words, even the 1980 interview on the *Today* show, which is short and thus specific words are not as evenly distributed as in longer texts.

We can observe that the interviews from around the time of Donald Trump taking office show high counts of vague pronouns and vague nouns in comparison to interview data of President Obama's. This large incidence of vagueness may be due to a personal rhetorical style, or it could be seen as in line with age effects as described by Wendelstein (2016).

4.4.2 Lexical Richness

As measure of lexical richness, we use MSTTR-1,000 (Mean Segmental Type–Token Ratio with 1,000-word segments), which we have explained in section 4.3. Commonly held assumptions are that lexical richness depends on text type (i.e., spoken, casual styles have lower TTR), individual style, and age. To keep the text type relatively constant, we only included interviews and discussions in our database. Concerning individual style, we compare Donald Trump's interviews to the interview of Barack Obama. Concerning language and age, we compare the interviews from the 1980s to our selection from the 2010s (see section 4.3).

4.4.2.1 *Individual Style*

The MSTTR-1,000 results are given in Table 4.2. The mean 1/MSTTR of Trump is 3.315 for 1987, and 3.227 for the period of 2016–18, showing a small increase in vocabulary richness, as it is expected for older speakers. Obama's 1/MSTTR is 2.718 (see Table 4.2), showing a considerably richer vocabulary. In order to be able to assess the magnitude

Table 4.2 Mean Segmental Type–Token Ratio of Spontaneous Speech

Interview	Year	1 / MSTTR	MSTTR	Segments	Means of 1/MSTTR
Trump 1980	1980	NA	NA	0	NA
Trump Late Nite 1987	1987	3.390	0.295	1	3.315
Trump LarryKing Live 1987	1987	3.240	0.309	3	
Trump NYT 2016	2016	3.311	0.302	9	3.227
Trump WSJ 2017	2017	3.274	0.305	7	
Trump Time 2017	2017	3.220	0.311	2	
Trump Fox 04-2018	2018	3.059	0.327	4	
Trump Fox 10-2018	2018	3.273	0.306	2	
Obama ABC 2017	2017	2.718	0.368	3	2.718

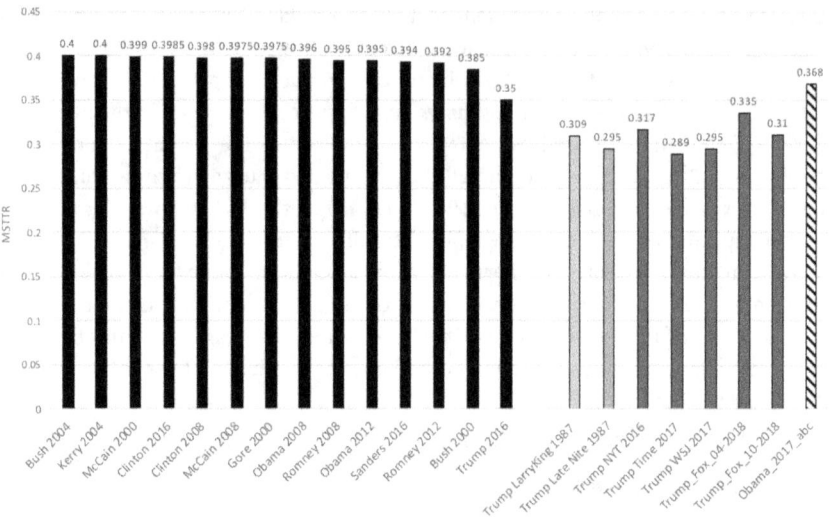

Figure 4.2 Type–token ratios of presidential debates compared to Trump and Obama data. (Values for Bush 2004 to Trump 2016 taken from Vrana and Schneider 2017.)

of this difference, we juxtapose our results to those of Vrana and Schneider (2017), who have measured MSTTR-1,000 of the presidential debates since 2000. The interviews take place in a more relaxed atmosphere than the decisive presidential debates, and thus generally have a slightly lower TTR. Donald Trump has a markedly lower TTR than any of the presidential candidates since 2000 (see Figure 4.2).

As the MSTTR delivers a separate TTR for each segment, we can also compare the fluctuation between individuals. We have compared the twenty-eight segments from Trump and the nine segments from Obama, using statistical significance testing in the form of a t-test, which confirms that the difference between Obama's style and Trump's style is highly significant ($p<0.001$).

While the difference in vocabulary richness between Donald Trump, Barack Obama, and other presidential candidates is strong, it is more difficult to assess the reasons for the difference. One reason for Trump's low TTR may be his populist approach with a strong tendency to repeat catchphrases for rhetorical impact. It may also be a partly conscious choice to refrain from using technical jargon, in order to remain relatable. Or it may be a sign of planning difficulties or concern age-related issues, as we discuss in the following.

4.4.2.2 TTR and Age

In a healthy aging process, vocabulary richness increases up to a very high age (Luo et al. 2019). This is in sharp contrast to patients with dementia, whose vocabulary richness decreases dramatically over time. Reduction in vocabulary richness has also been suggested as an early diagnostic of pathological aging effects, such as, for example, in the case of Iris Murdoch, whose vocabulary was observed to decrease significantly in her last novel (Evert, Wankerl, and Nöth 2017).

Table 4.2 shows that Donald Trump's vocabulary richness as measured by MSTTR has hardly changed between 1987 and 2018. The slight difference in mean MSTTR between Trump's 1987 interviews and the data from the 2010s is not significant. We thus find no evidence of age-related change in vocabulary richness in the data.

4.4.3 Sentence Complexity

Psycholinguistic research (Hartsuiker and Barkhuysen 2006) has shown that producing long and complex sentences places high cognitive demands on speakers. For the successful production of complex sentences, the speakers' working memory is strongly taxed. Therefore, aging speakers may find it increasingly difficult to produce long and complex sentences with subordinate clauses or other embeddings (Kemper 2015: 63; Luo et al. 2019) as their working memory deteriorates.

4.4.3.1 Sentence Structure

An overview of average sentence length in political debates shows that President Trump used the shortest sentences. This may, of course, be due to the fact that he is intentionally keeping his message simple for the voters to understand, which would be a typical feature of populist language (Wodak 2015).

Average sentence lengths from political debates show us that Donald Trump's sentence length is considerably shorter than that of other politicians (Figure 4.3). By comparison, Figure 4.4 shows that in the earliest recording investigated here, Trump 1980, an interview on the *Today* show, sentences were relatively long. This length of around twenty words per sentence is only matched by the contemporary phone-in interviews. Sentences in the other interviews are shorter, on average between eleven and thirteen words per sentence.

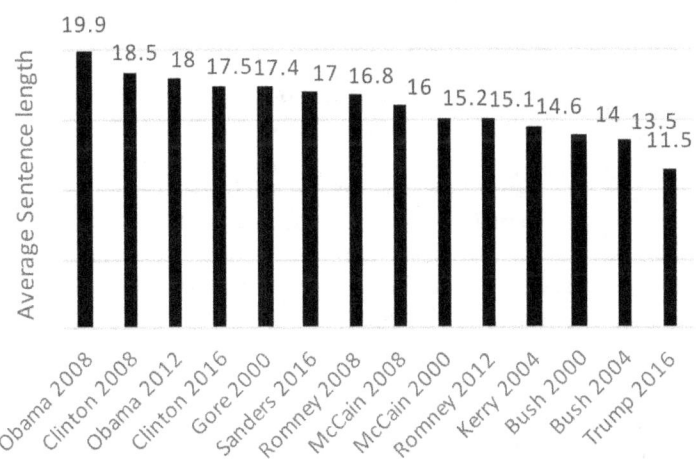

Figure 4.3 Average sentence length (mean) in political debates. (From Vrana and Schneider 2017.)

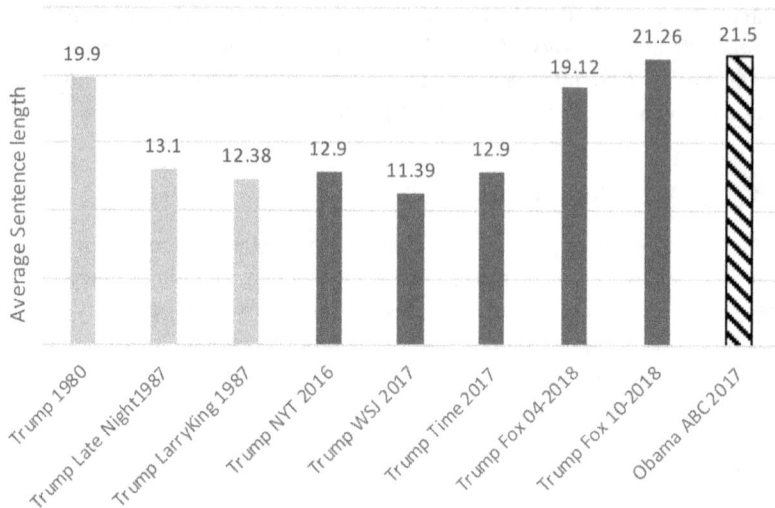

Figure 4.4 Average sentence length (mean) in Donald Trump's spontaneous speech.

An illustrative example from the transcript of a phone-in to *Fox and Friends* (April 2018) is given in (4). Coordinating conjunctions are given in **bold**, subordinated clauses are indicated by *italics*, discourse markers are given in brackets ( ), and clauses are annotated with labeled angular brackets [ ] for ease of reading. End of sentences (EOS) are also annotated.

(4)   main clause[yes dm(well) they do]. EOS 1
         main clause[dm(you know) I have known Kanye a little bit],
         coordinated main clause[**and** I get along with Kanye],
         main clause[I get along with a lot of people dm(frankly)]. EOS 2

         coordinated main clause[**but** Kanye looks]
         coordinated main clause[**and** he sees black unemployment at the lowest]
         subordinate clause[*it's been in the history of our country* dm(okay)]. EOS 3

         main clause[he sees Hispanic unemployment at the lowest]
         subordinate clause[*it's been in the history of our country*] EOS 4

         main clause[he sees dm(by the way) female unemployment
         self-correction[women unemployment] the lowest]
         subordinate clause[*it's been in now almost 19 years*]. EOS 5

         main clause[he sees that stuff],
         coordinated main clause[**and** he's smart]
         coordinated main clause[**and** he says:] EOS 6

         main clause["you know what?] EOS 7

$_{\text{main clause}}$[Trump is doing a much better job]
$_{\text{subordinate clause}}$[*than* the Democrats did"]. EOS 8

(Trump Fox 04 2018, at 0:30:00)

(4) illustrates the use of coordinating, paratactic *and* and *but*, which increase sentence length without introducing the multi-layered, hypotactic sentences that are created, for example, by subordinating *if*-clauses, relative clauses, or spatio-temporal *where*-clauses. Thus, here, sentence length is largely due to a coordinating, narrative sentence style rather than to a complex sentence structure. Furthermore, President Trump coordinates predominantly with *and* and overwhelmingly at the level of the main clause. The example contains five coordinated and four subordinate clauses. This rate of subordinate clauses per sentence (four subordinate clauses in eight sentences = rate of 0.5) is quite low, which is typical of Trump's language. Table 4.3 gives an overview of the ratio of subordinate clauses and coordinate clauses per sentence in the investigated examples of spontaneous speech by Donald Trump.

Table 4.3 indicates that Trump's sentences are more likely to contain coordinated clauses than subordinated clauses. The phone-ins to *Fox and Friends* stand out once more, as they show considerably higher rates of coordinated clauses than subordinated clauses. This is in contrast with the example taken from an interview with President Obama, where sentences on average have more than one subordinated clause, and about half of the sentences have a coordinated clause. A decreasing usage rate of subordinated clauses is in line with typical aging phenomena as described by Kemper (2015: 63), particularly if speakers are multi-tasking or otherwise under stress.

4.4.4 Word Classes

Pennebaker et al. (2014) show that the use of pronouns is related to informal language. In fact, so are verbs and most function words (Pennebaker et al. 2014: 5; Biber et al. 1999: 359). Nouns, on the other hand, are more frequent in formal language (Biber et al. 1999: 235). We therefore calculated the number of pronouns, nouns, and verbs per 1,000 words in Trump's and Obama's spoken language. The results are shown in Figure 4.5.

Table 4.3 Percentages of Subordinated versus Coordinated Clauses in Spontaneous Speech by Donald Trump

Occasion	Word count	Rate of subordinated clauses per sentence	Rate of coordinated clauses per sentence
Trump 1980	578	0.41	0.66
Trump Late Nite 1987	1,728	0.36	0.36
Trump LarryKing Live 1987	3,045	0.45	0.34
Trump NYT 2016	9,099	0.35	0.43
Trump WSJ 2017	7,028	0.30	0.30
Trump Time 2017	2,575	0.29	0.29
Trump Fox 04-2018	4,687	0.27	0.69
Trump Fox 10-2018	2,849	0.34	0.88
Obama ABC 2017	6,278	1.29	0.49

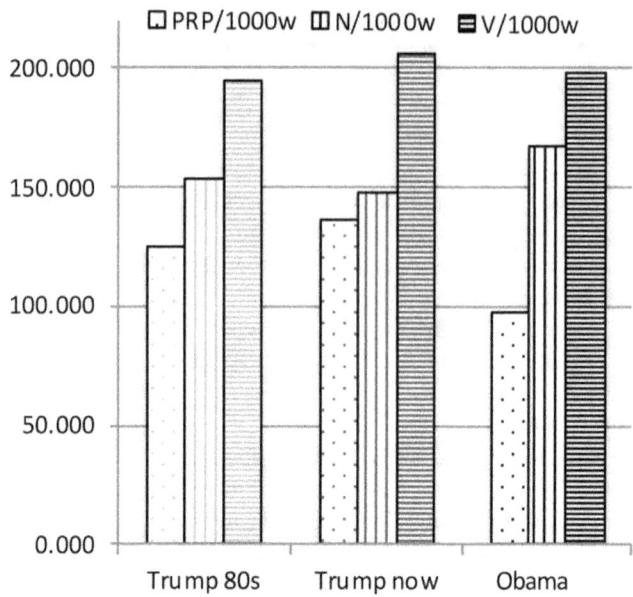

Figure 4.5 Distribution of personal pronouns (PRP), nouns (N) and verbs (V) in Donald Trump's speech from the 1980s and 2010s and in Barack Obama's 2017 speech.

Figure 4.5 shows that Donald Trump uses more personal pronouns overall than Barack Obama in the analyzed unscripted utterances. Furthermore, he uses increasingly fewer nouns and increasingly more pronouns. The numbers of verbs rise from the 1980s to the 2010s. These observations indicate that Trump's language is more informal than Obama's. The change in Trump's language between the 1980s and 2010s is in line with typical developments that have been observed in aging (Wendelstein 2016), but could also indicate that he uses even more informal language today than he did in the 1980s. The difference between Trump in the 1980s and Trump now is significant (Chi-square test, $\chi^2=6.56$, df=2, $p<0.05$), and the difference between Trump and Obama is very highly significant (Chi-square test, $\chi^2=24.54$, df=2, $p<0.001$).

Thus, overall we can see that Donald Trump's language is comprised of significantly shorter sentences—particularly as compared to language used by President Obama as he left office—that it has many verbs and pronouns but few nouns. These features are in line with typical aging features as observed by previous research (Wendelstein 2016; Luo et al. 2019). However, especially the low syntactic complexity of President Trump's language may, of course, be due to the fact that he wants to transmit a simple message to his voters. This last feature would be typical of populist rhetoric (Wodak 2015).

4.4.5 Repetitions and Incoherence

For the purposes of the current study, topic coherence is analyzed manually in the corpus texts. In particular, this study investigates the numbers of repetitions and false starts, as well as the amount of incoherence and irrelevance in the speeches. Only lack of coherence within Donald Trump's utterances is analyzed. Possible evasions of an interviewer's questions, which are a frequent feature in the discourse of many politicians, are not considered here.

4.4.5.1 Repetitions

While repetitions can be used as a rhetorical tool (see section 4.2), aging speakers may also show high degrees of unintentional repetition due to loss of working memory (Kemper 2015). Consider examples (5) and (6).

(5) Let me just tell you that Michael is uh in business, he's really a businessman. A fairly big business as I understand it, and I don't know his business but this doesn't have to do with me. Michael is a businessman, he's got a business. He also practices law. I would say probably the big thing is his business and they're looking at something having to do with his business. I have nothing to do with his business I can tell you he's a good guy. (Trump Fox 04-2018)
(6) Well he has a percentage of my overall legal work, a tiny, tiny little fraction. But Michael would represent me, and represent me on some things. He represents me like with this uh crazy Stormy Daniels deal, he represented me and you know from what I see he did absolutely nothing wrong. (Trump Fox 04-2018)

Particularly in situations of stress or multi-tasking, such repetitions may be related to overcharged working memory of the speaker. Of all speech samples analyzed here, we find the fewest repetitions in the earliest interview data. There also are few repetitions in the interview with the *Wall Street Journal*, which might suggest that President Trump may have been under less stress on that occasion. Figure 4.6 shows how many repetitions are found per 1,000 words in the investigated materials.

Looking at Figure 4.6, we see that such non-rhetorical repetitions are generally more frequent in the contemporary period than in the earlier texts, with the *Wall Street Journal* being an outlier. The short interview from 1980, like the Obama interview, has none of these disfluent repetitions. However, in comparison with other research on disfluency phenomena (Bortfeld et al. 2001), the numbers of repetitions remain low overall.

4.4.5.2 False Starts

In false starts, speakers return to a starting point to rephrase their sentences (Clark 1996). Illustrations of false starts from the speech of President Trump are provided in (7) and (8).

(7) **Well, I think we really came to recognize the** { } you know, I can say it from my standpoint, but he is viewing, I believe, Iran a lot differently than he did before he walked into the oval office. (Trump Fox 04-2018)
(8) **It's a total** { } it's all lies and it's a horrible thing that's going on. (Trump Fox 04-2018)

An overview of the false starts found in President Trump's analyzed interviews is given in Figure 4.7, which displays instances of false starts per sentence.

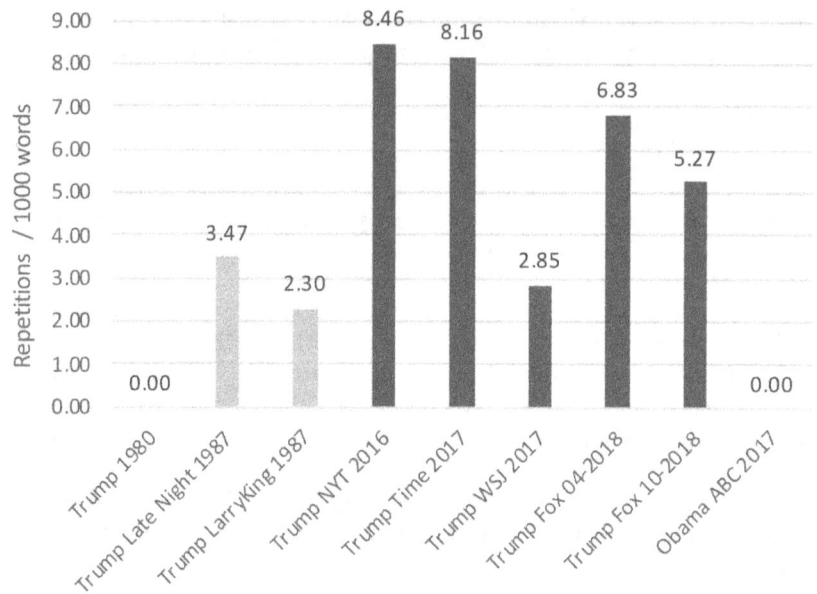

Figure 4.6 Repetitions per 1,000 words.

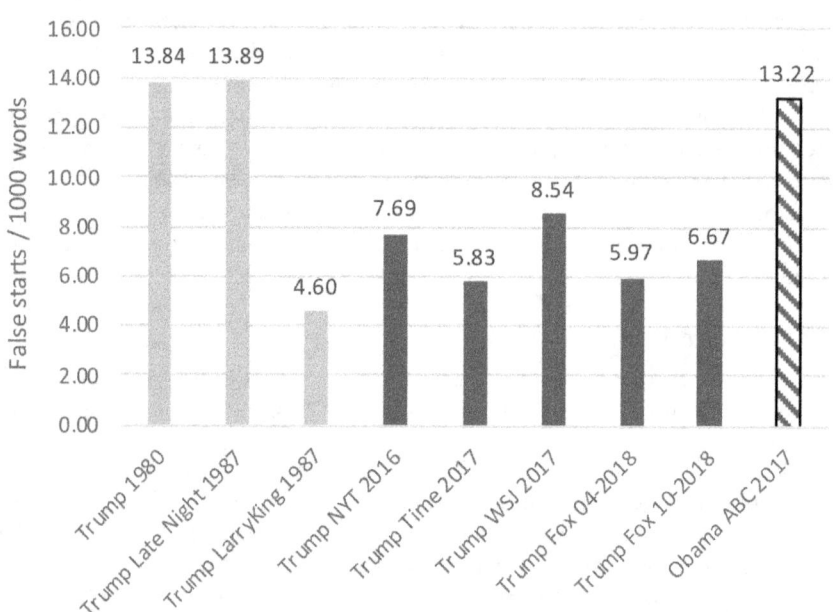

Figure 4.7 False starts in unscripted speech.

Figure 4.7 illustrates that false starts are particularly frequent in two early interviews with Donald Trump, as well as in the interview with President Obama. This is an interesting observation as we might have expected older or stressed speakers to have a higher need for self-corrections. However, this is not evidenced in the material studied here. In fact, in comparison with other research (Bortfeld et al. 2001), the numbers of false starts remain low overall.

4.4.5.3 Semantic Incoherence and Irrelevance

The last feature to be examined with respect to off-target verbosity is semantic incoherence and irrelevance. As explained by Kemper (2015: 67), these features are increasingly observed in the language of aging speakers. An example from the unscripted materials by President Trump is given in (9).

(9) Interviewer: So does the obstructionist win when—, when your nominees don't fight back?
Trump: Well I could say yes, I can also say no because Doc Ronny, you know, we call him Doc Ronny, we call him Admiral Ronny, he's an admiral, highly respected, a real leader, and I watched what Jon Tester of Montana, a state that I won by like over 20 points, so you know, really uh they love me and I love them, and I want to tell you that Jon Tester, I think this is going to cause him a lot of problems in his state. He took a man who was just an incredible man, an incredible man, respected by President Obama, he gave him his highest rating, you saw what President Obama said. (Trump Fox 04-2018)

This extract shows a tendency to jump between different topics, which has been observed by other authors (e.g., Sclafani 2018). An overview of the number of inconsistencies in the investigated unscripted speeches is given in Figure 4.8.

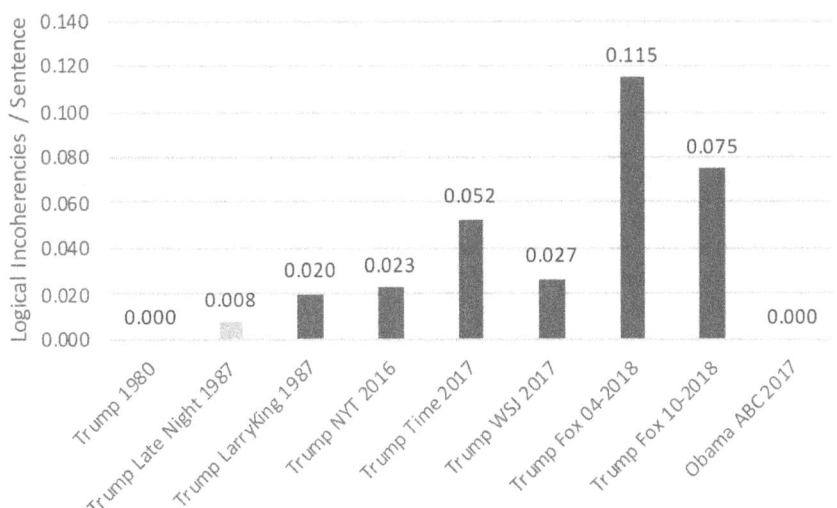

Figure 4.8 Numbers of incoherencies and irrelevance per sentence.

As we can see in Figure 4.8, President Trump has higher levels of such logical incoherencies in the analyzed data than in the data from the 1980s, or compared to the data in President Obama's ABC interview. As before, the 2017 data from the *Wall Street Journal* is more in line with earlier data. A possible reason for this could be that Trump's stress level could have been lower in this interview than in other interviews considered here.

As argued by Kemper (2015), decreasing cognitive control of aging speakers may lead to lower topic coherence and relevance of a speaker's utterance to the topic under discussion. Furthermore, increased issues with working memory may also manifest in memory difficulties concerning names, which seem to be visible in example (10).

(10) Trump: I can tell you there were Senate races that we weren't even going to contest, that we're actually leading in and I could mention names, I won't, eh maybe I mention one or two: Heidi, Heidi was gonna be you know when
Interview team: North Dakota
Trump: We have a man, North Dakota, we have a man who is fantastic and we asked him to run, the most popular, he's just a a great, great person.
Interview team: Kevin Cramer
Trump: Kevin is is just a great person he is running and he is up like thirteen points

(Trump Fox 10-2018)

Generally, the increase of incoherence between the 1980s and the 2010s could be an indication that President Trump's working memory may be increasingly challenged. This development has also been observed in the context of working memory restrictions in aging speakers (Kemper 2015) and may thus be a typical age phenomenon, which is likely to be compounded by stress and multi-tasking. This is an interesting observation and deserves further testing on large amounts of data.

4.5 Findings

Our analyses of President Trump's spontaneous language show that McWhorter's (2018) statement "that his current speech patterns . . . . [are] characteristics of casual speech as it has always existed" (McWhorter 2018) falls short. Indeed, we can find typical features of spoken language, which are also visible in the language of other politicians. But in addition, we can also find features that can be observed in the language of aging speakers.

In particular, these features are an abundance of pronouns (Tyrkkö 2016), low sentence complexity, and speech that is not related to the topic of conversation, so-called off-target verbosity. These features may be results of increasing restrictions on the working memory. However, there may be further, different reasons causing these features, such as tiredness, high stress levels, or pathological features. Stress must be considered an important factor here as it has been shown that older speakers perform less well under stress (Kemper 2015). Similarly, the data examined show multiple examples of incoherence, possibly uttered under stress or in contexts of multi-tasking.

A feature that is otherwise typical for the language of aging speakers is an increase in vocabulary richness over time: the more experienced the speakers become as language users, the more varied are the words that they use (Luo et al. 2019). We found no increase in vocabulary richness. Additionally, we observe an increase in the use of vague references like pronouns and imprecise references like *thing*. Vague reference is found in the language of aging speakers, but it can also be argued to be a feature of colloquial language (see previous chapters).

In comparison with findings on repetitions and false starts in laboratory conditions (Bortfeld et al. 2001, see section 4.2), President Trump's figures seem very much in line with normal rates, or even below those figures. However, instances of incoherence and irrelevance seem high in the data, and these are counterproductive to transporting a simple, populist message. Wanting to transport a simple message is an argument that is often used to explain why President Trump uses less complex language than many of his predecessors. The degree of incoherence and irrelevance found in the data is notable and seems to exceed normal spoken language use (see also Scalfani 2018). This feature rather points to the influence of factors like aging, which may be heightened by further factors such as stress.

4.6 Conclusion

It has been argued that a number of linguistic features of President Trump's language, especially when compared to the language used by other politicians, are similar to those typically found in the language of aging speakers. This holds in particular for increased incoherence, noticeable irrelevance, and increases in the use of personal pronouns and verbs with a concomitant decreased use of nouns, as well as a decrease in syntactically complex sentences, particularly subordinate clauses. What is not typical of aging speakers, but observed in the investigated data by President Trump, is that both lexical and syntactic complexity are not increasing while the speaker is becoming an increasingly experienced language user. Possible explanations for this may be working memory decline with increasing age, possibly compounded by high stress levels. Thus, the influence of age factors seems possible. Alternatively, a desire to transport simple messages may influence this latter point. It is noteworthy that even before becoming a politician in his thirties and forties, Donald Trump's language was simpler than that of many politicians investigated by this and other studies. This indicates that he has always favored a plain speaking style which may conceivably be due to him expressing an all-inclusive message that incorporates all his audience. However, clarity of messages is not increased by the abovementioned incoherencies and irrelevance found in the data.

Appendix

Table 4.4 Sources

Short Name	Source
Trump 1980	https://www.youtube.com/watch?v=0-w47wgdhso
Trump Late Nite 1987	https://www.youtube.com/watch?v=V3ssr2g_S1w&frags=pl%2Cwn
Trump LarryKing Live 1987	https://factba.se/transcript/donald-trump-interview-larry-king-september-2-1987
Trump NYT 2016	https://www.nytimes.com/2016/11/23/us/politics/trump-new-york-times-interview-transcript.html
Trump WSJ 2017	https://www.politico.com/story/2017/08/01/trump-wall-street-journal-interview-full-transcript-241214
Trump Time 2017	https://time.com/4710456/donald-trump-time-interview-truth-falsehood/
Trump Fox 04-2018	https://www.youtube.com/watch?v=_lu_Hgw60Ns
Trump Fox 10-2018	https://www.youtube.com/watch?v=XcxBCcv4iyc
Obama ABC 2017	https://abcnews.go.com/Politics/week-transcript-president-barack-obama/story?id=44630949

Notes

1 The statement Begley refers to is the following utterance Trump made at a press conference in 2017: "... there is no collusion between certainly myself and my campaign, but I can always speak for myself—and the Russians, zero" (quoted from Begley 2017).
2 As no audio sources are available for these three interviews, the correctness of the transcription unfortunately cannot be verified. Overall, the print versions give the impression of word-by-word transcriptions. Hesitations, however, are not marked in these transcripts, and thus preempt the overall analysis of this feature.
3 Thanks are due to Andrea Stammermann for making these transcripts.
4 The transcript provided by the news channel has been checked manually and corrected where necessary.

References

Beard, Adrian (1999), *The Language of Politics*, London: Routledge.
Begley, Sharon (2017), "Trump Wasn't Always so Linguistically Challenged: What Could Explain the Change?" *Statnews*, May 23. Available online: https://www.statnews.com/2017/05/23/donald-trump-speaking-style-interviews/ (accessed November 1, 2019).
Biber, Douglas (1988), *Variation across Speech and Writing*, Cambridge: Cambridge University Press.
Biber, Douglas, Stig Johansson, Geoffrey Leech, Susan Conrad, and Edward Finegan (1999), *Longman Grammar of Spoken and Written English*, Harlow: Pearson.
Birkner, Karin, Sofie Henricson, Camilla Lindholm, and Martin Pfeiffer (2012), "Grammar and Self-Repair: Retraction Patterns in German and Swedish Prepositional Phrases," *Journal of Pragmatics*, 44 (11): 1413–33.

Bortfeld, Heather, Silvia D. Leon, Jonathan E. Bloom, Michael F. Schober, and Susan E. Brennan (2001), "Disfluency Rates in Conversation: Effects of Age, Relationship, Topic, Role, and Gender," *Language and Speech*, 44 (2): 123–47.

Cheung, Hintat and Susan Kemper (1992), "Competing Complexity Metrics and Adults' Production of Complex Sentences," *Applied Psycholinguistics*, 13 (1): 53–76.

Clark, Herbert H. (1996), *Using Language*, Cambridge: Cambridge University Press.

Evert, Stefan, Sebastian Wankerl, and Elmar Nöth (2017), "Reliable Measures of Syntactic and Lexical Complexity: The Case of Iris Murdoch," *Proceedings of the Corpus Linguistics 2017 Conference*, Birmingham, UK. Available online: http://www.stefan-evert.de/PUB/EvertWankerlNoeth2017.pdf (accessed November 1, 2019).

Fox Tree, Jean E. (1995), "The Effects of False Starts and Repetitions on the Processing of Subsequent Words in Spontaneous Speech," *Journal of Memory and Language*, 34 (6): 709–38.

Gayraud, Frederique, Hye-Ran Lee, and Melissa Barkat-Defradas (2011), "Syntactic and Lexical Context of Pauses and Hesitations in the Discourse of Alzheimer Patients and Healthy Elderly Subjects," *Clinical Linguistics and Phonetics*, 25 (3): 198–209.

Gomez, Rowena G. and Desirée A. White (2006), "Using Verbal Fluency to Detect Very Mild Dementia of the Alzheimer Type," *Archives of Clinical Neuropsychology*, 21 (8): 771–5.

Hartsuiker, Robert J. and Pashiera N. Barkhuysen (2006), "Language Production and Working Memory: The Case of Subject-Verb Agreement," *Language and Cognitive Process*, 21 (1): 181–204.

Hendriks, Petra, Christina Englert, Ellis Wubs, and John C. J. Hoeks (2008), "Age Differences in Adults' Use of Referring Expressions," *Journal of Logic, Language and Information*, 17 (4): 443–66.

Horton, William S., Daniel H. Spieler, and Elizabeth Shriberg (2010), "A Corpus Analysis of Patterns of Age-Related Change in Conversational Speech," *Psychology and Aging*, 25 (3): 708–13.

Johnson, Ewa (2017), *Conversational Writing: A Multidimensional Study of Synchronous and Supersynchronous Computer-Mediated Communication*, Frankfurt: Peter Lang.

Kemper, Susan (2015), "Language Production in Late Life," in Annette Gerstenberg and Anja Voste (eds.), *Language Development: The Life-Span Perspective*, 59–76, Amsterdam: John Benjamins.

Kemper, Susan, Ruth Herman, and Cindy Lian (2003), "Age Differences in Sentence Production," *Journals of Gerontology: Psychological Sciences*, 58 (5): 260–8.

Kemper, Susan, Ryann Schmalzried, Ruth E. Herman, Skye N. Leedahl, and Deepthi Mohankumar (2009), "The Effects of Aging and Dual Task Performance on Language Production," *Aging, Neuropsychology, and Cognition*, 16 (3): 241–59.

Lakoff, George (2016), "Following Trump's Use of Language," *Berkeley Blog*, August 24. Available online: https://blogs.berkeley.edu/2016/08/24/following-trumps-use-of-language/ (accessed November 1, 2019).

Luo, Minxia, Gerold Schneider, Mike Martin, and Burcu Demiray (2019), "Cognitive Aging Effects on Language Use in Real-Life Contexts: A Naturalistic Observation Study," *Proceedings of CogSci 2019*, 24–27 July, Montréal, Canada: 714–20. Available online: https://cognitivesciencesociety.org/wp-content/uploads/2019/07/cogsci19_proceedings-8July2019-compressed.pdf (accessed November 1, 2019).

Maclay, Howard and Charles E. Osgood (1959), "Hesitation Phenomena in Spontaneous English Speech," *WORD*, 15 (1): 19–44.

McWhorter, John (2018), "What Trump's Speech Says about His Mental Fitness," *The New York Times*, February 6. Available online: https://www.nytimes.com/interactive/2018/02/06/opinion/trump-speech-mental-capacity.html (accessed November 1, 2019).

Moscoso del Prado Martín, Fermín (2016), "Vocabulary, Grammar, Sex, and Aging," *Cognitive Science*, 41 (4): 950–75.

Mulder, Kimberley and Jan H. Hulstijn (2011), "Linguistic Skills of Adult Native Speakers, as a Function of Age and Level of Education," *Applied Linguistics*, 32 (5): 475–94.

Pennebaker James W., Cindy K. Chung, Joey Frazee, Gary M. Lavergne, and David I. Beaver (2014), "When Small Words Foretell Academic Success: The Case of College Admissions Essays," *PLoS ONE*, 9 (12): e115844.

Schneider, Ulrike (2014), *Frequency, Chunks and Hesitations: A Usage-Based Analysis of Chunking in English*, Freiburg: NIHIN Studies.

Sclafani, Jennifer (2018), *Talking Donald Trump: A Sociolinguistic Study of Style, Metadiscourse, and Political Identity*, London: Routledge.

Tausczik, Yla R. and James W. Pennebaker (2010), "The Psychological Meaning of Words: LIWC and Computerized Text Analysis Methods," *Journal of Language and Social Psychology*, 29 (1): 24–54.

Tyrkkö, Jukka (2016), "Looking for Rhetorical Thresholds: Pronoun Frequencies in Political Speeches," in Minna Nevala, Ursula Lutzky, Gabriella Mazzon, and Carla Suhr (eds.), *The Pragmatics and Stylistics of Identity Construction and Characterisation*, Helsinki: VARIENG. Available online: http://www.helsinki.fi/varieng/series/volumes/17/tyrkko/ (accessed November 1, 2019).

Vrana, Leo and Gerold Schneider (2017), "Saying Whatever It Takes: Creating and Analyzing Corpora from US Presidential Debate Transcripts," *Extended Abstracts of Corpus Linguistics Conference*, July 24–28, Birmingham.

Wendelstein, Britta (2016), *Gesprochene Sprache im Vorfeld der Alzheimer-Demenz*, Heidelberg: Winter.

Wodak, Ruth (2015), *The Politics of Fear: What Right-Wing Populist Discourses Mean*, London: Sage.

Woolley, John T. and Gerhard Peters (1999–), "The American Presidency Project." Available online: https://www.presidency.ucsb.edu/documents/presidential-documents-archive-guidebook/presidential-candidates-debates-1960-2016 (accessed January 13, 2020).

Part II

Evaluation and Emotion

5

Very Emotional, Totally Conservative, and *Somewhat All over the Place*

An Analysis of Intensifiers in Donald Trump's Speech

Ulrike Stange

5.1 Introduction

It has been repeatedly claimed that Donald Trump is a heavy user of intensifiers, that is, elements such as *very* or *extremely* that modify other parts of speech to intensify their meaning. Such heavy usage of intensifiers seems to befit Trump's tendency to talk in extremes, characterized by an abundance of hyperboles (Abbas 2019). Danyushina (2016) counts intensifiers among the main characteristics of his speech, next to other features such as purposeful simplicity, colloquial manner (in terms of vocabulary, grammar, and style), or repetitions and parallelisms. As Hodges (2017) claims, Trump "sprinkle[s] intensifiers—semantically vacuous adverbs—over the message to enhance its emotional impact," with "Trump's most often tweeted intensifiers [being] (in order of popularity) *very, totally, so, really*." In *How to Talk like Trump*, Romano (2016) even makes this Rule #3: "Use intensifiers like 'very'—very, very often." These comments, although they are based on non-systematic observations rather than on empirical research, seem correct. Take, for instance, the following extract of an interview transcript[1] (interview conducted on May 11, 2017) where we find a wide array of intensifiers (marked in italics, including ambiguous *really*):

(1) **The Economist:** What is Trumponomics and how does it differ from standard Republican economics?
Donald Trump: Well it's an interesting question. I don't think it's ever been asked *quite* that way. But it *really* has to do with self-respect as a nation. It has to do with trade deals that have to be fair, and *somewhat* reciprocal, if not *fully* reciprocal. And I think that's a word that you're going to see a lot of, because we need reciprocality in terms of our trade deals. We have nations where—they'll get as much as 100% of a tax or a tariff for a certain product and for the same product we get nothing, OK? It's *very* unfair. And the *very* interesting thing about that is that, if I said I'm going to put a tax on of 10%, the free-traders, *somewhat*

foolishly, they'll say "Oh, he's not a free-trader," which I am, I'm *absolutely* a free-trader. I'm for open trade, free trade, but I also want smart trade and fair trade. But they'll say, "He's not a free-trader," at 10%. But if I say we're putting a reciprocal tax on, it may be 62% or it may be 47%, I mean massive numbers, and nobody can complain about it. It's *really sort of* an amazing thing.

Indeed, Trump uses intensifiers in at least every other sentence he produces (to be precise, 10 intensifiers in a text of 204 words). Some of the observed combinations seem odd: in "very unfair," for instance, *very* has an upscaling quality, but *unfair* is not gradable. Also, the exact intensifying function is unclear in combinations of intensifiers such as "*really sort of* an amazing thing."

To date, there is no systematic, corpus-based analysis of intensifiers in Trump's speech. Drawing on corpus data, the present study aims to fill this gap by sketching a profile of how Trump uses intensifiers in his tweets and in his remarks and by verifying whether his use really is different from the "average" American English speaker as well as other politicians. In line with previous research on intensification, the focus will be on the modification of adjectives (and adverbs).

The chapter is organized as follows: the next section offers an overview on important terminology and concepts pertaining to the field of intensification, including a summary of previous research on intensifiers. The presentation of the study design lists the research questions to be addressed in the analysis and provides details on the data used and the method employed. The analysis first focuses on amplifiers, a type of upscaling intensifiers that Trump is assumed to have a special penchant for. I first discuss observed frequencies (by giving an overview and comparing them to other data sets), then contrast collocational patterns, and highlight Trump-specific particularities. Also, I briefly discuss Trump's use of downtoners. These form a second type of intensifiers with a lowering quality. All findings are discussed in relation to the other data sets used in this study. The chapters are wrapped up by a short summary of the main results and a conclusion.

5.2 Intensifiers

Lexical items such as *so (cool)*, *very (bad)*, or *totally (dishonest)* are commonly referred to as *intensifiers* (see, for instance, Tagliamonte and Roberts 2005; Lorenz 2002; Stenström, Andersen, and Hasund 2002). They are typically defined as "a word, especially an adverb or adjective, that has little meaning itself but is used to add force to another adjective, verb, or adverb" (*Cambridge Dictionary*, s.v. *intensifier*). Intensifiers are "broadly concerned with the semantic category of DEGREE" (Quirk et al. 1985: 589) and are also called *intensive adverbs* (Stoffel 1901), *degree words* (Bolinger 1972), or *adverbs of degree* (Bäcklund 1973).

Intensifiers can be subdivided into amplifiers and downtoners. Amplifiers have an upscaling effect regarding "an abstractly conceived intensity scale," while downtoners have a lowering effect (Quirk et al. 1985: 589). Amplifiers can be split into *boosters* and *maximizers*. This split is closely related to the nature of the element they modify, that is, whether the element in question readily allows for comparative and superlative forms and is thus gradable. Boosters are used to intensify gradable elements such as *big, cold, expensive,* and *strong* (see Altenberg 1991: 129) and "denote a high degree, a high point on the scale" (Quirk et al. 1985: 590). Maximizers, such as *absolutely, extremely,* and *fully,* on the other hand, "express an absolute degree [and] are typically used to modify 'nonscalar' items, i.e. items that do not normally permit grading (e.g., *empty, impossible, wrong*) or already contain a notion of extreme or absolute degree (e.g., *disgusting, exhausted, huge, marvelous,* etc.)" (Altenberg 1991: 129). For downtoners, there is also a more fine-grained distinction based on the differences in lowering effects. The terms used are (from least to strongest lowering effect) *approximator* (e.g., *almost, nearly*), *compromiser* (e.g., *kind of, quite*), *diminisher* (e.g., *partially, somewhat*), and *minimizer* (e.g., *barely, hardly*; Quirk et al. 1985: 597).

The following examples from the Corpus of Contemporary American English (COCA) illustrate this range in meaning; note that intensifiers are italicized, whereas the part of speech thus modified is underlined. The overview is based on Quirk et al. (1985: 589–601).

INTENSIFIERS

(I) Amplifiers
   a. *Maximizers*: upper extreme of the scale—for example, *entirely, perfectly, extremely*

   (2) The whole city was *completely* empty. (COCA SPOK 2017)
   (3) By nightfall I was *totally* exhausted. (COCA FIC 2010)

   b. *Boosters*: high point on the scale—for example, *greatly, highly, so*

   (4) The hygienic situation is *very* bad. (COCA SPOK 2017)

(II) Downtoners
   a. *Approximators*: modified item expresses more than is relevant—for example, *nearly, virtually*

   (5) I'm *almost* certain the enormous cakes are fakes. (COCA MAG 2016)

   b. *Compromisers*: slight lowering effect—for example, *kind of, rather, sort of*

   (6) The vast majority of houses survived *more or less* intact . . . . (COCA NEWS 2008)

   c. *Diminishers*: low point on the scale—for example, *slightly, a bit, somewhat*

   (7) It's *partly* true and *partly* not true. (COCA MAG 2015)

   d. *Minimizers*: lower extreme of the scale—for example, *barely, scarcely*

   (8) His solution is *hardly* surprising. (COCA ACAD 2017)

Adjectives modified by intensifiers occur both in attributive position, as in examples (9) to (11), and in predicative position, as in examples (12) to (14):

(9) I have a *very* good feeling about the New Year. (COCA FIC 2017)
(10) But it was a *completely* crazy time. (COCA SPOK 2002)
(11) Acts of protest and acts of propaganda are *somewhat* different things. (COCA SPOK 2017)
(12) That was *very* good, young fella. (COCA FIC 2017)
(13) The mayor's idea is *really* interesting. (COCA NEWS 2017)
(14) I was *slightly* embarrassed because it was making a mockery out of me .... (COCA SPOK 2015)

Most intensifiers can readily be found in both syntactic environments. A prominent exception is *so*, which is still virtually restricted to co-occurring with adjectives in predicative position, as in (15). Instances like (16) to (18), where *so* co-occurs with adjectives in attributive position, are extremely rare in COCA (single digits in over 520 million words) and seem to work only in combination with demonstrative adjectives and the definite article.

(15) It's always *so* cool to see family members. (COCA SPOK 2017)
(16) ... and smiled this *so* beautiful smile. (COCA FIC 2002)
(17) ... and emoji or emoji, whatever, these *so* small images used in texts, which I like to use. (COCA SPOK 2015)
(18) July 17th ... shares an anniversary with the *so* mysterious crash of TWA Flight 800. (COCA SPOK 2014)

Although the examples listed so far all contain adjectives, intensifiers are also found with adverbs and verbs (as stated in the definition above). To list but a few examples:

(19) And he did it *completely* straight. (COCA MAG 1994)
(20) They're doing *very* well. (COCA NEWS 2017)
(21) ... he applied the jellylike salve, speaking *nearly* inaudibly to the horse, ... (COCA FIC 2005)
(22) And I *completely* denied everything, of course. (COCA SPOK 2000)
(23) I *almost* missed the flight because of an earlier flight. (COCA SPOK 2012)
(24) He had *hardly* slept the last two nights. (COCA FIC 2010)

Defined as a "functional category," intensifiers serve as "a vehicle for impressing, praising, persuading, insulting and generally influencing the listener's reception of the message" (see Partington 1993: 178). They are thus typically found in emotional language (Tagliamonte and Roberts 2005: 289). Importantly, there is a constant need for new intensifying items since "all means of emphasis quickly grow stale and need to be replaced" (Bolinger 1972: 18). As a result, intensifiers constitute an open class that readily admits new items that typically already exist as content words (e.g., *really*, *highly*, *terribly*, etc.). Their way from content word to intensifier involves, on the one hand, bleaching of the original semantic content (often referred to as delexicalization) and, on the other hand, grammaticalization (here defined as the restriction to the communicative functions as noted earlier; see the comments on *terribly* and *thoroughly* later on for an illustration of these processes).

Delexicalization and grammaticalization have been in the focus of studies conducted by Lorenz (2002), Partington (1993), and Ito and Tagliamonte (2003). These studies have shown that some intensifiers have lost more of their semantic content than others, and that a "partial state of delexicalization is by no means exceptional" (Lorenz 2002: 145). These differences in how advanced the process of semantic bleaching is for the individual intensifier is reflected in their collocational range (i.e., the words they readily combine with): lexical items that develop innovative intensifier uses at first have a rather restricted collocational spectrum, whereas (nearly or more) delexicalized ones extend their range of application and take more collocates (see Partington 1993: 183; Tagliamonte and Roberts 2005: 290ff.).

Terribly, for instance, originally only combined with adjectives that have a negative semantic prosody[2] (*terribly bad*, *terribly hungry*). Semantic bleaching enabled it to expand its use to adjectives with positive meaning, such as *terribly clever* or *terribly good* (see Partington 1993: 183–4). *Thoroughly*, on the other hand, still prefers collocates that allow a reading of *thoroughly* as 'through and through' (*thoroughly tired*, *thoroughly tested*), which is reminiscent of its original meaning. At the end of the delexicalization process, we find intensifiers devoid of semantic content and whose function is restricted to that of intensification. A relevant case in point is *very*, which originally meant 'truly, genuinely' (cf. *OED* online, s.v. *very*) and initially only had collocates that matched semantically (e.g., *very repentant* 'truly repentant'). Today, the original meaning of *very* is completely bleached so that it combines with all gradable adjectives and adverbs (*very good*, *very beautiful*, *very sad*, etc.) and even with a variety of non-gradable ones (*very pregnant*, *very dead*, *very unique*, etc., see also Partington 1993). With intensifiers, then, delexicalization and grammaticalization go hand in hand, and these processes apply automatically to new intensifiers in the language (see Lorenz 2002: 144–5).

5.3 Study Design and Research Questions

The following is an unbiased, exploratory study investigating the use of intensifiers in Trump's speech. The analysis focuses on both amplifiers and downtoners. The former serve to add force to the statement in question and have repeatedly been identified as a prominent feature in Trump's speech. Downtoners, by contrast, have a mitigating effect and might not be typically associated with Trump's speech. The spoken section of the COCA (Davies 2008–) will serve as a baseline for evaluating intensifier use in Trump's tweets and remarks (details on the different text types follow in the next section). To see whether potential discrepancies can be accounted for by the context (i.e., politics), intensifier use will also be analyzed in US Vice President Mike Pence's remarks and in tweets sent by US Democrats.

The present study addresses the following research questions:

(a) How frequently does Trump use intensifiers?
(b) Which intensifiers occur most frequently in his tweets and in his remarks?
(c) How frequently do intensifiers feature in his speech compared to other speakers' language?
(d) Are there any observable particularities in his use of intensifiers?

The first two questions aim at providing an overview of the use of intensifiers in Trump's speech, while questions (c)–(d) contrast his intensifier use with that of other speakers (the Democrats, Vice President Pence, and speakers as recorded for COCA Spoken 2010–17). The overall aim is to determine whether he really is different from other speakers where the use of words like *very* or *slightly* is concerned, or whether these repeated observations are actually based on misperceptions. For (d), potential differences in collocational patterns will be relevant; that is, does he use *very* or *really* differently compared to other speakers? Answering the questions listed earlier based on a corpus-based approach will provide (tentative) empirical (counter)evidence for the claims made about his use of intensifiers.

5.4 Data and Method

5.4.1 Data

Table 5.1 provides an overview of the different data sets used in the present study. As the data sets differ considerably in size, the normalizations will reflect the number of occurrences per 10,000 words in each data set to allow for a comparison of the observed frequencies across the different text types.

Table 5.1 Dataset

Dataset	Abbreviation	Time period	Corpus size	Comments
Trump (tweets)	TT	05/2009–07/2018	384,734	cleared of retweets
Trump (remarks)	TR	02/2017–09/2019	27,485	issue: energy and environment cleared of non-Trump speech
Democrats (tweets)	DT	01/2017–02/2018	589,082	cleared of retweets
Pence (remarks)	PR	06/2017–06/2019	6,111	issue: energy and environment cleared of non-Pence speech
COCA Spoken	COCA	2010–17	33,926,171	transcripts of unscripted conversation from more than 150 different TV and radio programs

The data set called "Trump (tweets)" contains the tweets posted from the account @realDonaldTrump only, while the data set "Democrats (tweets)" contains the tweets posted by a variety of Democrats (e.g., from the accounts @amyklobuchar, @SenatorDurbin, @SenWhitehouse). The tweets were sourced from the Trump Twitter Archive (Brown 2019) and with the help of TwitterCorpusQuery 2.0 (Scherl 2018). As Twitter does not guarantee that the search output yields all the tweets matching the search criteria, some tweets may be missing.

The remarks analyzed in this study are all taken from the energy and environment issue as published on the website of the White House (see Degani and Onysko, this volume, for details on this text type). The remarks amount to fourteen different texts in total (ten for Trump, four for Pence).

The spoken section of COCA contains transcripts of unscripted, (relatively) informal conversation from TV and radio programs. It was chosen as a baseline corpus because it has repeatedly been suggested that Trump's speech is relatively informal (e.g., Danyushina 2016; Hunston 2017; Ahmadian, Azarshahi, and Paulhus 2017). As the Trump data was gathered between 2009 and 2018, the data from the spoken section of COCA was restricted to the years 2010–17.[3]

5.4.2 Method

The tweets and the remarks were analyzed using the freeware tool LancsBox (Brezina, Timperley, and McEnery 2018). LancsBox provides a word list that helped identify all intensifiers used in Trump's tweets and remarks. In a next step, data extraction concentrated on those intensifiers that occur with sufficient frequency to allow for a detailed analysis. In line with previous research on intensification, the focus was on adjective and adverb modification (e.g., *really good/well*). Thus, if a different part of speech (or rather phrase) was modified, the element was discarded. This included, for instance, verb phrase modification as in example (25),[4] or noun phrase modification as in example (26). Tokens were also discarded if *really*, *totally*, and *so* had a different function, for example, when *so* was used anaphorically as in example (27), or when *so* was followed by *that*, introducing a purpose clause as in example (28).

(25) Remember Obama *so* loved the poor he created millions more! (@realDonalTrump, August 29, 2013)
(26) The failing @nytimes has been wrong about me from the *very* beginning. (@realDonaldTrump, January 28, 2017)
(27) I was recently asked if Crooked Hillary Clinton is going to run in 2020? My answer was, "I hope *so*!" (@realDonaldTrump, October 16, 2017)
(28) Get out tomorrow and vote *so* that we can all finally say those magic words. (@realDonaldTrump, November 5, 2012)

To retrieve relevant occurrences from the spoken section of COCA 2010–17, the search string used contained the respective intensifier plus a wildcard for adjectives (_j*) or adverbs (_r*). *Totally* _j* and *totally* _r* yielded, for instance, *totally different* and *totally differently*, among other adjectives and adverbs.

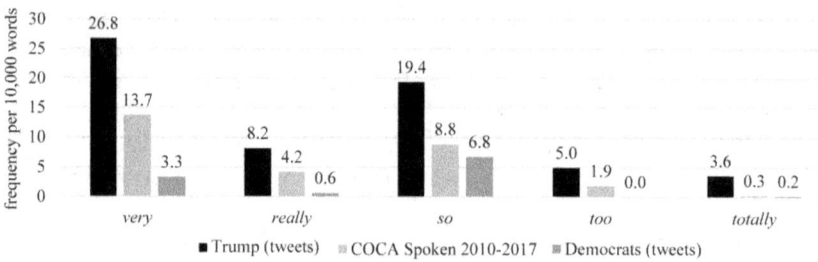

Figure 5.1 Frequency of selected intensifiers in tweets and in spoken language.

5.5 Intensifiers: Results and Discussion

5.5.1 General Observations on the Frequency of Amplifiers

In the tweet data, Trump frequently uses *very* (1,030 occurrences in 385,000 words; normalized frequencies displayed in Figure 5.1) and *so* (746[5]), followed by *really* (316), *too* (191), and *totally* (139; intensified adjectives and adverbs considered only). So the ranking is different from the one observed by Hodges (2017; *very, totally, so, really*).

In terms of intensifier classification, *very*, *really*, and *so* are boosters, denoting a high degree of the quality they modify. *Totally* is a maximizer (denoting the upper extreme end of the scale), while *too* denotes excessive degree (but, curiously, it is missing in Quirk et al.'s [1985] categorization of intensifiers).

Other amplifiers, as listed in Quirk et al., also occur, albeit rarely. These are as follows: *truly* (79), *highly* (72), *pretty* (15), *extremely* (13), *quite* (7), *badly* (5), *way too* (5), *fully* (4), *perfectly* (4), *quite* (4), *completely* (2), *deeply* (2), *severely* (2), *terribly* (2), *thoroughly* (2), *greatly* (1). Not attested were *absolutely, altogether, awfully, bitterly, enormously, entirely, intensely, real, strongly, utterly,* and *violently*. The following analyses will therefore concentrate on *very, so, really, too,* and *totally* as the top five intensifiers in Trump's tweets. *Truly* and *highly* are considered separately in section 5.5.4 as they, too, feature quite prominently in his speech.

5.5.2 Amplifier Frequencies across Datasets

In his tweets, Trump uses *very* most frequently (27 occurrences per 10,000 words), followed by *so* (20 occurrences per 10,000 words), *really* (8 occurrences per 10,000 words), *too* (5 occurrences per 10,000 words), and *totally* (4 occurrences per 10,000 words), which mirrors the ranks attested in COCA. Interestingly enough, Trump uses these intensifiers at least twice as frequently as usual in spoken English, as Figure 5.1 shows. In the Democrats' tweets, by contrast, *very, really,* and *too* are considerably less frequent than they are in COCA. The Democrats' use of *so* and *totally*, however, reflects the tendencies found in spoken English (see Table 5.6 in the Appendix for the raw frequencies).

The same overall tendencies can be observed in Trump's remarks, issued on a number of occasions on the general topic of energy and environment (Figure 5.2).

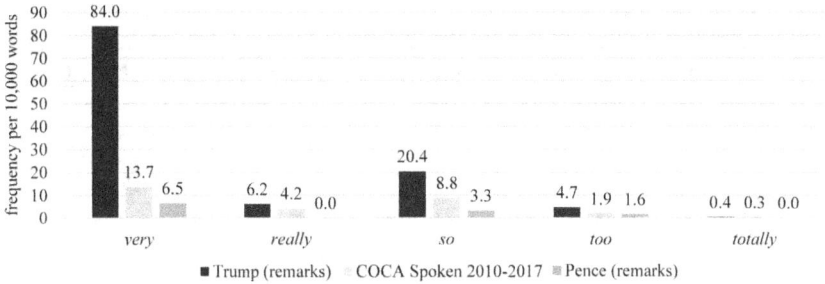

Figure 5.2 Frequency of selected intensifiers in remarks and in spoken language.

The frequency ranking is identical, but *very* is six times more frequent in Trump's remarks than it is in the spoken section of COCA (2010–17).

In short, both data sets suggest that Trump is indeed a prolific user of intensifiers in general, and that he exhibits a strong liking for *very*. Incidentally, *very* could be described as old-fashioned and conservative because it is the oldest intensifier English has, dating back to the fifteenth century (*OED online*, s.v. *very*). What is more, sociolinguistic studies have repeatedly shown that its use is associated with elderly and/ or (in a linguistic sense) conservative people (Ito and Tagliamonte 2003; Tagliamonte 2008; D'Arcy 2015).

5.5.3 Frequent Amplifier Bigrams

The following tables compare the collocational patterns for the individual intensifiers across the data sets used in the present study (i.e., Trump's tweets and remarks, the Democrats' tweets, Pence's remarks, and COCA Spoken 2010–17). Collocational patterns for intensifiers are most easily identified by running a corpus-based analysis on bigrams (that is considering two adjacent text fragments; here, it is the intensifier plus the modified adjective or adverb). The threshold for inclusion in the table was fifty occurrences of the intensifier in question in a given data set to allow for a sound analysis. As a result, I analyzed the collocates for *really*, *too*, and *totally* in Trump's tweets and the spoken section in COCA only—they were too rare elsewhere.

The percentages in the tables represent the proportion of bigrams for the respective collocate: the sequence *very much*, for instance, accounted for 30 percent of all occurrences of *very* plus ADJ|ADV in Trump's remarks (see Table 5.2). The presentation of the results will draw attention to striking similarities and/or strong differences in the collocational patterns, highlighting particularities.

5.5.3.1 *Very*

The top five collocates of *very* in Trump's remarks are almost identical to the ones found in COCA Spoken 2010–17 (viz. *much*, *well*, *important*, *good* overlap; Table 5.2). This shows that his use of *very* is rather like how other native speakers use it in terms of the lexical items it mainly collocates with. What is striking, however, is that the second most frequent collocate of *very* in his remarks is *very* (4.7 occurrences per

Table 5.2 Top Five Collocates of *Very*

Very	Trump's remarks		Trump's tweets		Democrats' tweets		COCA Spoken	
#1	*Much*	30%	*good*	5%	*happy*	10%	*much*	13%
#2	*Very*	6%	*nice*	>5%	*concerned*	7%	*good*	>5%
#3	*Well*	6%	*much*	>5%	*real*	6%	*important*	>5%
#4	*important*	5%	*sad*	>5%	*good*	>5%	*well*	>5%
#5	*Good*	>5%	*proud*	>5%	*important*	>5%	*difficult*	>5%
N_{total}		231		1,030		196		46,460

NB: Overlap in collocates marked in bold print.

10,000 words), which is a case of double intensification as it were. With respect to the proportions the individual bigrams account for, every third occurrence of *very* is in combination with *much* in his remarks.

A look at the remarks data reveals that this skew is caused by Trump using *very much* when expressing thanks (58/69 occurrences of *very much*).[6] If these occurrences are taken out of the equation, *very much* drops to 4 percent of all occurrences of *very* plus ADJ|ADV. In short, despite the overall differences in the frequency of *very* in Trump's speech and in COCA, the collocational pattern in his remarks is almost identical to the pattern in COCA Spoken, both with regard to the adjectives and adverbs featuring in the top five as well as the distribution of them relative to one another.

In the tweets, only two of the top five collocates overlap with the top five in COCA Spoken (Trump's tweets: *good* and *much*; Democrats' tweets: *good* and *important*), and overall, the adjectives have a more emotional quality (*good, nice, sad, proud, happy, concerned*). Why the tweets are different in this respect is a matter of speculation, and might have to do with Twitter as a medium for conveying messages and for establishing proximity to the people who follow Trump and the Democrats (after all, most Twitter users will access the tweets on their personal mobile devices). The remarks, on the other hand, are addressed to a much smaller audience, face to face, and are official in nature. What is observable in the collocational patterns here could thus be attributed to differences in audience design (Bell 1984)—this would mean that the use of *very* in Trump's remarks mimics the use of *very* in spoken English as recorded in COCA (which contains transcripts of unscripted conversations aired on television or the radio—so not that informal), while the use of *very* in his tweets seems more personal, as illustrated in (29) and (30):

(29) Congratulations to Andres Manuel Lopez Obrador on becoming the next President of Mexico. I look *very much* forward to working with him. (@realDonaldTrump, July 2, 2018)

(30) @hardball' very small audience is shrinking rapidly because people finally understand that he is *very very dumb*! (@realDonaldTrump, March 20, 2013)

5.5.3.2 So

Table 5.3 shows that the quantifying elements *much* and *many* are the top two adjectives/adverbs modified by *so* across the data sets. These examples are taken from Trump's tweets:

Table 5.3 Top Five Collocates of *So*

So	Trump's remarks		Trump's tweets		Democrats' tweets		COCA Spoken	
#1	*many*	23%	*many*	16%	*many*	28%	*much*	27%
#2	*much*	21%	*much*	15%	*much*	16%	*many*	12%
#3	*long*	7%	*badly*	>5%	*proud*	>5%	*good*	>5%
#4	*good*	>5%	*true*	>5%	*important*	>5%	*important*	>5%
#5	*happy*	>5%	*hard*	>5%	*hard*	>5%	*happy*	>5%
N_{total}		56		746		399		29,961

(31) Major Wall Street Journal opinion piece today talking about the Russian Witch Hunt and the disgrace that it is. *So* <u>many</u> people hurt, so bad for our country- a total sham! (@realDonaldTrump, June 24, 2018)

(32) Only 1 mill. dollars @mcuban? Offer me real money and I'd consider it. Your team and networks lose *so* <u>much</u> money I doubt you have much left! (@realDonaldTrump, November 5, 2012)

In the tweets, roughly every other *so many* referred to quantities of people (*people, friends, hypocrites, New Yorkers*, etc.), but only every third *so many* in Trump's remarks and in COCA Spoken (the last observation is based on a random sample of one hundred occurrences). *So much* showed more variation, but in all data sets considered, it frequently modified *more* in comparative constructions (*so much more expensive*) and *much* in the idiomatic expression *thank you so much*.

5.5.3.3 *Totally*

Figure 5.3 visualizes the collocational behavior of *totally* in Trump's speech. In fact, it is rather conservative in that the adjectives that *totally* modifies have a negative semantic prosody (with the sole exception of neutral *focused*, which occurred seven out of eight times in the imperative form *be totally focused*, see also Table 5.5):

(33) Just watched the *totally* <u>biased</u> and fake news reports of the so-called Russia story on NBC and ABC. Such dishonesty! (@realDonaldTrump, March 23, 2017)

(34) Wow, @CNN got caught fixing their "focus group" in order to make Crooked Hillary look better. Really pathetic and *totally* <u>dishonest</u>! (@realDonaldTrump, October 10, 2016)

Stange and Wagner (2018) have shown that *totally*, which originally combined with negative or neutral adjectives only, has recently been expanding its range to adjectives with positive meaning (e.g., *fine* and *true* on rank two and five in COCA Spoken 2010–17, Table 5.4). In Trump's tweets, *totally* combined with sixty-one different adjectives and only three of them are positive in meaning in context (*effective, electric, fair*). Thus, only 5 percent of the adjectives he uses with *totally* are positive. In COCA Spoken 2010–17, by contrast, 40 percent of the adjectives found in the top fifty collocates of *totally* are positive in meaning (as opposed to 28 percent in COCA Spoken 1990–4 and 4 percent in COHA[7] Fiction 1850s–90s). In sum, Trump's speech shows conservative traits where

Figure 5.3 Collocational behavior of *totally* in Trump's tweets (frequency threshold: three occurrences).

Table 5.4 Top Five Collocates of *Totally*

Totally	**Trump's tweets**		**COCA Spoken**	
#1	*biased*	13%	*different*	17%
#2	*dishonest*	7%	*fine*	>5%
#3	*focused*	6%	**wrong**	>5%
#4	*rigged*	>5%	*false*	>5%
#5	**wrong**	>5%	*true*	>5%
N_{total}		139		967

the collocational behavior of *totally* is concerned in that the ratio of positive versus negative adjectives reflects tendencies found in American English fiction in the second half of the nineteenth century.

5.5.4 *Truly* and *Highly*

A short note on *truly* (79 occurrences in Trump's tweets) and *highly* (72 occurrences) is in order, because they were also fairly frequent: in his tweets, *truly* collocates mainly with positive adjectives like (in alphabetical order) *amazing, beautiful, epic, fabulous, fantastic, great, magnificent, outstanding,* and *wonderful.* Among the negative adjectives were *defeated, dumb, evil, horrifying, incompetent, painful, stupid,* and *ugly.* The collocates show that the modified adjectives were typically either extremely positive or very negative in meaning.

In COCA Spoken 2010–17, we find fifteen positive adjectives and adverbs among the top thirty collocates (e.g., *great, amazing, stunning, extraordinary*). So when Trump uses *truly,* the overall tone is more positive than in the average American speaker's (in terms of types and tokens); the most frequent bigrams (in both data sets) *truly great* and *truly amazing* accounted for 37 and 5 percent of occurrences of *truly* in Trump's tweets, but only for 4 and 3 percent in COCA Spoken.

(35) George Steinbrenner was a great friend and a true legend. There will never be anyone like him in New York. We've lost a *truly* great man. (@realDonaldTrump, July 14, 2010)
(36) I am on my way to Singapore where we have a chance to achieve a *truly* wonderful result for North Korea and the World. (@realDonaldTrump, June 9, 2018)

Highly, on the other hand, although it most frequently modified positive *respected* (34 percent of all occurrences of *highly* in the tweets), was mainly used with negative adjectives like *discriminating, illegal, incompetent, neurotic,* or *overrated.* Positive collocates included *professional, sophisticated, competent,* and *gifted.* In COCA Spoken 2010–17, there are only two negative adjectives among the top thirty (*highly toxic, highly critical*), the rest is positive (*highly qualified*) or neutral (*highly variable*). It thus seems that the overall use of *highly* in Trump's speech is more negative than in spoken American English elsewhere.

(37) Current @NYMag really sad, not only boring but *highly* inaccurate. (@realDonaldTrump, March 29, 2013)
(38) Crooked Hillary's brainpower is *highly* overrated. (@realDonaldTrump, August 29, 2016)

In terms of frequency, at 2.1 occurrences per 10,000 words, *truly* is more than twice as frequent in Trump's tweets than it is in COCA Spoken 2010–17 (Figure 5.4). *Highly,* by contrast, is similarly frequent in COCA and in his tweets (1.9 vs. 2.2 occurrences per 10,000 words). *Truly* could thus be viewed as another prominent intensifier in Trump's speech. In the Democrats' tweets, neither amplifier plays a noticeable role (0.3 occurrences per 10,000 words; see Table 5.7 in the Appendix for the raw frequencies).

5.5.5 Particularities

This section draws attention to particularities observed in Trump's use of intensifiers. The first part is concerned with intensification rates (i.e., how often he uses amplifiers in contrast with other speakers), while the second part highlights distinctive features in the intensifier–adjective|adverb bigrams found in Trump's speech.

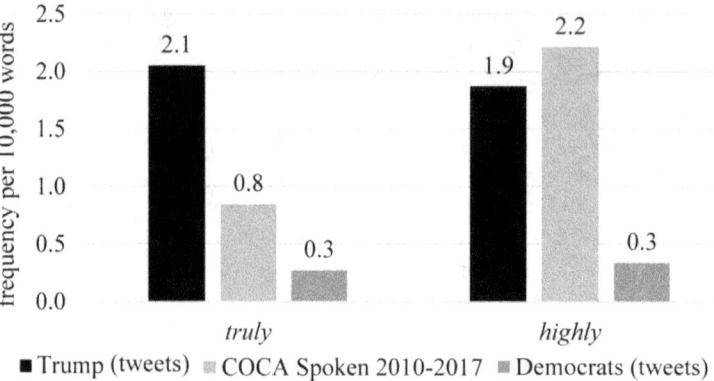

Figure 5.4 Frequency of *truly* and *highly*.

5.5.5.1 Intensification Rates

It is noteworthy that the quantifying adjectives *many* and *much* are very frequently intensified in Trump's speech and that they feature in the top five for *very* (*much* only), *so*, and *too*. This distribution is quite unlike spoken American English, where *much* is the most frequent collocate for *very* but accounts for only 13 percent of all modified adjectives (as opposed to 30 percent in Trump's remarks). *Many* and *much* are not among the top five collocates for *so* and *too* in COCA. In short, Trump quantifies a lot, and he also often adds more force to these quantifications by using intensifiers.

As stated in the introduction, there have been repeated claims that Trump is a heavy user of intensifiers. Figure 5.5 displays the intensification rates for the collocates most frequently found with intensifiers in the Trump data (the percentages were computed based on the frequency of co-occurring *very*, *really*, or *so*; for example, number of occurrences of *very much|really much|so much* * 100 / number of occurrences of *much*), and it shows that this claim is only partially true: for *much*, *many*, and *great* Trump uses fewer intensifiers in comparison to both the Democrats and the speakers

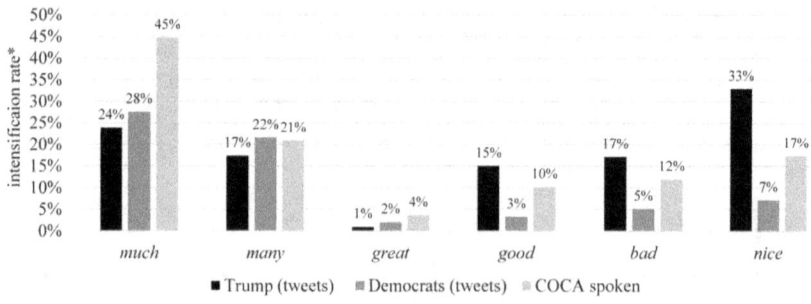

Figure 5.5 Intensification rates with *very|really|so*.

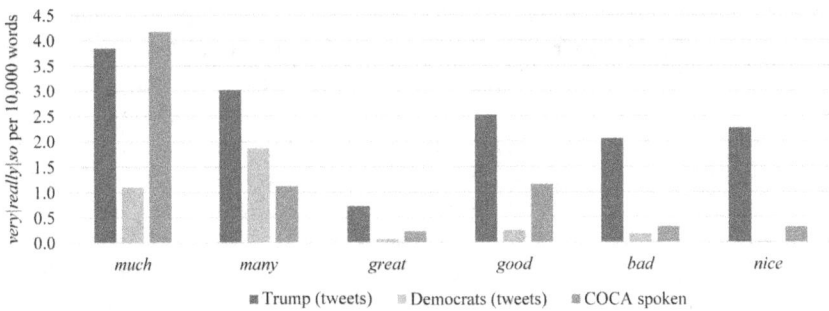

Figure 5.6 Frequency of intensifier–adjective|adverb bigrams.

Table 5.5 Frequencies per 10,000 Words

	much	many	great	good	bad	nice
Trump (tweets)	13.5	17.3	76.9	16.8	12.0	6.9
Democrats (tweets)	4.0	8.6	9.0	7.2	3.3	0.2
COCA Spoken	9.9	6.1	6.1	3.3	2.6	1.8

in COCA. In his tweets, for instance, *much* was modified by *very*, *really*, or *so* in 28 percent of the cases, while it has an intensification rate of 45 percent in COCA Spoken.

For evaluative *good*, *bad*, and *nice*, on the other hand, Trump shows higher intensification rates compared to the other data sets. His use of *nice* is accompanied by an intensifier in one out of three instances in his tweets (twice as frequent as in COCA). In short, Trump's intensification rates alone fail to offer sufficient explanatory power for the perception that he uses intensifiers all the time.

A look at normalized frequencies helps explain the discrepancy between perceived and actual intensification rates (Figure 5.6): Trump's intensification rates for *much*, *many*, and *great* are lower than the ones found in the other two data sets, but he is such a prolific user of these words that they end up occurring more frequently in the company of *very*, *really*, and *so* than they do in COCA or the Democrats' tweets (see Table 5.5 for the normalized frequencies).

5.5.5.2 Boosters Very and So plus Non-Scalar Adjectives

As a booster, indicating a high point on a scale, *very*, by definition, modifies gradable adjectives and adverbs. That is, the semantics of the intensified lexical item must allow for a degree reading. Of course, speakers are known to be creative and impose gradeability on non-gradable items (e.g., *you're so pregnant*; *this is very Star Wars*), but this is not the norm.

With respect to non-scalar adjectives found in combination with the booster *very*, there is no overlap between the ones found in Trump's tweets and in COCA Spoken

2010–17—at least where the top fifty collocates are concerned.[8] Ungradable adjectives attested in the Trump data include *dishonest* (rank 9), *unfair* (rank 20), *fair* (rank 31), *disloyal* (rank 38), and *true* (rank 46), with the bigram frequency varying between 0.6 and 0.1 occurrences per 10,000 words. In COCA, we find *first* (rank 20, 0.1 occurrences per 10,000 words), *latest* (rank 39), *real* (rank 45), *specific* (rank 48, 0.06 occurrences per 10,000 words). Non-scalar adjectives modified by *very* thus occur considerably more frequently in Trump's tweets than in spoken American English. These bigrams, frequently used by Trump in his tweets, are significantly less frequent in COCA Spoken 2010–17: *very dishonest* and *very disloyal* yield just 1 occurrence each (in 34 million words), *very unfair* 22, *very fair* 35, and *very true* 66 (which corresponds to 0.02 occurrences per 10,000 words). In conclusion, the collocational pattern for *very* as attested in Trump's tweets is indeed markedly different from the pattern in COCA Spoken 2010–17 if the scope is expanded from the top five collocates to the top fifty. The following examples illustrate the observed characteristic features:

(39) I'm not just running up against Crooked Hillary Clinton, I am running against the *very* <u>dishonest</u> and totally biased media – but I will win! (@realDonaldTrump, August 6, 2016)

(40) Obama was *very* <u>disloyal</u> to Wisconsin Democrats. @BarackObama he never showed up to help them . . . . (@realDonaldTrump, June 6, 2012)

(41) Thank you @JeffJlpa1 and @AmSpec for the wonderful and *very* <u>true</u> article, "Total Desperation on Iran" (@realDonaldTrump, April 20, 2015)

With respect to the booster *so*, which corresponds in meaning to 'very,' Trump's tweets contain seven non-gradable elements among the top fifty collocates (ordered from most frequent to least frequent): *great* (in the sense of 'markedly superior in character or quality'; rank 10), *dishonest* (rank 17), *biased* (rank 20), *amazing* (rank 34), *average* (rank 42), *corrupt* (rank 44), and *original* (rank 50), varying between 0.3 and 0.08 occurrences per 10,000 words. See, for instance:

(42) We are going to make our country so strong again, *so* <u>great</u> again. (@realDonaldTrump, August 20, 2015)

(43) Very little pick-up by the media of incredible information provided by WikiLeaks. *So* <u>dishonest</u>! Rigged system! (@realDonaldTrump, October 12, 2016)

(44) If crazy @megynkelly didn't cover me so much on her terrible show, her ratings would totally tank. She is *so* <u>average</u> in so many ways! (@realDonaldTrump, March 19, 2016)

In COCA Spoken 2010–17, the top fifty collocates of *so* contain four ungradable adjectives (*great* rank 5, *true* rank 35, *wrong* rank 36, and *amazing* rank 40), varying in frequency between 0.1 occurrences (*so great*) and 0.02 occurrences (*so amazing*) per 10,000 words. The Trump data thus suggests that Trump combines booster *so* with non-gradable adjectives more readily than the average American English speaker and does so considerably more frequently, too. So, in this respect, he is not conservative.

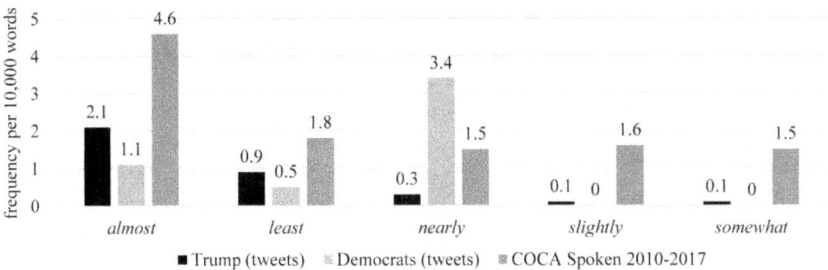

Figure 5.7 Top five downtoners in Trump's tweets.

5.5.6 Downtoners

With respect to downtoners modifying adjectives or adverbs, Trump's tweets contained occurrences of *a bit, a little, almost, at all, kind of, least, merely, nearly, practically, simply, slightly, somewhat,* and *sort of,* but none of *barely, fairly, hardly, mildly, partially, partly,* and *virtually*. The most notable finding pertaining to the use of downtoners in Trump's tweets is their conspicuous infrequency. They are extremely rare in the Trump data, and there is really not much to say about them. Figure 5.7 compares the frequency of the five most common downtoners in Trump's speech to their frequency in COCA Spoken 2010–17 (see Table 5.8 in the Appendix for the raw frequencies). The stark contrast is striking: even the most frequent downtoner in Trump's tweets is more than twice as frequent in spoken American English, while the other downtoners approach zero occurrences (or are not attested at all).

The top five downtoners in Trump's tweets include the approximators *almost* (80 occurrences) and *nearly* (12) as well as the diminishers *least* (35), *somewhat* (4), and *slightly* (4). Interestingly, the compromisers *kind of* and *sort of*, which feature in the top five in spoken American English (Figure 5.8), occur just one time each in Trump's tweets and are thus virtually non-existent. In their tweets, the Democrats are no fond users of downtoners either (with the exception of *nearly*, see Figure 5.7 and Figure 5.8). This finding suggests that downtoners (which weaken what is said, after all) occupy a tiny place in political discourse: while COCA Spoken 2010–17 contains twenty-eight

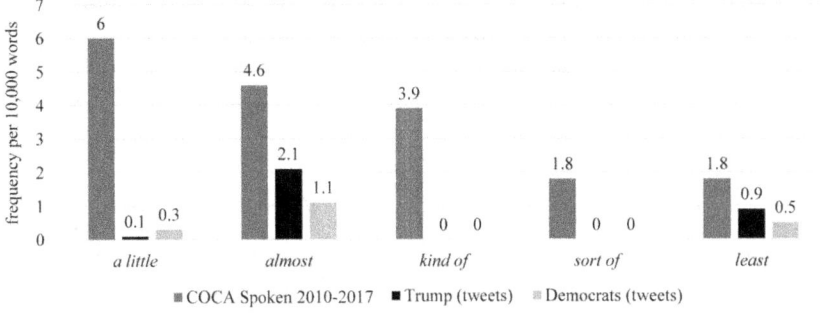

Figure 5.8 Top five downtoners in COCA Spoken 2010–17.

occurrences of downtoners per 10,000 words (see downtoner list above), the tweets only have three (Trump) and six (Democrats) occurrences per 10,000 words.

(45) One of the dumber and *least* <u>respected</u> of the political pundits is Chris Cillizza of the Washington Post @TheFix. (@realDonaldTrump, May 12, 2015)
(46) New polls out today are very good considering that much of the media is FAKE and *almost* <u>always</u> negative. (@realDonaldTrump, April 23, 2017)
(47) Get smart on knockout assaults and crime - we have to be *slightly* <u>more</u> vicious (and violent) than the assaulter-and crime would end FAST! (@realDonaldTrump, November 23, 2013)

5.6 Revisiting the Research Questions

This section summarizes the main findings and provides concise answers to the research questions presented earlier:

(a) How frequently does Trump use intensifiers?
(b) Which ones occur most frequently?
(c) How frequently do intensifiers occur in his speech compared to other users' language?
(d) Are there any observable particularities in his use of intensifiers?

In response to the first research question, the data has shown that Trump uses amplifiers twice as frequently in his remarks compared to his tweets (120 vs. 60 occurrences per 10,000 words, calculation based on top five intensifiers in his speech). His use of *very* in the remarks is quite peculiar in terms of frequency because he uses this intensifier very, very, very often (84 occurrences per 10,000 words).

This leads to the second question: the intensifiers most prominently featuring in his speech are (in order of decreasing frequency) *very*, *so*, *really*, *too*, and *totally*. As for the third question, comparing amplifier frequencies across data sets suggested the following ranking (high to low): Trump's remarks, Trump's tweets, COCA Spoken, the Democrats' tweets, Pence's remarks. This is indicative of register differences on the one hand, for the transcripts in COCA Spoken are less informal than Trump's speech (tweets and remarks) but not as formal as the Democrats' tweets and Pence's remarks. On the other hand, this also hints at highly emotional language where Trump is concerned, because intensifiers are typically associated with expressivity (Tagliamonte and Roberts 2005: 289).

As regards the last research question, the data has shown that overall intensification rates of adjectives and adverbs are not higher in Trump's speech. However, the adjectives and adverbs he modifies are more frequent in his tweets and remarks compared to the other data sets. This means that he intensifies these adjectives more frequently in absolute but not in relative terms. Consequently, the perception that he is a prolific user of *very* and the like is still accurate. With respect to the collocational patterns, the analyses have revealed that Trump tends to use the boosters *very* and *so* more readily

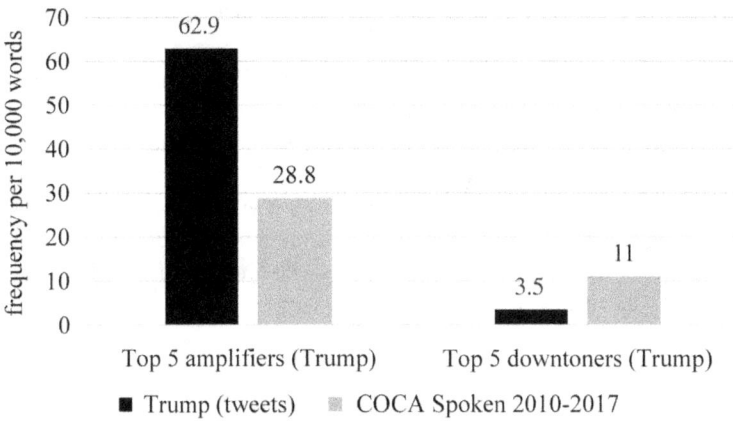

Figure 5.9 Frequency of intensifiers. Top five amplifiers: *very, so, really, too, totally*. Top five downtoners: *almost, least, nearly, slightly, somewhat*.

with non-gradable adjectives like *dishonest* or *true* (possibly to lend additional force to his statements) than the "average" American English speaker (COCA Spoken 2010–17). Traits of linguistic conservatism become apparent in how he uses *totally*—namely with predominantly negative adjectives, and favoring *very* strongly over all other intensifiers (as opposed to *really* or *so*, which younger/more innovative speakers prefer in spoken language—see, for example, Ito and Tagliamonte 2003; Tagliamonte 2008; D'Arcy 2015)

As for downtoners in Trump's speech, the data has shown that they are very infrequent compared to the spoken data in COCA 2010–17. They are also infrequent in the Democrats' tweets, however, which is indicative of political discourse disfavoring them in general (probably due to their weakening effect). Figure 5.9 visualizes the stark contrast in frequency where amplifiers and downtoners in Trump's speech are concerned—the former are very prominent in his tweets while the latter play only a minor role.

5.7 Conclusion

The present study was concerned with how Trump uses intensifiers. Drawing on corpus data (tweets, remarks, COCA Spoken), it has shown that he does use amplifiers markedly more frequently than other speakers, especially *very*. Thus, Rule #3 in *How to Talk like Trump*, "Use intensifiers like 'very'—very, very often" (Romano 2016), shows that Romano's perception of Trump's intensifier use is accurate. The high frequency of amplifiers in his speech shows that it is very informal and emotionally loaded. This is quite unlike more typical politicians' speech that aims at a formal register associated with power, respectability, and trustworthiness. Incidentally, amplifiers might be rarer in formal speech because, depending on the hearer's viewpoint, they can actually lessen the force of a statement (although they serve to add force): *this is good* (solid, powerful) versus *this is really good* (compensating, overstating?). A look at the collocational patterns revealed that Trump intensifies quantifying *much (time)* and *many (people)* quite frequently, which could be accounted for by the topics in his political discourse (vague but exaggerated quantifications as a means of illustrating the number of fake news, the severity of problems, people supporting something or opposing him, etc.).

In short, Trump is a prolific user of amplifiers, and the analyzed bigrams show that he speaks like an elderly, highly emotional man (with the exception of *so*, where he is quite innovative in that he readily combines it with non-scalar adjectives).The corresponding conspicuous infrequency of downtoners complements the picture in that it ties in with tentative claims by journalists who find that "Trump has never been prone to understatement" (Romano 2016).

Appendix

Table 5.6 Number of Relevant Hits for *Very|Really|So|Too|Totally* plus ADJ|ADV

Data set	Relevant hits
Trump (tweets)	2,421
Trump (remarks)	318
Democrats (tweets)	644
Pence (remarks)	7
COCA Spoken	97,984

Table 5.7 Number of Relevant Hits for *Truly* and *Highly* plus ADJ|ADV

	Trump's tweets	Democrats' tweets	COCA Spoken 2010–17
truly	79	16	2,870
highly	72	20	7,514

Table 5.8 Number of Relevant Hits for Top Five Downtoners plus ADJ|ADV

Top 5 among Trump's tweets	Trump's tweets	Democrats' tweets	COCA Spoken 2010–17	Top 5 COCA Spoken 2010–17	Trump's tweets	Democrats' tweets	COCA Spoken 2010–17
almost	80	67	15,641	a little	3	17	20,493
least	35	31	6,098	almost	80	67	15,641
nearly	12	200	4,937	kind of	1	1	13,246
slightly	4	0	5,271	sort of	1	2	6,262
somewhat	4	0	3,757	least	11	31	6,098

Notes

1 The full transcript is available at: https://www.economist.com/united-states/2017/05/11/transcript-interview-with-donald-trump (last accessed November 29, 2019).
2 In simplified terms, words with negative semantic prosody evoke negative associations. See Partington (1998) for a detailed treatment of semantic prosody.
3 Later data was not available at the time of submission. The subsections can be selected at five-year intervals (i.e., 2005–9, 2010–14, etc. plus the latest subset 2015–17).
4 Approximately 300 hits with the selected intensifiers were discarded because the modified item was a verb. Given the scarcity of research in the area of verb intensification, this could very well be an avenue worth pursuing in a different paper.
5 An additional nine occurrences of *so* occurred in lengthened form (with two to four additional <o>s), for example, "The Emmys are sooooo boring! Terrible show" (@realDonaldTrump, September 22, 2013). These lengthened forms seem to add even more expressive force to the intensifier and are very informal in writing.
6 Usually, intensification is a matter of choice as both the intensified and the non-intensified version of a phrase exist—compare *this is good* and *this is very good*. In the case of *very much* in *thank you very much*, the non-intensified version is, however, no viable alternative: **thank you much*.
7 The Corpus of Historical American English (Davies 2010–).
8 The discussion focuses on the contrast between Trump's tweets and COCA Spoken because there are not enough tokens to allow for a fruitful discussion of intensifier use in the Democrat's tweets and Trump's and Pence's remarks—at least where particularities in the collocational range are concerned.

References

Abbas, Ali H. (2019), "Super-Hyperbolic Man: Hyperbole as Ideological Discourse Strategy in Trump's Speeches," *International Journal for the Semiotics of Law*, 32 (2): 505–22.

Ahmadian, Sarah, Sara Azarshahi, and Delroy L. Paulhus (2017), "Explaining Donald Trump via Communication Style: Grandiosity, Informality, and Dynamism," *Personality and Individual Differences*, 107 (1): 49–53.

Altenberg, Bengt (1991), "Amplifier Collocations in Spoken English," in Stig Johansson and Anna-Brita Stenström (eds.), *English Computer Corpora: Selected Papers and Research Guide*, 127–47, Berlin: Mouton de Gruyter.

Bäcklund, Ulf (1973), *The Collocations of Adverbs of Degree in English*, Uppsala: Almquist and Wiksell.

Bell, Allan (1984), "Linguistic Style as Audience Design," *Language in Society*, 13 (2): 145–204.

Bolinger, Dwight (1972), *Degree Words*, The Hague: Mouton.

Brezina, Vaclav, Matthew Timperley, and Tony McEnery (2018), *#LancsBox v. 4.x [software]*. Available online: http://corpora.lancs.ac.uk/lancsbox (accessed November 12, 2019).

Brown, Brendan (2019), *Trump Twitter Archive*. Available online: http://www.trumptwitterarchive.com/archive (accessed November 12, 2019).

D'Arcy, Alexandra (2015), "Stability, Stasis and Change—The Longue Durée of Intensification," *Diachronica*, 32 (4): 449–93.

Danyushina, Yu (2016), "Lingua-Communicative Trumpology," in Anton Burkov (ed.), *Scientific Enquiry in the Contemporary Worlds: Theoretical Basics and Innovative Approach*, 86–8, San Francisco: B&M Publishing.

Davies, Mark (2008–), The Corpus of Contemporary American English: 600 million words, 1990–present. Available online: http://www.english-corpora.org/coca (accessed November 12, 2019).

Davies, Mark (2010–), The Corpus of Historical American English: 400 million words, 1810–2009. Available online: http://www.english-corpora.org/coha (accessed November 12, 2019).

Hodges, Adam (2017), "Trump's Formulaic Twitter Insults," *Anthropology News*, 58 (1): 14 June. Available online: https://doi.org/10.1111/AN.308 (accessed November 12, 2019).

Hunston, Susan (2017), "Donald Trump and the Language of Populism," University of Birmingham, Available online: https://www.birmingham.ac.uk/research/perspective/donald-trump-language-of-populism.aspx (accessed December 6, 2019).

Ito, Rika and Sali Tagliamonte (2003), "*Well Weird, Right Dodgy, Very Strange, Really Cool*: Layering and Recycling in English Intensifiers," *Language in Society*, 32 (2): 257–79.

Lorenz, Gunter (2002), "*Really Worthwhile* or *Not Really Significant?* A Corpus-Based Approach to the Delexicalization and Grammaticalization of Intensifiers in Modern English," in Ilse Wischer and Gabriele Diewald (eds.), *New Reflections on Grammaticalization*, 143–61, Amsterdam: Benjamins.

Partington, Alan (1993), "Corpus Evidence of Language Change—The Case of the Intensifier," in Mona Baker, Gill Francis and Elena Tognini-Bonelli (eds.), *Text and Technology: In Honour of John Sinclair*, 177–92, Amsterdam: Benjamins.

Partington, Alan (1998), *Patterns and Meanings*, Amsterdam: Benjamins.

Quirk, Randolph, Sidney Greenbaum, Geoffrey Leech, and Jan Svartvik (1985), *A Comprehensive Grammar of the English Language*, London: Longman.

Romano, Andrew (2016), "The Strange Power of Donald Trump's Speech Patterns," *yahoo! news*. Available online: https://www.yahoo.com/news/the-strange-power-of-donald-1397103083307062.html (accessed November 12, 2019).

Scherl, Magdalena (2018), *TwitterCorpusQuery 2.0* [software]. Mainz.

Stange, Ulrike and Susanne Wagner (2018), "*This Is so Totally Pathetic!* On the Diachronic Development of *So Totally*," paper presented at ICEHL XX, 27–31 August 2018, Edinburgh, United Kingdom.

Stenström, Anna-Brita, Gisle Andersen, and Ingrid K. Hasund (2002), *Trends in Teenage Talk: Corpus Compilation, Analysis and Findings*, Amsterdam: Benjamins.

Stoffel, Cornelis (1901), *Intensives and Down-Toners: A Study in English Adverbs*, Heidelberg: Carl Winter's Universitätsbuchhandlung.

Tagliamonte, Sali (2008), "*So Different* and *Pretty Cool!* Recycling Intensifiers in Toronto, Canada," *English Language and Linguistics*, 12 (2): 361–94.

Tagliamonte, Sali and Chris Roberts (2005), "*So Weird; So Cool; So Innovative*: The Use of Intensifiers in the Television Series *Friends*," *American Speech*, 80 (3): 280–300.

6

Crooked Hillary, *Lyin' Ted*, and *Failing* New York Times

Nicknames in Donald Trump's Tweets

Jukka Tyrkkö and Irina Frisk

6.1 Introduction

In a phone call with Mark Leibovich in 2016, then presidential candidate Donald Trump openly discussed his use of disparaging nicknames. According to Leibovich (2016), Trump acknowledged that the nicknames were part of his campaign strategy and something that comes very naturally to him. "It works, it flows," Trump is reported as saying. New nicknames were tested on the audiences of his campaign rallies, and the ones that got the audience chanting were kept while unsuccessful ones were quietly dropped. Once an opponent dropped out of the race, Trump told Leibovich, their nickname was retired. Even the occasionally non-standard spelling of nicknames came up in the interview, and Trump noted that "it matters as to the look and feel and touch."

Nicknames present an interesting object of study as they serve as social, cultural, and personal identity markers. As Adams (2009: 84) notes, "nicknaming carries a verdictive force: it judges, assesses, or ranks." This is not to say that the verdictive force is always or even predominantly negative. In order to maintain in-group ties and integrity, nicknames are often assigned to group members as terms of endearment and affection. However, they may equally well be assigned to out-group members, in which case they may also foster a sense of in-group membership among the speaker's own group. Importantly, like names, nicknames can be used either as terms of reference or as terms of address.

Trump's style of political nicknaming has been discussed widely over the last few years, with some journalists taking an active stand against these practices. Karen Tumulty of the *Washington Post* wrote in a recent article, "I hereby make a pledge: From this day forward, I will never again quote, repeat or otherwise dignify any of the asinine nicknames that President Trump gives his adversaries" (Tumulty 2019). This chapter takes a close look at the forms and functions of nicknames in Donald Trump's tweets from the time he took to Twitter in 2009 to the end of 2018. Through qualitative and quantitative analyses of a corpus comprised of Trump's tweets, we identify productive patterns in his nicknaming practices in the context of contemporary political discourse online. We comment on the semantics of Trump's nicknames, his gendered nicknaming practices, and the way moral judgments are communicated through nicknames.

6.2 Onomastics and Nicknaming

In linguistics, the field of study that examines names and naming practices is called *onomastics*. Although personal names and naming practices are found in every culture and part of the world (Alia 2009), their roles and functions differ considerably across the world: from an intimate ceremony at a local church that makes the newborn's given name(s) official to branding one's name in pursuit of socioeconomic power, thereby challenging the traditional view that "the holder [of a name] has little or no control over [its] designation and use" (Starks and Taylor-Leech 2011: 87).

Like names in general, nicknames serve to refer to an individual person; at the same time, they go beyond the common type of names in that they indicate a social relationship between two persons (Nübling, Fahlbusch, and Heuser 2012: 171). Descriptive nicknames are commonly indicative of the person's looks, personality, habits, quirks, and the like and thus "create expectations about the user" (Starks and Taylor-Leech 2011: 87). There are strong cultural norms at play when it comes to what descriptors are acceptable to use. Violating these norms is considered "politically incorrect" linguistic behavior and doing so can serve as a strong signal of the speaker's background and stance. For example, in present-day Western societies, it is generally considered unacceptable to use nicknames that refer to another person's appearance, sexual orientation, or abilities in a negative way, and even ostensibly positive descriptors may be considered inappropriate if they draw attention to features that are typically considered to be potentially hurtful (Croom 2013). For example, while it may be considered acceptable to distinguish between two co-workers as "Tall Jim" and "Short Jim," it would probably be unacceptable to call them "Smart Jim" and "Dim Jim," or "Fat Jim" and "Fit Jim," unless the workplace had a particularly informal culture and it was well-established that both men enjoyed the nicknames.

As Allsop (2017) notes, nicknames also serve the important function of simplifying and focusing our attention to one or two features of the named person. Examples of this effect are familiar to us all from children's fairytales: the Evil Queen is only evil, Prince Charming is, well, charming. This effect is related to the linguistic concepts of *collocation* and *semantic prosody*: two words that often occur together have a tendency to form bonds over time. The pairing begins to sound natural and hearing one of the items will easily bring the other to mind, especially in the right context (see Sinclair 1991: 70–5). When a new pairing has been formed, as in the case of multi-word nicknames, the words allude to one another, and this allows the often negative connotations of the descriptive item to affect the other. Thus, when the person's real name is mentioned, others may remember the nickname. In order for this so-called entrenchment to happen, the pairing needs to be repeated many times which, as we will show in section 6.5.6, is arguably one of the reasons behind Donald Trump's "tweetstorms."

In the US political arena, nicknames have been used as a "tool of influence" to elevate or insult political figures and can be traced back to George Washington's nickname *The Father of His Country* in the late 1700s (Gladkova 2002). Many presidents have been known by an initialism based on their name (e.g., Franklin Delano Roosevelt as FDR, John F. Kennedy as JFK, Lyndon B. Johnson as LBJ), and nearly all have had one or more benign nicknames derived from their name (e.g., Dwight D. Eisenhower was known as Ike, Theodore Roosevelt as Teddy). However, from the perspective of the present discussion, we are much more interested in descriptive nicknames, or indeed *mock names*, which highlight a supposedly recognizable or descriptive characteristic of the person. Coined during political campaigns, descriptive nicknames given to opponents are often fleeting affairs but occasionally they stick, especially when they are picked up by the national press: for example, Richard Nixon became "Tricky Dick," Bill Clinton was coined "Slick Willie" while Hillary Clinton was dubbed "Crooked Hillary" by Trump during his campaign.

Importantly, the dynamics of using nicknames change drastically when there is a power imbalance between the giver or user of a nickname and its recipient, or referent. Starting from a perfect power balance, such as would hopefully exist between best friends or spouses, we can go all the way to contexts where the power imbalance is not only extreme but, in fact, imposed by protocol and even law. In the case of absolute balance of power, both parties are free to create and use nicknames for each other. At the other extreme of the scale, only one party may do so, while the other has to maintain a formal and polite form of address at all times.

Finally, nicknames can be used either to directly address a person or to refer to an absent person. This dimension, unlike the other two, is less of importance, as in the case of Trump's tweets we are solely dealing with reference uses. Thus we can now describe situations of nickname use in terms of the three dimensions address/reference, negative/positive semantics, and power difference (see Figure 6.1).

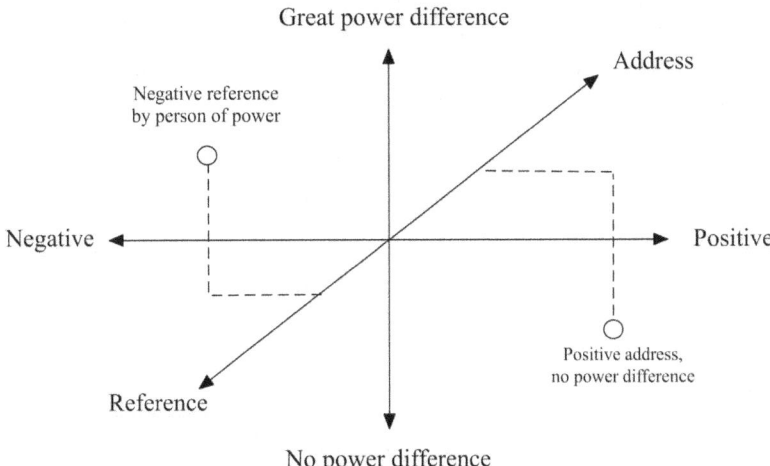

Figure 6.1 Schematic diagram of the three dimensions of nicknaming.

Following Adams's (2009: 84) assessment of the verdictive force of nicknames, that is, that nicknames are used to "judge, assess and rank" the named individual, they may, over time, come to stigmatize the person and have real-world consequences that go far beyond the simple labeling function. In the case of pejorative descriptive nicknames used habitually in public contexts, it is reasonable to expect that many members of the public will come not only to associate the person with the name but also to associate them with the qualities that the nickname implies. This effect, we may surmise, is likely to be stronger if the nickname is used by a person of great power and authority. When a trusted individual, such as an elected leader, uses a nickname that appears to evaluate, judge, or denigrate the targeted person, it is likely that a significant proportion of the public, in particular those who voted for that leader, will accept that label with relatively little assessment.

Perhaps the most prolific user of nicknames in recent political history before Donald Trump was George W. Bush, who was well known for assigning nicknames to almost everyone working in his vicinity (Adams 2008). Indeed, President Bush's habit of giving and using nicknames was not only prolific but also all the more notable because Bush did not shy away from using openly offensive nicknames, such as "Turd Blossom" for advisor Karl Rove. Discussing the issue of power imbalance, Adams (2008: 207) notes that "President Bush's exuberant naming practices are perhaps also unusually aggressive, and this is politically important, in the American context, because they assert a presidential right to put people into their places, as subjects under presidential authority. At the presidential level, nicknaming becomes political because of the office, because a president's authority is executive, not personal."

Against this theoretical background, our interest in the present study is in analyzing the nicknaming practices of Donald Trump both before and during his presidency. What makes the topic particularly noteworthy is the public nature of Trump's use of nicknames both referentially and when addressing individuals and his penchant for using openly offensive descriptors—it is important to emphasize that the tweets in which he uses such nicknames during the time he has been in office are, by declaration of the White House Press Office, official statements of the president of the United States.[1] While previous presidents may have occasionally used offensive nicknames during campaigns, within the working environment of the White House or in private conversation, Donald Trump has gone one step further and made a habit of using mocking nicknames in public tweets posted as president of the United States. These nicknames thus come with the official seal of approval of the highest executive in the land.

6.3 Trump's Nicknaming Practices on Twitter

This section provides a brief overview of Trump's use of Twitter as a channel for self-promotion and power practices online. Trump joined Twitter in March 2009. For the first couple of years, tweets from his account were infrequent and were mostly about himself and the products he was selling, such as his books and the Miss USA contest. Most notably, Trump was particularly fond of posting quotes of himself, such as the following, eerily prescient post from 2009:

(1) "My persona will never be that of a wallflower - I'd rather build walls than cling to them"–Donald J. Trump. (@realDonaldTrump, May 12, 2009)

In 2011, the topics addressed via the @realDonaldTrump account began to shift. Tweets from this time often commented on politics, although with a much less aggressive tone than what became standard during his political campaign in 2015–16. His early political tweets were particularly negative on China and Barack Obama, whom he regularly lambasted for wasting taxpayers' money, not getting results in negotiations with foreign countries, and being a boring and ineffective public speaker. He also blamed Obama for the so-called Operation Fast and Furious, where agents of the Bureau of Alcohol, Tobacco, Firearms, and Explosives allowed weapons to be sold to Mexican criminal cartels in order to trace them. For example, in October 2011, Trump posted:

(2) @BarackObama sold guns to the Mexican drug cartels. They were used in the murders of Americans. Where is the outrage? (@realDonaldTrump, October 2, 2011)

Another topic that Trump returned to over and over again was Barack Obama's birth place, as in this tweet from 2012:

(3) Let's take a closer look at that birth certificate. @BarackObama was described in 2003 as being "born in Kenya." http://t.co/vfqJesJL (@realDonaldTrump, May 18, 2012)

Themes familiar to present-day followers of the @realDonaldTrump account, such as other countries laughing at the United States and stealing American jobs, also emerged at this time. Although his style was still not as controversial as it would eventually become, he already started engaging in occasional ad hominem attacks, including the use of disparaging nicknames. We will discuss this in more detail in section 6.5.6, but to give an example, in December 2011, Trump tweeted about the diplomat Jon Huntsman:[2]

(4) A total lightweight: @JonHuntsman continues to give the worst responses on China in the debates. (@realDonaldTrump, December 16, 2011)

At the same time, Trump started getting into public feuds with other celebrities on Twitter. These seemingly inconsequential confrontations made headline news due to Trump's outrageous and often downright abusive language. One of the earliest examples is Trump's attack on Rosie O'Donnel, then co-host of the talk show *The View*.

(5) I feel sorry for Rosie 's new partner in love whose parents are devastated at the thought of their daughter being with @Rosie—a true loser. (@realDonaldTrump, December 14, 2011)

Later examples, targeted at actress Bette Midler, singer Cher, and host of the British version of *The Apprentice*, businessman Lord Alan Sugar, further illustrate the tone of the posts. The attacks were typically in response to negative comments made in public by the celebrities in question, but Trump's tweets were arguably more extreme in language and certainly incongruous with traditional ideas about statesmanlike behavior.

(6) @BetteMidler talks about my hair but I'm not allowed to talk about her ugly face or body — so I won't. Is this a double standard? (@realDonaldTrump, October 28, 2012)

(7) .@cher--I don't wear a "rug"—it's mine. And I promise not to talk about your massive plastic surgeries that didn't work. (@realDonaldTrump, November 13, 2012)

(8) Dopey Sugar @Lord_Sugar—you are the worst kind of loser—a total fool. (@realDonaldTrump, December 10, 2012)

After Donald Trump made the announcement in the summer of 2015 that he was running for president, Twitter quickly became a central feature of his strategy. He posted tirelessly about his opponents—almost 1,000 times about Hillary Clinton, more than 300 times about Ted Cruz—and although all other candidates during the 2016 election also used Twitter and other social media, none came close to Trump when it came to capturing and maintaining the public's attention. Trump served up a smorgasbord of content, sometimes praising the American military or God, then switching to thanking the audiences of his rallies or announcing the next one, constantly disparaging his political opponents and anyone else who happened to catch his eye in the wrong way.

While Obama had used social media to some extent, Trump was the first presidential candidate to make social media one of the cornerstones of his campaign and would later become the first president to express his seemingly private opinions on world affairs directly to the people. Tweeting has continued to be one of the most salient features of the Trump presidency, both during the election and the presidency itself.

6.4 Data and Method

6.4.1 Data

For the present study, we opted to use a pre-compiled collection of Donald Trump's tweets that is made available online by the Trump Twitter Archive (Brown 2019). The Trump Twitter Archive is a *monitor corpus* in the sense that it is constantly updated as new tweets are posted. We use this open-source version of the data in order to maximize transparency and verifiability. We used all tweets[3] posted between May 4, 2009 and December 31, 2018, on Donald Trump's private Twitter account (@realDonaldTrump), which has been active since March 2009. As president of the United States, Trump can also tweet using the official presidential account (@POTUS), which was first launched under President Obama and was passed on to Trump. As Trump rarely uses the official account, it was not included in the study. The collection of tweets comprises a total of 24,338 tweets, of which we used the 19,007 that are not retweets.

In order to find the nicknames in the corpus, we automatically annotated each word for part of speech (so-called tagging) using Treetagger (Schmid 1994) and then ran queries for sequences of two proper names or an adjective and a proper name. The resulting list of c. 7,000 items was manually pruned for nicknames. We made sure only to include true nicknames; proper nouns preceded by an adjectival premodifier were generally not included, unless capitalization and context made it clear that the adjective was, in fact, nominalized and functioned as the first element of a nickname. Additionally, we consulted the Wikipedia page for Trump's nicknames. As not all nicknames on the Wikipedia list appear in Trump's tweets, we added them to our list because they relate directly to Trump's nicknaming practices. Our final list of nicknames comprises 167 unique items (or "types") directed at 102 unique referents, which can be either individuals or groups of individuals. All examples given are from tweets.

6.4.2 Methodology

This study relies primarily on a methodology that has come to be known as *corpus-aided discourse analysis* (CADA)—see, for example, Partington, Duguid, and Taylor (2013). As we have seen in previous chapters, corpus linguistic methods allow linguists to examine language at a very large scale, which makes it possible to discover patterns and trends that would be impossible to see otherwise.

Discourse analysis, including the more specialized subfields of *critical discourse analysis* (CDA) and *political discourse analysis* (see Baker 2006; Partington, Duguid, and Taylor 2013), is a field of linguistics that is concerned with understanding how language is used in longer stretches of interaction, or *discourses*. The object of discourse analysis can be a specific instance of interaction, such as an individual political speech, or the common features of broad discursive contexts, such as academic writing or political speaking, understood as culturally and linguistically consistent and coherent phenomena. Discourse analysts are typically interested in uncovering patterns of linguistic behavior, as well as trends that appear to strengthen or weaken over time. In CDA, analytical approaches are motivated by a desire to reveal how linguistic means can be used to usurp or hold power and to create in-groups and out-groups, to coerce or mislead audiences into agreeing with the speaker, and to incite discord against specific groups of people. In this respect, CADA harnesses the power of large-scale corpus analysis and uses it to answer questions that arise from discourse analytical frameworks.

6.4.3 Semantic and Pragmatic Classification

In order to get an overview of the nature of nicknames used by Trump on Twitter, five distinctive uses of nicknames were identified, hereafter referred to as *categories* of nicknames. Every instance of a nickname was assigned to one of these categories, depending on its context of use.

Nickname Categories

1. Appearance
Refers to the referent's looks, height, and size: for example, *Horseface*
2. Personality
Refers to the referent's character traits and habits (Starks and Taylor-Leech 2011): for example, *Heartless Hillary, Fake News Media*
3. Intellect
Refers to the referent's IQ and judgment: for example, *Low-IQ Maxine Waters*
4. Behavior
Refers to the referent's actions: for example, *Leakin' Lyin' James Comey, Jeff Flakey*
5. Reference
Contains additional references to either events or people: for example, *Little Rocket Man*

Furthermore, every nickname in our data was analyzed in terms of whether it targets the moral value of the individual or media outlet nicknamed. More precisely, the morals variable assesses whether a nickname targets a referent's reputation or the credibility of a source based on national values as represented in the United States Constitution. The variable has been introduced in order to examine possible differences and similarities across the five categories of nicknames twittered by Trump. Each nickname token has been classified with respect to whether it displays a moral judgment or not. Examples (9)–(12) demonstrate how the nicknames are intended to suggest that the referent acts in an amoral manner, irrespective of whether they address the person's appearance, personality, or behavior. The element(s) addressing the individual's morals is given in italics.

(9) Miss *Piggy* (appearance)
(10) *Fake* Tears Chuck Schumer (personality)
(11) *Cheatin'* Obama (behavior)
(12) FBI *lover boy* (reference)

As shown in (9), *Miss Piggy* invokes muppet-like associations, allegedly assigned by Trump to White House correspondent April Ryan as opposed to the unmarked use of a nickname targeting someone's appearance in *Ugly Carly*. The *Fake* and *Lover Boy* elements in (10) and (12), used to show disapproval of the referents' morals, contrast with the nicknames that do not carry any moral judgment such as *No Talent Samantha Bee* (personality) and *Rocket Man* (reference). Interestingly, the nicknames labeled "intellect" do not contain any instances of moral assessment, while the opposite is indicative of the examples in the "behavior" category; that is, they all seem to target the referents' morals: *Leaking Dianne Feinstein, Lying James Comey, Failing New York Times*.

Finally, in the cases when Trump's nicknames were aimed at individuals, they were also labeled according to the gender of the referent, that is, "male" or "female." However, when the nickname referred to groups of people, organizations, or corporate entities, the variable *referent* was assigned the value "multiple." Examples include *Crooked Press* and *Corrupt New York Times*. The qualitative and quantitative results for the analytical categories outlined earlier will be provided and explained in the next section.

6.5 Results and Discussion

6.5.1 Word-Formation

Before plunging into a discussion of the main results of our study, it is worth taking a closer look at the structure of Trump's nicknames in terms of the word-formation processes used to create them and the level of word play involved. In Trump's tweets, the nickname quite often rhymes with the referent's first or last name, for example, *Wacky Jacky* and *Lamb the Sham*. If the name of the referent already includes an element which can be used in mockery, Trump often modifies the name so as to draw attention to this, like in *Sour Lemon* for Don Lemon (a CNN news anchor) and *Nutter of Philadelphia* for Michael Nutter (the ninety-eighth mayor of Philadelphia). Trump also makes use of derivational prefixes and suffixes to create sarcasm, as in *Deface the Nation* as a spin on the news show *Face the Nation*. Suffixed or compound nicknames that appear persistently in Trump's tweets involve former US senator Jeff Flake, exemplified in (13)–(15).

(13) Great to see that Dr. Kelli Ward is running against **Flake Jeff Flake**, who is WEAK on borders, crime and a non-factor in Senate. He's toxic! (@realDonaldTrump, August 17, 2017)

(14) **Jeff Flake(y)** doesn't want to protect the Non-Senate confirmed Special Counsel, he wants to protect his future after being unelectable in Arizona for the "crime" of doing a terrible job! A weak and ineffective guy! (@realDonaldTrump, November 9, 2018)

(15) Sen. **Jeff Flake(y)**, who is unelectable in the Great State of Arizona (quit race, anemic polls) was caught (purposely) on "mike" saying bad things about your favorite President. He'll be a NO on tax cuts because his political career anyway is "toast." (@realDonaldTrump, November 19, 2017)

As one of the biggest critics of Trump's immigration and economic policies, Flake has been a source of inspiration for Trump's nickname creations over the recent years. As shown in (13)–(15), Trump consistently refers to him as *Flakey* or *Flake Jeff Flake*, thereby creating and reinforcing the image of Flake being unreliable and irresponsible and therefore a non-deserving candidate for the presidential election of 2020. This illustrates the power structures of nicknaming in political discourse that we discussed in section 6.2, namely that nicknames "assert a presidential right to put people into their places" (Adams 2008: 207). Naturally, when Flake announced his retirement in October 2017, Trump's references to him on social media died out.

6.5.2 Semantic Analysis: Nickname Categories

The main focus in the present section lies on the categories of nicknames used by Donald Trump. We investigate whether he prefers different categories of nicknames for each of the genders. Figure 6.2 shows a breakdown of the nickname types. This means that all instances of *Crooked Hillary* were counted as a single type. First of all, we see that the opponents who received the largest share of Trump's attention in the form of nicknames are male individuals (ninety-seven types), followed by female individuals (thirty-six types) and multiple referents or organizations (twenty-four types).

The largest share of nicknames for both genders targets the referents' personality (female: 42 percent, male: 38 percent, and multiple/organizations: 50 percent). When we compare nickname categories, the differences between male and female referents are not statistically significant ($\chi^2 = 4.07$, df = 4, p = non-sig.), which means that, despite popular belief, Trump does not label genders differently in terms of nickname categories. Note, however, that we are discussing the relationship between gender and nickname type, not the frequency at which specific nicknames referring to each gender are used by Trump.

Let us now examine the nickname categories more closely. Examples from the two most productive categories overall (personality and reference) are given in (16)–(19). The nickname elements *Sneaky* and *Shady* refer to the referents' personality, while

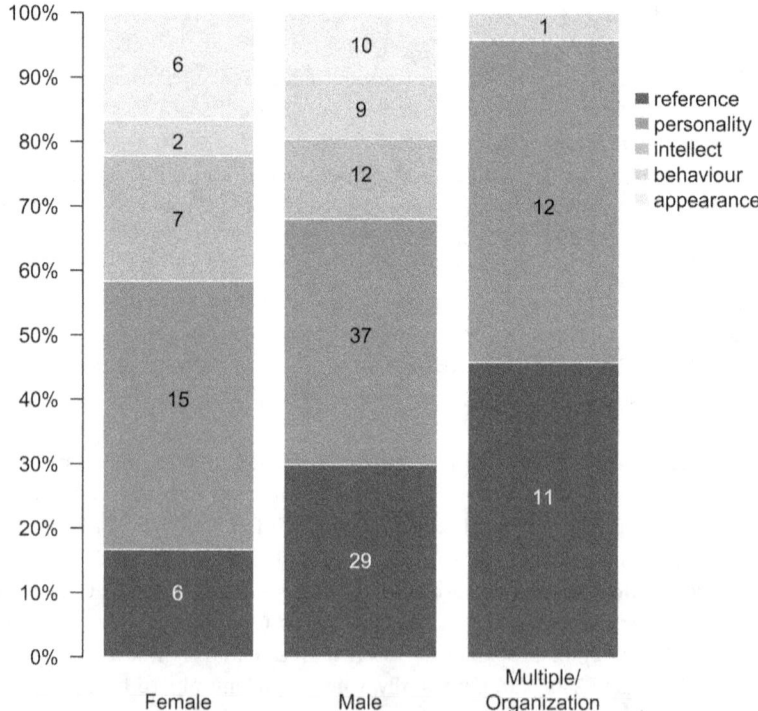

Figure 6.2 Trump's nicknames by category and referent.

High Tax, High Crime targets Pelosi's political positions (reference). Finally, the reference to *FBI lover boy* in (19) evokes connotations to Peter Storzok's marital infidelity and thus to his moral character (reference).

(16) The fact that **Sneaky Dianne Feinstein**, who has on numerous occasions stated that collusion between Trump/Russia has not been found, would release testimony in such an underhanded and possibly illegal way, totally without authorization, is a disgrace. Must have tough Primary! (@realDonaldTrump, January 10, 2018)

(17) Russia continues to say they had nothing to do with Meddling in our Election! Where is the DNC Server, and why didn't **Shady James Comey** and the now disgraced FBI agents take and closely examine it? Why isn't Hillary/Russia being looked at? So many questions, so much corruption! (@realDonaldTrump, June 28, 2018)

(18) Get the vote out in California today for Rep. Kevin McCarthy and all of the great GOP candidates for Congress. Keep our country out of the hands of **High Tax, High Crime Nancy Pelosi**. (@realDonaldTrump, June 5, 2018)

(19) The Rigged Witch Hunt, originally headed by **FBI lover boy Peter S** (for one year) & now, 13 Angry Democrats, should look into the missing DNC Server, Crooked Hillary's illegally deleted Emails, the Pakistani Fraudster, Uranium One, Podesta & so much more. It's a Democrat Con Job! (@realDonaldTrump, July 7, 2018)

The nicknames alone do not always suffice, and consequently they are often used in a patronizingly sarcastic way, as shown in (20)–(22).

(20) **Little @MacMiller**, I'm now going to teach you a big boy lesson about lawsuits and finance. You ungrateful dog![4] (@realDonaldTrump, January 31, 2013)

(21) Senator **Cryin' Chuck Schumer** fought hard against the Bad Iran Deal, even going at it with President Obama, & then Voted AGAINST it! Now he says I should not have terminated the deal - but he doesn't really believe that! Same with Comey. Thought he was terrible until I fired him! (@realDonaldTrump, May 10, 2018)

(22) **Lying Cruz** put out a statement, "Trump & Rubio are w/Obama on gay marriage." Cruz is the worst liar, crazy or very dishonest. Perhaps all 3? (@realDonaldTrump, February 12, 2016)

Nicknames in the categories appearance and intellect are similar across the male/female subsets. Trump's favorite descriptor is *little*, sometimes spelled "liddle," which has been used in nicknames for Marco Rubio, Adam Schiff, Jeff Zucker, Michael Bloomberg, George Stephanopoulos, Mac Miller, Donny Deutsch, Bob Corker, and Katy Tur. Although some of the referents may not be very tall, not all are: Adam Schiff's height is 179 cm and Marco Rubio's 175 cm. Notably, Trump uses the descriptor *big* when addressing Luther Strange, a Republican US senator from Alabama in a positive tone. Taken together, this indicates that Trump does not use *little* and *big* in reference to physical appearance, but rather metaphorically to indicate that the referents are (political) "lightweights" or "big players." In fact, the term *lightweight* is another stock expression in Trump's vocabulary. Over the years, it has been used in nicknames referring to, for instance, Marco Rubio, Bob Corker, Jeb Bush, Rand Paul, Kristen Gillibrand, Eric Schneiderman, Jon Huntsman, Al Neuharth, and Danny Zuker. As noted earlier, the term is intended to suggest that the person is not to be taken seriously and does not measure up to their position. Notably, Trump has used the term during his tenure as president of the United States in reference to four US senators (Rubio, Corker, Paul, and Gillibrand).

A particular subset of personality and behavior-related nicknames is reserved for individuals, often progressive politicians, whom Trump wishes to characterize as mentally unstable. Trump's favorite descriptors in this category are *wacky*, *crazy*, and *goofy*—see examples (23)–(25).

(23) **Wacky Omarosa**, who got fired 3 times on the Apprentice, now got fired for the last time. She never made it, never will. She begged me for a job, tears in her eyes, I said Ok. People in the White House hated her. She was vicious, but not smart. I would rarely see her but heard really bad things. Nasty to people & would constantly miss meetings & work. When Gen. Kelly came on board he told me she was a loser & nothing but problems. I told him to try working it out, if possible, because she only said GREAT things about me - until she got fired! (@realDonaldTrump, August 13, 2018)

(24) Looking more & more like the Trump Campaign for President was illegally being spied upon (surveillance) for the political gain of **Crooked Hillary Clinton** and the DNC. Ask her how that worked out - she did better with **Crazy Bernie**. Republicans must get tough now. An illegal Scam! (@realDonaldTrump, July 22, 2018)

(25) I hope that **Crooked Hillary** picks **Goofy Elizabeth Warren**, sometimes referred to as Pocahontas, as her V.P. Then we can litigate her fraud! (@realDonaldTrump, July 17, 2016)

One of the most infamous examples of Trump's online abuse was targeted at Joe Scarborough and Mika Brezinsky, hosts of a news and talk show on NBC and former friends of Donald Trump—there were even speculations that Scarborough, a former Republican congressman, might be Trump's running mate. The hosts became targets of his anger when they started criticizing him in the spring of 2016. Until then, Trump's tweets about the pair and their show had been positive (26), but by 2017, the relationship had soured which meant that Trump coined nicknames for them, as evident in (27) and (28).

(26) Thank you @Morning_Joe & @morningmika -- a great show! #Trump2016 #MakeAmericaGreatAgain (@realDonaldTrump, November 11, 2015)

(27) I heard poorly rated @Morning_Joe speaks badly of me (don't watch anymore). Then how come **low I.Q. Crazy Mika**, along with **Psycho Joe**, came to Mar-a-

Lago 3 nights in a row around New Year's Eve, and insisted on joining me. She was bleeding badly from a face-lift. I said no! (@realDonaldTrump, June 29, 2017)

(28) **Crazy Joe Scarborough** and **dumb as a rock Mika** are not bad people, but their low rated show is dominated by their NBC bosses. Too bad! (@realDonaldTrump, July 1, 2017)

6.5.3 Pragmatic Analysis: Moral Judgments

The results so far suggest that Trump uses nicknames as a "tool of influence" (Gladkova 2002) in order to diminish and/or discredit his opponents. We specifically annotated our Twitter data for the *morals* variable in order to be able to further analyze whether this is the case. As noted earlier, the morals variable assesses whether a nickname targets a referent's reputation or the credibility of a source based on national values. Trump's nicknames often build on these morals, which are deeply rooted in American history and culture. For instance, Trump repeatedly informs every US citizen of their moral duty to the country and urges them to act upon it, as seen in (29). However, as Trump points out, the road to "Mak[ing] America Great Again!" will be paved with hardships, and there will be an enemy wanting to sabotage this endeavor—the *Fake News*, see (30) and (31), and its associates, *Crooked Hillary*, *Lyin' Ted*, and *Crazy Megyn*.

(29) Thank you West Virginia! All across the country, Americans of every kind are coming together w/one simple goal: to **MAKE AMERICA GREAT AGAIN!** https://t.co/thRh7htVbH (@realDonaldTrump, August 3, 2017)
(30) The Fake News hates me saying that they are **the Enemy of the People** only because they know it's TRUE. I am providing a great service by explaining this to the American People. They purposely cause great division & distrust. They can also cause War! They are very dangerous & sick! (@realDonaldTrump, August 5, 2018)
(31) I win an election easily, a great "movement" is verified, and **crooked opponents** try to belittle our victory with FAKE NEWS. A sorry state! (@realDonaldTrump, January 11, 2017)

Figure 6.3 provides an overview of the moral dimension of Trump's nicknames. Like for Figure 6.2, each nickname type has only been counted once. It appears as if female referents are targeted proportionately more for what Trump suggests are moral transgressions than males, but the difference is not statistically significant (χ^2 = 1.42, df = 1, p = non-sig.).

When we look at the individual tokens, that is, each instance of a nickname used, and their context, we see that moral judgments are used by Trump when the referent has shown disloyalty to Trump or is accused by him of lack of character. Typical accusations are *leaking*, *lying*, *shady*, or *crooked*. *Crooked*, in the sense of "dishonest," is by far the most frequently used attribute ascribed by Trump to Hillary Clinton. It is usually used in combination with her name, *Crooked Hillary (Clinton)* or *Crooked H.*,

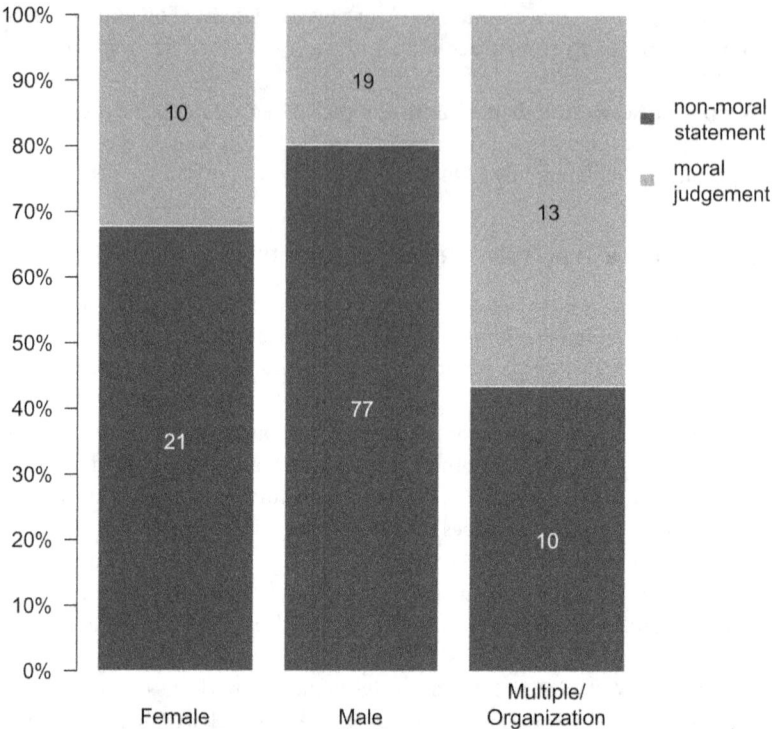

Figure 6.3 Breakdown of nicknames by referent and moral dimension.

or as a stand-alone item: *Crooked*, see (32). However, while *crooked* is more of a static characteristic, Trump keeps introducing more insulting and derogatory vocabulary to further discredit Hillary Clinton's reputation by creating a *dynamic* image of an utterly incompetent and corrupt politician who betrays her country and people on a daily (sometimes hourly, judged by the frequency of Trump's tweets) basis (see also Ahmadian, Azarshahi, and Paulhus 2017: 52). Examples (32)–(34), tweeted over the course of two days, exemplify this. These tweets are intended to expose what Trump considers Clinton's flawed character, judgment, and morals. It should be noted that (34) ends with a thirty-second video of still images with a voice-over laying out the story of the Clintons from poverty to "filthy rich"; the credits show that it is "PAID FOR BY DONALD J. TRUMP FOR PRESIDENT, INC., APPROVED BY DONALD J. TRUMP."

(32) So terrible that **Crooked** didn't report she got the debate questions from Donna Brazile, if that were me it would have been front page news!
(@realDonaldTrump, November 1, 2016)

(33) **Crooked Hillary Clinton** deleted 33,000 e-mails AFTER they were subpoenaed by the United States Congress. Guilty - cannot run. Rigged system!
(@realDonaldTrump, November 2, 2016)

(34) After decades of lies and scandal, **Crooked Hillary**'s corruption is closing in. #DrainTheSwamp! https://t.co/YivCacmkKq (@realDonaldTrump, November 2, 2016)

As former rivals in the race for the Republican Nomination for the 2016 presidential election, Donald Trump and Ted Cruz have exchanged a fair share of unpleasantries in the media and on Twitter. One of the nicknames originally coined by Trump that seems to have stuck with Cruz the longest is *Lyin' Ted*. As illustrated in (35) and (36), the character trait Trump persistently assigns to Cruz is weakness, which ultimately puts Trump himself in the position of power, being the strongest and most self-confident candidate in primaries (see also Jordan et al. 2019).

(35) **Lyin' Ted** and Kasich are mathematically dead and totally desperate. Their donors & special interest groups are not happy with them. Sad! (@realDonaldTrump, April 25, 2016)
(36) Shows how weak and desperate **Lyin' Ted** is when he has to team up with a guy who openly can't stand him and is only 1 win and 38 losses. (@realDonaldTrump, April 25, 2016)

However, power relationships between the two ex-rivals have been re-negotiated in the light of the upcoming 2020 election. Cruz, at the time of writing US senator for Texas, was referred to as *Beautiful Ted* and *Texas Ted* on Twitter before President Trump's visit to Texas in October 2018.

Finally, Donald Trump's Twitter attacks on Megyn Kelly, then Fox News anchor, began during his presidential campaign of 2016.[5] He started to publicly question her competence and professional skills, see (37), *before* giving her the nickname *Crazy Megyn* on Twitter in March, see (38). It is also worth mentioning that his tweets from that time were not limited to her professional duties, as shown in (39).

(37) I refuse to call Megyn Kelly a bimbo, because that would not be politically correct. Instead I will only call her a lightweight reporter! (@realDonaldTrump, January 27, 2016)
(38) Can't watch **Crazy Megyn** anymore. Talks about me at 43% but never mentions that there are four people in race. With two people, big & over! (@realDonaldTrump, March 15, 2016)
(39) If **crazy @megynkelly** didn't cover me so much on her terrible show, her ratings would totally tank. She is so average in so many ways! (@realDonaldTrump, March 19, 2016)

6.5.4 A Brief Remark on Absent Topics

It is fair to also say something about topics that do not come up in Trump's nicknames. For example, in the Twitter data we examined, Trump does not use a single nickname that directly references a person's sexual orientation. This is especially notable because there are many instances where Trump tweets about individuals who are known to be members of the LGBTQ community, such as the comedian and television personality Rosie O'Donnell and CNN journalist Don Lemon.

6.5.5 Combined Analysis of Nickname Categories, Morals, and Gender

A *Multiple Correspondence Analysis* (MCA) was carried out on the three variables, nickname category, moral judgment, and gender of the referent in order to see whether a particular pattern emerges. MCA is a method of statistical data analysis for the search of underlying correlations between several categorical variables (see, for example, Desagulier 2017: 268–76). The associations between the levels of the variables are indicated by points in a two-dimensional plot. Different variables are indicated by markers of different shape, and their proximity to each other and spatial orientation on the two-dimensional projection reflect the strengths of their associations.

The data for this study comprises all 669 nickname tokens in the Twitter data. The number of data points is much higher than in previous analyses because now we treat each instance when a nickname is used as a separate data point and no longer group them by nickname type; for example, *Crooked Hillary* is not counted as one type but as 286 tokens. In Figure 6.4, we present the results of the MCA. The lower left-hand quadrant of the plot shows a marker for the category 'personality', a marker for the gender label 'female', and a marker for moral judgment (represented as *y* for 'yes').

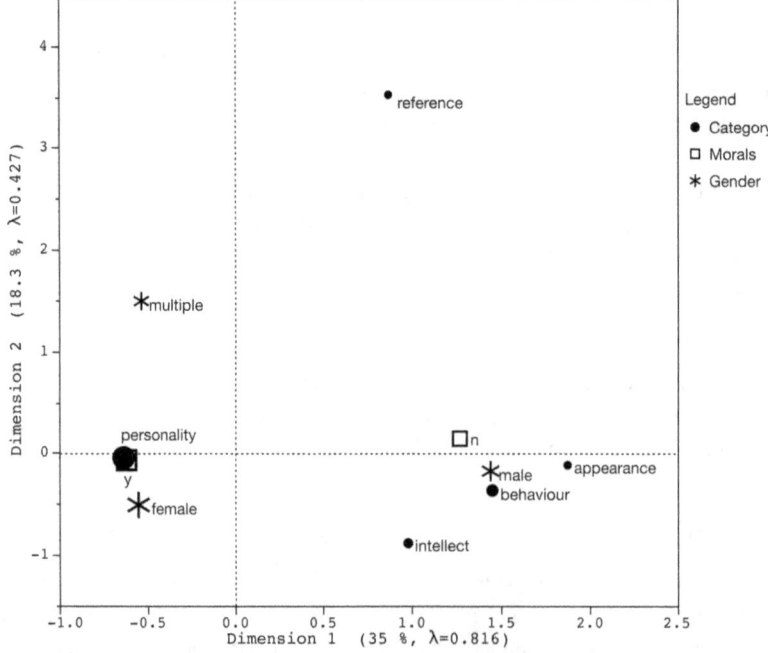

Figure 6.4 Multiple correspondence analysis of nickname features.

The marker 'multiple,' signifying multiple, institutional, and corporate references such as the *New York Times*, is also relatively close. The proximity of these markers to each other suggests that they tend to be strongly associated in Trump's nicknames. In other words, female referents, groups of people, and organizations are most likely to be given nicknames that relate to their personality and lack of morals. Male referents, on the other hand, cluster close to 'behavior,' 'intellect,' and 'appearance,' as well as the marker for no moral judgment, in the lower right-hand quadrant. This shows that the nicknames given to male opponents typically focus on behavior, intellect, or appearance, but do not tend to comment on their personality or morals (see also Preston and Stanley 1987 on gender-directed nicknames).

The analysis is, however, affected to a considerable degree by the highly frequent nickname *Crooked Hillary*, which is a moral personality reference to a female politician. However, given the frequency and distribution of Trump's nicknames in the data, we consider it noteworthy that the reality of his nicknaming practice is somewhat different from the folk linguistic impressionistic assumptions. Instead of mocking female opponents for their appearance or intellect, nicknames referring to these characteristics are more often used and repeated for male opponents, while nicknames focused on personality and lack of morals are more frequently used and repeated for females. Although it is certainly true that Trump does publicly evaluate women's appearance and behavior, when it comes to nicknames, those qualities are more likely to be found in male nicknames.

6.5.6 A Timeline of Nicknames

In this section, we want to look at the development of Trump's nickname use. Have his preferences for certain nickname categories changed over time? Were there events which prompted him to coin large numbers of new names? Like the previous one, this analysis is also performed on a token basis.

Trump started using nicknames on Twitter in 2011. With the exception of a burst of nicknames used in the second half of 2013, the practice was relatively limited until his presidential campaign started in the summer of 2015, at which point Trump seems to have made the calculated decision to start using nicknames. The notable cluster of nicknames in autumn 2013 are posts on *Lightweight @AGSchneiderman*, the sixty-fifth attorney general of New York, who filed a lawsuit against Donald Trump and Trump University in 2013. Trump has tweeted thirty-four times about Schneiderman using the same nickname thirty-three times. Figure 6.5 shows the nicknames tweeted during Trump's campaign and the beginning of his presidency, sorted by the semantic categories established in section 6.4.3. The gender symbols denote male and female referents, the asterisks stand for multiple/organizational referents.

The main target of Trump's nicknames in this period has been Hillary Clinton, with nearly one-third of all nickname tokens aimed at her. Marco Rubio, Ted Cruz, and Elizabeth Warren were the other main targets, and as the timeline shows, Trump worked through the field with considerable strategy. He started the nickname attacks on Marco Rubio (*Little Marco Rubio, lightweight Marco Rubio*), and when Rubio dropped out of the race in March 2016, Trump immediately switched to attacking Ted Cruz (*Lyin' Ted*). When Cruz ended his campaign a few months later in May 2016, Trump stopped using

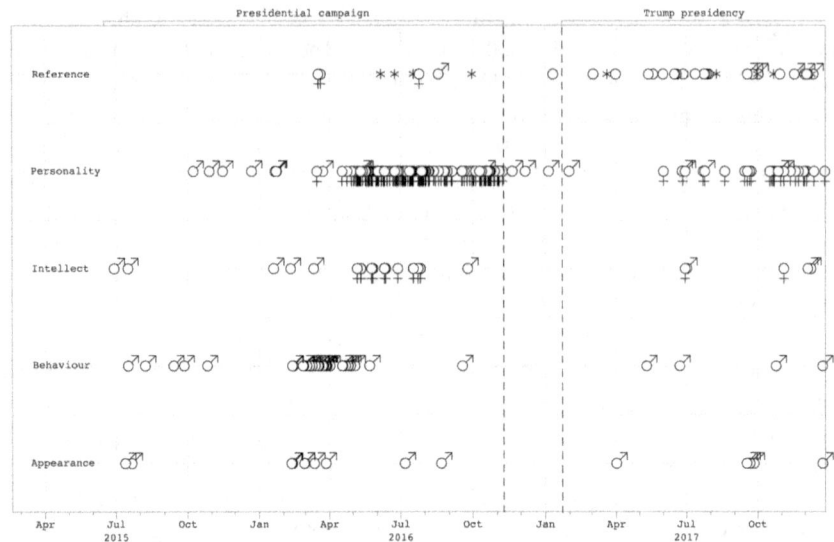

Figure 6.5 Nicknames tweeted between January 2015 and December 2017.

the nickname and switched to Elizabeth Warren (*Goofy Elizabeth Warren, Pocahontas*) and Hillary Clinton (*Crooked Hillary Clinton*). The other candidates did not receive similar attention, though Trump did fire off occasional tweets at Bernie Sanders (*Crazy Bernie*) and Jeb Bush (*Low Energy Jeb*).

As the timeline in Figure 6.5 shows, Trump's use of nicknames ceased almost completely for the period between the election and his inauguration. There was a period of almost seven months between the night before the election and May 31, 2017, during which he did not use the nickname *Crooked Hillary* a single time. Around June 2017, the nickname use started intensifying again and had once again reached a "baseline" by the end of the year. The one constant target throughout the otherwise quiet period was the media, especially *Fake News Media, Corrupt News Media,* and *Failing New York Times* (see also Schubert, this volume, for Trump's strategic fake news allegations).

One notable aspect of the total number of nicknames used by Trump on Twitter was that, despite popular belief to the contrary, he targeted men much more frequently than women. With the exception of Hillary Clinton (286 nicknames tweeted) and Elizabeth Warren (34 nicknames tweeted), Trump used nicknames relatively rarely when discussing female opponents. This may be in part because most of his political counterparts are male, but it is interesting nonetheless.

6.6 Conclusions

In this chapter, we have examined Donald Trump's nicknaming practices on the social media platform Twitter. The nicknames identified in the data have been analyzed both qualitatively and quantitatively in order to shed light on the interplay of self-promotion and power strategies in Trump's political discourse online. The results suggest that nicknames were by and large used to "out-group" individuals or groups of people, media outlets, and corporations, that is, anyone who "plays for the other team." By affording the opportunity to post messages at a rapid and sustained rate, Twitter allows a politician like Trump to paint their opponents as enemies, as dishonest and disreputable individuals, and as laughing stocks.

Our results further revealed that the largest number of nicknames was aimed at males, with females ranking second and multiple referents last. Naturally, certain nicknames were observed to have been more frequent, especially *Crooked Hillary*, as they saw consistent use for prolonged periods of time. Many others occurred sporadically over a period of time to eventually disappear or become replaced by the ones that fitted better into Trump's political agenda at the time, as was the case with *Lyin' Ted*, *Lying Cruz*, *Beautiful Ted*, and *Texas Ted*. In regard to multiple referents, a multitude of news outlets and TV shows was covered by the collective nickname *Fake News*, but some were afforded special attention, such as the *Fake News CNN*.

It may be argued that for a specific segment of the electorate, the uncouth messages indexed Trump's lack of membership in the Washington elite and helped forge an impression of a "straightshooter" or a "man of the people"—despite his privileged background and lifestyle. However, the continued use of such nicknames after the electoral victory arguably changed the dynamic of what could, at first, be regarded as a campaign strategy. While it may be argued that political opponents hurling insults at each other during a heated campaign is somewhat normal, and that there is nothing particularly striking if that type of activity takes place on social media as well as at campaign rallies, the power dynamic radically shifts when a national leader publicly and repeatedly refers to political opponents or institutions such as the media using nicknames that make fun of them or, worse yet, disparage their moral character. A statement by the president, whether at a press conference or on Twitter, is by definition news, and to use the presidential bullhorn for mocking opponents creates a significant power imbalance.

Therefore, Donald Trump's use of Twitter can be described as a culturally and historically significant phenomenon, shaping political discourse online today and perhaps in the years to come (see Ahmadian, Azarshahi, and Paulhus 2017; Soler, Cuatero, and Roblizo 2012). Trump's colorful language—which is one of his characteristic features and goes far beyond Twitter—has thus guaranteed him uninterrupted media attention since the moment he announced his run for president in the summer of 2015.

Notes

1 On June 6, 2017, White House press secretary Sean Spicer gave the official statement that as Donald Trump "is the President of the United States, so [his tweets are] considered official statements by the President of the United States." Importantly, the statement made no specific reference to the official Twitter account of the president of the United States (@POTUS), and the common interpretation of the statement is that the official nature of Trump's tweets also pertains to tweets from the account @realDonaldTrump (see Jenkins 2017).

2 Huntsman has served in every presidential administration since Ronald Reagan, and was appointed United States Ambassador to Russia by Donald Trump on March 8, 2017.
3 According to the compiler, the archive misses approximately 4,000 tweets, including retweets and those that Trump may have deleted prior to September 2016.
4 Calling people *dog* is another highly characteristic feature of Trump's offensive language use. People are *dumped like dogs* and *thrown out like dogs*, as well as described as *choking like dogs* and being *Obama lap dogs* (for an analysis of this and further metaphors in Trump's speech see Koth, this volume).
5 In the Republican primary in August 2015, Kelly asked Trump about the offensive language he had used describing women. In the days following the debate, Trump attacked her on Twitter and told a CNN reporter that during the debate "[t]here was blood coming out of her eyes, blood coming out of her wherever," which led to widespread speculation in the press that Trump had made a reference to menstruation, a charge he later denied.

References

Adams, Michael (2008), "Nicknames, Interpellation and Dubya's Theory of the State," *A Journal of Onomastics*, 56 (4): 206–20.

Adams, Michael (2009), "Power, Politeness and the Pragmatics of Nicknames," *A Journal of Onomastics*, 57 (2): 81–91.

Ahmadian, Sara, Sara Azarshahi, and Delroy L. Paulhus (2017), "Explaining Donald Trump via Communication Style: Grandiosity, Informality, and Dynamism," *Personality and Individual Differences*, 107 (1): 49–53.

Alia, Valerie (2009), *Names and Nunavut: Culture and Identity in the Inuit Homeland*, New York: Berghahn Books.

Allsop, Jon (2017), "Inside the Fairy Tale Mind of Trump," *Columbia Journalism Review*, September 27. Available online: https://www.cjr.org/special_report/trump-fairy-tale.php (accessed September 25, 2019).

Baker, Paul (2006), *Using Corpora in Discourse Analysis*, London and New York: Continuum.

Brown, Brendan (2019), *Trump Twitter Archive*. Available online: http://www.trumptwitterarchive.com/archive (accessed September 17, 2019).

Croom, Adam M. (2013), "How to Do Things with Slurs: Studies in the Way of Derogatory Words," *Language and Communication*, 33 (3): 177–204.

Desagulier, Guillaume (2017), *Corpus Linguistics and Statistics with R: Introduction to Quantitative Methods in Linguistics*, New York: Springer International Publishing AG.

Gladkova, Anna (2002), "The Semantics of Nicknames of the American Presidents," in Peter Collins and Mengistu Amberber (eds.), *Proceedings of the 2002 Conference of the Australian Linguistics Society*. Available online: http://www.als.asn.au/proceedings/als2002/Gladkova.pdf (accessed September 22, 2019).

Jenkins, Aric (2017), "Sean Spicer Says President Trump Considers His Tweets 'Official' White House Statements," *Time Magazine*, June 6. Available online: https://time.com/4808270/sean-spicer-donald-trump-twitter-statements/ (accessed September 25, 2019).

Jordan, Kayla N., Joanna Sterling, James W. Pennebaker, and Ryan L. Boyd (2019), "Examining Long-Term Trends in Politics and Culture Through Language of Political Leaders and Cultural Institutions," *PNAS*, 116 (9): 3476–81.

Leibovich, Mark (2016), "Donald Trump Shares His Opponent-Branding Secrets," *The New York Times*, May 9. Available online: https://www.nytimes.com/2016/05/09/magazine/donald-trump-shares-his-opponent-branding-secrets.html (accessed September 25, 2019).

Nübling, Damaris, Fabian Fahlbusch, and Rita Heuser (2012), *Namen: Eine Einführung in die Onomastik*, Tübingen: Narr.

Partington, Alan, Alison Duguid, and Charlotte Taylor (2013), *Patterns and Meanings in Discourse: Theory and Practice in Corpus-Assisted Discourse Studies (CADS)*, Amsterdam: John Benjamins.

Preston, Kathleen and Kimberley Stanley (1987), "'What's the Worst Thing . . .?' Gender-Directed Insults," *Sex Roles: A Journal of Research*, 17 (3): 209–19.

Schmid, Helmut (1994), "Probabilistic Part-Of-Speech Tagging Using Decision Trees," *Proceedings of International Conference on New Methods in Language Processing*, Manchester, UK.

Sinclair, John (1991), *Corpus, Concordance, Collocation*, Oxford: Oxford University Press.

Soler, Jose M., Fernando Cuartero, and Manuel Roblizo (2012), "Twitter as a Tool for Predicting Elections Results," *Proceedings of the 2012 International Conference on Advances in Social Networks Analysis and Mining*, 26–29 August, 2012, Kadir Has University, Istanbul, Turkey, 1194–200.

Starks, Donna and Kerry Taylor-Leech (2011), "Research Project on Nicknames and Adolescent Identities," *New Zealand Studies in Applied Linguistics*, 17 (2): 87–97.

Tumulty, Karen (2019), "Why I'm Swearing Off Trump's Nicknames," *The Washington Post*, May 28. Available online: https://www.washingtonpost.com/opinions/why-im-swearing-off-trumps-nicknames/2019/05/28/933f1c82-815e-11e9-95a9-e2c830afe24f_story.html (accessed September 25, 2019).

7

I'm Doing Great with the Hispanics. Nobody Knows It

The Distancing Effect of Donald Trump's *the*-Plurals

Ulrike Schneider and Kristene K. McClure

7.1 Introduction

For English speakers, it is easy to overlook *the*. Mostly, we do not think much about it—it is, after all, the most commonly used word in English. Use of *the* generally signifies a specific or known referent, perhaps one which has previously been referred to in the discourse. The function of signaling specificity starts to blur, though, when we consider the effect of adding *the* in some plural noun phrases, namely those that use *the* in combination with a plural to refer to a group, such as in (1).

(1) **The** Latinos love Trump, right? (Speech: Donald Trump in Pueblo, CO, October 3, 2016)

By this means, speakers tend to mark what they, consciously or not, identify as a homogeneous group which they do not associate with (Acton 2019: 38–9). This "distancing effect" (Acton 2019: 39) means that uses of *the* in combination with a plural reference to a group can be "acts of othering" (Acton 2019: 52). In other words, they can be a feature of discourse that creates and reinforces a distinction between a positively evaluated 'us,' often 'the people,' and a negatively evaluated and/or minoritized[1] 'other' (Reinfeldt 2000: 133; Kamenova and Pingaud 2017: 110–11; Otova and Puurunen 2017: 92; see also Partington and Taylor 2018: 83). Examples of such othering include phrases referring to ethnic groups, like *the blacks* or *the Hispanics*, or otherwise racialized groups, for example, *the Mexicans* or *the Muslims*.

Particularly during the news cycle for the 2016 Republican primary race, numerous US news outlets featured pieces that zoomed in on Trump's use of *the*-plurals. Graham (2016), for instance, argued that Trump's *the*-plurals stand in sharp contrast to "his supercharged used [sic] of 'we.'" While the frequent use of *we* "persuades people across the country that they are part of a larger movement," *the*-prefaced references to ethnic groups "suggest[ ] that for Trump, blacks and Hispanics aren't part of 'we'— 'they' constitute separate groups." The point about Trump's othering *the* was echoed in a range of other journalistic pieces during the 2016 primaries, including Holloway (2016), who concluded that it provides evidence of Trump's racist attitudes, as well as in an attention-grabbing headline by columnist Kathleen Parker—"Trump Can't Fake Love of 'the Blacks'" (Parker 2016). A few pieces additionally argued that *the*-plurals, beyond serving an othering function, suggest that the group referred to is a homogeneous, undifferentiated whole (e.g., Allen 2016; O'Connor and Marans 2016).

Thus, the journalistic coverage suggests not only that Trump frequently uses a definite article when referencing a demographic group but also that he does this particularly or even exclusively in reference to minoritized ethnic groups. Both of these claims raise various questions, warranting more careful consideration and quantitative investigation. Are phrases like *the blacks* and *the African Americans* so charged and therefore salient that a single use attracts a lot of media attention? Or could it be the case that Trump uses *the*-plurals (almost) consistently and indiscriminately of the group in question? In other words, does he use *the whites* just as often as *the blacks*? And does he refer not only to *the Muslims* but also to *the Christians*?

This chapter aims to answer these questions based on empirical evidence. We first detail a study by Acton (2019) who surveys whether American Democrats and Republicans use *the*-plurals to distance themselves from the opposing party. We later replicate the study based on Donald Trump's tweets in order to establish whether his use of *the*-plurals shows any kind of systematicity that points to (subconscious) use as a distancing device. We also briefly discuss previous findings on various signs of othering and distancing in Trump's language. Finally, we use material from the website Factba.se to study select instances of Trump's use of *the*-plurals, with the goal of understanding if and how using this construction to refer to minoritized populations serves to "other" those populations. Thus, we examine to what extent Trump uses particular ethnicity- and race-focused *the*-plurals and how his *the*-plurals may reflect attitudes toward the populations to which they refer.

7.2 *The Democrats* and *the Republicans*— Some General Notes on *the*-Plurals

The most comprehensive analysis of *the*-plurals to date has been undertaken by Acton (2019: 39), who argues that some uses of *the*-plurals tend to depict demographic groups "as separate, removed, or opposed," especially compared to plurals that refer to the same groups without a definite article. Thus, "a *the*-plural very often does suggest that the speaker is not a member of the relevant group, is deemphasizing their membership in the group, or is emphasizing their nonmembership" (Acton 2019: 38). Consequently, Acton (2019: 40) hypothesizes that Democrats should use higher rates of *the*-plurals when talking about Republicans than when talking about their own party. Of course, the same should be true for Republicans talking about Democrats. He tests this by analyzing data from a corpus of proceedings of the United States House of Representatives. The corpus yields more than 54,000 tokens of *Republicans* and *Democrats* after exclusion of pre-modified and post-modified tokens, such as (2) and (3); these cases had to be discarded because the modifying expressions more or less obligatorily trigger the definite article.

(2) (the) **liberal** Democrats
(3) (the) Republicans **in Congress**

Figure 7.1 visualizes Acton's results. Indeed, only about a third of plural references to the representatives' own party are *the*-plurals (30.4 percent and 26.1 percent for Democrats and Republicans respectively) while *the*-plurals are used in over 50 percent of references to the opposing party—a highly statistically significant difference (Acton 2019: 43).

Acton's results caution that *the*-plurals are not exclusively used for distancing, but he shows a robust trend: speakers are more likely to use *the*-plurals when talking about groups of which they are not members. This trend is so robust, in fact, that when replicating the study with transcripts from select episodes of The McLaughlin Group,

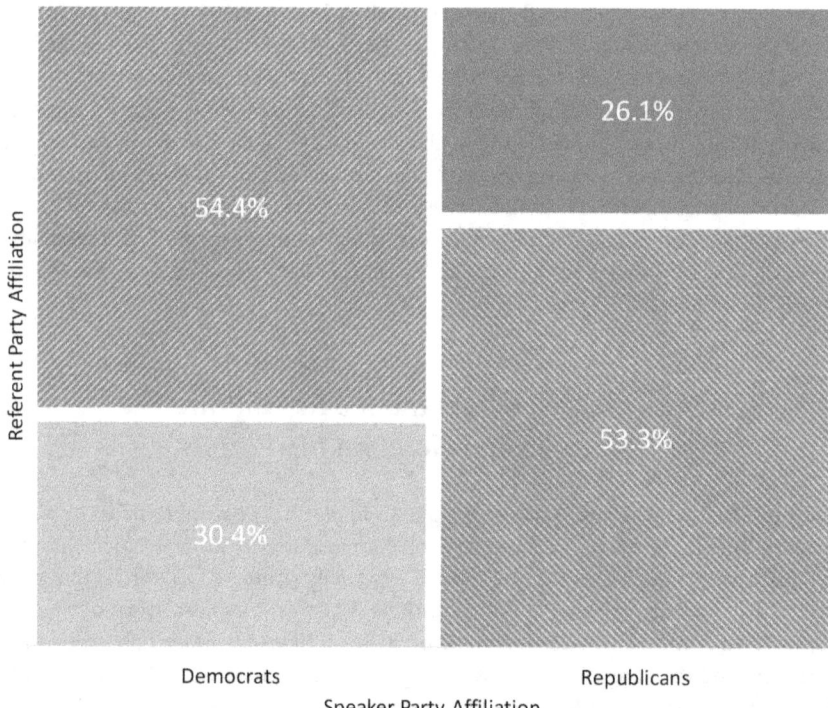

Figure 7.1 Graphical representation of Acton's (2019: 42) results. Democrats are shown as light gray and Republicans as dark gray; shaded areas represent members of one party talking about the other.

a syndicated political news program on which pundits are expected to be relatively objective, he finds the same "distancing effect of *the*" (Acton 2019: 46). Although the number of *the*-plurals was generally higher in the McLaughlin data than in the House corpus—"expected given [the] pundits' role as outside observers" (Acton 2019: 47)— they also used fewer *the*-plurals in reference to the party they associated with more closely.

Acton, however, warns against assuming that such *the*-plurals, though they are marked variants compared to bare plurals (Acton 2019: 56, 59), must inherently connote a negative stance. As he explains, "derogation does not simply logically follow from distancing. In fact, marking distance is also a way of showing respect or deference" (Acton 2019: 61). Why then do Trump's uses of *the*-plurals attract such negative attention? To understand this, we need to look at two factors that come into play—the associations speakers have with specific phrases and the homogenizing effect of *the*-plurals.

Let us first turn to speakers' associations. Acton argues that "[i]f an addressee has repeatedly heard a form in pejorative statements [i.e., statements which express contempt or disapproval], one can bet that those pejorative associations will color their interpretation of the use at hand" (Acton 2019: 61). He claims that *the blacks* and *the gays* have become so "loaded" (Acton 2019: 61) that they have "attained taboo or near-taboo status" (Acton 2019: 39) because they are associated with distancing (see also Zimmer as cited by Campbell 2016) which is, of course, no longer acceptable in contexts of race and sexual orientation.

More often, the argument that is put forward to explain speakers' negative perception of *the*-plurals is their homogenizing effect. This means that "[i]n addition to distancing the speaker from the group in question, pegging a group with the article 'the' suggests that members of that group act and think homogeneously" (Acton as cited in Abadi 2016). While some referents of *the*-plurals, like the parties discussed earlier, are actually organized in formally constituted groups and (loosely) ascribe to a core set of common values—in this case the party positions—this is mostly not true for ethnic and other minoritized groups. In those instances, "where the named group really is acting as a unit" there is also "an implicit team-like opposition," which, once more, is not applicable to ethnic groups (Liberman 2016). It is this effect of "pigeonhol[ing]" referents (Tagliamonte as cited by Abadi 2016) that makes *the*-plurals so problematic (see, for example, Murphy 2016). Gorski (2017: 343) concludes that "[i]n this way, social groups are reified into unitary entities, authorizing crude generalizations." This makes *the*-plurals surviving relics of a time when *man* and *mankind* were used to refer to any human being and humanity, and when political decision making prioritized the needs and benefits of white men (Sanchez 2016). In this worldview, "gender, nations, and borders were thought to be singular and whole.... Therefore, the use of the definite article seemed fitting" (Sanchez 2016). In the following section, we investigate the implications of these observations for Trump's use of *the*-plurals and discuss whether these plurals seem to be part of a larger repertoire of distancing language.

7.3 *The Muslims* and *the Latinos*— Trump's Use of Distancing Language

Donald Trump entered the presidential race of 2016 as the anti-establishment candidate. This is also reflected in his language and gestural choices. Sclafani (2018: 60) argues that the gestures accompanying Trump's speeches are part of "Trump's consistent projection of his own identity as the candidate who eschews political correctness in favor of 'getting real'—a quality that reinforces his self-branding as the 'authenticity' candidate."

However, not only does Trump distance himself from the Washington elite, but he also distances himself and "the American people" from a range of minoritized groups. One way of doing so is through the creation of the false binary opposition of a positively evaluated *us* and a negatively evaluated 'other' (or *them*), as in (4).

(4) I also said, **we** have to be extremely careful with radical Islamic terrorism and **we** have to look at **the Muslims** and **we** have to do something. **We** cannot stand by and be the stupid people while **our** country is destroyed. (Speech: Donald Trump in Rochester, NY, April 10, 2016).

As we have seen earlier, for many linguists and journalists, Trump's *the*-plurals also stand out as a distancing device. However, it would be overly simplistic to classify these plurals as "the rhetorical equivalent of the wall Trump keeps promising to build" (Hawhee 2018). This "most unusual speech tic[ ]" (Abadi 2016) seems to be used conjoined with other discourse tactics, which together create a more complex picture.

Sanchez (2016) draws particular attention to Trump's stump speeches, where he tries to win certain ethnic groups as voters. Sanchez points out the homogenizing effect of Trump's *the*-plurals in this particular context. He argues that in the mid-twentieth century, "[t]he insistence on singular identities [of ethnic minority groups] led to an insistence of singular problems and singular solutions" and that, ultimately, "[t]his is why Trump can refer to 'the blacks' and the inner-cities, while failing to comprehend that not every African American lives in the inner-cities" (Sanchez 2016). According to Sanchez, the use of the definite article in *the blacks*, *the women*, and *the Mexicans* presents them as "problems to be dealt with" rather than as people, let alone individuals: "They are objects without feelings. They are identifiers without identities" (Sanchez 2016). Sanchez (2016) therefore concludes that Trump's "reliance on the definite article hints at a dated understanding of identities and politics that is locked in the mid-20th century."

Even more perplexing than Trump's habit of using, for instance, **the** *African Americans* when talking to a group of African Americans are the semantic clashes in the constructions in which he uses these plurals. O'Connor and Marans (2016) sarcastically draw attention to this when they write "He claims to have 'a great relationship with the blacks,' which is totally something a normal person would say." In the expression *a great relationship with the blacks*, distancing language is juxtaposed with *great relationship*, which is intended to indicate proximity. Saul (2017: 104) labels the non-distancing parts of such juxtapositions "racial figleaves." She explains that "[a] racial figleaf is an utterance made in addition to an otherwise overtly racist one [which] serves the function of calling into question the racism of the speaker and the utterance. I use the term 'figleaf' because it is an utterance that provides a small bit of cover for something that is unacceptable to display in public" (Saul 2017: 98). In the following analysis, we also aim to see how pervasive such figleaves are in contexts where Trump uses *the*-plurals. Some studies in political science conclude that these and other linguistic and gestural tools, combined with Trump's aversion for political correctness, "work together to telegraph a white nationalist message to his followers without making them feel that he is, or they are, racist" (Maskovsky 2017: 433).

7.4 Data

The following analysis is based on two collections of texts that are used as corpora. These are, first, all tweets sent from Donald Trump's personal Twitter account @realDonaldTrump between March 2009 and early November 2019. And second, speeches provided by the website factba.se (FactSquared 2019). This selection was made in order to avoid media bias (see, for example, Sclafani 2018: 14), that is, to circumvent skewing due to the possibility that *the*-plurals highlighted in media coverage could be outliers selected for their ability to attract an audience rather than because they are an actual consistent feature in Trump's idiolect. In the case of the Twitter data, any potential bias can easily be avoided as we have the entirety of Trump's tweets available for analysis[2] and thus do not have to rely on a selection. Factba.se, on the other hand, states that it is their mission "to make available, unedited, the entire corpus of an individual's public statements and recordings" (FactSquared 2019, see "Mission"). Even though this may never be fully achievable, it at least encourages a neutral selection of material. The specific retrieval and coding procedures will be detailed together with the corresponding analysis.

7.5 Analyses and Results

7.5.1 *The Republicans* and *the Democrats* Revisited

In a first step, we need to establish how pervasive *the*-plurals are in Trump's language and whether he even uses them as othering devices. In order to do so, we generated data that can be compared to the use of *the Democrats* and *the Republicans* in the speech of other US politicians as reported by Acton (2019: 42). We can draw the conclusion that variation between bare plurals and *the*-plurals is not random if Trump, like other politicians, shows the tendency to use more *the*-plurals for the opposing party once he associates with the Republican Party.[3] Thus, we searched the Trump Twitter Archive for tweets sent from Trump's account that contained either *Democrats* or *Republicans*. Retweets were automatically excluded. Duplicates and tweets where the target words occurred in direct quotations were manually deleted. Tweets containing several instances of *Democrats* and/or *Republicans* were only included once in each dataset. This means that only the first mention of each party in a tweet was analyzed (for a similar approach see Acton 2019: 41). This resulted in a dataset of 1,065 tokens (700 *Democrats* and 365 *Republicans*).

In order to render the data as comparable as possible to Acton's (2019: 41) and to exclude contexts in which no (or little) variation between *the*-plurals and bare plurals could be expected, the following further restrictions were made. First, pre-modified and post-modified tokens were excluded. (5) and (6) show some examples of modifiers that led to exclusion from the Acton-comparable dataset.

(5) Angry Democrats, Congressional Democrats, corrupt Democrats, crazed Democrats, Crooked Hillary Democrats, Do Nothing Democrats, House Republicans, Lifelong Democrats, Louisiana Republicans, mean & despicable Democrats, Obstructionist Democrats, Open Border Democrats, Radical Left Democrats.

(6) Republicans in Congress, Democrats in the Senate, Democrats that ..., Republicans who ..., Democrats whose ..., Democrats working ....

Additionally, tokens preceded by the following quantifiers and partitives were excluded.

(7) numbers (whether given as numerals or spelled out, including zero), a few, (almost) all (of), band of, both, a "Lion's List" of, certain, dwindling number of, enough, many (more/other), millions of, more, most, only 15% of, other, over 50% of, some.

Two restrictions not mentioned by Acton (2019) needed to be made due to the nature of the Twitter data. First, Trump occasionally directly addresses one of the two party groups, such as in (8). As these contexts invariably require a bare plural, they were excluded. Second, in twenty-four instances, the plurals were possessives, sometimes with non-standard spelling as in (9) and (10). Although these cases permit some variation between bare plurals and *the*-plurals, they were nonetheless excluded, as it was unlikely that such cases would have been included in Acton's dataset.

(8) **Republicans** remember—debt ceiling, debt ceiling, debt ceiling—be smart and you will win! (@realDonaldTrump, December 27, 2012)
(9) End **the Democrats** Obstruction! https://t.co/tzBXilvW1b (@realDonaldTrump, January 22, 2018)
(10) I am growing the Republican Party tremendously - just look at the numbers, way up! **Democrats** numbers are significantly down from years past. (@realDonaldTrump, February 23, 2016)

After these exclusions, 445 tokens of *Democrats* and 277 tokens of *Republicans* remained. These were coded for the presence or absence of the definite article. In cases of coordination, we proceeded like Acton (2019: 42, fn.4): If only the first noun was preceded by a definite article, the article was considered to have scope over both nouns and thus either noun was coded as a *the*-plural. Although coordination was frequent in the dataset, this specific setting only occurred four times.

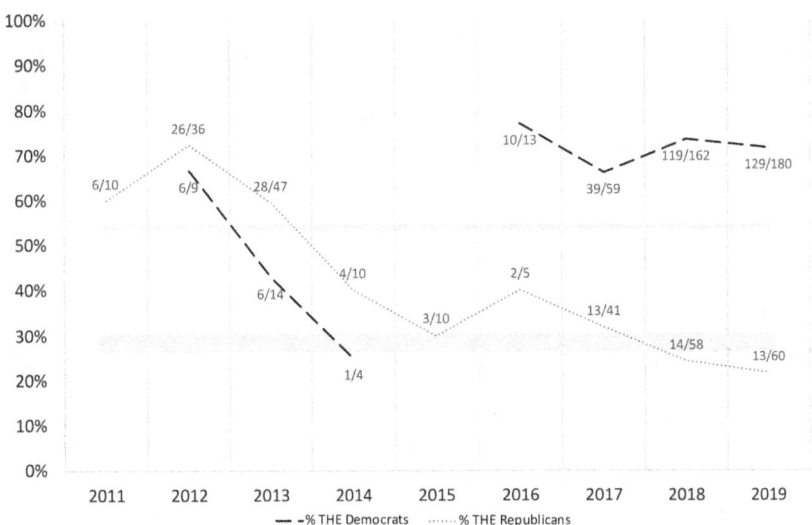

Figure 7.2 Percentage of *Democrats* and *Republicans* preceded by a definite article in tweets sent from Donald Trump's account.

Figure 7.2 shows our results. We will start with a brief look at the absolute number of references to *Democrats* and *Republicans* (as given in the labels in the graph). We see that in 2009 and 2010 the account was not used for political messages—in those years we find no mention of either *Democrats* or *Republicans*. Between 2011 and 2013, Republicans receive some attention (ninety-three tokens in the dataset), but Democrats are still hardly mentioned (only twenty-five tokens; Democrat data points for 2011 and 2015 are missing because [*the*] *Democrats* only occurred twice in each of those years). Interestingly, numbers dwindle in the years leading up to Trump's election in 2016. During the presidency (2017–19), references to both parties, and particularly references to Democrats (mostly unfavorable), rise considerably.

Let us now turn to the definite articles. We will assess Trump's rate of *the*-plurals with the help of the "baseline rates" established by Acton (2019). These are represented in the gray bands. The lower band represents the mean rates of *the*-plurals that members of the House of Representatives used in reference to their own party (or its members); the upper band represents the rate of *the*-plurals when referencing the opposing party. The lower band is wider than the upper one as the means of the two parties were further apart in this instance. Trump initially uses high rates of *the*-plurals in reference to both Democrats and Republicans. Between 2012 and 2014, Trump seems to be on the way to abandoning *the*-plurals in general, but after a brief interlude in 2015, where we have little data, *the*-plurals resurge and a clear split between the parties emerges. Particularly since taking office in 2017, it is evident that Trump is a Republican: his rates of *the Republicans* lie around the mean for own-party reference established by Acton, while his rates of *the Democrats* even exceed Acton's mean for opposing-party reference. In the tweets sent between 2017 and 2019, 71.7 percent of *Democrats* are preceded by a definite article, compared to 53.3–54.4 percent in Acton's data. This rate even exceeds that of the political commentators from the McLaughlin Group.

In conclusion, we have now established that *the*-plurals are not singular occurrences in Trump's speech, and neither does he use them exclusively in reference to ethnic groups. The data clearly shows that, once president, Trump uses *the*-plurals as othering devices. He is almost three times as likely to use *Democrats* with a definite article than *Republicans* (rates are 71.6 percent and 25.2 percent respectively).

7.5.2 *Muslims*, *Christians*, and *Evangelicals*— Demographic Groups in the Tweets

Now that we have established that *the*-plurals are not scattered randomly throughout Trump's tweets, we will investigate his plural references to different demographic groups. We hypothesize that he uses more *the*-plurals when tweeting about minoritized groups, like *Muslims*, *Hispanics*, and *African Americans*, than when talking about the contrasting majority groups which he belongs to, namely *whites* and *Christians*. For this purpose, we once more searched all tweets sent from the account @realDonaldTrump for plural references to a number of groups. The groups selected are mostly ethnic, namely *African Americans*, *blacks*, *Hispanics*, *Latinos*, and *whites*, as well as religious, namely *Christians*, *Evangelicals*, and *Muslims*. *Evangelicals* is an interesting case, as it is a group that Trump does not belong to but which has overwhelmingly expressed pro-Trump support; it is also a group that is not generally considered to be minoritized or stigmatized in US society. *Muslims* can be seen as both a religious and an ethnic reference, as the term has undergone a process of racialization, that is, "the extension of racial meaning to a previously racially unclassified relationship, social practice, or group" (Omi and Winant 2014: 111; see also Selod 2018), especially since September 11, 2001. Additional demographic groups have become similarly racialized, namely *immigrants*, *illegals*, and *Mexicans* and were therefore also included.

Looking at the total number of tokens listed in Table 7.1, we see that there are only 158 plurals referencing these particular racial, ethnic, and racialized groups in the tweets. After exclusion of pre-modified, post-modified, and quantified tokens (see method detailed in section 7.5.1) only eighty-one tokens remain, labeled as "Acton-comparable data" (ACD) in the table, due to the fact that Acton's (2019) criteria for exclusion were applied.

Despite the low number of data points, we can draw a few tentative conclusions. It appears that Trump generally avoids using *whites*, *blacks*, and *Latinos*. Furthermore, the highly charged phrase *the blacks* (Acton 2019: 39) never appears in the tweets. Instead of *blacks* and *Latinos*, he uses *African Americans* and *Hispanics*. None of these ever appear with a definite article in the Acton-comparable dataset. In fact, the entire dataset only contains six tokens of *the*-plurals. This means that only 7.4 percent of references to the selected demographic groups are preceded by a definite article. Thus, we must conclude that Trump is far more likely to use this othering syntax for members of his own party than for any demographic group when tweeting. One reason for the low rate of *the*-plurals in the tweets could be the syntax of the surrounding context.

Table 7.1 Plural References to Demographic Groups in Trump's Tweets[4]

Lexeme	Total	ACD total	ACD bare plural	ACD *the*-plural	Example
Minoritized groups					
African Americans[5]	17	16	16	0	**African-Americans** will vote for Trump because they know I will stop the slaughter going on! (@realDonaldTrump, August 29, 2016)
blacks	5	5	5	0	All time best unemployment numbers, especially for **Blacks**, Hispanics, Asians & Women. (@realDonaldTrump, September 13, 2019)
Hispanics	16	14	14	0	I love **Hispanics**! (@realDonaldTrump, May 5, 2016)
illegals	42	30	28	2	If only **the illegals** were Tea Party members then Obama would get them out of the country immediately. (@realDonaldTrump, July 9, 2014)
immigrants	51	2	2	0	Fake News Media had me calling **Immigrants**, or Illegal Immigrants, "Animals." (@realDonaldTrump, May 18, 2018)
Latinos	1	1	1	0	How much more crime, how many more shootings, will it take for African-Americans and **Latinos** to vote Trump=SAFE! (@realDonaldTrump, August 29, 2016)
Mexicans	1	1	0	1	**The Mexicans** are laughing at us as buses pass by. (@realDonaldTrump, July 10, 2014)
Muslims	6	4	3	1	Incompetent Hillary, despite the horrible attack in Brussels today, wants borders to be weak and open-and let **the Muslims** flow in. (@realDonaldTrump, March 23, 2016)
Total	**139**	**73**	**69**	**4**	
Non-minoritized groups					
Christians	10	3	3	0	**Christians** need support in our country (and around the world), their religious liberty is at stake! (@realDonaldTrump, September 19, 2015)
Evangelicals	8	4	2	2	Have great love for **the evangelicals** -- great respect for you. (@realDonaldTrump, September 11, 2015)
whites	1	1	1	0	Hates **Whites** & Cops! (@realDonaldTrump, July 29, 2019)
Total	**19**	**8**	**6**	**2**	

(11) I have known Al [**Sharpton**] for 25 years. [**I**] Went to fights with him & Don King, [**we**] always got along well. He "loved Trump!" He would ask me for favors often. Al is a con man, a troublemaker, always looking for a score. [**He is**] Just doing his thing. [**He**] Must have intimidated Comcast/NBC. [**He**] Hates **Whites** & Cops! https://t.co/ZwPZa0FWfN (@realDonaldTrump, July 29, 2019, material in brackets added by us)

(12) I will be in California this weekend making a speech for Clint Eastwood. Then [**I will move on**] to Arizona and Vegas. [**There will be**] Big crowds. [**We will be**] Discussing **illegals** & more! (@realDonaldTrump, July 8, 2015, material in brackets added by us)

All words given in square brackets in (11) and (12) are actually absent in the original tweets. Thus, the examples illustrate that the syntax is often incomplete, lacking (auxiliary) verbs and pronouns. In these types of contexts, we would expect determiners to be dropped. Trump may have developed this style due to the 140-character limit that Twitter imposed until 2017. However, in other cases, the syntax is complex and complete (see examples in Table 7.1). Furthermore, an argument along the lines of Trump's-syntax-in-his-tweets-is-incomplete-and-therefore-contains-few-determiners cannot explain why we find such high rates of *the*-plurals in tweets referencing *Democrats* and *Republicans*. We therefore decided to repeat the search for references to demographic groups in a different medium, in which they might be mentioned more frequently, namely Trump's spoken language.

7.5.3 *I Was Leading in the Latinos*—References to Latinos and Hispanics in Trump's Spoken Language

Due to the sparse Twitter data, we still do not know whether Trump actually uses *the*-plurals with some frequency in reference to minoritized groups, and/or whether he even prefers them in some contexts. We will tackle these questions with the help of an exemplary corpus study of *Latinos* and *Hispanics* based on the transcripts of speeches, interviews, and debates provided by the website Factba.se. Before we get to the results, we will first give a brief run-through of our method.

As mentioned in section 7.4, Factba.se aims to collect all publicly available speech samples of Donald Trump. This also includes his tweets and some written texts, both of which were not included in this part of the study, as it focuses on his spoken language. Factba.se usually provides spoken language in the form of aligned videos and transcripts. We thus first searched the transcripts for all instances of *Latinos* and *Hispanics* and then verified (and, where necessary, corrected) each token with the help of the corresponding video before transferring them to our dataset. This led to the exclusion of further data points, namely in the following cases:

- Where no video was available, for example, in the case of print interviews. (*The*-plurals might have been edited out prior to publication which would have skewed the data.)
- Where the transcript and the video were poorly aligned, which would have obliged us to watch long sequences of the video in order to find the token.

- Where the video was no longer available or inaccessible.
- Where it was impossible to determine whether Trump used a bare or a *the*-plural.
- Where Trump was merely reading out signs from the audience like "Latinos for Trump."

This extraction and verification process was undertaken between November 14 and 19, 2019. Any instances uttered after this date are, of course, not included. The resulting dataset consists of 35 tokens of (*the*) *Latinos* and 265 tokens of (*the*) *Hispanics*.

The data originates from 124 speeches, interviews, debates, and press conferences given between 2015 and 2019. As Table 7.2 shows, it is not evenly distributed; most of the data originates from campaign speeches given in 2016, many of these in states with a large Latino/Hispanic[6] population, like Florida, New Mexico, and Nevada. Before we turn to the definite article, we will look at the data a little more closely, particularly at Trump's use of the terms *Latinos* and *Hispanics* and the contexts in which he uses them.

Like in his tweets, Trump generally prefers to use *Hispanics*, and occasionally—especially between July and October 2016—he seems unsure which of the two terms is appropriate in a given context and often uses both:

(13) We wanna help **Hispanics, Latinos**. (Speech: Donald Trump in Raleigh, NC, July 5, 2016)
(14) I'm going to help **the Latinos, Hispanics**. (Debate: Second Presidential Debate between Donald Trump and Hillary Clinton, October 9, 2016)

The sentence in (15) is an interesting case. Here, Trump talks about a past event in Las Vegas and as a side note shares his knowledge about terminology. His statement seems muddled, though. While the beginning of the sentence suggests that he is talking about a single ethnic group which collectively prefers the term *Latinos* in Nevada, the latter part suggests that he wants to indicate that both terms are in use in the area. After November of 2016, he abandons the term *Latinos* altogether. The single use of the term in 2018, (16), seems like a slip he wishes to correct.

(15) A lot of **Hispanics—Latinos,** they like to be called in that area, you know that, right, Hispanics and Latinos. (Speech: Donald Trump in Sandown, NH, October 6, 2016)
(16) Because **the Latinos, the the Hispanic Americans** have the best unemployment numbers and employment numbers in the history of our country. (Interview: Laura Ingraham Interviews Donald Trump on Fox's The Ingraham Angle, October 29, 2018)

Table 7.2 Distribution of *Latinos* and *Hispanics* in the Factba.se Data

	2015	2016	2017	2018	2019
Latinos	5	29	0	1	0
Hispanics	54	154	4	28	25

Table 7.3 Contexts in which *Latinos* and *Hispanics* Are Used

	Latinos	*Hispanics*	**Total**
Poll result	11	92	103 (34%)
Employment	4	41	45 (15%)
Achievement		24	24 (8%)
Campaign promise	8	13	21 (7%)
Suffering	5	9	14 (5%)
Love (agent)		11	12 (4%)
Love/support (patient)	1	11	12 (4%)
Relationship (agent)		11	11 (4%)
Other	6	52	49 (17%)

These first glimpses at the data suggest that Trump is using *Hispanics* and *Latinos* interchangeably. A more systematic analysis confirms that this is mostly the case. Table 7.3 shows that roughly 80 percent of the data originates from only eight different semantic contexts. Talk about predicted or actual poll results, such as in (17) and (18), is the context in which Trump uses *Hispanics* and *Latinos* by far the most.

(17) And in Nevada, when I had the poll, I won Nevada, the state of Nevada in a landslide. **They did a poll of Hispanics. I won the Hispanics by a lot**, a lot, OK? (Speech: Donald Trump in Rochester, NY, April 10, 2016)

(18) Latinos, **we're doing well with the Latinos**. Nobody knows about it yet. (Speech: Donald Trump in San Jose, CA, June 2, 2016)

The tokens in many of the contextual categories not only share semantic properties; very often they are syntactically identical, as phrases or clauses are repeated almost unchanged. In the category of poll results, *(I/we) DO (well/great) with* and *I won (with)* are very common.

Trump also frequently emphasizes his good relationship with Hispanics (as an undifferentiated group). Depending on their focus, these claims fall into several different categories in Table 7.3. Instances where Trump refers to the relationship in general, like in (19) and (20), fall into the category Relationship. The more specific claim that he loves Latinos/Hispanics—see (21)—has received its own category. In both categories, the relationship is described from Trump's perspective; he is the subject or agent. He also makes claims about the reverse direction of the relationship, namely that Latinos/Hispanics love and support him, see (22). Interestingly, apart from a single token, all relationship/love-related statements are phrased with *Hispanics*, not *Latinos*. Trump frequently feels the need to provide evidence of this "great relationship." Very often, this evidence comes in the form of a reminder to his audience that, over the years, he has had "thousands of" Hispanic employees. These claims are usually either phrased with the verb *employ* or with *have* in combination with a relative clause or a non-finite clause, but in several cases, like the second token in (23), these clauses are missing, resulting in claims that sound oddly like a description of possession. Poll results, like (17) and (18), also frequently serve as evidence of the quality of his relationship with Hispanics.

(19) I mean, **my relationship with Hispanics** is great. (Speech: Donald Trump in Sioux City, IA, January 30, 2016)
(20) By the way, **I get along so great with the Hispanics**. (Speech: Donald Trump in Greenville, SC, February 15, 2016)
(21) **I love the Hispanics**. I love you. (Speech: Donald Trump Delivers a Speech in Orlando, March 5, 2016)
(22) **The Latinos love Trump,** right? (Speech: Donald Trump in Pueblo, CO, October 3, 2016)
(23) I **have thousands of Hispanics that work for me**. Over the years, I have tens of thousands of people working for me but **I have thousands of Hispanics**, thousands. (Speech: Donald Trump in Ottumwa, IA, January 9, 2016)

Finally, there are the related categories Suffering, Campaign Promise, and Achievement. In the first of these categories, Trump draws a picture of the worsening economic situation of Latinos/Hispanics and other ethnic groups under Obama as of 2016, as well as their generally poor living conditions since then. Latinos have "fallen into poverty" (Speech: Donald Trump in Akron, OH, August 22, 2016, and other tokens from August 2016) and Hispanics "are living in hell" in the inner cities (Debate: First Presidential Debate between Donald Trump and Hillary Clinton, September 26, 2016). Trump then proceeds to promise to change the situation, as seen in (24) and (25) (category: Campaign Promise). Note that in these descriptions of their suffering and promises of relief, Latinos/Hispanics are often grouped together with African Americans. Finally, once in office, Trump talks about his achievements in terms of improving economic conditions, such as in (26).

(24) And I love Mexico and I love the Hispanics and **I'm gonna get so many jobs for the Hispanics**, for the African-Americans, for people that can't get jobs now. (Speech: Donald Trump in Harrisburg, PA, April 21, 2016)
(25) We wanna help African-American youth. We wanna help African-Americans. **We wanna help Hispanics, Latinos**. (Speech: Donald Trump in Raleigh, NC, July 5, 2016)
(26) **Hispanics** are doing phenomenally well under my administration and under my policies of economic growth. (Interview: Geraldo Rivera Interviews Donald Trump on Geraldo in Cleveland, September 24, 2018)

This more detailed analysis has confirmed that Trump mostly uses *Latinos* and *Hispanics* synonymously. The only noteworthy exception is the contexts of Love and Relationship where he consistently uses *Hispanics*. Besides that, *Latinos* is also absent in the category Achievement. This category is, however, strongly correlated with time; Trump does not brag about the achievements of his presidency until 2018—by which time he has abandoned the term *Latinos* altogether. Therefore, it seems more an effect of a short-time diachronic change in his language than of the topic. In light of these minor differences between the use of the two terms and also due to the fact that the Latino dataset is rather on the small side, we decided to combine the two and analyze them together as one larger dataset.

In order to be able to analyze Trump's use of *the*-plurals, we once more need to exclude tokens occurring in syntactic contexts which attract or repel definite articles, irrespective of the speaker. In order to keep the data comparable to our previous analyses, we once more opted for Acton's (2019) criteria of exclusion, as described in section 7.5.1. In this case, this leads to the exclusion of entire semantic categories. In the category Employment, for instance, a sizeable twenty-one tokens are preceded by *thousands of*, after which a definite article is possible, but unlikely. Others are excluded because they are preceded by other numerals or *many* or because they are followed by relative clauses like *that work for me*. In the Acton-comparable dataset, only the single token "Hispanics worked for me" remains in the Employment category. Therefore, the two remaining data points from the categories Employment and Suffering are now included in the miscellaneous category Other.

Figure 7.3 shows changes in Trump's use of *the*-plurals of *Latinos* and *Hispanics* over time. The year 2017 is not represented in the graph, as the Acton-comparable dataset only contains a single token for this year (a bare plural). In the campaign years 2015 and 2016, his average rate of *the Latinos/Hispanics* was 58 percent. Due to the lack of comparable studies, it is difficult to assess what would constitute a "normal" or "non-distancing" rate for a speaker of American English. We can draw some tentative conclusions from a comparison to Acton's findings for *the Democrats* and *the Republicans*, although we would probably expect more *the*-plurals in reference to *Democrats* and *Republicans* than to *Latinos* and *Hispanics*, as the former may refer not only to (a subset of) the members of each party but also to the party as a whole. In the latter case, the homogenizing reading of *the*-plurals reflects real-world circumstances: the parties are officially constituted as units and appear as single blocks in Congress and so on. This reading is not possible for *Latinos* or *Hispanics*. "Membership" of an ethnic group is much more complex than membership in a party, in that there is no single public entity "the Hispanics." Against this background, the fact that Trump's rate of *the Latinos/Hispanics* slightly exceeds the rate of *the*-plurals used by politicians

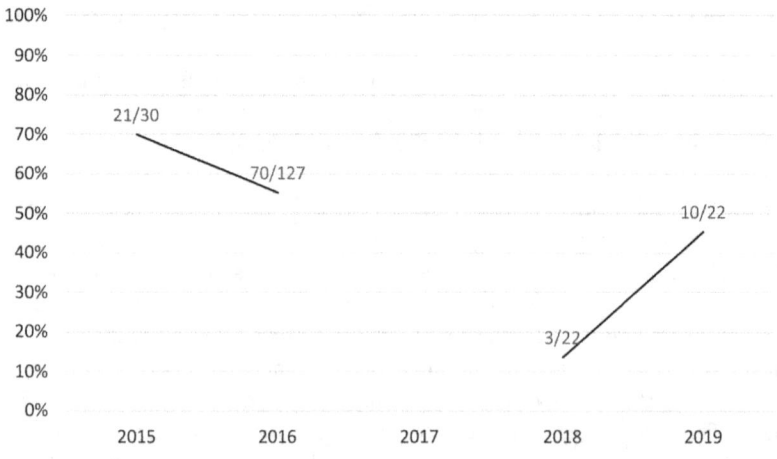

Figure 7.3 Rate of *the*-plurals in spoken references to *Latinos* and *Hispanics* over time.

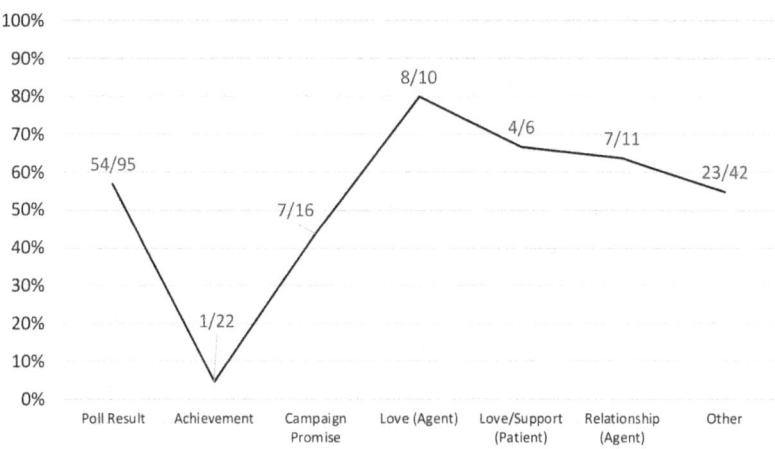

Figure 7.4 Rate of *the*-plurals of *Latinos* and *Hispanics* by semantic category.

to refer to (members of) the opposing party (see Figure 7.1) can be interpreted as an indicator that we are dealing with othering discourse.

The post-election plurals are even harder to interpret. Has Trump been counseled to avoid *the*-plurals? Has his new role as head of the nation temporarily changed his view on his constituents? Certainly, the topics of his speeches changed; campaign rallies were no longer of highest priority in 2018. Could a topic shift (partly) explain the decline in *the*-plurals? Figure 7.4 shows the rate of *the Latinos/Hispanics* by semantic category. Categories are presented in the same order in which they appear in Table 7.3. Immediately, the dent in the category Achievements stands out. It is the single context in which Trump uses almost no *the*-plurals. The category does not appear until after the election, because it is only then that Trump describes improvements in the employment and living conditions of Latinos/Hispanics. In 2018 and 2019, however, half of the data falls in this category. Once Achievement is excluded from the post-inauguration data, the rate of *the*-plurals jumps to 50 percent (eleven out of twenty-two tokens). We may therefore conclude that any apparent change in Trump's use of *the*-plurals in reference to *Latinos* and *Hispanics*, once he is president, is only due to his new topic of achievements.

Yet what causes this fundamental difference between talk about achievements and talk about other topics? Could it be that Trump tends to read his achievements off a script? The hesitation rates in examples (27) to (28) suggest otherwise. Another factor that sets Achievements apart from the other categories is Trump's use of adjectival forms in nominal positions—underlined in (27) and (28). These slips, which seem like the forms were lifted straight off a poll, are particularly common when Trump talks about his achievements.

(27) The economy is as good as it can be. Numbers have been fantastic. We're—we're just doing great. The—you look at the unemployment numbers, the best in 51 years, for individual groups like <u>African-American</u>, Asians, **Hispanics** the best

they've ever been, historic numbers. (Interview: Mark Levin Interviews Donald Trump on The Mark Levin Show, April 26, 2019)

(28) Something I'm very proud of: <u>the African American, Hispanic—Hispanic American</u>, and <u>Asian—Asian American</u>—the unemployment rates for all three have reached the lowest levels in the history of our country. Unemployment for <u>African American</u>, **Hispanics**, Asians, the lowest level in the history of our country. (Remarks: Donald Trump Delivers Remarks at Signing of McCain Defense Act, August 13, 2018)

In summary, we can rank Trump's use of *the Latinos/Hispanics* in speeches and so on by topic. He almost exclusively uses bare plurals when talking about his achievements (4.5 percent), alternates between the two plurals almost equally in most other contexts (rate of *the*-plurals: Campaign Promises 43.8 percent; Other 54.8 percent; Poll Results 56.8 percent), and uses most *the*-plurals when talking about his relationship with Latinos/Hispanics (combined rate of *the*-plurals for all love/relationship-related categories: 70.4 percent). Once achievement-related data points are excluded, we see no change in Trump's use of *the*-plurals over time. We will interpret these results in the next section.

7.6 Discussion and Conclusion

To conclude, we want to discuss our findings in light of the three broad claims that have been made about *the*-plurals, namely that they are distancing, derogatory, and homogenizing. Finally, we will discuss whether we found any evidence that Trump tries to mitigate the effect of his *the*-plurals with the help of racial "figleaves."

To many speakers, *the*-plurals in themselves are so clearly distancing that they appear to stand in contrast with the *we* in Trump's language, creating the impression that there are separate non-overlapping groups: *we Americans* versus *the Muslims, the Hispanics, the African Americans*, and so on (e.g., Graham 2016; Hawhee 2018). Our finding that Trump is much more likely to use a *the*-plural when tweeting about Democrats than when tweeting about Republicans supports this interpretation of distancing, though in a milder form. A single *the*-plural does not automatically indicate total separation between the speaker and the referenced group; however, non-membership in a group and possibly reservations against a group trigger more *the*-plurals in reference to that group. Thus, the rate of *the*-plurals seems to allow conclusions about a speaker's alliance, intentional or not, with a group; a low rate (probably ≤ 30 percent) signals no wish to distance oneself from the group, while a high rate (probably ≥ 50 percent) may signal distancing.

Some of the contexts in which we encountered uses of *Latinos/Hispanics* in Trump's spoken language were distancing in themselves. One example of such a distancing context would be one where Latinos/Hispanics are presented as "problems to be dealt with" (Sanchez 2016). Many of the tokens in the category Suffering fit this description. However, in terms of numbers, this category does not stand out. A more prominent distancing context is therefore the recurring situation where Trump talks about

Latinos/Hispanics as a trophy to be won, as expressed in pronouncements like (29) and (30), both included in the category Poll Result.

(29) I better win **the Hispanics** next time, right? (Remarks: Donald Trump Hosts Hispanic Heritage Month at The White House, September 17, 2018)
(30) I'm doing great with **the Hispanics**. Nobody knows it. (Speech: Donald Trump in Waterloo, IA, October 7, 2015)

While identification of an ethnic group as a "trophy" carries with it some potentially positive connotations, the distancing effect is nevertheless in place, as mentions along the lines of group-as-trophy or group-as-terrain-to-be-conquered suggest that Trump and Latinos/Hispanics are not on an equal footing. While the player can win the trophy, the trophy cannot win the player.[7] In spite of this, in our data, the rate of *the*-plurals in these contexts is no higher than in other contexts. This means that, ultimately, we have no evidence that distancing contexts trigger the use of *the*-plurals over bare plurals. In other words, the dominant pragmatic factor seems to be the speaker's power relationship with the referenced group.

The second strong claim put forward by observers of Trump's *the*-plurals is that these plurals are derogatory. Although Acton (2019: 61) cautions that "derogation does not simply logically follow from distancing," derogatory connotations can develop. We do not challenge this claim and neither did we set out to test it systematically. We can only proceed to analyze the data in the same way we did before, asking whether negative *contexts* trigger higher rates of *the*-plurals.

(31) **The Democrats** are getting ZERO work done in Congress. All they are focused on is trying to prove the Mueller Report wrong, the Witch Hunt! (@realDonaldTrump, May 22, 2019)
(32) **THE DEMOCRATS** ARE TRYING TO DESTROY THE REPUBLICAN PARTY AND ALL THAT IT STANDS FOR. STICK TOGETHER, PLAY THEIR GAME, AND FIGHT HARD REPUBLICANS. OUR COUNTRY IS AT STAKE! (@realDonaldTrump, September 26, 2019)
(33) Honduras, Mexico and many other countries that the U.S. is very generous to, sends [sic] many of their people to our country through our WEAK IMMIGRATION POLICIES. Caravans are heading here. Must pass tough laws and build the WALL. **Democrats** allow open borders, drugs and crime! (@realDonaldTrump, April 3, 2018)
(34) **Democrats** could solve the Shutdown in 15 minutes! Call your Dem Senator or Congresswoman/man. Tell them to get it done! Humanitarian Crisis. (@realDonaldTrump, January 12, 2019)

Certainly, tweets containing *the Democrats* are teeming with negative claims (see [31] and [32]), but so are tweets in which Trump writes about bare-plural *Democrats*, such as (33). In fact, even many statements that are positive on the surface at closer inspection tend to express negative sentiments, such as (34), which suggests Democrats could end a humanitarian crisis but deliberately do not do so.

When we turn to the Latinos/Hispanics dataset, we find that the situation is reversed. There is not a single token in which Latinos/Hispanics are the agents of undesirable action or in which they are described in any way as negative (within the same clause or sentence). Where negative statements occur, they always describe states that Latinos/Hispanics are in and which are out of their control: crime in their vicinity, unemployment, and poverty. Therefore, any *the*-plurals in the Latinos/Hispanics dataset were clearly not triggered by overtly negative claims within the same sentence or clause.

Let us turn back to Trump talking about his popularity among Latinos/Hispanics. He tends to refer to Latinos/Hispanics as a voting bloc that, per his characterization, was among his greatest supporters. This is evident in statements like (29) and (30), but also when he talks about his relationship with Latinos/Hispanics and their love for him—see (35).

(35) And I love the Mexican people. I employ thousands and thousands of **Hispanics** and I'm doing great in the polls. And by the way **the Hispanics** love me. You know why? They're here legally. **The Hispanics** that are here legally, they don't want their houses taken away. They don't want their jobs taken away. That's why I'm doing well with **the Hispanics** now. (Speech: Donald Trump Delivers a Campaign Speech in Lawrence Township, NJ, May 19, 2016)

These and similar claims position Latinos/Hispanics as some of his greatest fans, even though post-election analysis indicates that Trump secured only 29 percent of the Hispanic vote ("Reality Check: Who voted for Donald Trump?" 2016). Considering that voter turnout among Hispanics was only 47.6 percent (File 2017), actually only 13.8 percent of the Hispanic electorate voted for Trump. Thus, any statements presenting Hispanics as a group unanimously in favor of Trump are not supported by evidence—and are often a gross overgeneralization based on a single poll in Nevada in 2016. They frame Hispanics demographically as a homogeneous group acting in unison. Nevertheless, we need to be wary of attributing this homogenization (solely) to the definite article, as Trump alternates between bare plurals and *the*-plurals in these kinds of statements.

Finally, what about Trump's alleged love of the Hispanics—oddly enough the context with the most *the*-plurals? In political commentaries, Trump's *the*-plurals are not scattered at random, but appear more frequently when distancing himself from Democrats than when talking about Republicans. Does this make "I love the Hispanics" and "the Latinos love Trump" counterevidence to our conclusion that *the*-plurals are distancing? After all, a category of proximity rife with distancing syntax seems like an oxymoron. Yet, in light of the larger context in which Trump's statements about Latinos/Hispanics are often made, a different interpretation seems more fitting. (36) illustrates his discourse strategy. It is an excerpt from a lengthy answer given by Trump to a question at a town hall event in 2015. It has been split into several sections to illustrate how he alternates between positive and negative statements.

(36) We're going to stop drugs. Look, I told you before, Mexico forty-five to fifty billion, that's not including the drugs. The drugs that are coming across the border are beyond belief. Did you see the picture last week where they had a little wall this big, and they built a ramp for trucks to go over with drugs? Did you see the picture? They think we're playing games. And Mexico is not helping us. Mexico's not helping. You know, if you want to become a citizen of Mexico— — Negative statement

I love the Mexican people, I have many Mexican people and **Hispanics** working for me. In Nevada, I'm number one. I'm rated number one in the polls with **the Hispanics**. Everyone's shocked because **the Hispanics** that are here legally, those people, they want me—they know I'm gonna bring jobs and everything else. They don't want people pouring in. — Positive deflection

But I will tell you, Mexico has got to help us. You know, if you want to become a citizen of Mexico, if Todd wants to become a ci— — Negative statement

you can't get a more beautiful family. — Positive statement

If any of us wa- —if me, if I want to become a citizen of Mexico. Well, me, I know they won't take. OK. I was going to say I'm pretty good at getting in [unclear]. This wis what I mean. Do you know it's one of the hardest countries in the world to become a citizen of and yet people pour right through into us, into us. They call us the dumb Americans. (Speech: Donald Trump Holds a Town Hall-Style Event in Sioux City, IA, October 27, 2015) — Negative statement

Trump is about to make a negative statement about Mexico, but interrupts himself mid-sentence, injects a positive disclaimer aimed at communicating that he does not wish to discriminate against Hispanics living in the United States—that is, part of the electorate—and then proceeds to make the intended negative claim. What may first seem like a spontaneous interruption is, in fact, a repeating pattern—a deliberate argumentative strategy:

(37) We have a trade deficit with China this year, 505 billion, billion dollars. Think of it—505 billion dollars. We have trade deficit with Japan that's, that's shocking. We have, with—by the way, with Mexico— — Negative statements

I have great relationships with Mexico and with Hispanic people. I have thousands—I employ thousands of **Hispanics**. They're great. — Positive deflection

But we have, with Mexico, fifty-eight-billion-dollar trade deficit. And when I say we're gonna build a wall, which we will, by the way, but we're gonna build a wall. (Speech: Donald Trump in Hickory, NC, March 14, 2016) — Negative statement

(38) In China, the case of China, 500-billion-dollar trade deficit every single year. It's gonna end. Mexico.	Negative statement
I love the Mexican people. I love **Hispanics**. I love **Hispanics**. They're unbelievable people.	Positive deflection
We have now fifty-eight-billion-dollar trade deficit with Mexico. And our businesses sadly are leaving our country going to other countries. (Speech: Donald Trump in Bethpage, NY, April 6, 2016)	Negative statement

From this wider angle, his claims about Hispanics are not only homogenizing but clearly "figleaves," as they "provide[ ] a small bit of cover for something that is unacceptable to display in public" (Saul 2017: 98), namely at the very least a lack of understanding of minoritized groups and their concerns and at the most overtly racist attitudes and actions. To continue in the terms of the metaphor, *the*-plurals are the wormholes in the figleaf, letting Trump's lack of proximity to Hispanics shine through. However, we once more need to caution that, as illustrated by (37) and (38), the figleaf-character of a statement does not hinge on the use of a *the*-plural. However, statements relating to Trump's love for and relationship with Hispanics (as well as their love for him) are the broadest, most vague claims requiring little mental planning and are therefore only the most threadbare leaves.

Notes

1 The term *minoritized* highlights reference to groups who, sometimes regardless of population numbers, tend to be in a less dominant position of power than another more dominant group. For example, although African Americans outnumber other ethnicities in particular locations in the United States (and thus are not a minority in all contexts), they are still minoritized by way of continued systemic barriers preventing them from climbing the social ladder; similarly, according to the 2010 US Census, women slightly outnumber men—and are therefore not a minority—but they are still minoritized by way of being subject to systemic barriers with regard to wages, advancement opportunities, and other indicators of power.
2 Tweets were not retrieved directly from Twitter, but through the Trump Twitter Archive (Brown 2019), which states that the occasional tweet may be missing.
3 He has not always been a Republican; in 2000, he actually started a presidential campaign as a Reform Party candidate (Michigan Department of State Bureau of Elections 2019: 17).
4 Examples provided in the table are restricted to the sentence containing the search word; they do not represent entire tweets.
5 Tokens include both hyphenated and non-hyphenated spelling.
6 These terms are included together here although they are not always read as interchangeable, and there is an ongoing debate about which individual term, if either, is more appropriate. Broadly speaking, we accept the following distinction: *Latino*

refers to people with heritage from the geographic region known as Latin America, that is, the area south of the southern border of the United States; *Hispanic* refers to people with Spanish-speaking heritage. Because of this distinction, it is possible for someone to identify as Latino but not Hispanic and vice versa. Despite the intentional distinction adopted by the authors, it is worth noting that even some large, nonpartisan research think tanks such as the Pew Research Center use the terms *Latinos* and *Hispanics* interchangeably; as explained later, Trump also uses them as synonyms.

7 This is also reminiscent of the conceptual COMPETITION metaphor that underlies Trump's rhetoric (see Koth, this volume).

References

Abadi, Mark (2016), "'The Blacks,' 'the Gays,' 'the Muslims'—Linguists Explain One of Donald Trump's Most Unusual Speech Tics," *Business Insider*, October 17. Available online: https://www.businessinsider.com/donald-trump-the-blacks-the-gays-2016-10?r=DE&IR=T (accessed November 21, 2019).

Acton, Eric K. (2019), "Pragmatics and the Social Life of the Definite Article," *Language*, 95 (1): 37–65.

Allen, Jonathan (2016), "You're the Subhuman One, Donald," *Roll Call*, September 1. Available online: https://www.rollcall.com/news/opinion/youre-subhuman-one-donald (accessed November 21, 2019).

Brown, Brendan (2019), *Trump Twitter Archive*. Available online: http://www.trumptwitterarchive.com/archive (accessed November 7, 2019).

Campbell, Meagan (2016), "How Linguists Hear the US Election," *Maclean's*, October 21. Available online: https://www.macleans.ca/politics/worldpolitics/how-linguists-hear-the-u-s-election/ (accessed November 22, 2019).

FactSquared (2019), "Trump," *Factba.se*. Available online: https://factba.se/trump (accessed November 14 and 19, 2019).

File, Thom (2017), "Voting in America: A Look at the 2016 Presidential Election," *United States Census Bureau*, May 10. Available online: https://www.census.gov/newsroom/blogs/random-samplings/2017/05/voting_in_america.html (accessed December 13, 2019).

Gorski, Philip (2017), "Why Evangelicals Voted for Trump: A Critical Cultural Sociology," *American Journal of Cultural Sociology*, 5 (3): 338–54.

Graham, David A. (2016), "How Donald Trump Speaks to—and about—Minorities," *The Atlantic*, May 3. Available online: https://www.theatlantic.com/politics/archive/2016/05/the-way-donald-trump-speaks-toand-aboutminorities/481155/ (accessed November 21, 2019).

Hawhee, Debra (2018), "The Definite-Article Others," *The McCourtney Institute for Democracy, PennState College of the Liberal Arts*, July 23. Available online https://democracy.psu.edu/outreach/blog/the-definite-article-others-debra-hawhee (accessed November 21, 2019).

Holloway, Kali (2016), "Why Trump's Language Reveals His Racist Attitudes," *AlterNet*, October 22. Available online: https://www.alternet.org/2016/10/blacks-and-latinos-trumps-blatant-racism- visible- all-see/ (accessed November 21, 2019).

Kamenova, Denitza and Etienne Pingaud (2017), "Anti-Migration and Islamophobia: Web Populism and Targeting the 'Easiest Other,'" in Mojca Pajnik and Birgit Sauer (eds.), *Populism and the Web: Communicative Practices of Parties and Movements in Europe*, 108–21, London & New York: Routledge.

Liberman, Mark (2016), "The NOUNs," *Language Log*, September 5. Available online: https://languagelog.ldc.upenn.edu/nll/?p=26254 (accessed: November 22, 2019).

Maskovsky, Jeff (2017), "Toward the Anthropology of White Nationalist Postracialism," *HAU: Journal of Ethnographic Theory*, 7 (1): 433–40.

Michigan Department of State Bureau of Elections (2019), "Michigan Presidential Primary Facts and Statistics," February 20. Available online: https://www.michigan.gov/documents/MichPresPrimRefGuide_20863_7.pdf (accessed September 4, 2019).

Murphy, Lynne (2016), "Linguistics Explains Why Trump Sounds Racist When He Says 'the' African Americans," *Quartz*, October 11. Available online: https://qz.com/806174/second-presidential-debate-linguistics-explains-why-donald-trump-sounds-racist-when-he-says-the-african-americans/ (accessed November 22, 2019).

O'Connor, Lydia and Daniel Marans (2016), "Here Are 13 Examples of Donald Trump Being Racist," *Huffpost*, February 29. Available online: https://www.huffpost.com/entry/donald-trump-racist-examples_n_56d47177e4b03260bf777e83 (accessed November 21, 2019).

Omi, Michael and Howard Winant (2014), *Racial Formation in the United States*, 3rd edn, New York: Routledge.

Otova, Ildiko and Heini M. Puurunen (2017), "From Anti-Europeanism to Welfare Nation: Populist Strategies on the Web," in Mojca Pajnik and Birgit Sauer (eds.), *Populism and the Web: Communicative Practices of Parties and Movements in Europe*, 90–107, London & New York: Routledge.

Parker, Kathleen (2016), "Donald Trump and 'the Blacks,'" Chicago Tribune, August 31. Available online: https://www.chicagotribune.com/suburbs/daily-southtown/opinion/ct-sta-parker-trump-st-0901-20160831-story.html (accessed July 16, 2019).

Partington, Alan and Charlotte Taylor (2018), *The Language of Persuasion in Politics: An Introduction*, London and New York: Routledge.

"Reality Check: Who Voted for Donald Trump?" (2016), *BBC News*, November 9. Available online: https://www.bbc.com/news/election-us-2016-37922587 (accessed December 13, 2019).

Reinfeldt, Sebastian (2000), *Nicht-wir und Die-da: Studien zum rechten Populismus*, Wien: Wilhelm Braumüller.

Sanchez, Aaron E. (2016), "The History of Donald Trump's Definite Article," *Commentary and Cuentos: Thoughts on Race, Politics, and Pop Culture*, October 20. Available online: http://www.commentaryandcuentos.com/the-history-of-donald-trumps-definite-article/ (accessed November 21, 2019).

Saul, Jennifer M. (2017), "Racial Figleaves, the Shifting Boundaries of the Permissible, and the Rise of Donald Trump," *Philosophical Topics*, 45 (2): 97–116.

Sclafani, Jennifer (2018), *Talking Donald Trump. A Sociolinguistic Study of Style, Metadiscourse, and Political Identity*, New York: Routledge.

Selod, Saher (2018), *Forever Suspect: Racialized Surveillance of Muslim Americans in the War on Terror*, New Brunswick, NJ: Rutgers University Press.

Part III

Discourse and Metaphor

8

Either We WIN this Election, or We Are Going to LOSE this Country!

Trump's WARLIKE COMPETITION Metaphor

Anthony Koth

8.1 Introduction

Throughout the election, Trump often reduced the complexity of policy discussions down to the ideas of winning and losing, which evokes a sense of competition, with opponents vying against one another to achieve some goal. Winning and losing in a competition imply a zero-sum situation, that is, a mutually entailing relationship in which one competitor's win goes hand in hand with another's loss. In other words, one competitor's gain is by necessity tied to another competitor losing, and what is more, a win is defined as such only if there is a concomitant loss. Such a zero-sum, competition-driven thinking can be seen in the following tweet sent out by Trump near the end of the 2016 presidential campaign, albeit with an additional twist:

(1) Thank you Delaware County, Ohio! Remember- either we WIN this election, or we are going to LOSE this country! #DrainTheSwamp #TrumpPence16 (@realDonaldTrump, October 20, 2016)

Failing to win the election does not simply mean that he and his supporters lose the electoral competition; rather, failing to win the election is intolerable because it would result in the ultimate loss of America's exceptionalism and supremacy. Indeed, examining Trump's political rhetoric reveals his consistent use of such competitive terminology to convey his political views, encapsulated in his slogan "Make America Great Again." As the following analysis will demonstrate, this worldview reduces the complexity of policy issues to a simple demand: to reclaim American victory no matter the cost so that his supporters can once more be admired for their strength and conviction or otherwise be viewed with the contempt reserved for losers (Tännsjö 1998).

Trump's way of promoting his simplified ideological worldview draws on what is called a conceptual metaphor in cognitive linguistics. The basic idea behind conceptual metaphors is understanding one thing in terms of another, thus allowing people to make inferences about how and why the world works the way it does (Johnson and Lakoff 2002; Lakoff and Johnson 1980; Lakoff and Turner 1989). In the case of the conceptual metaphor underlying Trump's language under investigation here, we are dealing with an equation of life—or more specifically, business or politics—with competition. Using the zero-sum thinking of COMPETITION,[1] Trump engages in a form of common-sense thinking that invokes and reinforces forms of "folk knowledge" regarding political issues, that is, a layperson's understanding of politics that in most cases lacks an awareness of all its complex intricacies (Rubin 2003; Swedberg 2018). Moreover, Trump appropriates zero-sum thinking inherent to competitions in a way that gives victory a more warlike sense, which implies winning by any and all means necessary. Coupled with the value judgments connected to winning and losing (Tännsjö 1998), Trump shows off an excessive admiration for strength—usually his own or his supporters'—and an excessive contempt for weakness—usually everyone else's, particularly of those who oppose Trump. In this respect, the conceptual metaphor BUSINESS/POLITICS IS WARLIKE COMPETITION serves as a justification of who the American electorate should find deserving or undeserving of victory and respect, and what methods are necessary to achieve the end of winning.

To contextualize this line of argumentation, section 8.2 elaborates on the theory of conceptual metaphors, before the specifics of the conceptual metaphor BUSINESS/POLITICS IS WARLIKE COMPETITION are outlined in section 8.3. The actual analysis focuses on Trump's realizations of this particular conceptual metaphor. Section 8.4 gives information on the data taken into consideration, before section 8.5 provides a quantitative assessment of the COMPETITION metaphor in Trump's language (8.5.1) and a qualitative study of selected instantiations (8.5.2). Special emphasis will be put on the question of how the COMPETITION metaphor underlies Trump's treatment of immigration in his political discourse (8.5.3).

8.2 Essentials of Conceptual Metaphor Theory

Conceptual metaphor theory examines the link between cognition and language (Johnson and Lakoff 2002; Lakoff and Johnson 1980; Lakoff and Turner 1989). It has been used extensively in relation to politics (Bar-Lev 2007; Hernández 2013; Lakoff 2002; Lakoff 2004; Musolff 2006) and has recently been applied to Trump's rhetoric (Quinonez 2018; Stamenković 2017). Rather than being a literary device or embellishment, conceptual metaphors structure and organize our experiences. They also provide insight into how we perceive the world and think about it. The cognitive mechanism underlying conceptual metaphors is a mapping process in which a typically concrete and thus tangible source domain is projected onto a more schematic or abstract target domain, thereby facilitating the understanding and experiencing of one kind of thing, that is, an abstract phenomenon, in terms of another, that is, a more basic one. The fact that such mapping processes are indeed at work in the ways we perceive the world around us is manifested in linguistic instantiations of conceptual metaphors.

A classic example of a conceptual metaphor is IDEAS ARE FOOD, which maps the abstract notion of ideas onto food. The concrete source domain of FOOD comprises various conceptual elements like different types of food, the process of preparing and cooking, and the act of eating, chewing, swallowing, and digesting. The abstract target domain of IDEAS, on the other hand, has conceptual elements like claims or arguments, the process of thinking about or understanding ideas, and the act of accepting or rejecting them. We find the conceptual metaphor IDEAS ARE FOOD instantiated in expressions such as *stewing over ideas* or *devouring a book*, which, of course, do not mean that someone is actually stirring an idea in a pot or ingesting the actual paper of a book. Rather, they indicate that someone is thinking about an idea or readily accepting ideas as laid out in a book. Because of conceptual similarities between the two domains, metaphorical mapping is made possible. As the examples in Table 8.1 demonstrate, such metaphorical expressions are not simply random idiomatic phrases; instead, these linguistic realizations of the underlying conceptual metaphor reveal a structured and systematic way of understanding what an idea is.

The particular choice in terminology prompts distinct perspectives on the ideas being considered, based on varying sets of correspondences. Just as food needs to be prepared so that it can be consumed, ideas, too, have to be thought through and constructed properly in order to be more acceptable to an audience. Ideas being *stewed over* may be perceived as less likely to be palatable than those being *simmered on the back burner*. Such an evaluation is possible because of the conceptual element of 'doneness' in cooking. *Raw facts* and *half-baked* ideas may be less than acceptable for consideration, in the same way that raw meat or half-baked cakes are not yet ready to eat.

Another aspect relevant to this analysis is the partial nature of conceptual metaphors. Source domains (like FOOD) are complex structures of knowledge comprised of numerous conceptual elements (like preparation and degrees of doneness). However, few, if any, domains contain a sufficient set of conceptual elements that would be adequate to metaphorically grasp all facets of a target domain. IDEAS undergo a process to become acceptable just as FOOD does, but they can also be adhered to with

Table 8.1 IDEAS ARE FOOD

	Conceptual elements	
	Source domain (FOOD)	Target domain (IDEAS)
That's *food* for thought.	Food as nourishment	Considering ideas
Let me *stew* over that for a while.	Cooking	Thinking
Let's let that idea *simmer on the back burner* for a while.	Cooking	Thinking
All this paper has in it are *raw* facts, *half-baked* ideas, and *warmed-over* theories.	Properly prepared	Fully formed ideas
I just can't *swallow* that claim.	Fully consuming	Accepting
She *devoured* the book.	Fully consuming	Understanding
There are too many facts here for me to *digest* them all.	Digesting	Understanding

(Adapted from Kövecses 2010: 6–7)

great rigidity which is a conceptual element that the FOOD domain seems less suited to convey. There are other conceptual metaphors, for example, IDEAS ARE LOCATIONS (Lakoff, Espenson, and Schwartz 1991: 90–1), that can be used to highlight how ingrained ideas may become for someone who is *wrapped up in* or *tied to* a particular belief.

Even though conceptual metaphors grant access to abstract notions, there are two blind spots to be aware of. The first one concerns what Hamington (2008: 474–5) calls the "metaphoric fallacy." As pointed out before, conceptual metaphors serve to explain one concept in terms of another, which is reflected in linguistic instantiations of the mapping process. However, misconceptions may arise when the metaphor is taken too literally, thus blending out the analogical abstraction and causing "a conflation of definition with metaphor or the 'is' with the 'like'" (Hamington 2008: 475). Closely related to this problem is the second blind spot, which concerns a neglected awareness that a property inherent to metaphors is to necessarily reduce complex matters. Developing ideas can be reasonably likened to eating food, but the cognitive processes involved are ultimately more complex than what chewing, swallowing, and digesting imply.

As will be demonstrated in the next section, taking BUSINESS IS COMPETITION too literally can cause problematic inferences about ethics and morals, letting some businesspeople ignore the implications of their actions so long as they "hit their sales goals." Before problematizing the BUSINESS IS COMPETITION metaphor, it is crucial to identify the conceptual elements in the source domain of COMPETITION.

8.3 Zooming in on the Conceptual Metaphor of BUSINESS IS (WARLIKE) COMPETITION

8.3.1 COMPETITION as a Source Domain

The COMPETITION source domain is multifaceted, containing a number of conceptual elements such as the competitors involved, the kind of sporting event, the goal of a competition, the rules of the game, and so on. Of particular importance to competitions is indeed the regulatory framework since rules define the goals to strive for as "specific achievable state[s] of affairs" (Suits 2018: 24) and the win-condition that players seek to fulfill.

There are basically two different ways of approaching competitions which can be clustered into two groups or subdomains based on their manner of evaluation, broadly defined as generic versus more negative. The first type, which treats competition as a neutral source domain, harks back to the original meaning of *competition*, 'to strive with' or 'to seek with,' which implies "an enjoyable and mutual quest for excellence" as the primary purpose of holding a contest (Shields and Bredemeier 2011: 33); goals and victories have an undetermined or uncertain outcome since a win can be achieved by any participant who meets the given criteria. A more extreme type, which is akin to a warlike understanding of competition, is involved when competitions are rather seen as competitors striving 'against' each other. Shields and Bredemeier (2011: 33–5) refer to this more negative conceptualization as "decompetition,"[2] according to which competitors are absolutely sure about the outcome of the competition from the start, namely their own guaranteed win. Decompetition thus results in more aggressive behaviors on the playing field, an unwillingness to play by the rules, or an eagerness to exploit the rules to one's own benefit. In short, the opportunity to measure one's excellence turns into a fierce ambition to win at any cost, no matter what. Drawing on previous research of the COMPETITION domain and its use in various metaphors, Table 8.2 presents some of the terms and conceptual elements inherent to competitions, each of them spelled out for the generic/neutral sense of competition on the one hand and the more warlike sense of the decompetition subdomain on the other hand (Cudd 2007; FrameNet 2001; Hamington 2008; MetaNet Metaphor Wiki 2014; MetaNet Metaphor Wiki 2016; Shields and Bredemeier 2011). As can be seen from the DECOMPETITION subdomain, the more warlike sense is strongly characterized by an US versus THEM mentality, which makes the quality of competitions less playful.

The potential for evaluation is particularly salient in the COMPETITION domain precisely because competition is a means to evaluate people and their abilities to achieve

Table 8.2 Conceptual Elements of the COMPETITION Source Domain

Conceptual elements	COMPETITION domain	WARLIKE DECOMPETITION subdomain
Event	Sporting event such as football, soccer; players striving *with* each other for excellence	Players striving *against* each other, thus fighting in a warlike sense
Competitor 1	Self, home team	US
Competitor 2	(Friendly) rival	THEM, the enemy
Officials	Referees, umpires	Judges wrongly holding US back
Location	Stadium, (level) playing field	Battlefield
Means	Sporting equipment, baseball bat	Weapon-like instruments
Rules of the game	Constitutive rules defining how the game is played, imposing restraints	Restraints only partially tolerated, to be exploited for advantage in the game
Rules of fair play	Unwritten moral and ethical considerations about what is fair and foul play	
Outcome	Uncertain; result in terms of score or rankings	Pre-conceived: OUR victory as well as THEIR defeat and destruction are taken for granted
Prize	Medals, rankings	Admiration, glory
Winner	Competitor with the most points	The most deserving victor, preferably US, not THEM
Loser	Competitor with fewer points	The undeserving loser, preferably THEM, never US
Goals/purpose	Winning, fun, improving skills	Victory at all costs, avoiding defeat and humiliation
Zero-sum	A winner necessarily entails a loser	OUR victory entails THEIR defeat; THEIR victory is illegitimate

a given task. With the rules of the game codifying what constitutes success (e.g., certain actions gain or lose points) and thus determining who was more successful at the task at hand (e.g., the highest scorer wins), evaluation is essential in competitions. In the generic sense of competition, this rather objective evaluation of success is understood in zero-sum terms (Cudd 2007): the competitor who scored best is declared the winner which necessarily entails that the other competitors, who were less successful, are the losers. However, the more warlike sense of decompetition involves a kind of evaluation that happens outside of the codified rules, when one makes value judgments about the winner and the loser(s) laden with the emotional overtones evoked by victory and defeat. According to Tännsjö (1998), winners and losers are evaluated along a continuum: victors are highly cherished for their skill, ability, talent, and success while losers are viewed in a lower or contemptuous regard for their failure and weakness. This kind of evaluation is indicative of a shift in understanding of the zero-sum nature of competition, that is, a shift away from the basic entailment that a win begets a loss to a more moral judgment that winners are higher in value than the losers and thus better people who are the only ones deserving the glory of victory. These subjective evaluations push the zero-sum nature of winning and losing to an ideological extreme: a desire for victory no matter the costs because losing is tantamount to humiliation and a loss of significance.

Surely, these evaluations may seem not too problematic when it comes to a game. However, within conceptual metaphors such as BUSINESS/POLITICS IS COMPETITION, defining how success is measured and who achieves that success better can have far-reaching implications. An examination of the BUSINESS/POLITICS IS COMPETITION metaphor in the next section will further illuminate the implications of the (DE)COMPETITION source domain with respect to how it is metaphorically mapped onto the target domains of BUSINESS and POLITICS. Of particular interest for the conceptualizations of BUSINESS and POLITICS will be the three interrelated issues of (i) what defines success, (ii) the shift in zero-sum thinking from generic to warlike competition, and (iii) the value judgments made about winners and losers.

8.3.2 Mapping (WARLIKE) COMPETITION onto BUSINESS

In BUSINESS IS COMPETITION, which is a metaphor central to capitalism, businesspeople are mapped to competitors vying for profits, while profits, in turn, are mapped onto goals which the competitors need to achieve. Thus, maximizing one's market share at another company's expense can be understood through the zero-sum nature of competition. We find this conceptual metaphor instantiated in linguistic metaphors used in a business context, such as *winning strategies, playing hardball, leveling the playing field, being a team player*, or *playing by the rules* (Hamington 2008: 473).

However, taking the BUSINESS IS COMPETITION metaphor too literally, that is, as definitional rather than simply an explanatory cognitive routine, may lead to problematic inferences. Reducing the complexity of the business world to the singular focus on winning at all costs may allow a person (i) to disregard the moral and ethical implications of one's actions (Hamington 2008), (ii) to think in zero-sum terms that one's perceived losses come about because of another's perceived illegitimate gains (Burleigh 2016), and (iii) to think that only the winners deserve admiration, whereas the losers deserve contempt (Tännsjö 1998). Consequently, such metaphoric fallacies include a trivialization of complex business decisions as game moves, a truncation of moral or ethical considerations, a fixation on goals to the exclusion of other considerations, and a privileging of the adversarial nature of business relationships (Hamington 2008: 477–81). This fallacious thinking may to a certain extent be related to the partial nature of metaphors, since the source domain of COMPETITION inevitably flattens the complexity of the abstract target domain of BUSINESS. These fallacies may also be attributed to some people focusing more on the WARLIKE subdomain of COMPETITION. Note that Table 8.2 contains no equivalent to the rules of fair play within the WARLIKE DECOMPETITION subdomain. Fixating on the goal of profits and market share may make some people treat other considerations as trivial in comparison. Those people may feel justified in ignoring the idea of ethical behavior or the effects of actions on, for example, society or the environment.[3] Such thinking can turn business into a no-holds-barred, warlike competition for profit no matter the costs, with a disdain for limits or controls. People who think in these warlike terms have shifted the zero-sum aspect of competition from its more objective nature, that is, from simply determining who is gaining or losing resources, into a more subjective fear, that is, considering any losses as ill-gotten gains by rival companies or foreign countries.

According to the theory of "folk economics," which structures a layperson's understanding of the marketplace (Rubin 2003), wealth is understood in a zero-sum fashion, predicated on a belief in resource scarcity: given a finite amount of wealth in the world, one person's loss necessarily comes at another's gain. This conceptualization maps well onto the zero-sum condition of a generic competition between two competitors where only one win exists. However, as Burleigh (2016) demonstrates, people may think about resources via a resource entitlement belief: a person believes they alone know best how much of a given resource to allocate to various parties. A resource entitlement belief can become zero-sum when such an individual feels that one party deserves a certain portion of that resource, if not all of it, and that any less is an illegitimate gain by another party. Competitors who believe they were cheated out of their rightful points or their certain victory likely engage in this resource entitlement form of zero-sum thinking. In the same way that fixating on profits or winning at all costs may allow one competitor to ignore the rules of fair play, it may also permit such a competitor to accuse their opponents of cheating rather than accepting the possibility that their opponents may simply have performed better.

Ignoring the possibility that another team may have performed better and trivializing moral and ethical considerations are both indicative of the reduction in complexity of the abstract BUSINESS domain that can occur by taking the victory-at-all-costs mentality of the WARLIKE domain too literally. This goes along with what Tännsjö (1998: 27) refers to as "negligent" contempt for losers and their weakness, a form of neglect that shows itself in an effort to "think away" those we feel contempt for or "treat them as nonexistent." Indeed, the possibility that the rules of the game or of fair play could be disregarded is captured by Shields and Bredemeier's (2011: 35) comment that rules are understood as only "partially tolerated restraints" in a warlike competition, to be ignored when convenient or advantageous. In this respect, a zero-sum resource entitlement belief seems to tie in with such a form of negligent contempt in that one may categorically deny the legitimacy of other competitors' claims to a resource.

In a sporting event, such contempt may at worst make for a bad game, with lots of cheating by one competitor to maximize their score or full of insults and trash-talk disparaging the winner to question the validity of their victory. But when it comes to the conceptual metaphor BUSINESS/POLITICS IS WARLIKE COMPETITION, resources and victories become mapped to abstract concepts like life, rights, freedom, justice, or even citizenship, which are then measured in zero-sum terms. If people other than members of the in-group lay claim to them, they are viewed with contempt. According to Tännsjö (1998: 27), admiration for one's own strength and contempt for others' weakness are at the heart of fascist and nationalist ideologies, and people deemed weak can have their lives and claims to resources threatened by what he describes as the three distinct forms of contempt. Apart from the negligent form described earlier, which means the strong ignore the weak, there is an aggressive form that permits the strong to treat the weak violently, and a paternalistic form in which the strong "'take care' of those 'poor creatures'" (Tännsjö 1998: 27) out of pity.

In the remainder of this chapter, I describe how Trump's rhetoric and political discourse are heavily influenced by the more WARLIKE subdomain of the BUSINESS IS COMPETITION conceptual metaphor, which is thus extended to a conceptualization of POLITICS. Using data from the 2016 election, I demonstrate how Trump's words reveal the underlying mappings he makes between various political concepts and the conceptual elements of WARLIKE COMPETITION, how he engages in zero-sum resource entitlement thinking, and how he offers admiration for what he deems to be the right sort of Americans and utter contempt for the wrong sort of people, once more adhering to an US versus THEM mentality—all while he argues that he alone can "Make America Great Again."

8.4 Data and Methodology

Some data for this analysis are drawn from a corpus created for Koth (2019). The corpus contains the candidacy announcements and debate performances for all twenty-two candidates who ran for president during the 2016 primary and general elections, comprising approximately 515,000 words of which Trump's share is just over 69,000 words. I gathered publicly available transcripts and corrected them for accuracy and completeness adding hesitations, repetitions, false starts, common shortenings such as *gonna* and *wanna*, other vocalizations, interruptions, and a more accurate rendering of prosodic contours. These data were evaluated quantitatively. For a subsequent qualitative analysis, additional data were gathered from Trump's Twitter feed via the Trump Twitter Archive (Brown 2019), from the time between Trump's candidacy announcement and election day (from June 16, 2015 to November 8, 2016).

8.5 Analysis and Results

8.5.1 A Quantitative Analysis of Trump's Vocabulary

In a first step, I ran a comparative corpus analysis (Rayson and Garside 2000) focusing on the candidacy announcements and debate performances in order to determine to what extent the choice of competition-related vocabulary differentiated Trump's speaking style from the rest of the candidates' styles. In Table 8.3, the log-likelihood measure represents the relative difference between Trump and the other candidates. This measure can be applied across differently sized corpora. The higher the log-likelihood score, the more characteristic a word is of a particular corpus. Positive values indicate a word being more characteristic of Trump than of other politicians; negative values indicate the opposite. The *p*-values in the table refer to different thresholds of statistical significance and stand for a probability below 5 percent, 1 percent, or 0.1 percent, respectively, which allows us to refute the assumption that the observed differences are simply due to chance. Looking through the results, we find *losing*, *win*, and *competition* stand out.

Once Trump's preference for words related to COMPETITION became apparent, I analyzed the context surrounding those terms, both in the corpus and in his tweets, relating the data to the various features of COMPETITION described in sections 8.2 and 8.3.

In the next section, I demonstrate how Trump structures his rhetoric according to his worldview using the BUSINESS/POLITICS IS WARLIKE COMPETITION metaphor. I will point out the mappings he makes between political issues and the conceptual elements of both senses of COMPETITION. Some of these mappings can be readily seen, such as when other nations are conceptualized as opponents, while the reduction of complexity and the zero-sum resource entitlement belief might be less noticeable features.

8.5.2 Mapping out Trump's WARLIKE COMPETITION Metaphor

A closer, qualitative look at selected tweets and excerpts from debate contexts reveals that Trump frequently uses instantiations of the BUSINESS IS (WARLIKE) COMPETITION

Table 8.3 Trump's COMPETITION Word Choice

Word	Frequency		Log-likelihood	Significance
	Trump	Other candidates		
Losing	23	27	30.979	p<0.001
Win	64	198	22.476	p<0.001
Competition	15	17	20.788	p<0.001
Unfair	13	13	19.808	p<0.001
Lose	31	80	15.902	p<0.001
Compete	12	26	8.215	p<0.01
Winner	4	13	4.305	p<0.05
Defeat	5	86	−6.222	p<0.05
Fight	24	266	−7.682	p<0.01

conceptual metaphor in his rhetoric, which might not be unexpected given his status as businessman. Much like an athlete might argue they were robbed of points or a win, Trump would often criticize his political opponents for, among other things, not respecting the certainty of his victory and "stealing" his "win" in Iowa, see (2), or acting "selfishly" in their continued opposition to him, see (3).

(2) Ted Cruz didn't **win** Iowa, he **stole** it. That is why all of the polls were so wrong and why he got far more votes than anticipated. **Bad**! (@realDonaldTrump, February 3, 2016)
(3) I will **win** the election against Crooked Hillary despite the people in the Republican Party that are currently and **selfishly opposed** to me! (@realDonaldTrump, May 9, 2016)

Additionally, Trump extends this WARLIKE sense of victory as a certain or guaranteed outcome by giving it a temporal dimension: every victory should be America's precisely because Americans used to be the winners all the time. Throughout the campaign, Trump would link what he envisioned as America's recent lack of victories to various troubles, and even to its lack of continued greatness, as in his candidacy announcement:

(4) Our country is in serious trouble. We don't have **victories anymore**. We used to have **victories**, but we don't have them. When was **the last time** anybody saw us **beating**, let's say China, in a trade deal? They **kill** us. I **beat** China all the time, all the time. When did we **beat** Japan at anything? They send their cars over by the millions and what do we do? When was the last time you saw a Chevrolet in Tokyo? It doesn't exist, folks. They **beat** us all the time. When do we **beat** Mexico at the border? **They are laughing at us at our stupidity.** And now they are **beating** us economically. They are not our friend, believe me, but they are **killing** us economically. (Candidacy announcement, June 16, 2015)

Note how Trump juxtaposes generic competition terms like "beat" to positively evaluate his or America's side with the more warlike "kill" to negatively evaluate his or America's opponents. In this way, he evokes the impression that he and America are just trying to fight the good fight in order to be "Great Again," while other nations are seen as being out for America's blood.

For Trump, the only resolution to these injustices is to reverse the wrongful theft and loss America is experiencing at the hands of various enemies, whether foreign or domestic, and to make great again what should have been recognized as great all along. The power behind his slogan "Make America Great Again" can be found within this temporal extension of the WARLIKE sense of victory: because America used to be the winner all the time, such victories are a natural and continual outcome that America should experience in perpetuity. Thus, its alleged exceptionalism and supremacy must always be acknowledged whether in economic, military, or cultural terms. Any perceived or potential violation of this pre-specified outcome is deemed outright "(un)fair," (5), or "[im]proper" treatment (6), whether perpetrated by other candidates, other nations, or any other group Trump targets as his opponents.

(5) The media has not covered my **long-shot great finish** in Iowa **fairly**. Brought in record voters and got second highest vote total in history! (@realDonaldTrump, February 2, 2016)
(6) Remember this, the wall will be paid for by Mexico. We are **not being treated right**. We are **not being treated properly**. If we don't have borders, if we don't have **strength**, we don't have a country. (GOP Debate 9, February 13, 2016)

In WARLIKE metaphors, the focus on winning at all costs permits a neglect of other constitutive elements, by viewing the rules of the game and of fair play as only partially tolerated restraints, to be exploited for one's own advantage or to be ignored completely. Note in (7) how Trump emphasizes the importance of winning which makes "fighting back" a legitimate reaction, particularly if met with a challenge characterized as "unfair." Such an argument is predicated on the assumption that the other competitor cheated first, which in return justifies acting "brutal[ly]."

(7) When somebody challenges you unfairly, fight back - be brutal, be tough -don't take it. It is always important to WIN! (@realDonaldTrump, June 27, 2015)

In (8), Trump uses the same logic that 'they did it first' to justify his reasoning that America will "never ever knock out ISIS and all of the others that are so bad" unless "we . . . expand [our] laws" to permit waterboarding; after all, ISIS does not follow any "rules" or "regulations" against torture to begin with.

(8) First of all let me go back to the other just for a second in large mosques, w— all in all over the Middle East, you have people chanting death to the USA. . . . We have a law that doesn't allow right now waterboarding. **They**[4] **have no laws they have no rules they have no regulations** and they chop off heads. They drown forty fifty sixty people at a time in big steel cages, pull them up an hour later everyone dead. And we're working on a different set of of parameters. Now we have to obey the laws. Ok have to obey the laws. But we have to expand those laws because we [*applause*] have to be able to fight, on at least somewhat of an equal footing or we will never ever knock out ISIS and all of the others that are so bad. We better expand our laws or we're being a bunch of suckers and they are laughing at us they are laughing at us believe me. [*applause*] (GOP Debate 12, March 10, 2016)

The reason why such an undermining of morals and ethics becomes tolerable rests precisely in a belief that "[i]t is always important to WIN," as emphasized in (7). Such a win can be achieved by using any and all means necessary, whether by ignoring both the written rules of the game and the unwritten rules of fair play, or even by dismissing any referees or officials who are perceived as non-supportive. Ultimately, mapping POLITICS onto WARLIKE COMPETITION results in a problematic reduction in complexity, with the rules (9), the referees (10), and the opponents (11) all becoming one and the same: the ENEMY or OPPOSING FORCE whose objective is to deny Trump, the predestined winner, his rightful victory.

(9) Just to show you **how unfair Republican primary politics can be**, I **won** the State of Louisiana **and get less** delegates **than** Cruz-Lawsuit coming (@realDonaldTrump, March 27, 2016)
(10) Based on @MegynKelly's conflict of interest and bias **she should not be allowed to be a moderator of the next debate**. (@realDonaldTrump, January 23, 2016)
(11) While I believe I will clinch before Cleveland and get more than 1237 delegates, it is **unfair in that there have been so many in the race!** (@realDonaldTrump, March 23, 2016)

The WARLIKE version of victory is entwined not only with truncated ethics and morality but also with the privileging of the adversarial nature of relationships which allows conceptualizing any opposition, officials, or rules as an ENEMY or an OPPOSING FORCE. Throughout the election, Trump would often engage in name-calling against his opponents, for example, *Lyin' Ted* and *Crooked Hillary* (see also Tyrkkö and Frisk, this volume). While trash-talk about an opponent can be pretty standard fare in any competition, in its WARLIKE version such trash-talk can be used to dehumanize one's enemies. In (12), Trump uses the HUMAN IS ANIMAL metaphor to disparage Mitt Romney by mapping him onto a DOG, thereby downgrading Romney's status as a human being to animal condition to convey just how poorly he performed compared to the "failed president" Obama.

(12) Mitt Romney had his chance to **beat a failed president but he choked like a dog**. Now he calls me racist-but I am least racist person there is (@realDonaldTrump, June 11, 2016)

In (13), Trump uses a well-documented network of metaphors to remove any sense of agency from immigrants: his rhetoric evokes the conceptual metaphor of IMMIGRANTS ARE POLLUTANTS, which forms part of DIRT IS MATTER OUT OF PLACE within the NATION IS A HOUSE metaphorical mapping (Cisneros 2008; Kil 2014; Lizardo 2012; Santa Ana 1999). By describing immigrants as being "dump[ed]" in or "sen[t]" to America by Mexico and even "from more than Mexico," Trump ignores the possibility that they may be coming to America of their own accord and for their own reasons.

(13) When do we **beat Mexico at the border**? They're laughing at us at our stupidity. And now they are **beating us economically.** They are not our friend, believe me, but they are **killing us economically.** The US has become a **dumping** ground for everybody else's problems. [*Audience response*: That's why we need you. Yeah!] [*applause*] Thank you. It's true. And these are the best and the finest. When Mexico **sends** its people, they're not **sending** their best. They're not sending you. They're not sending you. They're **sending** people that have lots of problems, and they're bringing those problems with us [*sic*]. **They're bringing drugs, they're bringing crime, they're rapists**, and some, I assume are good people. But I speak to border guards and they tell us what we're getting. **And it only makes common sense. It only makes common sense. They're sending** us not the right people it's coming from **more than Mexico.** (Candidacy announcement, June 16, 2015)

Examples (12) and (13) quite literally demonstrate what Tännsjö (1998: 27) argues is at the center of the contempt felt for losers and the weak, who are "not treated as full persons." While the clearest examples may be the dehumanization and removal of agency in (12) and (13), the other ways in which Trump negatively evaluates his perceived opponents can offer cues to the electorate to feel contempt as well, for example, by calling Ted Cruz or nations like China thieves, see (2) and (4), respectively, or criticizing others for not treating him or America "right," "fairly," or "properly," see (5) to (7). This latter form of contempt stems from a belief in the illegitimacy of other people's victory, a conviction based on an US versus THEM mentality in which THEY are assumed to have wrongly stolen the admiration and respect that would normally be OURS. This form of contempt is more indicative of the aggressive form of contempt that seeks to eliminate weakness by beating losers in a "brutal" and "tough" manner, as evidenced in (3).

The HUMAN IS ANIMAL and IMMIGRANTS ARE POLLUTANTS conceptual metaphors instantiated by Trump in (11) and (12) are embedded within a larger system called The Great Chain Of Being metaphor that describes the relationships holding between things in the world (Kövecses 2010; Lakoff and Turner 1989). Like folk economics, it is a form of folk knowledge or, as Trump puts it, "common sense" (13). The Great Chain of Being structures the world hierarchically, situating humans above animals above natural physical objects (like dirt).

Throughout the election, Trump used several metaphors to negatively evaluate his opponents, immigrants, Muslims, and other nations in order to incite contempt for them, most notably for their attempts to "steal" (2) the victories that should belong to him, his supporters, and America, all while "they are laughing at us for our stupidity," see (4) and (8). As demonstrated in the next section, this theft of America's presupposed victories is closely linked to the zero-sum nature of COMPETITION shifting to a resource entitlement belief, which is at the core of Trump's theory of folk immigration.

8.5.3 The Zero-Sum Nature of "Folk Immigration"

The notion of "folk immigration" presented here harks back to "folk economics" (Rubin 2003) and other forms of folk knowledge, which serve laypersons to structure their understanding of how aspects of the world work. These aspects concern quite complex matters that only experts from the respective fields have studied in depth in order to possess a nuanced understanding, whereas folk-knowledge explanations are less sophisticated, ultimately based on simplifications. According to folk economics, one of the central means to understand economic interactions, which involves such a simplified reduction in complexity, is zero-sum thinking based on the scarcity of resources: there is only so much wealth or jobs in the world, therefore one's loss comes at another's gain. Throughout the election, Trump would justify his policy positions by using a series of folk theories, several of which are predicated on a zero-sum resource entitlement belief (Koth 2019): as Trump sees it, there is only so much wealth, safety, and "Great[ness]" available in America or the world, and all of it exclusively belongs to the right sort of Americans. In folk immigration, quantifiable resources like wages, wealth, and jobs are perceived as things put at risk by "not the right people" (13) coming into America. In (14), Trump offers an understanding of immigration in such zero-sum terms:

(14) Our inner cities have been left behind. We will never have the resources to support our people if we have an open border. (@realDonaldTrump, June 23, 2016)

"[O]pen border" immigration policies will result in a loss of "resources to support our people" in "our inner cities." Even though there are no overt COMPETITION terms within this tweet, several traces of that domain can still be discerned, namely an opponent laying claim on resources that are perceived as rightfully 'ours'. The sense of WARLIKE competition is also evoked through the palpable contempt for the immigrant opponents, who are conceptualized as thieves. As for those Americans in the inner cities, Trump shows a paternalistic form of contempt, requiring 'us' to "'take care' of those 'poor creatures'" (Tännsjö 1998: 27): with Americans in the inner cities "be[ing] left behind," they are unable to handle their own affairs, which legitimizes Trump's claim for "the resources to support [them]."

Against the backdrop of the nature of folk knowledge as a widely shared non-specialist belief system, Trump's argument may sound reasonable. From a layperson's perspective, it makes "common sense," as stated in (9), to compute changes concerning quantifiable resources like wealth or jobs in a zero-sum fashion and to blame immigrants or other nations for the losses America has experienced. When it comes to more abstract or less quantifiable concepts like safety, though, one could argue zero-sum thinking does not readily apply. However, Trump's line of argumentation in (15) in which "open borders" will not only "drive down wages for all Americans" but also their "safe[ty]" is indicative of a zero-sum resource entitlement belief after all: there is a certain amount or degree of "safe[ty]" Americans deserve, and immigration naturally and wrongfully reduces that level.

(15) Hillary Clinton's open borders immigration policies will drive down wages for all Americans - and make everyone less safe. (@realDonaldTrump, June 21, 2016)

Given this resource entitlement belief about safety and the competition over wages, this tweet also seems to evoke the aggressive form of contempt, targeted explicitly at Clinton for her policies, but also implicitly at those immigrants forcing down Americans' wages and endangering their safety.

The particular degree of safety that Trump claims Americans deserve can be understood similarly to the added temporal dimension of WARLIKE victory underlying Trump's slogan "Make America Great Again." Only Trump can make America "Safe Again for all Americans" (16), by restoring American exceptionalism that should never have been lost to begin with, whether in economic terms, see (4), (14), and (15), or cultural terms, see (16). Trump lays blame for this loss in exceptionalism on Clinton and her policies, as well as on immigration for "tearing American families apart":

(16) Hillary Clinton's open borders are tearing American families apart. I am
going to make our country Safe Again for all Americans. #Imwithyou
(@realDonaldTrump, June 23, 2016)

In several cases, Trump adapts the zero-sum resource entitlement belief to the issue of immigration by linking the loss of economic power, safety, and "Great[ness]" to a rise in "rampant problems" (17) caused by immigration. This goes along with a use of more common metaphors like IMMIGRANTS ARE POLLUTANTS, who are "bringing drugs, they're bringing crime, they're rapists," see (13), or a more novel spin on PEOPLE ARE MACHINES, in which immigrants are conceptualized as machines programmed only for "crime and killing":

(17) We must stop the crime and killing machine that is illegal immigration.
Rampant problems will only get worse. Take back our country
(@realDonaldTrump, August 10, 2015)

Placed prominently at the end of this tweet, Trump's admonition to "Take back our country" has a double meaning. On the one hand, Trump can claim that he is simply concerned about the situation at the border and therefore intends to tighten border security, that he is arguing to exclude only those people he deems "criminals" by following through on the oft-repeated chant at his rallies: "build the wall." On the other hand, Trump's statement can be understood through folk immigration: "Tak[ing] back our country" means reclaiming America's "Great[ness]" and exceptionalism which has been illegitimately stolen by people not worthy to be considered real Americans. While the dehumanizing way he talks about immigrants as in (13) or (17) could be interpreted as mere trash-talk or acting tough, his willingness to question the validity of some Americans' citizenship should raise concerns for its nationalist undertones, for example, when he was questioning Cruz's citizenship during the sixth GOP Debate (March 14, 2016) or that of children born on US soil to undocumented parents in (18).[5]

(18) How crazy - 7.5% of all births in U.S. are to illegal immigrants,
over 300,000 babies per year. This must stop. Unaffordable and not right!
(@realDonaldTrump, August 21, 2015)

Within the zero-sum resource entitlement belief of folk immigration, US citizenship—and its concomitant safety, wages, jobs, and "Great[ness]"—is a precious resource that only some Americans are entitled to. Those "300,000 babies," who are definitely US citizens, are simply an "unaffordable" percentage of newborns. For Trump, this drain on "resources" (14) and "safe[ty]" (15) is yet another example of what is "not right!" or "Bad!" (2): that good Americans are "not being treated right . . . properly" (6), or "fairly" (5), and are being put at risk of "LOS[ING] this country" (1).

Trump argues along the lines of folk immigration in order to reduce the complexity of the debate. By dehumanizing immigrants and generating contempt for them and their offspring as nothing but criminals, Trump attempts to discard possible counterarguments to his policies, even the US Constitution that defines citizenship in legal terms. In doing so, Trump's supporters, those "best and finest" (13), can feel assured that his tough talk and aggressive actions will "Make America Great Again" for "our" team.

8.6 Discussion and Conclusion

Without a doubt, Trump's strategy of speaking to the electorate through "folk" knowledges and as spectators of a competition helped him to differentiate himself from the other candidates in the 2016 presidential election. Using a WARLIKE COMPETITION metaphor, Trump would take the certainty of outcome in his favor for granted, conceptualize rules, officials, and other competitors as an ENEMY or OPPOSING FORCE, and invoke the value judgments of admiration and contempt within the cognitive frames of VICTORY and DEFEAT. In doing so, he was able to boil complex issues like terrorism, see example (8), or immigration, see example (13), down to a simplified folk theory of how the world is supposed to work: a zero-sum game with only one proper outcome, a belief that 'victory is only right when it is Our team's.' For a competitor with this WARLIKE mindset, a loss is not simply failing to achieve the game's goal or being bested by an opponent, it is rather having bad calls hamper their game, or even having a game "stolen" from them, as Trump claimed Cruz did in the Iowa caucus, see example (2). As it seems, anything that stands in the way of victory, admiration, and indeed America's supposed exceptionalism and supremacy is an immoral outcome brought about by others not understanding or accepting how the world is supposed to work. This particular sentiment gives the fullest explanation to Trump's claim that Cruz's "stealing" his Iowa caucus win was "Bad!," see (2). Trump's strong reaction does not appear to stem from either the possibility that Cruz had legitimately defeated him or that Cruz may have cheated to win, but rather, that he was denied his due victory, which, in his view, had already been granted to him by "all of the polls."

This belief in 'our rightful victory' is indicative of the shift in zero-sum thinking from resource scarcity, in which one win entails one loss, to a resource entitlement belief, in which victory is our due and anything less is an illegitimate theft. In a neutral competition, there is one reward, for example, first place or (in the political domain) the presidency, which only one competitor may attain by meeting the challenges more successfully than their opponents. In a warlike competition, respect and admiration, or a sense of self-worth, become rewards only the in-group can legitimately possess; experiencing the agony of defeat and contempt for weakness is simply unacceptable.

Using the tools of conceptual metaphor theory, it has been possible to demonstrate one way in which Trump's rhetoric has been unique during the pre-election speeches and tweets. The frequent use of the WARLIKE subdomain of COMPETITION reveals an underlying ideological core that accounts for his repeated negative appraisals of his opponents, his continual adulation for himself and his supporters, and ultimately his reduction of complex policies down to the simple choice that *either we WIN this election, or we are going to LOSE this country*!

Notes

1. Note that, following the conventions of conceptual metaphor theory, references to metaphorical concepts will be given in small capitals.
2. The prefix *de-* in the term *decompetition* as coined by Shields and Bremeier (2011: 33) is supposed to transport the sense of 'striving *against*.'
3. See also Degani and Onysko, this volume, for Trump's discourse on environmental issues and his use of conceptual metaphors in this context.
4. The antecedent of "they" is ambiguous. It may be "people chanting death to the USA" or perhaps "terrorists" or "Islam" from moderator Jake Tapper's immediate question for Trump or from a previous question to another candidate, John Kasich, respectively. On the issue of vague pronominal references see also Ronan and Schneider as well as Björkenstam and Grigonytė (this volume).
5. Note that Trump's arguments have no legal foundation. Cruz's mother is a US citizen by birth, which guarantees his US citizenship despite being born in Canada. Children born on US soil, regardless of their parents' status, are granted US citizenship at birth by the Fourteenth Amendment of the Constitution.

References

Bar-Lev, Zev (2007), "Reframing Moral Politics," *Journal of Language and Politics*, 6 (3): 459–74.

Brown, Brendan (2019), *Trump Twitter Archive*. Available online: http://www.trumptwitterarchive.com/archive (accessed February 10, 2020).

Burleigh, Tyler (2016), "'Your Gain Is My Loss': An Examination of Zero-Sum Thinking with Love in Multi-Partner Romantic Relationships and with Grades in the University Classroom" PhD diss., The University of Guelph, Ontario, Canada.

Cisneros, Josue D. (2008), "Contaminated Communities: The Metaphor of 'Immigrant as Pollutant' in Media," *Rhetoric and Public Affairs*, 11 (4): 569–601.

Cudd, Ann E. (2007), "Sporting Metaphors: Competition and the Ethos of Capitalism," *Journal of Philosophy of Sport*, 34 (1): 52–67.

FrameNet (2001), "Competition," *FrameNet*, November 21. Available online: https://framenet2.icsi.berkeley.edu/fnReports/data/frame/Competition.xml (accessed February 10, 2020).

Hamington, Maurice (2008), "Business Is Not a Game: The Metaphoric Fallacy," *Journal of Business Ethics*, 86 (4): 473–84.

Hernández, Carlos A.P. (2013), "The Constitutive Role of Emotions in the Discursive Construction of the 'People': A Look into Obama's 2008 'Race Speech,'" *Signs and Society*, 1 (2): 273–96.

Johnson, Mark and George Lakoff (2002), "Why Cognitive Linguistics Requires Embodied Realism," *Cognitive Linguistics*, 13 (3): 245–63.

Kil, Sang H. (2014), "A Diseased Body Politic: Nativist Discourse and the Imagined Whiteness of the USA," *Cultural Studies*, 28 (2): 177–98.

Koth, Anthony (2019), "Framing the 2016 Election: Politicians, Parties, and Perspectives," PhD diss., Rice University, Houston, TX.

Kövecses, Zoltán (2010), *Metaphor: A Practical Introduction*, 2nd edn, New York: Oxford University Press.
Lakoff, George (2002), *Moral Politics: How Liberals and Conservatives Think*, 2nd edn, Chicago, IL: University of Chicago Press.
Lakoff, George (2004), *Don't Think of an Elephant! Know Your Values and Frame the Debate: The Essential Guide for Progressives*, White River Junction, VT: Chelsea Green Publishing Company.
Lakoff, George, Jane Espenson, and Alan Schwartz (1991), *Master Metaphor List*, 2nd edn, Berkeley. Available online: http://araw.mede.uic.edu/~alansz/metaphor/METAPHOR LIST.pdf (accessed February 11, 2020).
Lakoff, George and Mark Johnson (1980), *Metaphors We Live By*, Chicago: University of Chicago Press.
Lakoff, George and Mark Turner (1989), *More than Cool Reason: A Field Guide to Poetic Metaphor*, Chicago, IL: University of Chicago Press.
Lizardo, Omar (2012), "The Conceptual Bases of Metaphors of Dirt and Cleanliness in Moral and Non-Moral Reasoning," *Cognitive Linguistics*, 23 (2): 367–93.
MetaNet Metaphor Wiki (2014), "Frame: Competition," *MetaNet Metaphor Wiki*. Available online: https://metaphor.icsi.berkeley.edu/pub/en/index.php/Frame:Competition (accessed February 10, 2020).
MetaNet Metaphor Wiki (2016), "Frame: War," *MetaNet Metaphor Wiki*. Available online: https://metaphor.icsi.berkeley.edu/pub/en/index.php/Frame:War (accessed February 10, 2020).
Musolff, Andreas (2006), "Metaphor Scenarios in Public Discourse," *Metaphor and Symbol*, 21 (1): 23–38.
Quinonez, Erika Sabrina (2018), "(Un)Welcome to America: A Critical Discourse Analysis of Anti-Immigrant Rhetoric in Trump's Speeches and Conservative Mainstream Media," MA diss., California State University, San Bernardino, CA.
Rayson, Paul and Roger Garside (2000), "Comparing Corpora Using Frequency Profiling," *Proceedings of the Workshop on Comparing Corpora*, 9: 1-6.
Rubin, Paul H. (2003), "Folk Economics," *Southern Economic Journal*, 70 (1): 157–71.
Santa Ana, Otto (1999), "'Like an Animal I Was Treated': Anti-Immigrant Metaphor in US Public Discourse," *Discourse & Society*, 10 (2): 191–224.
Shields, David and Brenda Bredemeier (2011), "Contest, Competition, and Metaphor," *Journal of the Philosophy of Sport*, 38 (1): 27–38.
Stamenković, Ivan (2017), "Stamping out ISIS: Metaphorical Expressions about Terrorism in Donald Trump's Campaign Speeches," *Facta Universitatis, Series: Linguistics and Literature*, 15 (2): 245–62.
Suits, Bernard (2018), "The Elements of Sport," in William J. Morgan (ed.), *Ethics in Sport*, 3rd edn, 33–44, Champaign, IL: Human Kinetics.
Swedberg, Richard (2018), "Folk Economics and Its Role in Trump's Presidential Campaign: An Exploratory Study," *Theory and Society*, 47 (1): 1–36.
Tännsjö, Torbjörn (1998), "Is Our Admiration for Sports Heroes Fascistoid?," *Journal of the Philosophy of Sport*, 25 (1): 23–34.

9

Silence and Denial

Trump's Discourse on the Environment

Marta Degani and Alexander Onysko

9.1 Introduction

Trump has not been hiding the fact that he is an explicit disbeliever in global warming, notwithstanding scientific evidence of melting ice caps, receding glaciers, thawing permafrost soil, and rising sea levels as well as the statistics about record-high temperatures globally accruing in the last few decades (e.g., Oreskes 2004, Hansen et al. 2010). A telling example of his stance on global warming can be gleaned from the following tweet:

(1) In the beautiful Midwest, windchill temperatures are reaching minus 60 degrees, the coldest ever recorded. In coming days, expected to get even colder. People can't last outside even for minutes. What the hell is going on with Global Waming [sic]? Please come back fast, we need you! (@realDonaldTrump, January 29, 2018)

Denial of this evidence paired with a lack of acknowledging the human contribution to global warming through the emission of fossil fuels can be expected to have a deep impact on the type of policies to be implemented and actions to be taken with regard to the environment—not to consider their implications for our society. Suffice it to say at this point that Trump has attempted many times to undo environmental laws and regulations from the Obama era, which has attracted a lot of public attention and was the target of media commentary. The *New York Times*, for instance, refers to eighty-three environmental rules rolled back under Trump (Popovich, Albeck-Ripka, and Kendra 2019) and *National Geographic* discusses fifteen ways in which the Trump administration has changed environmental policies, providing examples that testify to an impact on clean air, water, wild life, and public lands (Gibbens 2019).

While Trump's denial of global warming has been criticized and questioned on other occasions such as during a recent CBS interview (Stahl 2018), from a linguistic point of view, it is particularly interesting to investigate not only the argumentative construction of his stance but also the linguistic features that he employs to structure his discourse on the environment and related topics. Accordingly, the present contribution aims to shed light on these aspects of Trump's discourse on the environment. More specifically, the study adopts a discourse analytical approach to investigate Trump's framing of the environment. Critical attention is given to his lexical choices and to his discursive and rhetorical strategies, including the use of metaphors.

The data for analysis consist of presidential remarks from the "energy & environment" section of the White House Issues website.[1] These remarks are representative of Trump's public position as the president of the United States. From an outside perspective, lumping together energy and the environment appears as a slightly awkward match, as concerns with the environment are usually much larger than those of the energy sector. In fact, as this chapter will show, the first mention of energy in this combination alludes to Trump's priority to relate energy (consumption) to the US economy. By way of comparison, it is also interesting to observe that under the Obama administration, the White House website presented "advancing American energy," "climate change," and "our environment" as separate topic areas, and listed an "energy and environment" section as a virtual container exclusively for media contents (https://obamawhitehouse.archives.gov/energy).

To put Trump's discourse in a wider frame that explains its embedding in a specific political context, this chapter will first discuss environmental policymaking in the United States. After that, section 9.3 will provide some insight into major ideological framings that characterize US politics. Looking at Republican and Democratic ideologies helps to ground some of Trump's opinions and lines of argumentation that go against environmental concerns. Section 9.4 outlines the data of the president's remarks as published on the official White House website and the methods of analysis. The analysis of Trump's framing of the environment in terms of key topics, lexical choices, discursive strategies, and metaphors will follow in section 9.5. Special attention will be given to the speech announcing the US withdrawal from the Paris Climate Agreement. The general picture emerging from the analysis will be briefly summarized in the concluding section.

9.2 Environmental Policymaking in the United States

American presidents' authority over the bureaucracy and their related control over the implementation of laws give them the power to shape environmental policy. Thus, US commanders in chief can drive legislative agendas for protecting the environment and preserving the planet or they can block existing legislation through their veto power, pursue environmental deregulation, and issue executive orders that encourage the exploitation of natural resources. Presidents also have unilateral authority under specific statutes. A case in point is the Antiquity Act (1906), which gives presidents the authority to proclaim federal land as national monuments (Klyza and Sousa 2013).

Since the environment is currently challenged in multiple and interrelated ways (see EAA Web Team 2016), pro-environment action can be expected to be a top priority for political leaders across the globe. Scientists also warn that carbon emissions are destroying our planet (Muntean et al. 2019) and the constant rise of global average temperatures could have significant repercussions on human health in the near future (Balbus et al. 2016). Furthermore, there are prospects of increasing drought zones (Center for Climate and Energy Solutions 2020), and rising sea levels will afflict island inhabitants and communities in low-lying coastal areas (NOAA 2019, Gray and Merzdorf 2019). Even though the environment is in a critical state at present, current policymaking in the United States—the world's second largest contributor to carbon dioxide emissions—does not attempt to curb US production of greenhouse gases. Since Donald Trump took office in January 2017, his actions did nothing to reassure environmentalists' concerns. From the beginning, the new president has sent clear messages about the environment not being a priority in his political agenda. First, his cabinet appointments have reinforced ties with fossil-fuel industry and supported climate change denial (Hejny 2018). Scott Pruitt, attorney general of Oklahoma, an outspoken denier of climate change who had formerly fought against the Environmental Protection Agency (EPA) in support of fossil-fuel industry, became the head of the EPA. In a similar fashion, former Texas governor Rick Perry, an ally of the fossil-fuel industry, was appointed as the Head of the Department of Energy, the same agency he had promised to eliminate as a former Republican presidential contender. The nominee for secretary of the interior, a department that is in charge of protecting federal lands and resources, was Ryan Zynke, a man in favor of increased shale extraction and oil pipelines. While the actual list of Trump's anti-environmental political appointees is longer than this, his early picks for leading functions in the administration were first signs of his political vision and priorities in relation to the environment.

In addition to this, Trump also issued several executive orders addressing environmental regulations and dismantling Obama's climate policies (see https://www.whitehouse.gov/issues/energy-environment/). For example, in the opening of his "presidential executive order on promoting energy independence and economic growth" (March 28, 2017), Trump states that it is in the general interest of the nation to avoid "regulatory burdens that unnecessarily encumber energy production, constrain economic growth, and prevent job creation." Through executive action, Trump also initiated the repeal of the Clean Power Plan, which was part of Obama's climate change policy and was designed to significantly reduce US carbon emissions in the power sector. Trump's executive authority also involved releasing restrictions and granting permits for the construction of two major pipeline projects: the Keystone XL pipeline and the Dakota Access Pipeline.

At an international level, the US commitment to fight climate change and mitigate its effects in the years to come is no longer upheld. Irrespective of the communal efforts put together by the 196 nations (including the United States) that adopted the UNFCCC Paris Climate Agreement in 2015, Trump announced his intention to withdraw from it in June 2017 (the earliest effective date of withdrawal is November 2020).

The general picture might already appear as complex enough, and yet an additional element plays an important role in environmental policymaking in the United States: the increasing polarization of politics. As illustrated in McCarty, Poole, and Rosenthal (2006), partisan polarization has been present since the mid-1970s, but the phenomenon has become more and more tangible since the 1990s. The Republican and the Democratic Parties have never been as divided as nowadays. Furthermore, each of the two groups in the political spectrum tends to be more homogeneous, and most of the Republicans are turning more conservative. The rise of the Tea Party in 2009 combined with a markedly reduced number of moderates in the Republican Party translates into an overall anti-environmental political orientation. If we look at the League of Conservation Voters National Environmental Scorecard for 2016, we can get an idea of the type of partisan split characterizing US politics nowadays (see Hejny 2018). This scorecard measures pro-environment votes in Congress by giving to each of its members a score on a scale from zero to one hundred, in which one hundred equals a totality of pro-environment votes. Hejny reports that "[i]n 2016, the average score for Senate Democrats was 96, and for House Democrats, 94. The average score for Republicans in the Senate was 14, and in the House, 5" (Hejny 2018: 197). These numbers nourish the expectation that the current Republican leadership will not put environmental concerns high on their agenda. The next section will shed some more light on the ideological background beliefs and values that structure Republican and Democratic thinking.

9.3 Ideological Divides, Diverging Political Agendas, Different Framings

In the North American context, the debate on politics and ideology has been characterized by a few key publications. In his book *Culture Wars* (1991), the well-known sociologist James Davison Hunter put forward a theory about opposing views in American culture that has attracted a lot of attention among intellectuals (especially in the fields of political science and sociology). Hunter refers to a "values divide" in US culture, which he explains in terms of cultural oppositions motivated by diverging moral priorities that also affect political orientation and behavior. Other scholars embraced Hunter's theory of increasing cultural and political polarization in the United States (see Bowman 2010). According to Hunter, American people's visions of morality and moral authority are led by orthodox or progressive idea(l)s as opposites on a continuum of moral worldviews. Orthodoxy is defined as a "commitment on the part of adherents to an external, definable and transcendent authority" (Hunter 1991: 44). This authority defines all the boundaries between right and wrong, good and bad, proper and improper. For progressivism, on the other hand, "moral authority tends to be defined by the spirit of the modern age, a spirit of rationalism and subjectivism" (Hunter 1991: 44). In this case, moral authority is transient and is linked to personal experience and rationality. When Hunter applies these notions to the political domain, he sees moral orthodoxy as coherent with conservative thinking and progressive morality as in line with a liberal political agenda. In politics, Hunter's "culture wars" translate into morally motivated divisions between Republicans and Democrats. As he points out,

> [e]ach side operates from within its own constellation of values, interests and assumptions. At the center of each are two distinct conceptions of moral

authority—two different ways of apprehending reality, of ordering experience, of making moral judgments. Each side of the cultural divide, then, speaks with a different moral vocabulary. Each side operates out of a different mode of debate and persuasion. Each side represents the tendencies of a separate and competing moral galaxy. They are, indeed, "worlds apart." (Hunter 1991: 128)

Hunter's words suggest that moral inclinations not only have an influence on people's perception and understanding of reality, but they also affect the use of language as well as the type of argumentation strategies and rhetorical devices that are adopted.

As mentioned earlier, these ideas have been influential in and beyond academic circles. In particular, it is in the domain of cognitive linguistics that one can find the closest connection to Hunter's theory. Lakoff's ideas on the relation between politics and morality as first expressed in his book *Moral Politics* (1996) appear to complement from a linguistic point of view Hunter's sociological investigation of a cultural divide in the United States. Lakoff elaborates a theory based on metaphorical cognitive models that account for conceptual differences between American conservatives and liberals. While Hunter looked at the cleavage between conservatives and liberals as a chiefly cultural and social phenomenon, Lakoff considers the conceptual-linguistic dimension of the phenomenon and focuses on framing, rhetorical habits, and lexical choices. Lakoff's discussion revolves around divergent conceptualizations and opposing metaphorical systems that are informed by different moral priorities and are reflected in language in multiple ways (e.g., frames, narratives, metaphors, and lexical preferences). Lakoff (1996) provides an explanation of the political behavior and linguistic habits characterizing prototypical conservative as opposed to liberal Americans in terms of two divergent models of political morality—the Strict Father (SF) and the Nurturant Parent (NP). While the SF model fits the conservatives and is associated with the Republican Party, the NP model coheres with the liberals and is linked to the Democratic Party.

This theory has been influential and has stimulated further research in linguistics (see Ahrens 2011; Ahrens and Yat Mei Lee 2009; Cienki 2004, 2005a, 2005b; Degani 2015) and other disciplines including communication science and social psychology (see Deason and Gonzales 2012; Moses and Gonzales 2015; Ohl et al. 2013). Given the relevance of Lakoff's theory for investigating the relation between ideological leaning, political behavior, and linguistic framing in US politics, this approach is adopted here as a general theoretical framework. Drawing on Lakoff's seminal work (1996), the present study mainly refers to Lakoff (2010) since this later publication investigates discourse on the environment from the same theoretical vantage point of an SF versus NP model.

As Lakoff (1996, 2010) points out, several conservative moral considerations act against environmentalism. First, one needs to be aware of how nature is conceptualized. The conservative moral view entails the notions of moral order and moral authority, according to which man stands above nature. The basic idea is that humans are superior to and have dominion over nature, and this justifies the exploitation of the environment. Nature is seen as being at the service of humanity, as an important resource for human prosperity and profit.

Second, the market is viewed as the highest moral authority as far as the environment is concerned. The market is morally entitled to decide on courses of action. Hence, political agendas that promote few or almost no regulations, taxes, and protections for workers are justified. Along analogous lines of reasoning, the support for renewable energy development and environmental-friendly technology as well as the creation of new jobs in the green sector ideologically figure as instances of governmental interference in the market. If market principles rule and constant accretion is the goal, then the environment comes second to the economy.

An example of a market principle that guides environmental decisions is cost–benefit analysis. This principle requires quantifying in monetary terms the costs and the benefits of a proposed regulation. The regulation is justified only in cases when the benefits clearly exceed the costs. Since most regulations concerning the environment are difficult to measure in straightforward numerical terms, conservatives can use cost–benefit analysis to block regulation aimed at reducing climate change. At the same time, complex systemic processes such as climate change go beyond simple explanations of direct cause and effect, which leaves more room for potentially alternative outcomes and implications. This space can be used by conservatives to question scientific evidence on climate change (cf. Lakoff 2010).

As mentioned earlier, Lakoff describes prototypical progressives as standing on the opposite side of this ideologically driven political spectrum. The progressive moral view gives priority to nurturance over discipline, and becoming nurturers of others is seen as an accomplishment in life. Empathy as the capacity to relate to and to project oneself onto others extends to the environment too, and it is expected to generate an attitude of care, respect, and protection toward our natural surroundings.

Improving the environment then also demands forms of personal commitment in terms of, for instance, conserving energy and recycling, whenever possible. Consonant with this moral worldview, liberal politics is in favor of environmental preservation by making major investments in renewable energy and by promoting regulation to keep control of threats such as global warming, air/water pollution, and (nuclear) waste. Thus, in sharp contrast to the prototypical conservative agenda, the market and its principles do not dictate progressive political action, and liberal politicians see the government as essential for improving environmental conditions.

In addition to informing political action, ideologies also find expression in the discourse of politicians. As stated by Lakoff (1996, 2010), conservative rhetoric on the environment is very different from that of progressives. Lakoff (2010) explains that framing environmental reality in line with conservative moral values involves, for instance, describing EPA regulations as threats to the most vulnerable sections of society and associating them with large job losses. For conservative rhetoric, it would also be common to silence the fact that factory farming has negative effects on our environment and figures among the chief contributors to global warming.

Besides these observations, Lakoff (2010) points out that Republicans—with the help of think tanks—have been very successful in shaping the public discourse on the environment in the United States. By way of exemplification, he refers to a well-known language adviser of the Republicans, Franz Luntz, who suggested to reframe the public discourse on the environment by replacing the expression *global warming* with *climate change* (Lakoff 2010: 71). The reason for that "rebranding" might lie in the fact that *climate change* is a more general (i.e., vaguer) term compared to *global warming*. While the nominal participle *warming* has a processual meaning, *change* is a static category label. In addition, change is not in itself a negative notion and can also evoke connotations of something beneficial. Numerical evidence from the Corpus of Contemporary American English (COCA, Davies 2008–) confirms the more frequent use of *climate change* (36.35 tokens per million words from 2015 to 2019 versus *global warming* 6.74 tokens per million words from 2015 to 2019).

Against this background of ideologically motivated divergences between Republican and Democratic political actions and discourses, we can consider Hejny (2018: 198), who writes, "the Trump Administration's actions on the environment can be seen as an evolution of the Republican Party's (anti-)environmental ideology." Hejny also refers to specific political strategies that appear as coherent to the Republican, ideologically driven, environmental policy. They include "cutting regulations, promoting cost–benefit analysis, appointing pro-industry heads of environmental agencies, reducing enforcement, and rhetorically challenging environmentalism" (Hejny 2018: 197–8). As Hejny makes clear, President Reagan, who can be seen as setting a clear model for subsequent Republican presidencies, used all of these strategies. According to Hejny, Trump not only follows Reagan's example, but his call for deregulation has become stronger and his anti-environmental discourse is both harsher and characterized by "an explicit attack on the environmental administrative state" (Hejny 2018: 204).

There is yet further proof of Trump's anti-environmental stance as expressed in his rhetoric. The president's concern for the environment is stated unequivocally in his notorious claim that climate change is a "hoax," which he reiterated during his run for the presidency in 2016. Clearly, once climate change is presented as fraudulent, it soon turns into a topic not worthy of any public discussion. This silencing strategy indeed proved successful since, as reported by the Pew Research Center (2016), the issue of the environment only scored eleventh among the relevant issues for voters during the 2016 presidential campaign. The environment received a low salience ranking after the economy, terrorism, foreign policy, health care, gun policy, immigration, social security, education, Supreme Court appointments, treatment of racial and ethnic minorities, and trade policy. The fact that EPA websites have been altered under the Trump Administration to remove discussions on climate change is in line with this strategy (Milman and Morris 2017).

The chapter will now proceed with a more fine-grained linguistic analysis targeted at Trump's official remarks on the topic area "energy and environment" in order to identify specific ways of his (non)dealing with environmental issues.

9.4 Data and Methodology

In order to investigate Trump's official discourse on the environment, we consulted the government website "Energy & Environment" (https://www.whitehouse.gov/issues/energy-environment/). The website collects all presidential communications related to the topics of energy and the environment. It also contains a range of different text types, among which "remarks" are particularly interesting and were therefore selected for analysis. A remark is an instance of a political speech, and as such it can be defined as "a coherent stream of spoken language that is usually prepared for delivery by a speaker to an audience for a purpose on a political occasion" (Charteris-Black 2014: xiii). Thus, a remark draws on a written draft, but it is also a text that is performed in public and later transcribed in a way that (semi)authentically reproduces its oral delivery. Beyond the customary greetings and thanking formulas, a remark also contains direct addresses to the people in the audience as well as their responses. The remarks analyzed in this chapter are delivered by the president for important events such as the signing of executive orders or the announcement of government measures that have an impact on the areas of energy and environment. These remarks can be classified as chiefly deliberative, that is, as policymaking (Charteris-Black 2014: xiii), since they provide the president with an argumentative space to give reasons and convince his listeners of his policies.

Since the remarks are event-based, they are spread unevenly throughout the period of investigation (January 2017 to mid-June 2019), with the year 2018 not containing any instances. Table 9.1 provides information on the occasions, the dates of delivery, and the length (word count) of the remarks on environmental and energy-related issues given by Trump.

In many of his remarks, Trump calls upon other people such as workers and other state officials and representatives to comment on the proposed plans or legislative actions. Apart from the title, date, and location of delivery, all words not uttered by

Table 9.1 Details of Trump's Remarks on Energy and Environment

Occasion	Date of delivery	Word count
Remarks by President Trump at Signing of H. J. Resolution 38	February 16, 2017	1,015
Remarks by the President in TransCanada Keystone XL Pipeline Announcement	March 24, 2017	665
Remarks by President Trump at Signing of Executive Order to Create Energy Independence	March 28, 2017	1,580
Statement by President Trump on the Paris Climate Accord	June 1, 2017	2,931
Remarks by President Trump and Secretary of Energy Rick Perry at Tribal, State, and Local Energy Roundtable	June 28, 2017	1,204
Remarks by President Trump at the Unleashing American Energy Event	June 29, 2017	2,485
Remarks by President Trump During a Visit to Lake Okeechobee and Herbert Hoover Dike	March 29, 2019	1,575
Remarks by President Trump at Signing of Executive Order on Energy and Infrastructure	Crosby, TX	April 10, 2019	2,275
Remarks by President Trump on Promoting Energy Infrastructure and Economic Growth	Hackberry, LA	May 14, 2019	6,084
Remarks by President Trump on Renewable Energy; Council Bluffs Iowa	June 11, 2019a	4,790
Remarks by President Trump Before Marine One Departure	June 11, 2019b	3,041
Total		27,645

Trump were removed from the texts. The numbers in Table 9.1 show the count of Trump's words per speech.

In light of the adopted discourse analytical approach, and in consideration of the overall amount of data under investigation, the orientation of the study is primarily qualitative, even though some quantitative data are also provided. All texts were subjected to close reading by both authors.

The analysis is structured in two levels. The macro-level of analysis consists in identifying ways in which Trump lexically frames his discourse on the environment. Attention is devoted to singling out preferred and dispreferred lexical choices as well as discussing examples of typical environment-related vocabulary not to be found in the remarks (i.e., negative lexical evidence). For this part of the analysis, the texts were processed with Wordsmith Tools. At the micro-level, the analysis was twofold. On the one hand, we focused on discursive strategies that sustain Trump's framing of the environment and occur across his speeches. On the other hand, we investigated the conceptual metaphors employed by Trump to refer to the Paris Climate Agreement. This last analysis was conducted on the Statement by President Trump on the Paris Climate Accord (June 1, 2017).

9.5 Analysis

This section provides a threefold perspective on Trump's remarks on energy and environment. A first look at how Trump frames energy and environment in terms of topic selection and lexical choices is given in section 9.5.1. This is followed in section 9.5.2 by a close-up on a range of discursive strategies that he employs. Trump's announcement of the US withdrawal from the Paris Agreement, which led to international controversy, is a special case among the remarks. Section 9.5.3 focuses on this important speech and analyzes Trump's line of argumentation and his metaphorical depiction of the Paris Agreement.

9.5.1 Energy and Environment: Framing through Topic Selection and Lexical Choices

When reading Trump's remarks, the first striking observation concerns the imbalance between the mentions of *energy* and *environment*. Numerical evidence in our corpus shows that the term *environment* is used 6 times while *energy* occurs 149 times (uses of the words *energy* and *environment* in proper nouns, for example, *Sempra Energy*, and titles, for example, *Secretary of Energy*, were excluded from the count). Thus, while environmental concerns represent a marginal topic in the texts, Trump highlights the need for energy production and transportation in order to "fuel" the economy in all of his remarks. At the same time, Trump's conception of energy is extremely limited and can be captured in three words: *coal* (33 hits), *gas* (33), and *oil* (29). These fossil fuels are portrayed as the energy resources on which the country should count now and in the future. The quote in (2) exemplifies this discursive focus.

(2) We're here today to usher in a new American energy policy.... Americans' quality of life was diminished by the idea that energy resources were too scarce to support our people.... The truth is that we have near-limitless supplies of energy in our country. Powered by new innovation and technology, we are now on the cusp of a true energy revolution. Our country is blessed with extraordinary energy abundance, which we didn't know of, even five years ago and certainly ten years ago. We have nearly 100 years' worth of natural gas and more than 250 years' worth of clean, beautiful coal. We are a top producer of petroleum and the number-one producer of natural gas. We have so much more than we ever thought possible. We are really in the driving seat. (June 29, 2017)

For Trump, America's way forward is through the exploitation of these environmentally dangerous resources (coal, oil, and natural gas), and his political actions speak accordingly. This can be seen, for example, in the lifting of restrictions on the production of oil, natural gas, and shale energy, on the completion of oil and gas pipeline projects, and on creating incentives for offshore drilling.

Trump's positive framing of fossil fuels as energy resources is also reinforced by his emphasis on the economic and social benefits that would derive from a continued use of oil, natural gas, and coal. In his rhetoric, Trump establishes a causal link between fossil-fuel exploitation and the economy, which is exemplified in (3).

(3) we will create millions of good American jobs—also, so many energy jobs—and really lead to unbelievable prosperity all throughout our country. (March 28, 2017)

The word *jobs* is used eighty times in the corpus, and it contributes to create an image of the president as the one who will sustain the economy by creating millions of new jobs in the energy sector. Thus, more extensive exploitation of the environment is justified by the prospect of making the economy grow and thrive.

In addition, Trump envisions that American families will benefit from the investment in the fossil-fuel industry. The idea that this will directly affect the lives of American families because it will cut down the costs for fueling cars is transmitted, for instance, in (4). Furthermore, Trump suggests that investing more in fossil fuels would make Americans pay less for heating their houses. This type of argumentation is present in claims such as (5).

(4) The fuel you produce brings down prices at the pump for millions of American drivers. Those savings go straight into the pockets of hardworking families all across our land. (June 11, 2019)
(5) We need help with New York. New York is hurting the country because they're not allowing us to get those pipelines through, and that's why they're paying so much for their heating and all of the things that energy and our energy produces. (April 10, 2019)

Trump's positive framing of fossil fuels also supports his political agenda and his vision of national economic growth. This idea is captured in his key phrase of "energy independence." By relying more and more on American energy resources such as coal, gas, and oil, and by developing the relevant infrastructure for their transportation, the nation is not just reducing its dependence on foreign countries for energy supplies but also securing its leadership in energy production and exportation internationally. While collocations such as *energy production* (7 hits), *energy revolution* (6), *energy infrastructure* (6), *energy industry* (4), *energy wealth* (4), *energy resources* (4), and *energy reserves* (4) are coherent with a conservative ideology and the related exploitative attitude toward the environment, the expression *energy independence* (8) along with *energy dominance* (6) and the concept of economic *sovereignty* (6) describe Trump's ideological approach more accurately. The latter three expressions encapsulate Trump's vision that the United States shall play a leading role globally as a provider of energy and that they shall be independent from other countries. All of that chimes in with the larger picture of the United States as an economic and industrial superpower in the world.

Another distinctive feature of Trump's framing of fossil fuels concerns their depiction via adjectival pre-modification. Frequently, he provides an inaccurate depiction of what these substances really are and what their overuse does to the environment. Collocations such as "clean coal," "clean, beautiful coal," "clean, natural gas," and "clean, beautiful, natural gas" make people believe that he talks about sustainable ways of using energy. These expressions are oxymoronic in that they consist of a combination of contradictory and incongruous words. As such, they are dangerous because they misinform by creating false assumptions. Furthermore, with the exception of *clean coal*, these collocations are unusual in American English and thus appear as characteristic of Trump's own way to talk about energy and the environment. The COCA (Davies 2008–) does not contain any examples of the nominal phrase *clean, beautiful, natural gas*, and only one instance of *clean, beautiful coal*, used by Trump during an interview. The phrase *clean, natural gas* occurs 7 times, first occurrence in 1990, while there are 219 hits for *clean coal*.[2]

When Trump refers to coal, he also affirms that in the recent past "we haven't treated it with the respect it deserves" (February 16, 2017), and he even adopts a belligerent tone when he metaphorically describes his predecessor's concern about coal as Obama's "warfare" against this resource. In Trump's terms, Obama conducted a "war on coal" and, more generally, a "war on American energy," against which he [Trump] now needs to fight fiercely.

This type of argumentation is in line with Trump's conservative (Republican) ideological leaning, according to which Obama attacked a "natural order" (the depletion of natural resources) and this order needs to be restored for the well-being of US citizens. Trump also accuses the previous administration of having blocked the economic development of the nation because of the "job-killing regulations/barriers/restrictions" (nine hits in his remarks) imposed on the use of fossil fuels. This economy-driven interpretation of past environmental regulation motivates Trump's use of another metaphorical expression, *unlock(ing)* (seven hits), to describe his political actions as liberating. Accordingly, Trump talks about "unlocking the restrictions," "unlocking the power of America," "unlocking vast treasures of energy," "unlocking our nation's resources," "unlocking the full oil and gas potential," and so on.

Apart from fossil fuels, the only other energy resource that Trump refers to positively in his speeches, though only once, is nuclear energy. Trump describes nuclear power as producing "clean, renewable, and emissions-free energy" (June 29, 2017). In a way that is reminiscent of his discursive construal of fossil fuels, Trump's approbatory depiction of nuclear energy hides other important aspects related to the use of this resource. In particular, any harmful side effects such as nuclear waste and the pending risk of radioactive pollution appear as discursively silenced by this positive depiction.

As pointed out earlier, Trump's remarks on energy and the environment deal primarily with energy issues, while dismissing environmental concerns. In these texts, many important topics related to the current state of the environment and the need to protect it are muted. Thus, notwithstanding the discursive focus on energy, no mention of methods to reduce energy consumption is made. None of the 149 examples in which the word *energy* is used is about ways, ideas, or proposals for containing, conserving, or saving energy. In a similar fashion, the remarks do not contain any instance of the phrases *green energy* and *thermal energy*.

Further negative lexical evidence (in the sense of missing lexical items) characterizes the depiction of environmental challenges. Selecting from online lists of environment terminology,[3] we found that the following key terms never occur in the remarks: *acid rain, biodiversity loss, climate change, contamination, deforestation, desertification, draught, endangered species, flood, food supplies, fumes, greenhouse effect, heat wave, natural resources depletion, natural resources drain, ozone layer, pollutant, pollution, sea level, sewage, soil degradation, soil erosion, species extinction, waste*, and *water crisis*. The expression *global warming* is mentioned only once and dismissively in the sentence "they were saying it was global warming" (June 11, 2019), an example that will be discussed in the following section. Another low frequency term is *emission*, which occurs three times in the corpus but is looked at critically only once, when the president talks about "emissions-free energy" to refer to nuclear power (see discussion above).

These findings also cohere with the discursive silencing of measures that could be taken to protect the environment. In the corpus, the following words are absent: *biodegradable, biodiversity, conserve, recycle, reuse, solar power/panel, sustain, sustainable, thermal activity, tidal power, wave power*. Furthermore, *reduce/reducing* (6) and *preserve* (1) are never used in relation to the environment, and *renewable* only occurs twice. Wind power, as an example of sustainable and renewable energy, is referred to as *wind* and used three times in the same speech to criticize political opponents and their environmentalist agendas (see section 9.5.2). Notwithstanding this discursive void on many important environmental matters, Trump uses the word *environment* three times in combination with the verb *protect* to describe environmental protection as a political objective, see, for example, (6). He also employs the term *environment* once to denounce environmental rules put forward by his predecessor, see (7), and twice for self-appraisal, see, for example, (8). Trump's actual goals of environmental action are captured in two phrases, *clean air* (two hits) and *clean water* (three), which will be discussed in the next section.

(6) We have to protect the environment. (April 10, 2019)
(7) ... which [clean power plan] would have made the environment less clean (May 14, 2019)
(8) ... as someone who cares deeply about the environment, which I do. (June 1, 2017)

Overall, the speeches provide an image of a president who is a strong supporter of fossil fuels, who does not believe in renewable resources, and who does not address important environmental issues concerning the state of the environment, current environmental challenges, and measures of environmental protection. This silencing of major environmental concerns is compensated with a form of rhetoric that celebrates the potency of an industrial economy based on fossil fuels and honors the imperatives of capital accumulation.

9.5.2 Energy and Environment: Framing through Discursive Strategies

Trump's discourse on the environment is characterized by the use of discursive avoidance strategies. As already pointed out in the preceding section, Trump's lexical preferences and the substantial lack of environment-related vocabulary indicate that many environmental concerns are not given due consideration in his remarks. In fact, most environmental issues are disregarded and this strategic silencing contributes to the creation of a rhetoric of denial. Trump's claims on the environment, and on environmental protection more specifically, serve the function of denying the existence of any environmental problems. Considering problems and offering solutions is a common argumentative strategy that allows speakers to focus on positive aspects of their actions. In the case of Trump's rhetoric, in which environmental problems are portrayed as non-existent, political solutions do not need to be provided, and maintaining the status quo appears as a justified behavior. This strategy is exemplified in (9).

(9) ... we're strongly protecting the environment. We have to protect the environment. The United States has among the very cleanest air and water developments in the world. And also we have the cleanest air and water, they say, in the world. We are the best. And you want that and I want that. I want clean air and beautiful, crystal-clean water. (April 10, 2019)

Through a sequence of short, assertive claims, Trump provides a very positive depiction of the United States' standing on environmental issues. The assertiveness of this message results from the lack of any hedging or mitigating linguistic devices. Trump's personal opinions on the excellent conditions of the environment in the United States are presented as indisputable facts (see the use of the verbs *have* and *be*). Furthermore, the tone of his message about the current political engagement with environmental protection is encomiastic (i.e., praising), and this is conveyed through the combined use of a manner adverb (*strongly* to connote the act of protecting) and three superlatives (*very cleanest, cleanest, the best* to evaluate US air and water, and the nation at large).

At the same time, Trump's framing of environmental protection in (9) masks the actual complexity of environmental protection by making people believe that protecting the environment means caring about air and water exclusively. In addition to this, the reality of air and water pollution is hidden since Trump's words describe US air and water as the *cleanest*. Thus, the selective focus on air and water combined with the positive evaluation of their status appears as further instances of denial both in relation to the scope of environmental protection and with respect to the current conditions of air and water. This passage also shows how Trump's rhetoric of denial is typically sustained by discursive strategies of positive (self-)presentation, also of the United States as a whole (e.g., *the world's leader in environmental protection*, June 1, 2017).

Overall, this discursive orchestration also sustains a politics of non-intervention, in other words, maintaining the status quo is rhetorically justified. Accordingly, the texts neither describe nor allude to possible ways to achieve these objectives concretely. Interestingly enough, the vacuity that characterizes Trump's discourse on environmental protection contrasts with the accuracy transmitted by the constant use of numbers for measuring aspects of American economic growth, as in (10). The rhetorical appeal to logos (rational thinking) that is achieved in this case by providing numbers to support the argumentation and hence be persuasive is a further discursive indication of the priorities in his political agenda and the areas of concrete political intervention.

(10) We've added $3.3 trillion in stock market value to our economy, and more than a million private sector jobs. (June 1, 2017)

As scientific research demonstrates, investing in renewable resources (e.g., solar power, wind, rain, tides, waves, and geothermal activity) represents one tangible way of protecting the environment and of incentivizing economic growth that is driven by technological progress and work opportunities in emerging sectors of energy production (see, for example, Yi 2014). Trump's model of the economy, however, is reminiscent of the age of industrialization when fossil fuels turned into major energy resources. What is more, Trump even presents renewable forms of energy as major impediments to the economic development of the nation, see (11).

(11) At 1 percent growth, renewable sources of energy can meet some of our domestic demand, but at 3 or 4 percent growth, which I expect, we need all forms of available American energy, or our country will be at grave risk of brownouts and blackouts, our businesses will come to a halt in many cases, and the American family will suffer the consequences in the form of lost jobs and a very diminished quality of life. (June 1, 2017)

Similar to (9), Trump's words in (11) pursue a discursive strategy of positive (self-) presentation as a form of denial. The prospects on the economic growth of the nation provide the rationale for negating support to renewable energies. Renewables are portrayed as inadequate resources given the impetus of US economic progress. Then, President Trump adopts a rhetoric of fear ("we need all forms of available American energy") that is based on a slippery slope argument. The slippery slope argument, also referred to as slippery slope fallacy (cf. Walton 2015), consists in asserting that a relatively small first step or action will lead to either a series of (negative) events or a (negative) result. In (11), Trump constructs his message against renewable resources by stating that if renewables were used as major energy resources, there would be a chain of negative events following: brownouts and blackouts, businesses having to come to a halt, job losses, and diminished quality of life for American families. The series of dramatic scenarios that are foreseen serve the general purpose of raising fear in the audience at the idea that other forms of energy could supplant fossil fuels. In addition, emotional engagement is also triggered by the use of emotionally charged language (*grave risk, suffer, very diminished quality*) to describe the bad consequences that would follow if renewables were taken as prime energy sources.

Trump's discourse on renewables is dismissive, and the potential usefulness of these resources for the future economic well-being of the nation is denied. Wind power is the only instance of a renewable energy that is mentioned (only once), and it is objected to because of its presumed "collateral" effects. As Trump claims,

(12) They [politicians in favor of The Green New Deal] don't like anything. They don't know what they like. They sort of like wind, even though it kills all the birds. You want to see a bird cemetery? Go under a windmill sometime. You'll see the saddest—you got every type of bird. You know, in California, you go to jail for five years if you kill a bald eagle. If you go under a windmill, you see them all over the place. Not a good situation. But that's what they were counting on: wind. And when the wind doesn't blow, you don't watch television that night. Your wife said "What the hell did you get me into with this Green New Deal, Charlie?" (May 14, 2019)

As (12) illustrates, Trump's argument against wind power is built upon discursive strategies of denigration and dissimulation. The quote starts with disparaging comments about the president's political opponents who are in favor of green energy ("they don't like anything, they don't know what they like, they sort of like wind"). In a less direct manner, Trump also accuses his political adversaries of incongruity when he refers to their support for endangered species (the bald eagle) in California (a typical stronghold of the Democrats) and contrasts this attitude to their allowing of bird cemeteries under windmills. This belittlement of wind power supporters is accompanied by a trivialization of the topic, which is achieved through dissimulation strategies.

First, wind (power) is described as the cause of birds' death. Second, wind power is portrayed as an unreliable source of energy because it cannot guarantee constant electricity. In both cases, Trump relies on the strategy of storytelling, a common rhetorical device to create an emotional engagement (i.e., a pathos appeal) in order to bring his political message across and win the support of his audience. Furthermore, the emotional effect of storytelling is amplified by the use of emphatic, emotionally charged expressions such as *the saddest, every type of bird, all over the place,* and *what the hell.*

Like *wind power, global warming* is mentioned only once—in passing and dismissively—when Trump explains that the actual cause of forest fires is bad forest management, a problem he claims to have addressed promptly and effectively in California. As he asserts,

(13) Remember I went to California? I saw something that nobody has ever seen. It was like a blowtorch. It was 80-mile-an-hour winds and the death and destruction was incredible. And I said, "You need forest management." They were saying it was global warming. Could have had something to do with it. But you need forest management. You can't let 15 and 20 years of leaves and broken trees and deadwood—that after the first 18 months is dry as a bone—you can't let that be there. You have to clean it. You have to clean those floors of the forest. And you're going to see a big difference. And, actually, they mocked me. They said, "Oh, what's he doing? He's talking about sweeping the floors." Well, I don't use the word "sweeping," but you have to have forest management. And all of a sudden, about four weeks after that happened, they learned I was right. (June 11, 2019a)

At the beginning of this excerpt, Trump communicates his efficiency and capacity to come up with straightforward solutions. This is transmitted chiefly by the combination of verbs that he selects to describe his actions: *I went, I saw, I said*. The last verb in particular is followed by a claim, *you need forest management*, which has the communicative effect of an order. What follows is an instance of rhetorical refutation, which consists in presenting the opponents' argument in the form of a counter position (*they were saying it was global warming*), refuting it and offering an alternative (*could have had something to do with it. But we need forest management*). At this point, Trump can present forest management as the solution to the problem of forest fires.

Another general feature underlying Trump's discourse is the nostalgic celebration of a glorious past when things were supposedly better and America was great (tellingly, his election campaign slogan was "Make America Great Again"). This orientation toward the past that must be revived is also evident in the way he deals with energy and the environment. Thus, he evokes images of a highly industrialized society run by heavy machines and factories, where pipelines invade the soil, and oilrigs, pumps and boilers dominate the landscape. In this image of economic growth and alleged progress thanks to increased investments in the fossil-fuel industry, energy workers (the ones working in the oil, natural gas, and coal sectors) also play an important role. Trump is full of praise for them, using adjectives such as *incredible, special, great, amazing, wonderful,* and *tremendous,* and his flattery systematically addresses their contribution to bring prosperity back to the American people and to the nation. In a vivid manner, Trump describes the energy workers' efforts as follows:

(14) Your workers embody the skill, grit, and courage that has always been the true source of American strength. They are great people. *They break through rock walls, mine the depths of the earth, and reach through the ocean floor*, to bring every ounce of energy into our homes and commerce and into our lives. Our nation salutes you. You're brave and you are great workers. Thank you very much. Thank you, fellas. . . . *American hands will bend the steel and pour the concrete* that brings this energy into our homes and that exports this incredible, newfound energy all around the world. And American grit will ensure that what we dream, and what we build, will truly be second to none. We will be number one again all the way. We're going to make America great again. (June 29, 2017, authors' emphasis)

As this passage reveals, besides putting industrial work on a pedestal, Trump's praise of the skillful, strong, and courageous American energy workers discloses an alarming eulogy of environmental exploitation. As exemplified here, when Trump talks about energy workers *unleashing* the great potential of the nation, *fueling* the economy to *make America great again* and start *the golden era of American energy*, the subtext is one of an abusive relation to the environment and its precious resources.

On top of this, Trump creates an image of himself as a strong leader, making statements such as (15) or using recurrent phrases such as *fight for you* (American workers), *fight for energy, fight for the American farmer*, and *fight for our interest*.

(15) I'm fighting every day for the great people of this country (June, 1, 2017)

Trump's discourse is also imbued with forms of self-appraisal. Thus, beyond metaphorically portraying himself as a hero-like figure the country needs, he emphasizes his trustworthiness by repeating phrases like *I promised* or *I made my promise and I keep my promise*. Sometimes, Trump's discourse is also double-voiced in a Bakhtinian sense (Bakhtin 1981). This happens, for instance, when he emulates other voices praising him, as in (16).

(16) that's this guy right here, and he'll do it better than anybody (June 29, 2017)

The use of the third person to address himself appears as strategic linguistic distancing, which has the effect that the praising claim sounds more objective. Later, in the same speech, Trump claims: "when I go around, there are so many people that say thank you. You saved the sovereignty of our country. You saved our wealth." Again, he reports other people's voices with the aim of aggrandizing his own political persona.

9.5.3 Withdrawal from the Paris Climate Agreement

Among the topics addressed by Trump, the Paris Accord[4] appears as central, not just given its relevance in absolute terms, but also because it sums up the president's personal approach to the environment. The analysis will thus now consider Trump's remark on this international agreement (June 1, 2017) and focus on how he frames it. What is most striking in Trump's portrayal of the Paris Agreement is the reiterated accusation of unfairness. The Accord, in Trump's words, is unfair to the United States, its businesses and its workers because it disadvantages the United States to the benefit of other nations. Thus, for strictly economic reasons, the US withdrawal from the Accord is presented as necessary and as a form of protection of the nation and its citizens. The following two paragraphs from the speech exemplify this stance.

(17) As President, I can put no other consideration before the wellbeing of American citizens. The Paris Climate Accord is simply the latest example of Washington entering into an agreement that disadvantages the United States to the exclusive benefit of other countries, leaving American workers—who I love—and taxpayers to absorb the cost in terms of lost jobs, lower wages, shuttered factories, and vastly diminished economic production. (June 1, 2017)

(18) In short, the agreement doesn't eliminate coal jobs, it just transfers those jobs out of America and the United States, and ships them to foreign countries. This agreement is less about the climate and more about other countries gaining a financial advantage over the United States. The rest of the world applauded when we signed the Paris Agreement—they went wild; they were so happy—for the simple reason that it put our country, the United States of America, which we all love, at a very, very big economic disadvantage. (June 1, 2017)

Trump's discourse on the Paris Agreement is also characterized by distinctive metaphorical depictions that can be expected to activate emotional involvement and, hence, gain the favor of his audience. The very notion of fairness, crucial for motivating the withdrawal, is conveyed by relying on the sports metaphor of the "level playing field." In terms of conceptual metaphor theory,[5] the expression can be analyzed as FAIRNESS IS A FLAT SURFACE. In other words, the abstract concept fairness (i.e., the target domain) is metaphorically understood by comparing it to the concrete image of a level playing field (source domain), which provides the playing teams with the same even terrain, that is, with the same basic conditions to win the game. This metaphorical expression also occurs in other remarks when he complains about 'unfair' conditions. The president describes his actions as motivated by his intention to give the United States a "level playing field" against other nations. The fact that the Paris Accord is depicted as detrimental to the United States appears as the result of a number of metaphors that emphasize related negative aspects characterizing the agreement. As Trump's use of language indicates, the treaty is represented as a metaphorical AGENT, BURDEN, THIEF, WEAPON, DISEASE, PRISON, PHYSICAL OBSTACLE, and INVASION. Each of these metaphorical conceptualizations plays a role in Trump's overall strategy of making the audience believe that the United States should by no means be part of this international agreement. Table 9.2 provides an overview of the different metaphors Trump uses when talking about the Paris Accord.

Table 9.2 Metaphors Defining the Paris Accord

Conceptual metaphors	Examples
THE ACCORD IS A HARMFUL AGENT	"it *put* our country . . . at a very, very big economic disadvantage" "The Paris Accord would *undermine* our economy, *hamstring* our workers, *weaken* our sovereignty, *impose* unacceptable legal risks, and *put* us at a permanent disadvantage to the other countries of the world" "As someone who cares deeply about the environment, which I do, I cannot in good conscience support a deal that *punishes* the United States—which is what it does—the world's leader in environmental protection, while *imposing* no meaningful obligations on the world's leading polluters"
THE ACCORD IS A BURDEN	"the draconian financial and economic *burdens* the agreement imposes on our country" "the *onerous* energy restrictions it [the Accord] has placed on the United States"
THE ACCORD IS A WEAPON	"[By remaining in the agreement] we continue to suffer this self-inflicted major economic *wound*"
THE ACCORD IS A THIEF	"including *funds raided out* of America's budget for the war against terrorism" "under the Paris Accord, billions of dollars that ought to be invested right here in America *will be sent to* the very countries that have taken our factories and our jobs away from us"
THE ACCORD IS A DISEASE	"No responsible leader can put the workers—and the people—of their country at this *debilitating* and tremendous disadvantage" "The Paris Agreement *handicaps* the United States economy" "further *decimation* of vital American industries on which countless communities rely"
THE ACCORD IS A PRISON	"Yet, under this agreement, we are effectively *putting* these reserves *under lock and key*" "foreign lobbyists wish to keep our magnificent country *tied up* and *bound down* by this agreement"
THE ACCORD IS A PHYSICAL OBSTACLE	"Staying in the agreement could also *pose* serious *obstacles* for the United States"
THE ACCORD IS AN INVASION	"And exiting the agreement protects the United States from future *intrusions on* the United States' *sovereignty*"

Another aspect of Trump's line of argumentation against the climate agreement draws on American patriotic feelings. Thus, he calls upon American ideals and the American Constitution, which, according to him, are not respected by the agreement. In his words,

(19) Not only does this deal subject our citizens to harsh economic restrictions, it fails to live up to our environmental ideals. . . . Thus, our withdrawal from the agreement represents a reassertion of America's sovereignty. Our Constitution is unique among all the nations of the world, and it is my highest obligation and greatest honor to protect it. And I will.

This quotation exemplifies another reason that Trump gives to morally justify his actions: the Paris Agreement is presented as a threat to US sovereignty. In Trump's view, the Accord causes the nation to lose its independence and to become subject to the will of other nations. Consequently, as Trump claims, the withdrawal from the agreement is a way of protecting the United States, reasserting its undisputed sovereignty and, most fundamentally, respecting the principles of freedom and independence stated in its Constitution.

9.6 Conclusion

Investigating Trump's official presidential discourse of the environment has drawn a bleak picture of a US leader who recalls the imagery of an early twentieth-century fossil-fuel-based industrialized society. At the same time, references to real environmental concerns are non-existent being submerged by his continuous mention of economic growth, the creation of jobs in the fossil-fuel sector and the accompanying exploitation of fossil resources. Oxymoronic collocations such as *clean coal* and *clean, beautiful natural gas* are a symbol of his attempt to reframe pollutant energy sources and to deny their dangers notwithstanding conclusive scientific evidence about their relation to global warming. While his line of reasoning and some of the concepts he evokes, in particular those that depict human dominance over their natural environment and those related to the United States as independent, sovereign, and striving for global leadership, are very much in line with a general moral framing along the lines of Republican (conservative) ideology, his disregard toward concrete measures of real environmental protection is alarming and possibly unrivalled among US presidents.

On the surface level of language use, Trump's remarks on energy and environment confirm observations on his simple, plain, and conversational style in earlier research (e.g., Degani 2016; Lakoff 2017; Demata 2017; Pilyarchuk and Onysko 2018) and in contributions to the present volume (see Egbert and Biber as well as Ronan and Schneider, this volume). In the current study, for example, Trump's negative metaphorical conceptualizations of the Paris Accord and other metaphors that he evokes are voiced through repetitive expressions and choice of plain words.

Overall, the analysis of Trump's discursive stance in relation to the environment has shown that his lexical choices and discursive strategies frame the environment as being in a healthy state. Trump claims that the United States has the cleanest air and water in the world and that there are no environmental issues. His strategy of remaining silent on any kind of environmental concerns also emerges from the lack of using terms referring to the environment and its protection. Emission-based energy production, on the other hand, is Trump's main concern and he presents fossil fuels as the necessary way forward for the United States. The state of the environment as Trump paints it is thus in stark contrast to scientific evidence and to current social developments of increasing consciousness toward global warming that has become manifest, among others, in protests by young people across the world.

Notes

1. https://www.whitehouse.gov/issues/energy-environment
2. Looking at the use of clean coal in context, it is interesting to note that about 31 percent occur in Trump and Republican discourse while 9 percent are part of proper names (for example, American Coalition for Clean Coal Electricity). Sixty percent of the hits for clean coal occur in wider public discussions. The term appeared in 1990 for the first time and occurs consistently up to 2017 (when it peaks in COCA) except for four years (1995, 1996, 1997, and 1999).
3. "Environment—Vocabulary List and Sentences in English"; "3000 Core Vocabulary words—The Environment" (Merriam-Webster Learner's Dictionary); "Vocabulary—Environment"
4. For general information on the Paris Agreement see https://unfccc.int/process-and-meetings/the-paris-agreement/the-paris-agreement
5. See Koth, this volume, for more extensive commentary on conceptual metaphor theory.

References

"3000 Core Vocabulary Words—The Environment," Merriam-Webster Learner's Dictionary. Available online: http://learnersdictionary.com/3000-words/topic/the-environment (accessed January 22, 2020).

Ahrens, Kathleen (2011), "Examining Conceptual Metaphor Models through Lexical Frequency Patterns: A Case Study of U.S. Presidential Speeches," in Sandra Handl and Hans-Jörg Schmid (eds.), *Windows to the Mind: Metaphor, Metonymy and Conceptual Blending*, 167–84, Berlin & New York: Mouton De Gruyter.

Ahrens, Kathleen and Sophia Yat Mei Lee (2009), "Gender versus Politics: When Conceptual Models Collide in the US Senate," in Kathleen Ahrens (ed.) *Politics, Gender and Conceptual Metaphors*, 62–82, Basingstoke: Palgrave Macmillan.

Bakhtin, Mikhail M. (1981), *The Dialogic Imagination: Four Essays* (translated by Caryl Emerson and Michael Holquist), Austin, TX: University of Texas Press.

Balbus, John, Allison R. Crimmins, Janet L. Gamble, David R. Easterling, Kenneth E. Kunkel, Shubhayu Saha, and Marcus C. Sarofim (2016), "Ch. 1: Introduction: Climate Change and Human Health," in *The Impacts of Climate Change on Human Health in the United States: A Scientific Assessment*, 25–42, Washington, DC: US Global Change Research Program.

Bowman, Carl D. (2010), "The Myth of a Non-Polarized America," *The Hedgehog Review*, 12 (3): 65–77.

Center for Climate and Energy Solutions (2020), "Drought and Climate Change," *Center for Climate and Energy Solutions*, January 16. Available online: https://www.c2es.org/content/drought-and-climate-change/ (accessed January 22, 2020).

Charteris-Black, Jonathan (2014), *Analysing Political Speeches: Rhetoric, Discourse and Metaphor*. Basingstoke: Palgrave Macmillan.

Cienki, Alan (2004), "Bush's and Gore's Language and Gestures in the 2000 US Presidential Debate: A Test Case for Two Models of Metaphor," *Journal of Language and Politics*, 3 (3): 409–40.

Cienki, Alan (2005a), "Metaphor in the 'Strict Father' and 'Nurturant Parent' Cognitive Models: Theoretical Issues Raised in an Empirical Study," *Cognitive Linguistics*, 16 (2): 279–312.

Cienki, Alan (2005b), "The Metaphorical Use of Family Terms Versus Other Nouns in Political Debates," *Information Design Journal*, 13 (1): 27–39.

Crippa, Monica, Gabriel Oreggioni, Diego Guizzardi, Marilena Muntean, Edwin Schaaf, Eleonora Lo Vullo, Efisio Solazzo, Fabio Monforti-Ferrario, Jos Olivier, and Elisabetta Vignati (2019), *Fossil CO2 and GHG Emissions of all World Countries—2019 Report*, Luxemburg: Publications Office of the European Union.

Davies, Mark (2008–), "The Corpus of Contemporary American English (COCA): 600 Million Words, 1990–present." Available online: https://www.english-corpora.org/coca/ (accessed January 22, 2020).

Deason, Grace and Marti H. Gonzales (2012), "Moral Politics in the 2008 Presidential Convention Acceptance Speeches," *Basic and Applied Social Psychology*, 34 (3): 254–68.

Degani, Marta (2015), *Framing the Rhetoric of a Leader: An Analysis of Obama's Election Campaign Speeches*, Basingstoke: Palgrave Macmillan.

Degani, Marta (2016), "Endangered Intellect: A Case Study of Clinton vs Trump Campaign Discourse," *Iperstoria*, 8: 131–45.

Demata, Massimiliano (2017), "'A Great and Beautiful Wall.' Donald Trump's Populist Discourse on Immigration," *Journal of Language Aggression and Conflict* 5 (2): 274–94.

EAA Web Team (2016), "State and Outlook 2010," *The European Environment Agency*, June 3. Available online: https://www.eea.europa.eu/soer/synthesis/synthesis/contents (accessed January 22, 2020).

"Environment—Vocabulary List and Sentences in English," *englisch-hilfe.de*. Available online: https://www.englisch-hilfen.de/en/words/environment.htm (accessed January 22, 2020).

Gibbens, Sarah (2019), "15 Ways the Trump Administration Has Changed Environmental Policies," *National Geographic*, February 1. Available online: https://www.nationalgeographic.com/environment/2019/02/15-ways-trump-administration-impacted-environment/ (accessed January 22, 2020).

Gray, Ellen and Jessica Merzdorf (2019), "Earth's Freshwater Future: Extremes of Flood and Drought," *Global Climate Change: Vital Signs of the Planet*, June 13. Available online: https://climate.nasa.gov/news/2881/earths-freshwater-future-extremes-of-flood-and-drought/ (accessed January 22, 2020).

Hansen, James, Reto Ruedy, Makiko Sato, and Ken Lo (2010), "Global Surface Temperature Change," *Review of Geophysics*, 48 (4): RG4004.

Hejny, Jessica (2018), "The Trump Administration and Environmental Policy: Regan Redux?" *Journal of Environmental Studies and Sciences*, 8 (2): 197–211.

Hunter, James D. (1991), *Culture Wars: The Struggle to Define America*, New York: Basic Books.

Klyza, Christopher M. and David J. Sousa (2013), *American Environmental Policy: Beyond Gridlock*, Cambridge MA: MIT Press.

Lakoff, George (1996), *Moral Politics*, Chicago, IL: University of Chicago Press.

Lakoff, George (2010), "Why It Matters How We Frame the Environment," *Environmental Communication*, 4 (1): 70–81.

Lakoff, Robin T. (2017), "The Hollow Man: Donald Trump, Populism, and Post-Truth Politics," *Journal of Language and Politics*, 16 (4): 595–606.

McCarty, Nolan, Keith T. Poole, and Howard Rosenthal (2006), *Polarized America: The Dance of Ideology and Unequal Riches*, Cambridge, MA: MIT Press.

Milman, Oliver and Sam Morris (2017), "Trump is Deleting Climate Change, One Site at a Time," *The Guardian*, May 14. Available online: https://www.theguardian.com/us-news/2017/may/14/donald-trump-climate-change-mentions-government-websites (accessed January 22, 2020).

Moses, Jennifer F. and Marti H. Gonzales (2015), "Strong Candidate, Nurturant Candidate: Moral Language in Presidential Television Advertisements," *Political Psychology*, 36 (4): 379–97.

Muntean, Marilena, Diego Guizzardi, Edwin Schaaf, Monica Grippa, Efisio Solazzo, Jos Olivier, and Elisabetta Vignati (2019), "Fossil CO_2 Emissions of all World Countries, 2018 Report," *Emissions Database for Global Atmospheric Research*, October 9. Available online: https://ec.europa.eu/jrc/en/publication/fossil-co2-emissions-all-world-countries-2018-report (accessed January 22, 2020).

NOAA (2019), "Is Sea Level Rising?," *National Ocean Service*, October 9. Available online: https://oceanservice.noaa.gov/facts/sealevel.html (accessed January 22, 2020).

Ohl, Jessy J., Damien S. Pfister, Marty Nader, and Dana Griffin (2013), "Lakoff's Theory of Moral Reasoning in Presidential Campaign Advertisements, 1952–2008," *Communication Studies*, 64 (5): 488–507.

Oreskes, Naomi (2004), "The Scientific Consensus on Climate Change," *Science*, 306 (5702): 1686.

Pew Research Center (2016), "Top Voting Issues in 2016 Election: 2016 Campaign: Strong Interest, Widespread Dissatisfaction," *Pew Research Center*, July 7. Available online: http://www.people-press.org/2016/07//07/4-top-voting-issues-in-2016-election/# (accessed January 22, 2020).

Pilyarchuk, Kateryna and Alexander Onysko (2018), "Conceptual Metaphors in Donald Trump's Political Speeches: Framing His Topics and (Self-)Constructing His Persona," *Colloquium: New Philologies*, 3 (2): 98–156.

Popovich, Nadja, Livia Albeck-Ripka, and Pierre-Louis Kendra (2019), "83 Environmental Rules Being Rolled Up under Trump," *New York Times*, June 7. Available online: https://www.nytimes.com/interactive/2019/climate/trump-environment-rollbacks.html (accessed January 22, 2020).

Stahl, Lesley (2018), "President Trump on Christinne Blasey Ford, His Relationships with Vladimir Putin and Kim Jong Un and More," *CBS News*, October 15. Available online: https://www.cbsnews.com/news/donald-trump-full-interview-60-minutes-transcript-lesley-stahl-2018-10-14/ (accessed January 22, 2020).

"Vocabulary—Environment," *My English Pages*. Available online: https://www.myenglishpages.com/site_php_files/vocabulary-lesson-environment.php (accessed January 22, 2020).

Walton, Douglas (2015), "The Basic Slippery Slope Argument," *Informal Logic*, 35 (3): 273–311.

Yi, Hongtao (2014), "Green Businesses in a Green Energy Economy: Analysing Drivers of Green Business Growth in the U.S. States," *Energy*, 68, 922–9.

10

Donald Trump's "Fake News" Agenda
A Pragmatic Account of Rhetorical Delegitimization

Christoph Schubert

10.1 Introduction: Constructing Fakeness

Since Donald Trump took office in January 2017, investigative journalists have repeatedly argued that the president's utterances are not always entirely accurate. For instance, on June 10, 2019, the *Washington Post* noted that "President Trump has made 10,796 false or misleading claims over 869 days" (Kessler, Rizzo, and Kelly 2019), concerning such issues as immigration, economy, or trade. On the other hand, Trump has continuously employed the catchphrase *fake news* in order to reduce the credibility of news companies like CNN or the *New York Times*. As the following two extracts show, this fixed expression appears in diverse genres of presidential discourse, including press conferences and Twitter posts.

(1) JIM ACOSTA (CNN): Mr. President-elect, can you give us a question?
    DONALD TRUMP: No, I'm not going to give you a question. You're fake news.
    (Media conference on January 11, 2017, quoted in McNair 2018: 1)
(2) The Fake News is working overtime. Just reported that, despite the tremendous success we are having with the economy & all things else, 91% of the Network News about me is negative (Fake). Why do we work so hard in working with the media when it is corrupt? Take away credentials? (@realDonaldTrump, May 9, 2018)

The exchange with CNN reporter Jim Acosta, which took place during Trump's first press conference as president-elect, indicates that Trump uses the defamatory label *fake news* to avoid having to deal with inconvenient journalists. In the Twitter message, Trump equates the attribute *fake* with the feature 'negative', revealing his distinctive approach to the concept of fakeness. Moreover, he strategically employs the allegation of fakeness as a justification to potentially suspend press passes. Accordingly, Trump uses the brand *fake news* as a powerful political tool (McNair 2018), popularizing it mainly by means of Twitter (Davis and Sinnreich 2019). Since Trump's fake news label is additionally rendered particularly newsworthy and relevant by extensive media coverage, it plays a major role in public agenda-setting (Carveth 2019).

The phenomenon that media are accused of misinformation is not new, but the term *fake news* became a regular buzz word in mainstream and social media during the presidential election race of 2016 (Barclay 2018: 29). In broad terms, it signifies "journalism that should not be taken seriously because it [is] false, fabricated or little better than fiction" (McNair 2018: 6), so that the concept is often used as part of a specific political agenda. After his inauguration in January 2017, Trump boosted the popularity of the catchphrase on Twitter, where it has since served as "a rhetorical device for discrediting unfavorable coverage of his presidency" (Davis and Sinnreich 2019: 149). As there is evidence that in some cases real news has been labeled *fake news* by Trump, the term is not to be understood as serious political criticism of journalistic inaccuracy but rather as a "discursive weapon in Trump's reputation management arsenal" (Davis and Sinnreich 2019: 163). It thus appears that *fake news* has been reinterpreted as "anything that reports something I don't want to believe" (Barclay 2018: 29) instead of actual misinformation.

The present chapter intends to show that allegations of dishonesty against the critical press loom large in Trump's discourse already in presidential primary debates during his election campaign. It will furthermore be pointed out that accusations of fakeness are also applied to his competitors in the presidential race, who are repeatedly accused of lying. Along these lines, the aim of this chapter is to analyze the ways in which allegations of misrepresentation are strategically used to influence public opinion and to delegitimize critical journalists and political opponents (Chilton and Schäffner 2011). Delegitimization is here understood as the practice of presenting adversaries in a negative light with the rhetorical aim of damaging their reputation and trustworthiness, so that they are no longer accepted as authorities by the public (van Leeuwen 2018). Moreover, the present study explores to what extent Trump uses the construction of fakeness as a rhetorical strategy enabling him to evade inconvenient questions and to initiate counterattacks, thus exercising control over the political negotiation of fact and fiction.

10.2 Pragmatic Approaches to Lying

In order to analyze Trump's fake news agenda, it is necessary to give an account of lying from a pragmatic perspective. In general, a prototypical lie meets three criteria (Aitchison 2012: 71; Meibauer 2014: 42): the speaker (a) utters something that is false, (b) believes that it is false, and (c) intends to deceive the hearer. Accordingly, it is possible to distinguish between different degrees of lying, depending on the beliefs and intentions of the speaker (Saul 2012: 3–10). For instance, if criterion (c) is not fulfilled, such a statement is usually called a "white lie," which is not intended to mislead. However, when Trump accuses journalists or adversaries of spreading "fake news," he claims that they utter prototypical lies according to all three criteria.

This clearly applies, for instance, when he speaks of "the total dishonesty of the press," see example (4), section 10.5.1, or when he calls another candidate "the single biggest liar," see example (15), section 10.5.5.

In order to shed further light on what the phenomenon of lying involves in more precise terms, it is useful to take various pragmatic approaches into consideration. In speech act theory, which considers verbal utterances as a type of action, several conditions for the successful performance of speech acts are postulated. Among them, one important requirement is the "sincerity condition," which means that speakers commit themselves to the truth of an utterance (Searle 1969: 63). In Austin's terminology, insincerity implies that speakers do not have the appropriate "thoughts, feelings, or intentions" (Austin 1975: 39), which leads to an "abuse" of the speech act, since the hearer is not aware that the act is performed without the requisite attitude. Along these lines, dishonest speech acts are carried out in an abusive way (Huang 2014: 132), which corresponds with the kind of behavior Trump accuses journalists of, who allegedly abuse their position by misinforming and deceiving the public.

Another relevant pragmatic approach is the cooperative principle established by Grice (1975, 1989), according to which communicative partners interact rationally and expect mutual cooperation. More specifically, the cooperative principle can be subdivided into the four conversational maxims of quality, quantity, relevance, and manner, among which the first two are particularly relevant to the analysis of lying. Each of the maxims is divided into two submaxims that provide additional specification:

MAXIM OF QUALITY: try to make your contribution one that is true

1. Do not say what you believe to be false.
2. Do not say that for which you lack adequate evidence.

MAXIM OF QUANTITY

1. Make your contribution as informative as is required (for the current purposes of the exchange).
2. Do not make your contribution more informative than is required.

(Grice 1975: 45–6)

If speakers blatantly fail to meet the quality maxim, this does not necessarily mean that they are lying. Rather, the maxim is "flouted," as in the case of irony, where speakers literally say something that is false but at the same time give irony signals that tell the hearer that something else is meant. If, however, no such signals are provided, this is a "violation" of the quality maxim and results in actual lying (Grice 1975: 49). In other words, the distinction between flouting and violating is one between "overt untruthfulness and covert untruthfulness" (Dynel 2011: 141). With respect to the quantity maxim, a violation means that not the whole truth is provided but significant facts are withheld or concealed, so that this is "deception without lying" (Dynel 2011: 162). In other approaches, the practice of giving half-truths is labeled "misleading" (Saul 2012: 4), or it is considered a type of "indirect lying" (Meibauer 2014: 28–30).

On the basis of these distinctions, the term *fake news* is used to accuse the press of non-cooperative communicative behavior owing to supposed violations of the quality and quantity maxims.

Lastly, it is worthwhile to investigate the effects of Trump's fake news agenda from the vantage point of impoliteness research (Bousfield 2008; Culpeper 2011). Whenever Trump denounces journalists or political opponents as liars, this is an act of impoliteness in the more narrow linguistic sense, since he attacks the addressee's figurative "face," which is defined by politeness theory as "the public self-image that every member [of a society] wants to claim for himself" (Brown and Levinson 1987: 61). Every interactant has a "positive face," which is the desire for appreciation and approval, as well as a "negative face," which is the wish for personal freedom and non-interference through others. If interactants are part of an institution in society, such as the press, their individual face is complemented by an institutional face that pertains to the professional reputation of the organization.

Impoliteness is generally defined as "the communication of intentionally gratuitous and conflictive verbal face-threatening acts (FTA) which are purposefully delivered" (Bousfield 2008: 72). Thus, allegations of dishonesty are FTAs that chiefly damage the addressee's positive face, since they are harsh accusations that display strong disagreement and aim to discredit the hearer. For instance, among impolite formulae the insulting address form *liar*, occasionally used by Trump, is a "personalized negative vocative" (Culpeper 2011: 135–6). Depending on the discursive context, allegations of dishonesty may also threaten the recipients' negative face if they attack the sovereignty of the press and pressure journalists to change their way of reporting. In this way, the free press is disparaged in its role as the "fourth estate," whose role it is to manage the perception of political decisions and to shape public opinion (Kellner 2018: 97). As Dailey, Hinck, and Hinck (2008: 18) note, face threats in presidential debates between the years 1960 and 2004 chiefly referred to the opponent's faulty character, to incompetence in leadership, to weak political proposals, and to "incorrect use of data." Hence, the last of these items indicates that allegations of fakeness have a long tradition, but they have recently found a new powerful outlet in the form of social media platforms.

In his study of offensive discursive behavior, Culpeper distinguishes between the three types of affective, coercive, and entertaining impoliteness (2011: 221; see also Huang 2014: 150). Trump's verbal attacks against the press mainly have a coercive function, since they are employed to discredit media companies in the eyes of the public for the sake of political persuasion. In doing so, Trump accepts the risk that his own public face is damaged as well, as the attacks could make him appear rude. However, this danger is somewhat reduced in Trump's case due to his past role as a reality TV personality in the NBC show *The Apprentice* from 2004 to 2015. In this program, the very direct and brusque catchphrase *You're fired!* was one of his trademarks and served as a form of entertainment through impoliteness. Moreover, a certain degree of verbal aggression is expected by the audience of the highly competitive primary debates, making the debates contexts in which impoliteness is contextually "appropriate," at least to some extent (Watts 2003: 25). Ultimately, although Trump's impolite accusations are literally directed toward the press and his political adversaries, the actual addressees are the voters as the prime target of his persuasive efforts.

10.3 Fake News and (De-)Legitimization in Political Discourse

Trump has used the fake news label for renowned and highly respected media outlets such as the *New York Times*, the *Washington Post*, the BBC, and MSNBC, so that every news provider critical of Trump's politics can be potentially included (McNair 2018: 2). This makes fake news an important ingredient in the so-called "post-truth" approach to politics. In this framework, facts and their verification are neglected in favor of subjective impressions and personal emotions with the goal of political persuasion and dominance (McIntyre 2018: 1–15). By and large, "fake news" is a popular soundbite and a belligerent slogan Trump utilizes in his campaign against news providers:

> To this day, Trump and his staff continue to dismiss reporting they don't approve of as "fake news." The Trump base have labeled the mainstream and increasingly anti-Trump press as "false news" tout court, marking the first time that a president has so broadly delegitimized the mainstream media. (Kellner 2018: 97–8)

In contradistinction to the "fake news media," Trump emphasizes his own trustworthiness with his stereotypical appeal "believe me," which in debates additionally fulfills the functions of involving the audience and eliciting applause (Sclafani 2018: 39).

Another key term in the post-truth era is *alternative facts*, famously coined in a news interview by Trump consultant Kellyanne Conway on January 22, 2017. Thus, Trump's presidency started with an allegation of dishonesty against the press, as he claimed that the media misrepresented the size of the crowd that attended his inauguration ceremony (Kellner 2018: 96). Regarding discursive levels, the fake news allegation is generally a metadiscursive feature of Trump's idiolect, since it is a comment on news reporting, thus representing discourse *about* previous discourse.

Furthermore, it is necessary to consider the fake news agenda in a wider framework of political discourse analysis, which distinguishes three pivotal strategic functions in political communication (Chilton 2004: 45–7; Chilton and Schäffner 2011: 311–12):

(a) COERCION AND RESISTANCE: As indicated in the discussion of "coercive impoliteness" (see section 10.2), Trump exerts political power by repeatedly persuading the electorate to distrust the news media and to accept him as the most reliable source of information. By dismissing and rejecting selected news items, Trump exercises control over the topics discussed and thus influences public agenda-setting. Labeling news as *fake* is one way of "making assumptions about realities that hearers are obliged to at least temporarily accept in order to process the text or talk" (Chilton and Schäffner 2011: 311). Resistance to fake news allegations may be put up by media outlets giving evidence that the accusations are unfounded.

(b) LEGITIMIZATION (OF THE SELF) AND DELEGITIMIZATION (OF THE OTHER): The fake news label is a strategy of negative other-presentation that accuses news providers of dishonesty and thus deprives them of their institutional integrity. If legitimization includes the "right to be obeyed" (Chilton and Schäffner 2011:

312), delegitimization means that the public is persuaded not to pay attention to the delegitimized organization or institution. Correspondingly, the more vehemently critical news coverage is delegitimized, the more Trump's position is legitimized and fortified.
(c) REPRESENTATION AND MISREPRESENTATION: The fake news accusation is the allegation of political misinformation in terms of quality (i.e., lying) or quantity (i.e., telling half-truths) (Bakir et al. 2018: 538). Having control over the distribution and provision of information is an important instrument of exercising power for both politicians and media institutions. As a result, the strategic presentation of politically relevant opinions and events is a hotly disputed issue in society.

Thus, in a nutshell, all three strategic functions can be identified in the fake news agenda: Trump accuses journalists of misrepresentation in order to delegitimize the press and to coerce audiences to vote for him.

Since the delegitimization of critical journalism is the main objective of Trump's fake news agenda, a closer look at related techniques is in order. In general, political legitimization is defined as "the principal goal of the political speaker seeking justification and support of actions which the speaker manifestly intends to perform in the vital interest of the hearer" (Cap 2006: 7). In inverse logic, Trump aims to deprive investigative media outlets of their justification and public support, claiming that journalists try to harm the American people. Hence, the fake news agenda has a delegitimizing function on three levels, according to the model by van Leeuwen (2018: 220):

(a) AUTHORITY: The expert knowledge of established newspapers is doubted and assaulted, which includes the journalists acting as moderators and panellists in the primary debates.
(b) MORAL EVALUATION: Depending on culture-specific ethical value systems, allegations of dishonesty contribute to the moral disqualification of news providers (Chilton 2004: 47).
(c) RATIONALIZATION: Selected news items are called into question through biased reasoning, founded on ideological arguments that support the persuasive goal.

On the basis of the aforementioned distinctions, the exemplary analyses in section 10.5 will illustrate that Trump's use of the label *fake news* is a versatile and multifaceted discursive strategy to win voters over to his side. In preparation of these detailed examinations, section 10.4 gives an overview of the dataset and provides details on the methodological approach taken to analyze the texts.

10.4 Data and Methodology

The study is based on the full-text transcripts of eleven Republican primary debates. Presidential primary debates are an important stage in the US election process, giving presidential candidates the opportunity to advertise their political profiles and to set themselves apart from their competitors. Since the debates are broadcast on television and other digital media outlets, it is necessary to distinguish between first-frame interaction, which includes everyone present in the TV studio, and second-frame interaction, which refers to audiences that watch the event on the screen (Fetzer 2011: 124). While the second frame encompasses the majority of voters, the first frame comprises the studio audience, the presidential candidates, as well as the moderators, usually well-known anchorpersons and other influential journalists of news companies, who may also be part of debate panels (Schroeder 2016: 205).

By posing investigative questions, journalists intend to uncover weaknesses and argumentative inconsistencies, which may be further elucidated by the competitors attacking each other. Accordingly, contributions to the debates fulfill the three main functions of attacks, defenses, and acclaims, which are assertions displaying the speaker's positive sides (Benoit 2014: 13–15). Owing to Trump's rather aggressive verbal behavior, known to many viewers through his reality TV background, "the Republican primary debates became [a] media spectacle dominated by Trump" (Kellner 2018: 91). In terms of (im-)politeness, attacks do not only aim at the candidates' personality but also at their public image, since the debaters are representatives of a specific political value system (Dailey, Hinck, and Hinck 2008: 10–11).

The primary debates under investigation were held between August 6, 2015 and March 10, 2016. The debate from January 28, 2016, could not be included since Trump did not participate, owing to an alternative campaign event on the same day. The transcripts were retrieved from the comprehensive web archive of the American Presidency Project (APP), compiled by the political scientists John Woolley and Gerhard Peters (1999–) at the UC Santa Barbara. As random comparisons with the broadcast debates show, the transcripts are highly accurate and also provide annotations of audience reactions through square brackets such as "[*laughter*]" or "[*applause*]." Table 10.1 gives an outline of all dates, presidential candidates, and numbers of words,

Table 10.1 Republican Debates in the Dataset

Date	Candidates	Size
August 6, 2015	J. Bush, B. Carson, C. Christie, T. Cruz, M. Huckabee, J. Kasich, R. Paul, M. Rubio, D. Trump, S. Walker	19,326
September 16, 2015	J. Bush, B. Carson, C. Christie, T. Cruz, C. Fiorina, M. Huckabee, J. Kasich, R. Paul, M. Rubio, D. Trump, S. Walker	34,794
October 28, 2015	J. Bush, B. Carson, C. Christie, T. Cruz, C. Fiorina, M. Huckabee, J. Kasich, R. Paul, M. Rubio, D. Trump	21,698
November 10, 2015	J. Bush, B. Carson, C. Christie, T. Cruz, J. Kasich, M. Rubio, D. Trump	20,525
December 15, 2015	J. Bush, B. Carson, C. Christie, T. Cruz, C. Fiorina, J. Kasich, R. Paul, M. Rubio, D. Trump	24,069
January 14, 2016	J. Bush, B. Carson, C. Christie, T. Cruz, J. Kasich, M. Rubio, D. Trump	22,796
February 6, 2016	J. Bush, B. Carson, T. Cruz, C. Fiorina, J. Kasich, R. Paul, M. Rubio, D. Trump	25,290
February 13, 2016	J. Bush, B. Carson, T. Cruz, J. Kasich, M. Rubio, D. Trump	18,632
February 25, 2016	B. Carson, T. Cruz, J. Kasich, M. Rubio, D. Trump	24,903
March 3, 2016	T. Cruz, J. Kasich, M. Rubio, D. Trump	21,340
March 10, 2016	T. Cruz, J. Kasich, M. Rubio, D. Trump	22,404
Total		255,777

which add up to over 250,000 tokens altogether, thus allowing for substantial and representative analyses.

As far as the methodological procedure is concerned, Trump's fake news agenda was investigated in a qualitative analysis based on a succession of several steps: (i) the transcripts were downloaded from the APP archive; (ii) by way of a thorough reading of the texts, all utterances by Trump accusing adversaries of lies and fakeness were manually identified and (iii) classified according to the target of his accusations, which can be either the journalists or other presidential candidates; (iv) all utterances that contained allegations of dishonesty were grouped in distinctive categories with regard to pragmatic maxims and subsequently examined in their respective contexts; (v) representative and prototypical extracts were singled out in order to illustrate characteristic discursive techniques of denouncing critical remarks as lies.

10.5 Delegitimization through Allegations of Misrepresentation

Trump's fake news agenda relies on allegations of misrepresentation that can be classified according to the target of the accusations, the pragmatic dimensions of quality and quantity within the cooperative principle, and the type of political content. By using these criteria, it is possible to identify the five categories (a) to (e), as displayed in Figure 10.1.

As far as the target is concerned, Trump's allegations in the debates are either directed toward other presidential candidates (e), such as Ted Cruz, Jeb Bush, and Marco Rubio, or toward the news media whose output is framed as "fake news." Furthermore, accusations may refer to the conversational maxims of quality or quantity: if journalists, according to Trump, violate the quality maxim, this may pertain to either his personal image (a) or to public opinion (b). If the media allegedly violate the quantity maxim, this can manifest itself in underrepresentation (c), that is, the omission of relevant information, or in overrepresentation (d), realized by an exaggerated focus on a specific news item. The five categories will be outlined with the help of illustrative examples in the following.

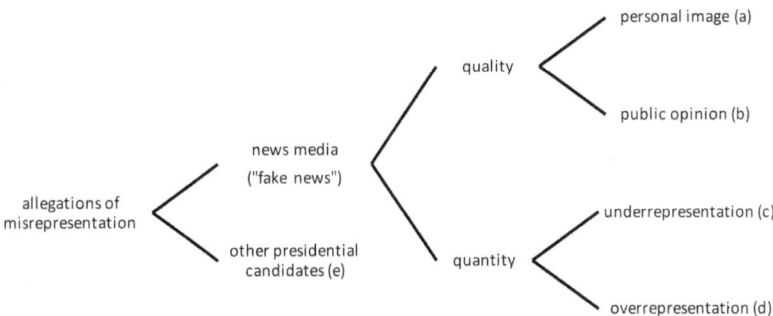

Figure 10.1 Trump's allegations of misrepresentation in primary election debates.

10.5.1 Allegations of Misrepresentation Concerning Trump's Personal Image (Category a)

According to Carson (2010: 257–65), lying is used by politicians for two main reasons: to get support for their individual agenda and to control public opinion. This corresponds with the fact that Trump's accusations refer either to his personal image or to the presentation of opinion polls. Whenever Trump's own utterances or actions are criticized by journalists, his defensive moves become particularly vigorous. In (3), when Trump is questioned by Neil Cavuto from the Fox Business Network, he claims that the *New York Times* misquoted him on economic relations with China.

(3) CAVUTO: Mr. Trump, sometimes maybe in the heat of the campaign, you say things and you have to dial them back. Last week, the *New York Times* editorial board quoted as saying that you would oppose, "up to 45 percent tariff on Chinese goods."
TRUMP: That's wrong. They were wrong. It's the *New York Times*, they are always wrong.
CAVUTO: Well--
TRUMP: They were wrong.
CAVUTO: You never said because they provided that--
TRUMP: No, I said, "I would use—" they were asking me what to do about North Korea. (January 14, 2016)

Trump's statement "they were wrong" refers to a report by the *New York Times* which, in turn, quoted a statement by Trump. Although Trump does not use the catchphrase *fake news* here, his verdict "It's the *New York Times*, they are always wrong" amounts to the same absolute disqualification and delegitimization, which is reinforced by the evaluative attribute *wrong* being used four times. Through this form of impoliteness, he attacks the institutional positive face of the newspaper and coerces the audience to take his side. With the adverb *always*, the expert authority of the respected news provider is entirely negated. By claiming that his utterance was misrepresented in the report, Trump manages to evade Cavuto's critical question and redirects the criticism toward the *New York Times*. This means that Trump denies the premise that he made a particular assertion, which cannot be immediately verified during the debate, thereby putting the very foundation of the investigative inquiry into doubt.

In another debate, Trump complains about the way in which the media covered violent scenes and related events that occurred during some of his campaign speeches. In this case, the discussion is about Trump having asked his audience to raise their hands in order to support him, which was supposedly misrepresented on NBC's *Today Show*, where he was portrayed as a fascist leader.

(4) TRUMP: It shows the total dishonesty of the press. We were having—on a few occasions, again massive crowds. And we're talking and I'm saying who is going to vote on Tuesday? Who is going to vote? The place goes crazy. Then I say, hey, do

me a favor. Raise your right hand. Do you swear you're going to vote for Donald Trump? Everyone's laughing, we're all having a good time. That's why I have much bigger crowds than Ted, because we have a good time at mine. [*applause*]

But we're all having a good time and the next day, on the *Today Show* and a couple of other place [*sic*], not too many. Because when you look at it, everyone's smiling, laughing. Their arms are raised like this. They had pictures, still pictures of people and they tried to equate it to Nazi Germany. [*bell rings*] It is a disgrace. It was a total disgrace. And I've had reporters, people that you know, come up to me and said that—what they did on the *Today Show* was a disgrace. [*applause*] (March 10, 2016)

In similar ways to the adverb *always*, the adjective *total* in the phrase "the total dishonesty of the press" has a superlative meaning that does not allow for any exceptions and thus delegitimizes journalists by attacking their credibility and authority. In addition, Trump claims that the media coverage was "a total disgrace," using this noun three times for the sake of emphasis. Semantically, the concept 'disgrace' has strong implications of shame and loss of respect, so that in this case delegitimization is based on moral evaluation as well. The blame put on Trump by the *Today Show* and by related programs is thus denied and redirected toward these media outlets. Trump's attack against this show is additionally underscored with the help of anonymous "reporters," introduced as "people that you know." In Trump's argument, these are journalists who took his side against the aforementioned reports written by their colleagues.

As in (3), the face-threatening maneuver is not directed toward journalists in the first frame of interaction but attacks media representatives potentially watching the debate in the second frame. Moreover, it persuasively addresses potential voters, the majority of whom are also situated in the second frame. With regard to the submaxims of the quality maxim, the depreciative characterizations "always wrong" and "total dishonesty" both imply that the reporters lack the necessary evidence. The latter phrase also indicates that the text producers deliberately say what they believe to be false, so that they supposedly lie to the public. Trump's supporters in the TV studio reinforce his argumentation with applause, inciting him to continue speaking after the bell rings. In both (3) and (4), Trump uses one particular instance of alleged misrepresentation in order to make generalized assertions about the fakeness of the media at large.

10.5.2 Allegations of Misrepresentation Concerning Public Opinion (Category b)

During the presidential election process, various news companies regularly conduct public opinion polls that are subsequently covered by the media and discussed in the debates. These polls play an important role since they not only reflect current ratings of candidates but also have an effect on the debates: candidates with low results will drop out of the campaign, as reflected by the decreasing number of contestants throughout the eleven debates (see Table 10.1). One particularly delicate topic for Trump is his relationship with the Hispanic population, since he repeatedly labeled Hispanics as criminals, which is a central argument for him to erect a wall at the southern US border.[1] In (5), he is confronted with poor ratings by panelist Maria Celeste Arrarás from the Spanish-language network Telemundo.

(5) ARRARÁS: But a brand new Telemundo poll says that three out of four Hispanics that vote nationwide have a negative opinion of you. They don't like you. Wouldn't that make you an unelectable—
TRUMP: No.
ARRARÁS: —candidate in a general election?
TRUMP: First of all, I don't believe anything Telemundo says.
ARRARÁS: You used to say that you love— [*laughter*]
TRUMP: Number one. Number two, I currently employ thousands of Hispanics, and over the years, I've employed tens of thousands of Hispanics. They're incredible people. They know, and the reason I won in Nevada, not only won the big one, but I also won subs, like, as an example, I won with women. . . .
ARRARÁS: For the record, you have said publicly that you loved Telemundo in the past. But it is not just a Telemundo poll. We have—
TRUMP: I love them. I love them. [*applause*] (February 25, 2016)

By retorting that he does not "believe anything Telemundo says," Trump again uses a generalizing assertion by means of the indefinite pronoun "anything," leaving no room for exceptions. With this reply, the question is utterly invalidated since its argumentative foundation is discarded, so that this type of delegitimization renders any justification on Trump's side superfluous. In this case, Trump does not literally assign the attribute of fakeness to the news company but rather states his own incredulity and thus indirectly discredits Telemundo. As it is a face-to-face conversation, he performs impoliteness in first-frame interaction, directly attacking a representative of the network. His utterances do not only address the recipients' positive face by means of stark disagreement and hostility but also indirectly target their negative face, assaulting the company's institutional status and professional freedom.

In consequence, Trump frames himself as a political and media authority entitled to question the credibility of polls. Arrarás, however, counterattacks with an emotional move, quoting Trump's past statement that he "loved Telemundo." The blatant contradiction between Trump's past and present utterances leads to a discrepancy that triggers involuntary humor and laughter in the audience, now threatening the candidate's trustworthiness and reputation. As a result, Trump first prevaricates with reference to alternative polls, and when confronted once again with his past expression of affection, he eventually backpedals with the words "I love them. I love them." The pronoun "them" here most probably refers to "Telemundo," since in the previous exchange Arrarás twice mentions Trump's love for this TV network. Thus, in this example Trump's hasty and generalizing fake news accusation results in damage to his own negative face, undermining his image as a reliable candidate.

In addition, Trump's attribution of fakeness to media companies may be selective when favorable reporting comes from an outlet usually classified as "fake." For instance, during the debate on March 3, 2016, Ted Cruz calls other Republicans to join him in a coalition against the potential nominee Donald Trump. As an argument, Cruz points out that 65 percent of Republicans reject Trump as presidential candidate and that Trump was beaten in five states by other competitors during the presidential race. In (6), Trump replies to Cruz's attack with reference to a favorable poll by CNN, which is commonly his prototype of a "fake news" network (Davis and Sinnreich 2019: 152). Trump here argues that Cruz is rejected by 85 percent of Republicans, while Trump himself won ten states, as opposed to the five states won by Cruz.

(6) TRUMP: CNN spent a lot of money on a poll, just came out. I'm at 49. He's at 15. He tells me about 65 percent of the people. It's not 65 percent of the people. If you go by that, 85 percent of the people. Then he goes, we have five. And—well, excuse me, I won 10. I won 10 states. If you listen to him, it's like—I won 10 states. Everybody knows that on Super Tuesday Trump was the winner. There wasn't one person that didn't say that. (March 3, 2016)

As in the tweet in (2), it appears that in the presidential debates Trump already equates fake news with unfavorable news, while positive news is excluded from the allegation of misrepresentation even if the news provider is generally labeled as "fake." This leads to ambivalence and inconsistency not only in Trump's self-presentation but also in delegitimization, since authority is sporadically attributed to journalists otherwise discredited as dishonest. Thus, it is an integral part of Trump's fake news agenda that the defamatory label is assigned inconsistently and strongly depends on the context, serving his campaign as a flexible and adaptable tool.

10.5.3 Allegations of Underrepresentation (Category c)

The label *fake news* does not always refer to blatant lies but may also include allegations of omitting and concealing relevant facts, which means Trump feels that his actions are underrepresented in the media. Thus, according to the first submaxim of quantity, Trump accuses journalists of making their contributions less informative than is required by their professional ethics, which demand a comprehensive account of all facts. In (7), he is asked by Chris Wallace from *Fox News* whether he has proof that the Mexican government actually sends criminals to the United States.

(7) WALLACE: . . . and you have repeatedly said that you have evidence that the Mexican government is doing this, but you have evidence you have refused or declined to share. Why not use this first Republican presidential debate to share your proof with the American people?
TRUMP: So, if it weren't for me, you wouldn't even be talking about illegal immigration, Chris. You wouldn't even be talking about it. [*applause*] This was not a subject that was on anybody's mind until I brought it up at my announcement. And I said, Mexico is sending. Except the reporters, because they're a very dishonest lot, generally speaking, in the world of politics, they didn't cover my statement the way I said it. The fact is, since then, many killings, murders, crime, drugs pouring across the border . . . (August 6, 2015)

Trump manages to evade the investigative request for evidence by means of two techniques: first, he claims that the media neglected the issue of illegal immigration and prides himself on disclosing respective problems and attracting attention to them. He thereby insinuates that he is actually doing the job of the press by addressing urgent social issues. Second, he retorts that his original words were misquoted, since he did not refer to the "Mexican government" but to "Mexico" sending criminals such as rapists and drug dealers across the border. Based on these two strategies, the media are delegitimized by the claim that they ignore pressing questions, which ultimately implies that they deceive the public. In this way, Trump assaults not only their professional authority but also their moral integrity since they purportedly fail to inform their readers about impending harm. With the phrase "a very dishonest lot" he again combines an emphatic stance in the form of the intensifying adverb *very* with the practice of generalization, which he makes explicit with the metadiscursive adverbial *generally speaking*.

In several debates, Trump portrays himself as the straightforward and outspoken messenger of inconvenient truths, while claiming that the press hold back information owing to political correctness that does not allow them to provide the public with all necessary facts. This is illustrated in Trump's reply to the question whether he has reconsidered his proposal of banning Muslims from entering the United States. His answer implies that the mainstream media do not sufficiently address the threat posed by Muslim immigrants.

(8) TRUMP: Look, we have to stop with political correctness. We have to get down to creating a country that's not going to have the kind of problems that we've had with people flying planes into the World Trade Centers . . . (January 14, 2016)

Example (9) is Trump's reaction to CNN reporter Jake Tapper, who inquired about Trump's assertion that Islam hates America. Once again, Trump accuses the media of neglecting or playing down the danger emanating from Muslim terrorism, in contrast to himself, who openly addresses the issue.

(9) TRUMP: Now you can say what you want, and you can be politically correct if you want. I don't want to be so politically correct. I like to solve problems. We have a serious, serious problem of hate. [*applause*] (March 10, 2016)

In this way, Trump additionally promotes his image as an anti-politician who is opposed to the allegedly treacherous establishment in Washington. By constructing a divide between passive and deceitful political correctness on the one hand and sincere determination on the other, he coerces viewers to take his side. In a more intricate way, allegations of underrepresentation may be contrasted with accusations of overrepresentation, as shown by (10), where Trump is questioned about tax laws that he benefited from.

(10) TRUMP: . . . virtually every person that you read about on the front page of the business sections, they've used the law. The difference is, when somebody else uses those laws, nobody writes about it. When I use it, they say, "Trump,

Trump, Trump." The fact is, I built a net worth of more than $10 billion. . . .
Four times, I've taken advantage of the laws. And frankly, so has everybody else in my position. (August 6, 2015)

Trump here complains about quantity-related deception by the media from a double perspective. In regard to other, lesser-known businessmen, the first submaxim of quantity is allegedly breached, since less information is provided about their activities than is required. As far as Trump himself is concerned, he claims that the second submaxim is disregarded by the media, for more information on his affairs is given than is seemingly required. While the negative pronoun *nobody* claims absoluteness without any exception, the stance adverbial *frankly* creates a contrast to the supposedly misleading news reports.

10.5.4 Allegations of Overrepresentation (Category d)

The purported non-observation of the second submaxim of quantity by the press is criticized by Trump in other contexts as well. He claims that selected items of information are particularly foregrounded by journalists, while other facts are suppressed and located in the background of news reporting. Thus, in (11), David Muir from ABC News addresses the excessive force used by police against minorities.

(11) MUIR: You have said police are the most mistreated people in America. As president, how do you bridge the divide?
TRUMP: Well, there is a divide, but I have to say that the police are absolutely mistreated and misunderstood, and if there is an incident, whether it's an incident done purposely—which is a horror, and you should really take very strong action—or if it is a mistake, it's on your news casts all night, all week, all month, and it never ends. The police in this country have done an unbelievable job of keeping law and order, and they're afraid for their jobs, they're afraid of the mistreatment they get . . . .
MUIR: Great. Mr. Trump, I did ask about bridging the divide though as president. (February 6, 2016)

By way of prevarication, Trump first highlights the merits and achievements of US police officers and then accuses the media of exaggerating police brutality through unceasing reports on such incidents. This alleged overrepresentation is rhetorically underscored by the climactic sequence "all night, all week, all month" as well as by the hyperbolic adverb *never*. In Trump's words, media misrepresentation of the police is based on the fact that officers are "mistreated" by journalists and consequently "misunderstood" by the public. In this way, Trump insinuates one-sided and biased news coverage, which means that he performs delegitimization by undermining journalists' authority as impartial reporters and by doubting their moral integrity. Since the media are supposedly responsible for the fact that police officers are "afraid" while maintaining law and order, reporters are even portrayed as a threat to law enforcement. Although Muir briefly acknowledges Trump's lengthy attack as "great," he then explicitly indicates that he noticed the candidate's evasive maneuver. This discussion proves that the construction of newsworthiness is a matter of perspective and can thus be assessed differently by the media on the one hand and by news actors such as politicians on the other (Bednarek and Caple 2017: 3–5).

Alternatively, allegations of overrepresentation may refer to Trump himself, as already hinted at in (10). Consider (12), in which he complains that moderators in the debates frequently ask other competitors about their attitude toward Trump. In this case, Hugh Hewitt from the Salem Radio Network asks Trump how, as future commander in chief, he would deal with Vladimir Putin.

(12) HEWITT: Mr. Trump?
TRUMP: I think it's very sad that CNN leads Jeb Bush, Governor Bush, down a road by starting off virtually all the questions, "Mr. Trump this, Mister"—I think it's very sad. And, frankly, I watched—I think it's very sad. And, frankly, I watched the first debate, and the first long number of questions were, "Mr. Trump said this, Mr. Trump said that. Mr. Trump"—these poor guys—although, I must tell you, Santorum, good guy. Governor Huckabee, good guy. They were very nice, and I respect them greatly. But I thought it was very unfair that virtually the entire early portion of the debate was Trump this, Trump that, in order to get ratings, I guess. (December 15, 2015)

By addressing the way in which reporters initiate their questions, Trump moves to a metadiscursive level that allows him to evade the actual question. He claims that by frequently mentioning his name, moderators overrepresent some of his past statements in order to appeal to television viewers. Consequently, Trump attacks media authority by doubting journalistic neutrality with the obvious aim of delegitimization. While he insinuates with the idiom "lead . . . down a road" that journalists try to steer candidates in a preordained and thus "unfair" direction, he underlines his own righteousness with the repeated stance adverbial *frankly*, concomitantly displaying disappointment ("sad") and compassion ("these poor guys"). Once again, the accusations are expressed on the basis of a highly generalizing quantifier, in this case "[virtually] all," which hardly allows for positive exceptions.

10.5.5 Allegations of Misrepresentation by Other Presidential Candidates (Category e)

In addition to the media, Trump also accuses his competitors and fellow party members of disseminating misinformation. In his attempt to disassociate himself from the established political elite, he generally disqualifies the other candidates with the sweeping statement "I don't believe these politicians. All talk, no action" (March 3, 2016). More specifically, since Ted Cruz, Jeb Bush, and Marco Rubio are his direct rivals, he tries to diminish their trustworthiness without the discursive detour via the news media. Thus, in (13), Trump aggressively accuses Bush of lying after the latter attacked him in his preferred role as a businessman.

(13) BUSH: And we need ... someone that doesn't brag, for example, that he has been bankrupt four times and it was great, because he could use the legal system. Someone—
TRUMP: That's not—let me respond. That's another lie. I never went bankrupt! [*crosstalk*]
DICKERSON: Hold on, Mr. Trump. [*crosstalk*]
TRUMP: No, but it's another lie.
DICKERSON: Hold on, Mr. Trump.
TRUMP: No, but it's another lie. This guy doesn't know what he's talking about. Just a lie. (February 13, 2016)

The orderly progression of the exchange is disturbed by Trump's interruptions and overlapping contributions, so that moderator John Dickerson from CBS News has trouble restoring order. By retorting three times that his former bankruptcy is "another" lie, Trump presupposes that Bush lied before, thus characterizing him as a dishonest and treacherous politician. When fellow party members are attacked, the face-threatening act takes place in first-frame interaction and is addressed not to an abstract media company but to a specific individual, so that face damage and corresponding delegitimization appear much more immediate and severe. In some cases, the accusations are additionally supported by personalized defamatory vocatives, as demonstrated by (14), where Rubio claims that Trump hired many foreign workers, and by (15), which is Trump's reply to Cruz criticizing him for his wavering views on abortion.

(14) RUBIO: ... let me finish the statement. This is important.
TRUMP: You haven't hired one person, you liar.
RUBIO: He hired workers from Poland. And he had to pay a million dollars or so in a judgment from—
TRUMP: That's wrong. That's wrong. Totally wrong. (February 25, 2016)
(15) TRUMP: You probably are worse than Jeb Bush. You are the single biggest liar. This guy's lied—let me just tell you, this guy lied about Ben Carson when he took votes away from Ben Carson in Iowa, and he just continues.... This guy will say anything, nasty guy. (February 13, 2016)

When Rubio is called a "liar" (see 14) and Cruz is labeled the "single biggest liar" and a "nasty guy" (see 15), this equals a strong moral devaluation, since Trump denigrates the very character of the addressees by placing them in the undesirable category of untruthful and deceitful individuals. In this way, he perpetuates and reinforces the widespread public perception that the "stereotypical politician is conniving, egotistical, and dishonest," as pointed out by research on social stereotypes (Lakoff 1987: 85). Trump's hyperbolic rhetoric once again surfaces in the maximizing adverb "totally" (see 14) as well as in the comparative *worse*, the superlative *single biggest*, and the indefinite pronoun *anything* (see 15). In this fierce political competition, the more the other is discredited as unreliable and corrupt, the more the self is profiled as trustworthy and appealing.

10.6 Conclusions

The analyses have shown that credibility and trustworthiness, which are of tremendous value in election campaigns, are hotly disputed and negotiated in presidential primary debates. Trump's fake news agenda manifests itself in diverse allegations of misrepresentation that are strategically used in order to exercise discursive power and persuade the voters in favor of his candidacy. This strategy is common already in the debates, before *fake news* became a catchphrase in presidential tweets and was thus established as an integral lexical item in the Trumpish idiolectal discourse.

In the televised debates, Trump's accusations of fakeness may refer either to the media or to his competitors in the presidential race. In the latter case, personalized attacks are directed toward individuals, portraying them as liars and deceivers. If news media are in focus, Trump addresses either a supposed violation of the quality maxim—which equals downright lying—or a violation of the quantity maxim—which does not necessarily imply lying but other types of deception. A purported violation of the quality maxim may refer to Trump's personal image or to opinion polls reflecting public perception. As regards the quantity maxim, accusations either pertain to the underrepresentation of information due to political correctness or to the overrepresentation of news items that are unwelcome from Trump's perspective. We can therefore conclude that, in such cases, news providers and Trump have deviating approaches to the newsworthiness of particular reports. Moreover, Trump's attribution of fakeness is highly selective, since favorable polls by media outlets otherwise rejected as "fake" may be accepted as reliable by him.

In terms of social interaction, allegations of misrepresentation are a form of impoliteness, which threatens the addressees' positive face through disagreement and hostility and harms their negative face by attacks on their institutional integrity and independence. Most importantly, however, the fake news agenda aims to delegitimize news providers that publish critical reports about Trump and his political practices. Delegitimization is then based on (a) the minimization of media authority by doubting trustworthiness, (b) moral devaluation by insinuating low ethical standards and dishonesty, and (c) rationalization by way of biased arguments such as exaggerated political correctness.

While the general function of the fake news agenda is delegitimization, it also fulfills more specific functions in the conversational interaction of the debates: by blatantly rejecting premises that critical questions are based on, these inquiries can be conveniently evaded. Simultaneously, the accusation of misinformation serves Trump as a powerful 'counterstrike' that attracts attention through generalization and hyperbole, and additionally portrays him as a vigorous and determined leader. All in all, as regards the negotiation of factuality, Trump obviously intends to enhance the credibility of his own statements by casting doubt on unfavorable media reports. Thus, in the primary debates, the fake news agenda was a decisive tool for Trump to undermine the power of critical journalism as the fourth estate, aiming to legitimize his claim for the presidency.

Note

1 For a further analysis of this and similar references to Hispanics, see Schneider and McClure, this volume.

References

Aitchison, Jean (2012), *Words in the Mind: An Introduction to the Mental Lexicon*, 4th edn, Chichester: Wiley-Blackwell.
Austin, John L. (1975), *How to Do Things with Words*, 2nd edn, Oxford: Clarendon.
Bakir, Vian, Eric Herring, David Miller, and Piers Robinson (2018), "Lying and Deception in Politics," in Jörg Meibauer (ed.), *The Oxford Handbook of Lying*, 529–40, Oxford: Oxford University Press.
Barclay, Donald A. (2018), *Fake News, Propaganda, and Plain Old Lies: How to Find Trustworthy Information in the Digital Age*, Lanham: Rowman & Littlefield.
Bednarek, Monika and Helen Caple (2017), *The Discourse of News Values: How News Organizations Create Newsworthiness*, Oxford: Oxford University Press.
Benoit, William L. (2014), *Political Election Debates: Informing Voters about Policy and Character*, Lanham: Lexington Books.
Bousfield, Derek (2008), *Impoliteness in Interaction*, Amsterdam: John Benjamins.
Brown, Penelope and Stephen C. Levinson (1987), *Politeness: Some Universals in Language Usage*, Cambridge: Cambridge University Press.
Cap, Piotr (2006), *Legitimisation in Political Discourse: A Cross-Disciplinary Perspective on the Modern US War Rhetoric*, Newcastle: Cambridge Scholars.
Carson, Thomas L. (2010), *Lying and Deception: Theory and Practice*, Oxford: Oxford University Press.
Carveth, Roth (2019), "Setting the 'Fake News' Agenda: Trump's Use of Twitter and the Agenda-Building Effect," in Michele Lockhart (ed.), *President Donald Trump and His Political Discourse: Ramifications of Rhetoric via Twitter*, 170–89, New York: Routledge.
Chilton, Paul (2004), *Analysing Political Discourse: Theory and Practice*, London: Routledge.
Chilton, Paul and Christina Schäffner (2011), "Discourse and Politics," in Teun A. van Dijk (ed.), *Discourse Studies: A Multidisciplinary Introduction*, 303–30, London: Sage.
Culpeper, Jonathan (2011), *Impoliteness: Using Language to Cause Offence*, Cambridge: Cambridge University Press.
Dailey, William O., Edward A. Hinck, and Shelly S. Hinck (2008), *Politeness in Presidential Debates: Shaping Political Face in Campaign Debates from 1960 to 2004*, Lanham: Rowman & Littlefield.
Davis, Dorian H. and Aram Sinnreich (2019), "Tweet the Press: Effects of Donald Trump's 'Fake News!' Epithet on Civics and Popular Culture," in Michele Lockhart (ed.), *President Donald Trump and His Political Discourse: Ramifications of Rhetoric via Twitter*, 149–69, New York: Routledge.
Dynel, Marta (2011), "A Web of Deceit: A Neo-Gricean View on Types of Verbal Deception," *International Review of Pragmatics*, 3 (2): 137–65.
Fetzer, Anita (2011), "'Here is the Difference, here is the Passion, here is the Chance to be Part of a Great Change.' Strategic Context Importation in Political Discourse," in Anita

Fetzer and Etsuko Oishi (eds.), *Context and Contexts: Parts Meet Whole?*, 115–46, Amsterdam: John Benjamins.

Grice, H. Paul (1975), "Logic and Conversation," in Peter Cole and Jerry L. Morgan (eds.), *Syntax and Semantics*. Vol. 3: *Speech Acts*, 41–58, New York: Academic Press.

Grice, H. Paul (1989), *Studies in the Way of Words*, Cambridge, MA: Harvard University Press.

Huang, Yan (2014), *Pragmatics*, Oxford: Oxford University Press.

Kellner, Douglas (2018), "Donald Trump and the Politics of Lying," in Michael A. Peters, Sharon Rider, Mats Hyvönen, and Tina Besley (eds.), *Post-Truth, Fake News: Viral Modernity & Higher Education*, 89–100, Singapore: Springer.

Kessler, Glenn, Salvador Rizzo, and Meg Kelly (2019), "President Trump Has Made 10,796 False or Misleading Claims over 869 Days," *The Washington Post*, June 10. Available online: https://www.washingtonpost.com/politics/2019/06/10/president-trump-has-made-false-or-misleading-claims-over-days/?noredirect=on&utm_term=.c689836af19f (accessed June 11, 2019).

Lakoff, George (1987), *Women, Fire, and Dangerous Things: What Categories Reveal about the Mind*, Chicago: The University of Chicago Press.

McIntyre, Lee (2018), *Post-Truth*, Cambridge, MA: MIT Press.

McNair, Brain (2018), *Fake News: Falsehoods, Fabrication and Fantasy in Journalism*, New York: Routledge.

Meibauer, Jörg (2014), *Lying at the Semantics-Pragmatics Interface*, Berlin & Boston: De Gruyter Mouton.

Saul, Jennifer M. (2012), *Lying, Misleading, and What Is Said: An Exploration in Philosophy of Language and in Ethics*, Oxford: Oxford University Press.

Schroeder, Alan (2016), *Presidential Debates: Risky Business on the Campaign Trail*, 3rd edn, New York: Columbia University Press.

Sclafani, Jennifer (2018), *Talking Donald Trump: A Sociolinguistic Study of Style, Metadiscourse, and Political Identity*, London: Routledge.

Searle, John R. (1969), *Speech Acts: An Essay in the Philosophy of Language*, Cambridge: Cambridge University Press.

Van Leeuwen, Theo (2018), "Legitimation and Multimodality," in Ruth Wodak and Bernhard Forchtner (eds.), *The Routledge Handbook of Language and Politics*, 218–32, London: Routledge.

Watts, Richard J. (2003), *Politeness*, Cambridge: Cambridge University Press.

Woolley, John and Gerhard Peters (1999–), "The American Presidency Project." Available online: http://www.presidency.ucsb.edu/ (accessed February 15, 2019).

11

Sorry Not Sorry

Political Apology in the Age of Trump

Jan David Hauck and Teruko Vida Mitsuhara

In memoriam Jennifer Jackson

11.1 Introduction

Donald Trump's well-known trademark and self-proclaimed key to success is to never apologize. This principle is known as "the John Wayne code," after the American Western actor embodying a predominant archetype of strong, unregretful masculinity from a bygone era, where apologies are tantamount to weakness (Battistella 2014: 172–3). Indeed, Trump is rarely heard uttering words of regret, and one looks in vain for genuine apologies. If the need arises to repair or retract a statement or action, Trump denies, deflects, retreats, or repeats the offense in modified form (Fisher 2018). While such rhetorical strategies are not unique among American politicians, in this chapter we will show that Trump uses them in a specific way to accomplish two things: (1) to distinguish himself from the class of recent politicians such as Bill Clinton or Barack Obama (see Battistella 2014: 173–4) whom he frequently derides as weak, and (2) to appeal to a particular kind of "general public," constructed in opposition to the "establishment."

Trump's discursive practices stand in contrast to what has become a canonical form of public apology in the United States, likewise designed to achieve alignment with the general public while absolving the apologizer from misconduct: the Christian personal testimonial. This form of apology has gained visibility in recent years in US politics through mass-mediatized apologies for extramarital affairs of prominent politicians. As analyzed by Jennifer Jackson (2012), these testimonials construct multiple versions of the speaker's self, producing a temporal disjuncture between past and present self through the construction of an opposition of sinner and redeemed. For example, President Clinton (1993–2001) issued an apology regarding his affair with White House intern Monica Lewinsky, in which he quoted from the Bible and highlighted his "determination to change and to repair breaches of my own making." By quoting scripture, politicians "extricate the sinner from his sin through a relationship with

God and recenter the Saved Self through forgiveness" (Jackson 2012: 51). Invoking the Christian narrative of redemption, the penitent not only seeks absolution for himself but demonstrates the power of repentance for others, that is, for the American public. The public apology becomes the vehicle through which the sinner transcends his past transgression and rejoins that public as saved and redeemed (Jackson 2012: 49). In Jackson's words, the repentant politician presents himself as a generalized "Everyman"[1] who is prone to sinning but can be saved.

We argue in this chapter that Trump also uses elements of the apologetic discourse from the Christian testimonial in order to produce identification with "the Everyman." However, he avoids a central element that is crucial for apologies to be perceived as genuine: the disjuncture of past and present self. As we will show, he replaces the contrast between a politician's past and present selves with a seemingly analogous contrast between himself and his opponents—for example, claiming that the latter have done "far worse" things or accusing them of "running the country into the ground." This allows him to bolster the public's perception of him as authentic and always unwaveringly himself, while at the same time aligning with that very public against his political opponents.

Instead of presenting himself as "the Everyman sinner" whose transformation to the better demonstrates the potential of redemption to others, he aligns with "the Everyman victim," that is, a victim of the politics of his adversaries. He achieves this by means of what Gunn (2018) has called "perverse rhetoric," that is, a discursive strategy that establishes moral equivalencies between his or his supporters' behavior and that of critics, thus drawing attention away from the actual point of criticism. Besides the data we analyze later, such rhetoric is most visible in his remarks about the Charlottesville violence in August 2017, when Trump identified "very fine people" on "both sides" and thereby presented the protest against White supremacist hate groups as a violent act against those groups. As a consequence, protestors and White supremacists were cast as equally responsible for the violence that occurred.

This "both sides" logic is a crucial element of Trump's rhetorical strategies in the (non-)apologies we will analyze here. As a sitting president, Trump has never apologized, neither for his response to Charlottesville—despite mounting public pressure—nor for extramarital affairs of which he has been frequently accused, but which he has denied.[2] However, there are a few public and televised apologies by Trump as a presidential candidate concerning the misogynistic *Access Hollywood* tape, in which, among other things, he bragged about how he is able to grab women's genitals because he is a celebrity. Though this was not an affair, the remarks were made when Trump was already married to Melania (who was pregnant at the time). Trump is heard saying that he had attempted to have sexual intercourse with a married woman, and the actions Trump describes on the tape amount to illegal sexual misconduct, which warrants comparison of Trump's apology to the Christian testimonials discussed by Jackson (2012). However, as Trump has not yet been found guilty of sexual misconduct, he designs his apology in a way that deviates from the canonical US politicians' Christian testimonial, which we analyze in section 11.4. We approach Trump's apologetic discourse from a linguistic anthropological perspective, informed by semiotics, pragmatics, as well as narrative and conversation analysis.

11.2 Apologies

Apologies are part of "remedial interchanges," that is, communicative sequences that serve the purpose of changing "the meaning that otherwise might be given to an act, transforming what could be seen as offensive into what can be seen as acceptable" (Goffman 1971: 109). Multiple strategies have been identified and categorized in the literature (e.g., Ware and Linkugel 1973; Benoit [1995] 2014), ranging from outright denials over attempts to mitigate and give justifications to reduce the offensiveness, to full-scale admissions of wrongdoing and asking for forgiveness. What they all have in common is that they address the "face" of the offended party, but also of the offender.[3]

Goffman (1971: 112) makes a crucial distinction between apologies and accounts. While apologies acknowledge an offending act as morally wrong and establish agency and responsibility of the offender, accounts minimize the act by denying its occurrence, pleading ignorance, or claiming it was not supposed to be taken seriously and certainly not meant as an expression of someone's moral character. However, this is no strict dichotomy since apologies mostly also require accounts, and accounts can include elements of apology.

Through their acknowledgment of wrongdoing, apologies involve a splitting of the "self," with "self" referring to the reflexive awareness of one's existence in time and space and how that existence is perceived by others (Ochs and Capps 1996). The speech act of apology splits the self into "a blameworthy part and a part that stands back and sympathizes with the blame giving," and it is this aspect of sympathy that makes the offender "worthy of being brought back into the fold" (Goffman 1971: 113). Such a separation between the offending and the apologizing self corresponds to the separation between the time and place of the past offense and the time and place of the present apology. Both parts of the split self are brought in relation to one another in the narrative event of the apology (Jackson 2012).

This splitting of self is a necessary prerequisite for apologies to be perceived as genuine. However, as the offender's present self is distanced from the one committing the offense, it also entails a certain risk, particularly in the case of public apologies, and especially in political contexts. Public apologies imply the official acknowledgment of wrongdoing (Leech 2014: 132; Murphy 2019: 204). As such, the outcome may go beyond the desired effect of repairing the relationship between the offender and the offended, in the sense that public apologies may trigger subsequent requests for reparations beyond the verbal apology itself. For this reason, public apologies are often carefully constructed to minimize responsibility, calculating their benefits and costs (Kampf 2009). The use of formal apology tokens such as *I apologize* or *I am sorry* may be avoided in favor of more vague formulations that merely provide an account or express sympathy.

Responses to public apologies may be temporally and spatially removed, involve a variety of actors, or remain absent altogether. For example, a national government may issue a statement apologizing to a group of people for past injustices suffered. Both the actual offenders and the offended may no longer be alive and often there are no clear recipients entitled to "accept" the apology, although the descendants of those affected or certain institutions may be understood as recipients. This means that the recipients of a politician's apology for an offending statement, a racist remark for example, may be an entire population, and responses are often distributed across a wide range of public individuals, media outlets, and institutions. Politicians have to carefully calibrate their words in order to control how different publics perceive their apology (Jackson 2012; Ancarno 2015).

11.3 Coherence and Authenticity of the Political Self

In public pronouncements, politicians frequently make use of personal narratives to craft a particular public persona, a "political self" (Duranti 2006: 468). These narratives are accounts from their life that in one way or another speak to the kind of person a politician purports to be. Public apologies fall into this genre; they are narrative events. Discourse analysts have shown that narratives, as ubiquitous elements of everyday talk, provide crucial resources for the presentation and calibration of the self. They "imbue events with a temporal and logical order" (Ochs and Capps 2001: 2), giving coherence to experience for narrator and audience alike. There are a number of constraints that narrators must deal with in the telling of their stories (Ochs and Capps 2001: 1–58). For example, narrators must work to maintain alignment between the narrated self and the narrative self, such that the (present) self that is evoked in the telling of the story is not radically at odds with the (past) self in the story. Narrators must also strive to be as authentic and accurate as possible in retelling a personal experience, while at the same time telling it in a way that is consistent and follows a coherent narrative logic.

The contrast between coherence and authenticity is particularly salient in the construction of the political self. Political candidates "worry about how to project and maintain an image of themselves as beings whose past, present, and future actions, beliefs, and evaluations follow some clear basic principles, none of which contradicts another" (Duranti 2006: 469)—that is, they worry about how to display "existential coherence" (Duranti 2006: 472). After all, lack of coherence is a common charge in the arena of politics, including accusations of inconsistencies, contradictions, lies, or failure to keep a promise. Candidates must appear as authentic as possible while guaranteeing coherence, both in terms of the kind of person they project and in the evaluation of their past actions.

Apologies are particularly vulnerable to charges of incoherence and inauthenticity. To some extent this is because their main purpose is facework and they are highly dependent on factors outside of the speech event, that is, the offense and the context in which it occurred, the offended party, and the context of the apology. But mostly it is due to an inherent disjuncture in the apology itself, as apologies split the self into two as elaborated in section 11.2. Indeed, authenticity of the apology *requires* the apologizing party to acknowledge and thus objectify a past (version of) self as distinct from the present self—such as when the offended party is assured, "I won't do it again"—but distancing oneself from one's own past actions inevitably makes the self vulnerable to the charge of inauthenticity. There is, however, a canonical form of the political apology that circumvents this double bind through the invocation of the larger moral order of Christianity: the Christian testimonial.

11.4 Public Apology as Christian Testimonial

The Christian testimonial is the prototypical form of apology in that it requires a split self. At the core of the doctrine of Christianity is the assumption that no one is born a Christian but must become one through redemption. The penitent is forgiven by God's grace and accepted back into the community of the saved.

> To apologize for one's sin is seen as a form of witnessing to others the redemptive power of God and the power of one's belief system shaping the everyday life of man. . . . Transgression's subsequent rote narrative of apology is the allegorical journey of the Lost but Found, the speaker the embodiment of the Reborn. Sin is a sanctioned act of the very moral code that denounces it and serves as a requisite social act to perpetuate moral alignments to Christianity, its ideologies and the moral institutions it manifests. (Jackson 2012: 59)

The Christian testimonial has become an institutionalized rhetorical staple for politicians to display how they have risen from sinner to saved. It shaped US public apology such that "the sinning and confessing men become the bodily incarnations of a whole moral order, making sin itself requisite for the continuation of this order" (Jackson 2012: 50). In other words, being a sinning or morally imperfect politician is part of how US politicians participate in the moral framework of being "the Everyman." The repeated use of this format has made it "accessible and deployed as a plug-and-play idiom of God's moral order" (Jackson 2012: 50). This format is most evident in public apologies for extramarital affairs.

As the hallmark feature of the Christian testimonial, the person issuing the apology in the present disavows the actions of the past in an attempt to redeem themselves, with the narrative effect of a split self. There are several ways in which such a splitting is achieved. One is by shifting between first- and third-person references. To illustrate this point, Jackson (2012: 53) refers to the public apologies of American Pentecostal minister Jimmy Swaggart who was caught having extramarital affairs: "I, Jimmy Swaggart . . . I have asked myself that 10,000 times through 10,000 tears. Maybe Jimmy Swaggart has tried to live his entire life as though he were not human." Another common strategy is to alternate between versions of the self where the private man who has committed a sin is distinct from the public one who is faultless and has served his constituency well. This split is usually done to minimize the public gaze on anything the apologizer deems "private" while foregrounding their public achievements (see section 11.5.1 for an example).

A third strategy works by either verbally or physically showcasing the "true" self (see also Gruber 2014: 93; Benoit [1995] 2014: 24) as opposed to the one that emerges in public media discourse. For example, politicians often strategically stage alibis and witnesses, usually the wife and the children, in the background of the mediatized apology, evoking a public image of the apologizer as first and foremost a family man. The split self here is subtle and implied via careful crafting of the broadcast image, with the wife and family usually referred to at some point in the apology. Also, the apology contains references to time and space, which become chief ways to split the "true" self from the past offending one. The theatricality of this apology drama sets up the politician as not only a public figure but as a husband who privately made mistakes but has importantly been forgiven as evident in the visible support of his family, most importantly the offended woman, his wife. If done well, these strategies of dismantling the self in the public apology can save a political career, as the following example of Bill Clinton shows.

11.5 Contrastive Analysis of Two Cases of Political Apologies

In what follows we analyze two televised statements by Bill Clinton in which he apologizes for his affair with the then twenty-two-year-old White House intern, Monica Lewinsky, and several instances of Trump's apologies for the *Access Hollywood* tape. We provide the Clinton case to illustrate the canonical form of political apology as Christian testimonial and show that while Trump invokes this genre and appears to be following the same pattern he diverges from it in crucial ways, most importantly avoiding a split self.

11.5.1 "I Have Sinned"—Bill Clinton's Testimonial

Between 1995 and 1997, Clinton and Lewinsky had an affair that became public and resulted in an impeachment trial in 1998. After months of not acknowledging his infidelity, the evidence was proven indisputable, and Clinton apologized to the American public for what he called "the spectacle of the last seven months." He issued a televised statement on August 17, 1998, addressing the affair as well as a deposition made in January that year where he did not "volunteer information" about it.

(1) *Clinton's statement on national television, August 17, 1998*[4]

> I answered their questions truthfully about my private life, questions no American citizen would ever want to answer. Still, I must take complete responsibility for all my actions, both public and private. . . . I know that my public comments and my silence about this matter gave a false impression. I misled people, including even my wife. I deeply regret that. . . . This matter is between me, and the two people I love most—my wife and daughter—and our God. . . . I intend to reclaim my family life for my family. It's nobody's business but ours. Even presidents have private lives. It is time to stop the pursuit of personal destruction and the prying into private lives and get on with our national life.

While he does say he "regrets" that he "misled people, including even [his] wife," other apology tokens are missing, and the statement must be understood as an account for self-defense but not an apology, most importantly because the American public did not accept it as one. And while he invokes God, Clinton avoids the sinner–saved framework, characteristic of the Christian testimonial. Instead, the statement relies on the second tactic discussed earlier, the distinction between private and public self. However, instead of aligning with the American public, the self-defensive passages, "questions no American citizen would ever want to answer" and "nobody's business but ours," place him against that very public. He emerges as a victim of the public gaze, not as a private man in need of forgiveness from the public he wronged. The statement was not received as a real apology and public opinion remained negative.

Eventually, Clinton himself acknowledged this and issued a second apology at the White House Annual Prayer Breakfast three weeks later on September 11, 1998:

(2) *Clinton's statement at the White House Annual Prayer Breakfast, September 11, 1998 (excerpt 1)*[5]

I agree with those who have said, that in my first statement ... I was not contrite enough. I don't think there is a fancy way to say that I have sinned. It is important to me that everybody who has been hurt know that the sorrow I feel is genuine.

Here he follows the format of the Christian testimonial that frames his transgression in the sinner–saved dynamic. He then proceeds to specify recipients of the apology including not only his wife and family but also Monica Lewinsky, her family, and the American people, whom he has asked for forgiveness. He continues:

(3) *Clinton's statement at the White House Annual Prayer Breakfast, September 11, 1998, continued (excerpt 2)*

But, I believe, that to be forgiven, more than sorrow is required—at least two more things. First, genuine repentance—a determination to change and to repair breaches of my own making. Second, what my Bible calls a broken spirit; an understanding that I must have God's help to be the person that I want to be.

In quoting the Bible, the Prayer of St. Francis, and the Yom Kippur liturgy, Clinton summons "the work and guidance of God as a means to extricate the sinner from his sin" (Jackson 2012: 51), which makes his apology appear genuine and helps aligning himself with the Everyman.

In Clinton's first statement, he attempts to split the self between private and public by affirming that the matter is a private affair that does not affect the American public. In this way, he defends his non-repentant and non-transformed self. His apology also lacks a temporal or spatial distinction between the self that wants privacy and the self that publicly announces that America should worry about other things, thus resulting in a non-successful apology. By contrast, in the second statement Clinton no longer excludes the American public from his private affair, but instead invites them to witness his transformation. He emerges a repentant man who is sorrowful for misleading the public. Clinton received a standing ovation by the many men of faith in attendance for the White House Annual Prayer Breakfast.

11.5.2 "I've Never Said I'm a Perfect Person"— Donald Trump's Video Statement

"To win, one must never apologize," Fisher (2018) succinctly characterizes Trump's basic rule of behavior. If the need arises to pull back on a statement or action, "he has crafted a method of apology that is equal parts retreat and doubling down." Trump avoids the verb *apologize* in his public statements—his retreats contain typical strategies of self-defense (Benoit [1995] 2014: 22–4), including denial, evasion, and mitigation, claiming he misspoke, meant something else, or was misunderstood or misquoted by the press.

As a presidential candidate for the 2016 elections, Trump seemingly departs from his own principles when reacting to the misogynistic *Access Hollywood* tape. His televised statements about the situation included formal apology tokens such as the verbs *apologize* and *regret*. On the tape, recorded in 2005, Trump is heard saying that he attempted to have sexual intercourse with a married woman, is able to grab women's genitals, and would kiss women "automatically" because "when you're a star, they let you do it. You can do anything." After the tape surfaced on October 7, 2016, there was public outcry as Trump's statements about his behavior could be read as an admission of sexual harassment, a criminal offense.

The first reaction by the Trump campaign was a written statement issued on the campaign website the same day:

(4) *Written statement on Trump's campaign website, October 7, 2016*[6]

This was locker room banter, a private conversation that took place many years ago. Bill Clinton has said far worse to me on the golf course—not even close. I apologize if anyone was offended.

This short statement is composed of an account and an apology. The account comprises elements that are strategically aimed at coding the offense and highlighting particular issues in order to control the narrative frame. We follow Goodwin's (1994) technical use of the terms "coding" and "highlighting" as strategies through which the perception of a given phenomenon is modified. "Coding" refers to a set of practices through which the world is classified into categories, such as Trump's labeling of the offense as a "private conversation" and "locker room banter." We will explore the "locker room" euphemism later, but we note here that Trump utilizes the same public versus private distinction we have already seen in Clinton's first statement. A "private" conversation in the locker room is not meant for the public ear and therefore should not be held to the same standards. The second strategy of modifying perception is "highlighting," that is, making a particular phenomenon stand out, whether it is a linguistic element or something in the physical environment. In the written statement, Trump emphasizes that the offense occurred "many years ago," thereby temporally removing it from the present (also by the use of past tense *was*) and diminishing its present relevance. He is thus able to reduce the offensiveness by minimizing the offense (see Benoit 2017: 249). Lastly, Trump claims that Bill Clinton has said "far worse" things. As we will see, this comparison with Clinton is a crucial part of Trump's strategy to bolster his authenticity and coherence of self while constructing a radical opposition between himself and his opponent, Hillary Clinton, whom he conflates with her husband.

The actual apology is also mitigated. While his statement contains the explicit "I apologize," it is followed by a conditional clause complement, "if anyone was offended." As Battistella (2014: 38) argues, "conditionals allow speakers to qualify the act of apologizing.... The *if* clause ... places the onus on the offended party to say whether an offense has occurred." Moreover, the apologizer "does not commit themselves to the truth of the proposition" (Murphy 2019: 210)—that is, they do not necessarily admit that the offense actually occurred. It furthermore creates an opposition in his audience between those offended and those not, thereby removing focus from him and the alleged offense and leaving it to the public to debate whether it was offensive.

Later the same day, Trump issued a video statement. At first glance, this video seems like a genuine apology and even exhibits the same features that are prominent in Christian testimonials. However, while Trump uses apology tokens and appropriates elements of the narrative structure of a testimonial, he diverts from it in crucial ways that avoid the creation of a split self, necessary for a successful confession (Jackson 2012).[7]

(5) *Trump's Video Statement, October 7, 2016 (excerpt 1)*[8]
 1 I've never said I'm a perfect person, nor pretended to be someone that I'm not.
 2 I've said and done things I regret, and the words released today,
 3 on this more than a decade-old video, are one of them.
 4 Anyone who knows me, knows these words, don't reflect, who I am.
 5 I said it, I was wrong, and I apologize.

His references to the offense are "semantically bleached" in the sense of Gruber (2014: 76); that is, he uses words such as "things" and "words" that do not specify the offense. But he acknowledges the "words" as a possible offense for which he apologizes. One could analyze this as the classic split-self structure: Trump's present self is regretful and apologizes for past words and deeds that were "wrong." At the same time, however, Trump preempts any impression that he once was a different person who has now changed for the better.

The video starts with the words "I've never said I'm a perfect person, nor pretended to be someone that I'm not." This opening statement constitutes existential coherence and continuity of self and at the same time shifts the focus away from an offensive statement referencing illegal actions to an issue about honesty and pretense. While he never specifies the offense, he highlights that he has never "pretended to be someone" he is not. He is always authentically himself, implicitly disavowing any change he might have undergone. If he had said he was a good guy and then the video had turned up, he could be charged with dishonesty. But he has not. Not (pretending) to be a "perfect person" further serves to align him with the Everyman—not Everyman "sinner" but the Everyman who does not pretend to be perfect (as in "nobody's perfect").

Thus, the overarching opposition that he introduces in the beginning is, on the one hand, being "perfect" and not saying derogatory things in private (which has already been established as "pretentious"), and on the other hand, occasionally saying derogatory—or, as he qualifies later, "foolish"—things, but at least being honest about it. He successfully frames the issue as a matter of (mere) words versus personhood by dissociating what his statements denote—their "denotational content"—from the kind of identity they may imply—their "indexical references"[9]—thus erasing any truth-value one might attempt to attach to "words" (see next section).

This is part of a broader rhetorical strategy that has been described as a "discourse of theater," opposed to a "discourse of truth" through which utterances are usually evaluated in Western folk theory, especially by the media (Hill 2000).[10] The discourse of truth relies on Western concepts of personalism, which imply that talk should be understood as expressing a speaker's intentions or knowledge (see Duranti 2015). It is particularly relevant for politicians' utterances, which are evaluated in terms of their being informative and truthful. The discourse of theater, by contrast, does not focus on truth but on "the message," which means a "set of themes deployed through performance" (Hill 2000: 264), and is indispensable for political campaigning.

However, there is always the risk that statements from the discourse of theater will be evaluated in terms of the discourse of truth. One could conclude that Trump has in fact built a trap for himself. Since he has admitted to the charge and apologized, the conclusion that lends itself would be that the statements on the *Access Hollywood* tape are true and represent "exactly who he is." In the second presidential debate, Hillary Clinton argues along these lines—and she has a point, Trump never denounces the actions that his words on the tape describe. While this implies continuity of self, it is not a very favorable self that emerges. At the same time, though, Trump claims that the words do *not* reflect "who I am"—following the common mitigation strategy of invoking a "true character" in order "to deflect negative character attributions" (Gruber 2014: 93) associated with an offense. How does he manage to get away with such a blatant contradiction?

In order to understand how he skillfully camouflages this contradiction, we examine the parallel structure of lines 1 and 4 of his statement. What is implied in line 1 is that Trump has never said he would *not* sexually offend women. Within a discourse of truth, this contradicts the claim in line 4 that bragging about sexually offending women is not who he is. The contradiction becomes less noticeable because each statement contributes to communicating the "message" of Trump's existential coherence and authenticity. Evaluated within the discourse of theater, however, what emerges is a picture of Trump as not being pretentious (line 1) on the one hand and as a man of action not of words (line 4) on the other.

In the discourse of theater words neither have to map onto individuals' intentions or motives, nor correspond to actual states of affairs. We may extend this to include contractual words such as marriage vows or campaign promises, and inflammatory racist, sexist, or classist words. Words are not who Trump is. This furthermore aligns with common Western understandings of language as inherently deceitful (see Bauman and Briggs 2003: 19–26) and that "actions speak louder than words," which may contribute to the appeal that he has for many voters.

Once the offense has been moved into the realm of (mere) words, the opposition that emerges is between honest and dishonest people, no longer between a sexual offender and a repentant person. Beginning with his first statement about the tape, Trump codes the offense as mere words and highlights honest actions as the relevant issue to attend to, thereby establishing a narrative frame that sets the stage for the subsequent attacks on Hillary and Bill Clinton's actions.

Nonetheless, on both of these levels Trump remains vague. The question of who Trump actually is is left to be answered by "anyone who knows [him]." In public Christian testimonials, "sinning" politicians invoke specific members of their private and public life, mainly family, friends, clergy, and colleagues, to align with their Everyman side, that is, to show themselves as family men and most importantly as persons who can sometimes sin like we all do. Trump, by contrast, remains nonspecific here. But his vagueness and use of semantically bleached references are precisely what allows him to maintain the appearance of existential coherence while still formally performing an apology. This becomes even clearer when we look at the lines that follow.

(6) *Trump's Video Statement, October 7, 2016, continued (excerpt 2)*
    6 I've travelled the country talking about change for America,
    7 but my travels have also changed me.
    8 I've spent time with grieving mothers, who've lost their children,
    9 laid off workers, whose jobs have gone to other countries,
    10 and people from all walks of life, who just want a better future.
    11 I have gotten to know the great people of our country,
    12 and I've been humbled by the faith they've placed in me.
    13 I pledge to be a better man tomorrow, and will never, ever let you down.

Here, Trump appears to be talking about personal transformation. He claims that his travels have "changed" him and pledges to be a "better man tomorrow." At first sight, these two statements seem to follow the canonical strategy of repentance where one sins and promises to never do so again. However, the simple mention of "change" leaves open which kind of transformation he is talking about. Moreover, when we look at the intervening lines, we note that Trump, seemingly veering off topic, returns to issues of his campaign. Lines 8 to 12 do not make any reference to the original offense. Thus, this section does not seem to refer to the transformation of him as a repentant person. Instead, it accomplishes two things.

First, the vagueness of his previous abstract discussion of "words" gives way to concrete references of "grieving mothers" or "laid off workers." While it is hard to see how they could have anything to do with the sexual transgressions of a reality TV star, mothers, children, and workers are useful as political symbols because they have an aura of specificity that helps him evoke the impression of a connection with the audience, "localiz[ing] an otherwise anonymous national mass-mediated public" (Jackson 2012: 49).

Second, lines 8 to 12 alter the implied, indexical referents of the verb *change* and the adjective *better* in lines 7 and 13. The statement that travels have "changed" Trump sounds like an announcement or a preface to an account and thus raises the expectation that an explanation of how exactly he has changed will follow. Such an assumption is due to the maxim of relevance, that is, the general pragmatic principle that a speaker's subsequent statements are relevant to previous conversational contributions (Levinson 1983: 102). Following the maxim of relevance, we would expect the following section to have a bearing on the kind of change he is talking about. However, the lines that follow do not address the offense at all. Therefore, Trump's use of the word *change* in line 7 does not refer to a prior self that uttered the words captured on the *Access Hollywood* tape and that has now changed, but rather to his agenda of "changing" (line 6) and creating a "better future" (line 10) for the United States. Through its sequential positioning the statement subtly shifts the focus from personal change to the context of a presidential candidate who is listening to the concerns of his voters.

Such a reading is supported by the fact that he says he would "never, ever let you down" (line 13). Had he ended that sentence with *again*, the statement could have been interpreted as a backreference to his prior offense; yet, the word *again* is conspicuously missing. He is not talking about personal change, but rather about the change his campaign is promising. He has not "let down" the American people; rather, the only thing that is implied is *that* they have been let down—by whom is left open. Moreover, his pledge to be a "better man" (line 13) does not mean he is a repentant sinner, but rather a politician who is better than his adversaries.

In short, by invoking the moral public of mothers and workers, and by modifying the context in which his "change" is to be interpreted, Trump achieves alignment with the Everyman while at the same time setting himself off from his opponents. Trump has hijacked the canonical format of apologies to subtly shift the focus from his offense to the difference between him and others, first and foremost Hillary Clinton. It is this difference that takes center stage in the remainder of the statement. The remaining section of the video makes explicit the second dimension of glossing his offense as mere "words."

(7) *Trump's Video Statement, October 7, 2016, continued (excerpt 3)*
   14 Let's be honest. We're living in the real world.
   15 This is nothing more than a distraction
   16 from the important issues we are facing today.
   17 We are losing our jobs. We are less safe than we were eight years ago
   18 and Washington is totally broken.
   19 Hillary Clinton and her kind have run our country into the ground.
   20 I've said some foolish things, but there is a big difference
   21 between the words and actions of other people.
   22 Bill Clinton has actually abused women,
   23 and Hillary has bullied, attacked, shamed, and intimidated his victims.
   24 We will discuss this more in the coming days.
   25 See you at the debate on Sunday.

Whereas in the first sections, the counterpart of his offensive words is personhood, here his words become opposed to the "actions of other people," a direct attack on Hillary Clinton. This opposition of words versus actions informs the remaining statements in the video. First, he lists "important issues" (line 16) that his campaign is supposed to address (lines 17 and 18), for which he makes Hillary Clinton responsible, standing in for "her kind" (line 19), a metonymic index of the political establishment. He then explicitly contrasts his verbal offense with a list of alleged abusive actions by both Clintons (lines 22 and 23).

In summary, we argue that Trump is able to maintain the appearance of existential coherence while performing an apology because he subtly replaces the difference between past and present self with the difference between his opponents and his own (continuous) self. Differentiation from others who have said or done things that are "far worse" is, of course, a common strategy in self-defense (Benoit [1995] 2014: 24, 2017: 249–50) that contributes to a rehabilitation of the present self. Thus, to a certain extent, the outcome is similar to the process of differentiating oneself from past sins resulting in the split self of the Christian testimonial. However, the kind of self that emerges is radically different in the two cases. In the narrative structure of Trump's apology, Bill and Hillary Clinton come to occupy the slot that the testimonial traditionally reserves for the past repentant self; as a consequence, Trump's own distinction of past and present selves disappears, and he emerges unscathed as existentially coherent and authentic.

11.5.3 "This Was Locker Room Talk"— The Second Presidential Debate

The *Access Hollywood* tape became a major talking point in the second presidential debate that took place on October 9, 2016. We limit our analysis to the two responses by Trump which include apologies in order to show how these statements similarly contribute to maintaining continuity of self and existential coherence.

The debate begins with a question from a schoolteacher in the audience asking whether the candidates feel they were "modelling appropriate and positive behavior for today's youth." After first general responses by Clinton and Trump, moderator Anderson Cooper addresses a follow-up question to Trump, asking explicitly about the *Access Hollywood* tape:

(8) *Second Presidential Debate, October 9, 2016 (excerpt 1)* [11]
    1 You called what you said "locker room banter."
    2 You described kissing women without consent, grabbing their genitals.
    3 That is sexual assault. You bragged that you have sexually assaulted women.
    4 Do you understand that?

Trump responds:

(9) *Second Presidential Debate, October 9, 2016, continued (excerpt 2)*
    5 No, I didn't say that at all, I don't think you understood what was said.
    6 This was locker room talk. Uhh, I am not proud of it?
    7 I apologize to my family. I apologized to the American people.
    8 Certainly, I'm not proud of it, but this is locker room talk.
    9 You know when we have a world, where you have ISIS chopping off heads,
    10 where you have, and frankly, drowning people in steel cages.
    11 ((Several lines omitted. Trump mentions "wars," "horrible sights all over," "the carnage all over the world" before continuing with:))
    12 Yes, I am very embarrassed by it, I hate it, but it's locker room talk,
    13 and it's one of those things.

Coding his words as mere "locker room talk," Trump effectively precludes them from any scrutiny under the discourse of truth. The reference to "locker room talk" makes the words part of a context-dependent speech genre the primary function of which is the performance of masculinity, virility, and sexual prowess. The interpretive frame that is created thus shifts the focus away from the denotational content of the words (i.e., what the words literally mean) and toward their indexical entailments (i.e., what is implied by using these words). Whether the statement is true is no longer in question.[12] At the same time, the implication that this genre is reserved for the intimate context of the locker room creates a distinction between those that have access to such spaces and simply "get" this kind of talk, and those who do not.

Against this backdrop, we can understand why Cooper's attempts to press Trump on the issue of whether or not he has actually abused women—he reiterates the question three further times—fail from the very start. Cooper evaluates the words within the discourse of truth, that is, as statements about actions of Trump, and asks him repeatedly whether or not he has actually done any of the actions he mentioned. His goal is to corner Trump into either admitting he did not, which would cast his words as lies in the discourse of truth, or, conversely, admitting to sexual assault. However, Trump completely dismisses Cooper's propositional framing of the offense and instead casts it as a misunderstanding (line 5). "I didn't say that at all" does not refer to the actual words on the tape (there is little doubt that it was him who uttered them), but to Cooper's framing of the words as "sexual assault." Moreover, by depicting him as not understanding that it was locker room talk, Trump also pushes Cooper out of the community of those who understand this speech genre—perhaps excluding Cooper because he is homosexual and thus cannot know what this type of talk is about.

Cooper's repeated attempts to corner Trump into specifying whether his words refer to actions fail for this reason. Half a minute later, after repeatedly mentioning ISIS and deflecting Cooper's questions with statements such as that he has "tremendous respect for women," Trump finally responds to Cooper's fourth rephrased version of the question whether he has "ever done those things" with "No I have not." But this response is a short remark made as an aside that almost goes unnoticed among remarks that he will make the country safe. It also follows a strategy of semantic bleaching by omitting any referent whatsoever (although, admittedly, Cooper's question about "those things" is itself already semantically bleached). One may interpret Trump's statement as a denial of having "done those things." While this interpretation is consistent within the discourse of truth, it fails to see how Trump manages to control the narrative framing which allows him not to answer the questions directly.

The *Access Hollywood* tape comes up again about five minutes later in response to a different question. While in Cooper's question, as in the video statement (see section 11.5.2), the main issue was whether Trump's words represented actions, the focus now is on whether Trump has actually changed, which is particularly illuminative for our present purposes. Moderator Martha Raddatz refers to a question posted on Facebook that reads, "Trump says the campaign has changed him. When did that happen?" In addition, Raddatz asks explicitly whether he was a "different man" back then, thereby directly addressing the question of a split self. Trump's response is as follows:

(10) *Second Presidential Debate, October 9, 2016 (excerpt 3)*
    1 It was locker room talk as I told you. That was locker room talk.
    2 Uh I'm not proud of it. I am a person who has great respect for people,
    3 for my family, for the people of this country, and certainly I am not proud of it,
    4 but that was something that uh happened.
    5 If you look at uh Bill Clinton? Far worse,
    6 mine are words and his was action. His was, what he's done to women,
    7 there's never been anybody in the history of politics, in this nation
    8 that's been so abusive to women.
    9 So, you can say, any way you wanna say it,
    10 but Bill Clinton was abusive to women.
    11 Hillary Clinton attacked those same women, and attacked them viciously,
    12 four of them here tonight. One of the women, who is a wonderful woman,
    13 at twelve years old was raped. At twelve.

Trump reiterates it was locker room talk (line 1), "something that uh happened" (line 4). But then instead of addressing Raddatz's question, he turns to an attack on Bill and Hillary Clinton with a more extended version of the points already raised in the video statement.

In the video statement as in the debate, Trump uses two strategies, scaling down to the immediate local public and aligning with specific witnesses (Jackson 2012). In naming the four women he cites as witnesses against the Clintons and pointing out that they are "here tonight" (line 12), Trump appropriates yet another element of the Christian testimonial although for a very different purpose.[13] Bill Clinton and other politicians used the strategy of personal reference and the presence of key individuals as witnesses to their true character and repentant self. Trump's invocation of the women is used to directly attack his opponent, Hillary Clinton. It is telling that this is Trump's response to a question about whether he has changed or is a "different man" from the one who bragged about sexually assaulting women.

Nowhere in Trump's discourse are we able to find a split self. The overarching opposition that emerges is that between his own steadfast self, aligned with the Everyman victim, and the actions of his and America's alleged opponents: the Clintons and everything he associates with them.

11.6 Conclusion

This chapter has investigated how Trump invokes the canonical apology format of US politicians, the Christian testimonial, and transforms it into a vehicle for deflection from his transgressions. By describing the practices Trump used to seemingly apologize for his remarks in the *Access Hollywood* tape, this study contributes to a growing body of research on Trump's language use. It is also of more general relevance to the study of the relationship between the pragmatics of apologies and the narrative construction of self in political oratory.

Acts of contrition in the form of mass-mediatized apologies for sexual transgressions were once a marker of how US male politicians expressed how they have learned from their mistakes and emerged as better men and public servants. This genre of political oratory stems from the Christian testimonial that allows a sinner to become saved and voice their new self to the American public. In the two public reactions to the *Access Hollywood* tape, Trump draws on the genre of political apology but mutates it. While the Christian testimonial equates the politician's former self with the Everyman-as-sinner—his transformation demonstrating the redemptive power of God to everyone—Trump's strategy works through aligning himself with the Everyman-as-victim, that is, a victim of his opponents' actions, while maintaining existential coherence and continuity of self.

By transforming the public apology into a genre for attacking his opponents, Trump avoids displaying a split self and thus circumvents a potential pitfall that anyone who genuinely apologizes is confronted with, namely endangering the integrity of the present self by confessing to a past sin. Moreover, not apologizing becomes a way to maintain his political persona as unchanging and always himself, evoking reliability and stability. Yet, that persona is fundamentally at odds with reality. Trump is notorious for contradicting himself—sometimes in the same sentence. But he reminds his critics that anything he says is "just words." In this respect, this chapter also contributes to understanding political oratory in the Age of Trump where words are bleached of meaning, must not map onto individuals' intentions or motives, and where the question arises whether a president must ever adhere to a discourse of truth.

Notes

1 We follow Jackson (2012) in using the term *the Everyman* as well as masculine pronouns in order to highlight the fact that part of the rhetorical strategy of political apologies (for extramarital affairs) is to appeal to the "men who sin." This is of course part of a larger gender asymmetry in American politics, where men hold office in the majority of elected positions. The capital <E> underlines the term as a macro-category referring to a traditional archetype of American heterosexual masculinity.
2 We do not count his apology "on behalf of our nation" to Supreme Court justice Bret Kavanaugh (see Bierman and Savage 2018).
3 The concept of "face" refers to our self-perception that we want others to support, to be appreciated and not be imposed upon (Goffman 1967). Acts that attack someone's positive self-image or affect their freedom are "face-threatening." By apologizing, the offender addresses the offended party's face-needs in order to remedy the offense and maintain or restore social harmony (Tavuchis 1991). For the offender who apologizes, apologies are face-threatening and face-saving at the same time: they are face-threatening because taking responsibility for wrongdoing calls into question one's moral character; they are face-saving because they mitigate the offense and reclaim the offender's morality (see Meier 1998; Leech 2014; Murphy 2019). See also Schubert, this volume, for more extensive commentary on the notion of face with respect to impoliteness in fake news accusations.
4 The transcript is accessible here, https://edition.cnn.com/ALLPOLITICS/1998/08/17/speech/transcript.html, the video under https://www.youtube.com/watch?v=ajJMQG4Bmxo, both accessed on February 29, 2020.

5 The transcript is accessible here, https://edition.cnn.com/ALLPOLITICS/stories/1998/09/11/transcripts/clinton.prayer.html, the video under https://www.youtube.com/watch?v=B2_EzLLIPNg, both accessed on February 29, 2020.
6 This statement was originally posted at https://www.donaldjtrump.com/press-releases/statement-from-donald-j.-trump, but is no longer available. It has been archived under https://web.archive.org/web/20161007210105/https://www.donaldjtrump.com/press-releases/statement-from-donald-j.-trump.
7 News outlets were careful about describing the statement as an apology (e.g., Haberman 2016). Trump's wife, Melania, issued a statement claiming that while she did find the words of her husband "unacceptable and offensive," they did not "represent the man that I know," and that she hopes "people will accept his apology, as I have" (Collins 2016).
8 The video and transcript were published at https://www.facebook.com/DonaldTrump/videos/10157844642270725/; the video is also available at https://www.youtube.com/watch?v=ycfARBsz6_Y; both accessed on February 29, 2020.
9 Indexicality is a central concept in linguistic anthropology that allows for the specification of the distinction between the "content" that a particular utterance is understood to refer to (the semantic or denotational value of words, such as an actual room in a gym that is evoked by using the words *locker room*), and the particular contexts they may "point to" or "index," such as a particular accent that may index a person's provenience or the context of their upbringing, the use of a respect term that may index the relationship of the speaker to the addressee, or the invocation of "locker room banter" that may index male prowess.
10 We thank Paul Kroskrity for drawing our attention to this point.
11 The video of the debate is accessible under https://www.youtube.com/watch?v=FRl I2SQ0Ueg; a full transcript has been published at https://www.politico.com/story/2016/10/2016-presidential-debate-transcript-229519; both accessed on February 29, 2020.
12 We are indebted to Alexander Thomson and Nicco La Mattina, who both independently pointed out these issues to us.
13 Trump had also already held a surprise press conference with these women earlier the same day.

References

Ancarno, Clyde (2015), "When Are Public Apologies 'Successful'? Focus on British and French Apology Press Uptakes," *Journal of Pragmatics*, 84 (1): 139–53.
Battistella, Edwin L. (2014), *Sorry about That: The Language of Public Apology*, Oxford & New York: Oxford University Press.
Bauman, Richard and Charles L. Briggs (2003), *Voices of Modernity: Language Ideologies and the Politics of Inequality*, Cambridge: Cambridge University Press.
Benoit, William L. ([1995] 2014), *Accounts, Excuses, and Apologies: Image Repair Theory and Research*, 2nd edn, Albany, NY: SUNY Press.
Benoit, William L. (2017), "Image Repair on the Donald Trump 'Access Hollywood' Video: 'Grab Them by the P*ssy,'" *Communication Studies*, 68 (3): 243–59.
Bierman, Noah and David G. Savage (2018), "Trump Apologizes to Kavanaugh 'on Behalf of Our Nation,' Asserting He Was 'Proven Innocent,'" *Los Angeles Times*, October 8. Available online: https://www.latimes.com/politics/la-na-pol-trump-kavanaugh-20181008-story.html (accessed July 18, 2019).

Collins, Eliza (2016), "Melania Blasts 'Offensive' Trump, Says She Accepts Apology," *USA TODAY*, October 9. Available online: https://www.usatoday.com/story/news/politics/onpolitics/2016/10/08/melania-trump-urges-america-forgive-trump-vulgar-comments/91791400/ (accessed February 29, 2020).

Duranti, Alessandro (2006), "Narrating the Political Self in a Campaign for U.S. Congress," *Language in Society*, 35 (4): 467–97.

Duranti, Alessandro (2015), *The Anthropology of Intentions: Language in a World of Others*, Cambridge: Cambridge University Press.

Fisher, Marc (2018), "How Trump Retreats: Grudging Apologies, Plus a Wink and a Nod to the Original Insult," *Washington Post*, July 17. Available online: https://www.washingtonpost.com/politics/how-trump-retreats-grudging-apologies-plus-a-wink-and-a-nod-to-the-original-insult/2018/07/17/ea7ac346-89f9-11e8-8aea-86e88ae760d8_story.html (accessed July 18, 2019).

Goffman, Erving (1967), *Interaction Ritual: Essays on Face-to-Face Behavior*, New York: Pantheon Books.

Goffman, Erving (1971), *Relations in Public: Microstudies of the Public Order*, New York: Basic Books.

Goodwin, Charles (1994), "Professional Vision," *American Anthropologist*, 96 (3): 606–33.

Gruber, M. Catherine (2014), *I'm Sorry for What I've Done: The Language of Courtroom Apologies*, Oxford & New York: Oxford University Press.

Gunn, Joshua (2018), "Donald Trump's Perverse Political Rhetoric," in Ryan Skinnell (ed.), *Faking the News: What Rhetoric Can Teach Us about Donald J. Trump*, 160–73, Exeter: Imprint Academic.

Haberman, Maggie (2016), "Donald Trump's Apology That Wasn't," *New York Times*, October 8. Available online: https://www.nytimes.com/2016/10/08/us/politics/donald-trump-apology.html (accessed February 29, 2020).

Hill, Jane H. (2000), "Read My Article: Ideological Complexity and the Overdetermination of Promising in American Presidenital Politics," in Paul V. Kroskrity (ed.), *Regimes of Language: Ideologies, Polities, and Identities*, 259–92, Santa Fe, NM: School of American Research Press.

Jackson, Jennifer L. (2012), "'God's' Law Indeed Is There to Protect You from Yourself: The Christian Personal Testimonial as Narrative and Moral Schemata to the US Political Apology," *Language and Communication*, 32 (1): 48–61.

Kampf, Zohar (2009), "Public (Non-)Apologies: The Discourse of Minimizing Responsibility," *Journal of Pragmatics*, 41 (11): 2257–70.

Leech, Geoffrey N. (2014), *The Pragmatics of Politeness*, Oxford & New York: Oxford University Press.

Levinson, Stephen C. (1983), *Pragmatics*, Cambridge: Cambridge University Press.

Meier, A.J. (1998), "Apologies: What Do We Know?," *International Journal of Applied Linguistics*, 8 (2): 215–31.

Murphy, James (2019), *The Discursive Construction of Blame: The Language of Public Inquiries*, London: Palgrave Macmillan.

Ochs, Elinor and Lisa Capps (1996), "Narrating the Self," *Annual Review of Anthropology*, 25 (1): 19–43.

Ochs, Elinor and Lisa Capps (2001), *Living Narrative: Creating Lives in Everyday Storytelling*, Cambridge, MA: Harvard University Press.

Tavuchis, Nicholas (1991), *Mea Culpa: A Sociology of Apology and Reconciliation*, Stanford, CA: Stanford University Press.

Ware, B. Lee and Wil A. Linkugel (1973), "They Spoke in Defense of Themselves: On the Generic Criticism of Apologia," *Quarterly Journal of Speech*, 59 (3): 273–83.

Part IV

Conclusion

12

Great Movement versus *Crooked Opponents*

Is Donald Trump's Language Populist?

Ulrike Schneider and Matthias Eitelmann

12.1 Introduction

In lieu of a conclusion, we would like to discuss the one big question that, so far, has only occasionally been touched upon in this volume: namely, is Donald Trump a populist? In other words, do all his different linguistic traits, described in this volume, boil down to being features of populist language?

This is certainly a popular topic of discussion online: a combined Google search for *Trump* and *populist* yields over fourteen million results (at the date of writing, February 2020). Surprisingly, though, the verdict is very often that Donald Trump is *not* a "real populist" (Krugman 2019), or that "Trump is doing populism all wrong" (Nicolaci da Costa 2017). So, what is he "doing wrong"? Krugman's (2019) short answer in the *New York Times* is that Trump "seems determined to betray his base." He points out that

> [i]n 2016, on the campaign trail, Trump sounded as if he might be a European-style populist, blending racism with support for social programs that benefit white people. He even promised to raise taxes on the rich, himself included. Since taking office, however, he has relentlessly favored the wealthy over members of the working class, whatever their skin color. His only major legislative success, the 2017 tax cut, was a huge break for corporations and business owners; the handful of crumbs thrown at ordinary families was so small that most people believe they got nothing at all.

Thus, to Krugman, it is actions that make a populist. To be "engaged in even a smidgen of actual populism" (Krugman 2019), a politician would have to initiate legislation that benefits their voter base. In this view, Trump betrayed his base and therefore "isn't a populist, unless we redefine populism as nothing but a synonym for racism" (Krugman 2019). But this is not the only sense in which the word *populism* can be used. For instance, Beinard (2019), writing for *The Atlantic*, adheres to a slightly wider definition as he speaks of "the utter *emptiness* of Trump's populism" (our emphasis). This suggests two components of populism: packaging and content. To Beinard, the former is constituted by the "economic populism that he [Trump] touted during the 2016 campaign." It is empty populism because Trump did not follow the campaign promises with actions benefiting the people. Instead, Beinard sees an "old story" unfolding, namely that of an "alliance between Big Business and authoritarian demagogues," resulting in political actions that exclusively benefit the rich.

According to this packaging-and-content—or promise-and-action—definition, non-empty populism, that is, a politician "living up to his populist promise," may actually be positively evaluated, as Olsen's (2019) opinion piece for *The Washington Post* shows:

> President Trump's politics are often labeled as "populist." Three recent executive actions show he's delivering on the promise of that label.
>
> Populist politics invariably involve some version of the slogan "the people vs. the powerful." Whether from the left or the right, populist policies try to help ordinary people to make their own way or to get a better deal by restricting powerful people or entities from exerting market or monopoly power. Trump's latest orders and proposed regulations do exactly that.

Taken together, these three examples show that assessments of whether Trump *is* a populist come with their own set of complications. Not only can his actions be evaluated in different ways but also are there several yardsticks of populism around. In this chapter, we will therefore first take a step back and survey the range of definitions of populism currently in use. We need to keep in mind that the aim of the chapter is to evaluate whether the linguistic properties of Trump's *language* described throughout this volume are actually pieces of a jigsaw that, once put together, create a larger picture, namely that of a populist. Our first endeavor is therefore to find out whether it is even possible to assess whether someone is a populist based on their language and largely independently of their actions. Thus, our view on populism is contrary to the viewpoint taken by the authors writing for the *New York Times*, *The Atlantic*, and *The Washington Post*: What they take for granted (namely, the conviction that Trump's rhetoric is populist) is evaluated here, while what they take as a yardstick (his actions) cannot be considered. We will then proceed to see how other linguists went about the task of identifying populist traits in Trump's language and which conclusions they drew before developing our own working definition of populist language based on Moffitt (2016) and Hawkins (2009) and evaluating the evidence accumulated in this volume.

12.2 What Is Populism?

The question "what is populism?" is currently hotly debated among the specialists in the field of political science, and the verdict is still out. Nevertheless, one definition has become the de facto standard, as it is the most cited one and consequently the most widely known, namely Mudde and Rovira Kaltwasser's (2012: 8) "minimal definition" of populism as "a thin-centred ideology that considers society to be ultimately separated into two homogeneous and antagonistic groups, 'the pure people' and 'the corrupt elite,' and which argues that politics should be an expression of the *volonté générale* (general will) of the people" (emphasis in the original; see also Mudde 2007; Mudde and Rovira Kaltwasser 2017). Since this definition is actually very complex, we will peel it apart layer by layer.

First of all, it contains the component that is at the heart of populism and gave it its name: the distinction between people and elite. We are deliberately skipping the usual definite articles before *people* and *elite* here, as they would suggest that these are clearly defined concepts—which they are not; they are therefore usually put in inverted commas to indicate that we are merely talking about conceptualizations (as in the abovementioned definition). As Mudde and Rovira Kaltwasser (2012: 8) point out, "both categories are to a certain extent 'empty signifiers' . . ., as it is the populists who construct the exact meanings of 'the elite' and 'the people.'"[1] The authors argue that to do so, populists draw on "*moral* [criteria] (i.e. pure vs. corrupt), not situational (e.g. position of power), socio-cultural (e.g. ethnicity, religion), or socio-economic (e.g. class)" ones (Mudde and Rovira Kaltwasser 2012: 8–9; our emphasis).

Second, the categorical split of the populace into just 'the elite' and '*the* people' not only plots these two groups against each other—at a more basic level, it means that there essentially *are* only two groups. '*The* people' have *one* (majority) will—the general will of the people, or *volonté générale*. Populists adhere to the belief in this general will, which implies that they are "clearly on the side of majority rule" and at the same time "hostile towards pluralism and the protection of minorities." As a consequence, "any other institutional center of power, including the judiciary, is believed to be secondary. After all, 'the general will of the people' cannot be limited by anything, not even constitutional protections" (Mudde and Rovira Kaltwasser 2012: 17).

Third—and maybe most importantly—Mudde and Rovira Kaltwasser (2012) deem populism an ideology—albeit a "thin-centered" one. The 'thickness' of an ideology is determined by the number of political concepts at its core. The authors argue that the populist core consists of only the three aforementioned concepts, namely "the people, the elite, and the general will" (Mudde and Rovira Kaltwasser 2012: 9). As a thin ideology, populism may then attach itself to "host ideologies," "be they thick (e.g. liberalism, socialism) or thin (e.g. ecologism, nationalism)" (Mudde and Rovira Kaltwasser 2012: 9). Crucially, no matter the host ideology, populism itself is still seen as an ideology in its own right—"whether the populist really believes in the message distributed or whether populism is a strategic tool is largely an empirical question" (Mudde and Rovira Kaltwasser 2012: 9).

For a linguistic study of populism, this minimal definition provides few criteria that can be applied. It allows for some clear predictions concerning lexicon and semantics: we would expect mention of *people* and *elite*, contrasts between *us* and *them*, and so on. However, it gets much harder to formulate concrete hypotheses about populist pragmatics based on this definition, let alone populist syntax or populist word-formation. What is more, it does not even mention a figure like Donald Trump, as Mudde and Rovira Kaltwasser (2012: 2) strictly distinguish between populism and "the person who expresses it." Thus, for a linguistic working definition, we need one that specifies more elements.

Reinfeldt (2000: 47; drawing on Canovan 1981), for instance, does not separate the leader from the ideology and instead asserts that the dramatis personae of populism often include a special figure (*besondere Figur*) besides 'the people' and 'the elite.' He mentions that many descriptions of populism further include the notion that populist demands are overly simplifying and insufficiently complex (*übersimplifizierend* and *unterkomplex*; Reinfeldt 2000: 49), and that some see populism as an anti-intellectual ideology (Reinfeldt 2000: 59). The latter points give some first indications of the kind of syntax we might expect from a populist, namely simple and unlike formal academic language.

Whereas less restricted definitions may have their benefits for applied studies, they bear the risk of being so wide that they essentially encompass all politicians. Considering populism as synonymous with politics may be useful to grasp elements of political logic (see, for example, Laclau 2005), but it is unsuitable for the identification of distinct political styles (see criticism by Moffitt 2016: 24–5 and Truan 2019: 309). Luckily, the solution may lie in the word *style* itself: while the definitions discussed so far were either by proponents of populism-as-ideology (Mudde and Rovira Kaltwasser 2012) or of populism-as-logic (Reinfeldt 2000), a third set of definitions is based on the view that populism is a political *style*. We will see that this angle on populism, which is focused on rhetoric and discourse, serves well as a linguistic working definition of populism as it allows for concrete linguistic hypotheses beyond the levels of lexicon and semantics. The style-based criteria of populism detailed in section 12.4 are mostly based on Moffitt (2016) and occasionally draw on Hawkins (2009).

At the heart of the view of populism as a political style is, of course, still the (constructed) rift between 'the people' and 'the elite' and the aim to appeal to the people (Moffitt 2016: 8). However, instead of focusing on the particulars of this rift, advocates of populism-as-style zoom out and describe how the rift is "performed" and how the media are used to transmit this performance. In this theatrical scenario, "the leader is seen as the performer" and "'the people' as the audience" (Moffitt 2016: 5). The performance itself relies on "slang, swearing, political incorrectness" (together referred to as "bad manners") and involves instilling a sense of "crisis, breakdown or threat" (Moffitt 2016: 44, 8). Thus, we have "three necessary and sufficient characteristics" (people/elite, bad manners, and crisis) of a populist style and two "key elements of the performative relationship" (the leader as performer and the media as stage; Moffitt 2016: 8, 43).

We will later apply the populism-as-style definition in our analysis of whether the findings detailed throughout this volume paint the picture of a politician using populist rhetoric. Before we do so, we will cast a brief look at previous linguistic assessments of Trump's speech style within a populist framework.

12.3 Populist or Not?

While analyses of the populist qualities of Trump's politics abound (e.g., Bonikowski 2019; Weyland and Madrid 2019), these usually take it as a given that he uses "populist rhetoric" or "discursive strategies comparable to those of populist radical-right parties in Europe" (Bonikowski 2019: 110). Truly linguistic analyses of potential populist traits in Trump's rhetoric, however, are rare. This is mostly due to the fact that—as we have seen earlier—many definitions of populism focus on actions and sideline the rhetorical means used to achieve them.

Not everyone settles the matter quite as swiftly as Lakoff (2017) does, though. She argues that Trump's upper-class lifestyle of luxury and his upper-class social circle make it impossible for him to be a populist (Lakoff 2017: 598–9). In addition, she holds that only politicians who truly believe in "power to the people" can be populists, and she is firmly convinced that Trump does not hold this belief—or, in fact, any belief (Lakoff 2017: 599). In a final sweep, she declares all semantic and pragmatic analyses of Trump's language vain endeavors as "[h]is grammar does not contain a semantic component relating linguistic forms to extra-linguistic referents" (Lakoff 2017: 600).

Luckily enough, others have still made a sustained effort to analyze the degree of populism in Trump's rhetoric. Hawkins (2009), an advocate of populism-as-style, developed a grading scheme which allows for "elite discourse," that is, discourse by (political) leaders (Hawkins 2009: 48), to be rated for its inherent degree of populism and, together with Littvay, applies it to Trump and several other candidates of the 2016 presidential campaign (Hawkins and Littvay 2019). They propose that holistic human coding that assigns an entire speech a single grade is the best solution to determine whether a speech shows pluralist, mixed, or populist traits (Hawkins 2009: 1050). To make an informed judgment, the graders are provided with a rubric of six criteria according to which they evaluate the speeches. In essence, these criteria measure "the two core elements of populist discourse: a reified will of the common people and an evil, conspiring elite" (Hawkins and Littvay 2019: 13; as we incorporated these criteria into our own hypotheses, more information can be found when we develop the hypotheses one by one later on). Hawkins and Littvay (2019: 15) find that all candidates show relatively stable degrees of populism throughout the campaign; for example, Clinton scores low and Sanders scores high, with one exception: Trump's populism score oscillates strongly.

> Closer analysis of this inconsistency reveals a great deal about his likely sincerity.... Our educated guess is that variability in Trump's populism is the product of his speechwriters. The fact that his debate scores are so low, and that his scores trended more upward after he adopted a new campaign team in May 2016, suggests that Trump himself is not all that populist, and hence receives low scores when speaking extemporaneously. (Hawkins and Littvay 2019: 15)

To inspect these inconsistencies even more closely, they split the data into speeches and debates where Trump had a teleprompter script available and those where he did not, and had these rated with separate scores for "anti-elitism" and "people-centrism." They find that "anti-elite messages" are present in both categories while "people-centrism" increases significantly in the speeches with a teleprompter script (Hawkins and Littvay 2019: 15–18). They interpret this difference as evidence that Trump is a "half populist," that is, that he "has key elements of populism even in his extemporaneous speeches, and they are strong" (Hawkins and Littvay 2019: 16). Interestingly enough, while many politicians actually become less populist once elected, Trump's level of populism did not decrease (Hawkins and Littvay 2019: 19).

McCallum-Bayliss's (2019) analysis of Trump's metaphors comes to a similar 'half-and-half' conclusion, namely that "he is not motivated by populist principles," but "uses populist tactics" (McCallum-Bayliss 2019: 243). Drawing on results from a variety of studies, McCallum-Bayliss comes up with five points that position Trump within the realm of populist rhetoric: namely,

(i) He declares himself *the voice* of the people . . . .
(ii) He criticizes the political establishment . . . and condemns its institutions . . . .
(iii) He denigrates opponents and detractors to delegitimize them . . . .
(iv) He provokes fear and anxiety in 'the people': the corrupt elites have *cheated them* . . . .
(v) He plays on fears of cultural change, fostering racism, xenophobia, white supremacy . . . . (McCallum-Bayliss 2019: 255; emphasis in the original)

She contrasts these with four counterarguments to the theory that Trump is a populist, derived from her own results:

1. A Conqueror [a metaphor that Trump uses frequently] does not need to represent the people and Trump does not. Large diverse segments of society protest against his administration . . . .
2. He mobilizes the masses through entertainment, not civic engagement. His *incredible movement* is about him, not the people.
3. He is a narcissist, convinced of his self-importance and unequaled qualities and abilities. . . .
4. Ill-considered actions result in negative outcomes for the people . . . .
   (McCallum-Bayliss 2019: 255; emphasis in the original)

All of the counterarguments have in common that they do not concern Trump's rhetoric. Instead, they are founded on the assumptions that a true populist (a) believes in their claims and (b) puts their money where their mouth is—both of which are contested.

Pérez, Román, and Lorenzo Rodríguez's (2019) study of populist rhetoric in viral tweets puts these findings into perspective. They analyze 188 "top tweets" (as determined by Twitter) on such topics as economy, immigration, and health care sent from Donald Trump's and Hillary Clinton's accounts between their nomination as candidates for their respective parties and the election in 2016. A familiar picture emerges: Trump's viral tweets are more likely to contain attacks on the elite and the media, criticism of the system, promises to restore the power balance, a "preference of perceived legitimacy over the established legal order," and self-promotion—in short "typical populist discursive strategies" (Pérez, Román, and Lorenzo Rodríguez' 2019: 20–1). Yet, once again, it is not Trump who stands out as "a champion of street-level Americans," because Clinton's tweets are far more likely to present her as an "advocate of the people" (Pérez, Román, and Lorenzo Rodríguez' 2019: 20–1). Nevertheless,

"Trump clearly exceeds Clinton in all metrics of audience response" (Pérez, Román, and Lorenzo Rodríguez' 2019: 27). In fact, it seems like the message of a Trump tweet is not actually very relevant in determining whether it 'goes viral.' Instead, Trump appears to capitalize on form: while Clinton's viral tweets hardly contain exclamation points, all caps, hyperbole, or direct addresses to specific people, Trump's contain an abundance of these features. The authors therefore conclude that "form matters more than content" in making populist discourse 'go viral' and that Trump's "aggressive, hyperbolic, and polarizing tone might have pressed the right emotional keys" (Pérez, Román, and Lorenzo Rodríguez' 2019: 27).

Across these studies, what prevails is the image of a wavering 'half populist,' who picks from the populist toolkit—preferentially the more emotional tools—but does not really believe in populist ideology. We will see whether our analysis leads to similar results.

12.4 Hypotheses

Before we evaluate the findings about Trump collected in this volume, we will return to the five components of populism-as-style. We will fill them in with details described in the literature and derive linguistic hypotheses from these descriptions.

12.4.1 Appeal to 'the People' versus 'the Elite'

As we have seen earlier, the populist vision of the world is Manichean, that is, moral and dualistic (e.g., Hawkins 2009: 1063; Moffitt 2016: 43). Hawkins (2009: 1063) goes so far as to say that "everything is in one category or the other, 'right' or 'wrong,' 'good' or 'evil'" with "nothing in between"—"no shades of gray." The bad is represented by a minority elite while the good is represented by "the common man (urban or rural) [who is] seen as the embodiment of the national ideal" (Hawkins 2009: 1063). Many other definitions also mention that particularly right-wing populism also tends to single out and to 'other' further 'bad' groups (e.g., Wodak 2017: 556; Norris and Inglehart 2019: 76–8). Moffitt (2016: 43) specifies that "[p]opulists may also target particular Others—such as asylum seekers, immigrant workers or particular minority groups—as enemies of 'the people,' *but these Others will be linked to 'the elite'*" (our emphasis). Based on this conceptualization, we can postulate the following hypotheses:

H_1 Trump's rhetoric shows a dualistic worldview consisting of the positively connoted people and the negatively connoted elite.
H_2 As *people* and *elite* are constructed categories, boundaries may shift and are unlikely to be spelled out. Instead, category boundaries remain fuzzy and vague descriptors are used.
H_3 Where other people, groups, or entities are singled out as evil or as a threat to 'the people,' Trump clearly connects these 'others' to 'the elite.'
H_4 Political actions are presented as being in the common interest of 'the people'; minority interests are disregarded.

12.4.2 The Leader–Performer

Populist leaders have a balancing act to do: on the one hand, they construe themselves as the voice of the people and must thus appear "ordinary," simply as one of the people. On the other hand, they must justify their role as the leader and therefore appear "extraordinary" and "beyond" the people (Moffitt 2016: 52). The performance of ordinariness also serves to distance the leader from the elite (whether they actually are a member of the elite "does not seem to matter too much if the performance is suitably convincing," Moffitt 2016: 58). The performance of extraordinariness may elevate the leader "to a celebrity or even messiah-like status" (Moffitt 2016: 55). Moffitt (2016: 64) takes the messiah metaphor even further and argues that in populism, the leader becomes a physical "incarnation of 'the people.'"[2] This role of the leader leads to the following hypotheses:

- H_5 While 'elite' politicians present themselves as educated and rational using complex syntax and a large vocabulary, Trump presents himself as ordinary, using less complex syntax and other features of spoken conversation like hesitations, discourse markers, more verbs, and fewer nouns.
- H_6 To boost his extraordinary status, Trump never uses self-denigrating language and instead prefers self-aggrandizing expressions.

12.4.3 Bad Manners

One particular element of the performance of ordinariness is a disregard for appropriate behavior. On the form side of the discourse, these mannerisms may consist of "slang, swearing, ... and being overly demonstrative and 'colourful'" (Moffitt 2016: 44, 58, 61). In terms of the content of the discourse, 'bad manners' may manifest in political incorrectness, taunts, over-the-top claims, a "denial of expert knowledge," and "ready resort to anecdote as 'evidence'" (Moffitt 2016: 44, 60). Sincerity is of no importance—rather, "the aim is to get a reaction," even if it is a negative one (Moffitt 2016: 61). Therefore, we stipulate:

- H_7 Claims made by Trump are often emotional and/or run counter to factual evidence.
- H_8 "The language will show a bellicosity toward the opposition that is incendiary and condescending, lacking the decorum that one shows a worthy opponent." (Hawkins 2009: 1064)

12.4.4 Crisis

An important element in the rise of populism is a sense of crisis or imminent catastrophe. Crucially, this crisis is not a pre-existing trigger for populism, but an inherent part of the performance of populism itself (Moffitt 2016: 45, 119–20). For this performance, an issue is singled out, framed as a failure of the elite, and elevated to "cosmic proportions" (Hawkins 2009: 1063). Consequently, this crisis requires urgent action, possibly systemic change to protect the people from its effects. The populist then propagates simplistic short-term solutions. Since the agents made responsible for the crisis (often minorities benefiting from elite decisions) are amoral according to populist logic, "nondemocratic means may be openly justified" (Hawkins 2009: 1064; Moffitt 2016: 45, 126–8). This leads to the additional hypotheses:

- H_9 War, conflict, and crisis not only feature as topics of Trump's discourse, but also in his choice of metaphors.
- H_{10} Complex social, political, economic, and environmental issues are presented as simple matters with clear solutions.

12.4.5 The Media–Stage

Finally, this complex performance would be in vain without an audience. The modern-day populist makes use of intense mediatization to reach this audience. This reliance on (the right kind of) media attention makes the media equally populism's "'friend' and 'foe'" (Moffitt 2016: 72). On the one hand, populists take advantage of storytelling techniques employed by the media (e.g., simplification, anti-establishment attitude, focus on scandal, and conflict) and may use non-elite tabloid media to "bring them closer to 'the people,'" or even set out to make themselves "celebrity politician[s]" thus "blurring the line between politics and entertainment" (Moffitt 2016: 74–6, 84–5). On the other hand, they often portray the media as a "tool of 'the elite' that is used to discredit them, marginalize 'common sense' opinions, and mislead 'the people'" (Moffitt 2016: 75, 81–4). This leads some populists to circumvent traditional media altogether and focus their attention on social media "to speak 'directly' to and for 'the people'" (Moffitt 2016: 88). We see both the love for social media and for celebrity in Trump's presidency. In terms of his language, this leads to two final hypotheses:

- H_{11} Trump attempts to control (people's perception of) elite media by demonizing and criticizing it.
- H_{12} Trump's language is shaped to make ideal 'media sound bites'; that is, he has a tendency towards simple clear slogans and towards repeating those.

12.5 Analysis of Populist Traits in Trump's Language

12.5.1 *Great Movement* versus *Crooked Opponents*— The Players in Trump's World

Perhaps the most expectable title for this section would have been *Hard-working Americans* versus *the Washington Swamp* as both of these are certainly groups drawn up by Trump and whom he mentions frequently. However, it became clear throughout this volume that the dominant rift is a different one. First of all, the most persistent finding was the vagueness of Trump's descriptors and references. All third-person pronouns (singular and plural) are used more frequently than in "average" political communication, and very often with only a vague link to the actual referent(s) (see Egbert and Biber; Björkenstam and Grigonitė; Ronan and Schneider). These pronouns are complemented by a range of vague descriptors (e.g., *things, thing, something, millions and millions, much, many*, see Ronan and Schneider; Egbert and Biber; Stange); thereby the task of defining in-group and out-group, friend and foe is delegated to the audience. In Trump's discourse, the vague almost imperceptibly shades to the absolute and generalizing (e.g., *everything, anything, virtually all, always, total*, see Ronan and Schneider; Schubert). These generalizing terms suggest that there are no shades of gray; people, groups, and media outlets are either friend or foe; their status may change over time, but they are never just neutral (see Schubert). Boundaries between good and bad are often drawn on moral grounds (e.g., the media as a *disgrace, Crooked Hillary, Lyin' Ted*, see Schubert; Tyrkkö and Frisk; Koth).

Consequently, the picture that emerges is not so much that of 'the people' unitedly fighting 'the elite' above them, but rather that of Trump and 'America' surrounded by "crooked opponents" on all sides; what unites the latter is that they are all against Trump and his "great movement." Of course, as stated earlier, the image of *(hardworking) Americans* versus *the Washington swamp* is used by Trump, but in light of the evidence accumulated in this volume, it seems more like a means to an end. Membership in these groups is fickle. The central and permanent dichotomy is that of Trump and his supporters versus everyone else.

A good example of the shifting prerequisites for membership in "the American people" is immigrants. On the one hand, "border security" and "border issues" feature large on Trump's agenda (see Egbert and Biber) and immigrants are presented as pollutants dumped on America (see Koth). On the other hand, we saw that Trump has only positive things to say about Latinos/Hispanics in his speeches (see Schneider and McClure). This means that once the (descendants of) said immigrants become part of the electorate, Trump vies for their vote, apparently pulling them into the in-group. Yet Trump's language does not suggest fighting on their behalf. Instead Hispanics, African Americans, and "people in the inner cities" themselves become problems to be solved (see Schneider and McClure; Koth). As if on a board of *Risk*, they are terrain to be conquered (see Schneider and McClure).

In summary, we have seen rhetoric that drew a dualistic worldview of a positively connoted 'Team Trump' and a negatively connoted opposition. As these categories loosely overlap with 'the people' and 'the elite,' H_1 is partially confirmed, though we would argue that 'Team Trump' is the superordinate, larger, and possibly more important category and that 'the people' appear to be a component of 'Team Trump.' Team membership is often only vaguely spelled out and may shift—it is often not self-assigned, but assigned by Trump—confirming H_2. Particularly the 'opposing team' is very heterogeneous; a connection between the various groups and 'the elite' is occasionally drawn, but ultimately not necessary due to membership being negatively defined as non-membership in 'Team Trump' (see Koth; Tyrkkö and Frisk), thus refuting H_3. Finally, minority interests may, in fact, be taken up, but apparently only when this is in the common interest of 'Team Trump.'

12.5.2 *Tremendous Success*—Donald Trump as the Leader

Ever since publications about Trump's politics and rhetoric skyrocketed during his presidential campaign in 2016, one of the central points has been that he came in as the anti-establishment candidate who threw political correctness to the wind. The contributions to this volume show that this is measurable in core linguistic areas of Trump's language, that is, in his grammar and lexicon, and across a variety of different speech genres. Compared to the public speaking style of other politicians, Trump's is much more akin to spontaneous conversation: Trump's sentences are shorter; clauses are more likely to be coordinated and less likely to be subordinated than other politicians' (see Ronan and Schneider). The sentences and clauses, in turn, contain more verbs and pronouns and fewer nouns than other politicians' language (see Egbert and Biber; Ronan and Schneider). Overall, the vocabulary is smaller, less specialized, repetitive, but highly distinctive (see Egbert and Biber; Björkenstam and Grigonitė; Ronan and Schneider). And the list of features of a colloquial speaking style goes on: Trump repeats more (see Björkenstam and Grigonitė), coins nicknames for his adversaries (see Tyrkkö and Frisk), uses contractions (see Egbert and Biber), and pairs intensifiers with non-gradable adjectives (see Stange). Overall, he simply permits himself a lot more spontaneity, which results not only from more conversational scripts for his speeches but also from long off-script passages (see Björkenstam and Grigonitė).

Overall, this "casual speaking style" (Björkenstam and Grigonitė) creates the impression that Trump is 'ordinary', in the sense of being a "man of the people" (Tyrkkö and Frisk). This effect is boosted by direct interaction with the audience, which, by extension, suggests interaction with the public at large (e.g., "let me tell you," "I'll tell you," see Egbert and Biber). Furthermore, as Björkenstam and Grigonitė point out, the large number of vague pronouns "create a sense of inclusion" and proximity, because they suggest that Trump and his audience have shared knowledge. In summary, H_5 is so strongly confirmed that we might conclude that his "performance of the low" is what makes the 'Trump brand'.[3]

A populist leader must strike a balance between performing as an "ordinary man of the people" yet also being perceived as extraordinary. Indeed, Trump is not shy when it comes to self-praise, which he phrases in more grandiose terms than other politicians (see Egbert and Biber) and often in the third person to create an impression of objectivity (see Degani and Onysko). Moreover, to underline his extraordinary status, he avoids certain rhetorical behaviors of 'ordinary' politicians. Most famously, political correctness falls into this category, as Trump equates it with deceitfulness (see Schubert). Second, Trump takes an unconventional (for politics) approach to expressing his attitude or standpoint: he uses more stance adverbs (e.g., *clearly*, *obviously*), but fewer other expressions of stance (e.g., *I believe that*) than other politicians. As the former indicate that what is said is a generally accepted fact, they make Trump appear highly certain. The latter link an opinion directly to the speaker—therefore eschewing them avoids being held accountable for what was said (see Egbert and Biber). Finally, Trump emphasizes that he is unlike other politicians in that he has always unwaveringly stayed true to himself. This is carried through to his apologies.

While US politicians commonly revert to the Christian testimonial in which they create a split between their past sinning self and the present redeemed self, Trump takes up elements of this style of testimonial, but instead of creating a split self, he creates a split between himself and other politicians, who are presented as having sinned far worse (see Hauck and Mitsuhara). In this way, Trump comes out not only on top but also with a continuous unscathed self. A second split he uses to replace the one commonly made is that between "mere words" or "locker room talk" and personhood. While the words may have been inappropriate or untrue, they are not who he is—and in the case of locker room talk could not even reasonably be expected to be true (see Hauck and Mitsuhara). Thus, we find ample evidence in support of the hypothesis that Trump uses linguistic means to boost his extraordinary status (H_6).

12.5.3 *The People . . . that are Selfishly Opposed to me—Trump's Manners*

Many of the features that make Trump's language so conversational are certainly very uncouth if used by a statesman in official contexts. It transpired that "conversational" needs to be complemented by emotional and hyperbolic. Trump's language is peppered with intensifiers (e.g., *very, very very*, and *so*, see Stange), quantifiers (e.g., number + number, *much, many, great*, see Egbert and Biber; Stange), as well as "emphatic, emotionally charged expressions" (see Degani and Onysko). This already hints at a speaker reaching for emotional rather than factual arguments (H_7). While fact-checking Trump has not been at the heart of this volume, we certainly saw that many of Trump's claims are vague or generalizing (as discussed in section 12.5.1) and that counterarguments may be ignored or remain unaddressed (see Degani and Onysko). Schubert shows that Trump evades requests for evidence, and Degani and Onysko even argue that some of his self-praise may be a form of denial.

Emotions run particularly high in the face of opposition. We saw Trump insulting opponents (see Egbert and Biber), often with moral judgments like *deceitful* (see Schubert). Tyrkkö and Frisk's analysis of Trump's nickname use reveals that he strategically worked his way through his opponents, presenting them as morally bad (e.g., *crooked*), mentally unstable (e.g., *crazy*), or simply irrelevant (e.g., *lightweight*), and often embedded the nicknames in "patronizingly sarcastic" contexts (see Tyrkkö and Frisk).

The analysis by Koth ties together a lot of the findings described so far. He shows that in Trump's view, any kind of win or loss—whether in an election, a trade deal, or in a debate—is tied to moral judgments. "[W]inners are higher in value" and consequently deserve glory. This leads to two crucial consequences: (a) Trump's "excessive admiration for strength" and "excessive contempt for weakness" and (b) his assumption that past—glorious(!)—winners are *entitled* to be future winners. Ergo America's past greatness absolutely guarantees future greatness, and his own win is a certainty. From this view any opposition to Trump's victory and agenda is not playing by the rules. Such deceitful lack of fair play legitimizes moral judgments and a bellicose attitude. This explains why Trump does not feel the need to treat adversaries as "worthy opponent[s]" (H_8).

12.5.4 *I am Fighting for YOU!—*
War, Conflict, and Simple Solutions

War, conflict, and crisis feature frequently in Trump's rhetoric, as hypothesized in H_9. His view on winning is based on the conceptual metaphor POLITICS IS WARLIKE COMPETITION (see Koth). Interestingly, actions of 'Team Trump' and 'America' are often described in "generic competition terms" (e.g., *beat*) while actions of opponents are "described in more war-like terms" (e.g., *kill*, see Koth; also Degani and Onysko for Obama's alleged "war on coal"). This indicates that in Trump's view, he and 'America' are "trying to fight the good fight," while "the rules, the referees, and the opponents" are "the ENEMY or OPPOSING FORCE" (Koth).

In true fashion of a politician, Trump, of course, proposes solutions to the conflicts and crises he draws up. We hypothesized (H_{10}) that these issues are presented as simple matters with clear solutions—and there is evidence to support this: campaign promises were often vague or lacked justification, and were presented with more certainty than, for instance, in the rhetoric of Barack Obama (e.g., *they have to*, *I'm going to* instead of *could* or *may*, see Egbert and Biber). Once president, Trump often dismisses or ignores arguments that run counter to his opinions and policies, for example, concerning global warming or wind energy (Degani and Onysko).

Once more, it transpired that Trump's statements and rhetorical devices are based on a set of folk theories and cognitive metaphors. First, Trump's view relies on the notion of the "Great Chain of Being [that] structures the world hierarchically, situating humans above animals above natural physical objects" (Koth). In this setup, it is natural for humans to exploit nature. This is why Obama's opposition to coal equals an attack on "a natural order" (Degani and Onysko). Second, Trump acts as a businessman, applying principles of business and economy to politics. Among those is his high regard for (measurable) economic success (see Degani and Onysko). Third, "[a]s Trump sees it, there is only so much wealth, safety, and 'Great[ness]' available in America or the world, and all of it exclusively belongs to the right sort of Americans" (Koth). This "zero-sum" thinking explains why any concession to others comes at a loss to the "right sort of Americans" (Koth).

12.5.5 *Fake News*—Trump on Stage

Finally, we get to Trump's double-edged relationship with the media. We hypothesized that as a true populist, he should demonize particularly mainstream media (H_{11}), while at the same time relying on his own celebrity status through constant presence in the media, and "shaping" his language to this purpose (H_{12}). We find clear evidence for both of these claims.

Trump redefined *fake news*, no longer applying it to misreporting, but to "unwelcome information" (Schubert). At times, his campaign against unwanted news is moral and highly emotional. "Fake News" outlets become the "enemy of the people" (see Tyrkkö and Frisk) who are "totally dishonest" and "always wrong." By means of such claims, the respective outlets or journalists are delegitimized, morally devaluated, and lose authority (see Schubert). Crucially, the fake news label is not fixed. Instead, it strategically shifts depending on who 'needs' to be accused of overrepresenting, underrepresenting, or misquoting Trump (Schubert).

At the same time, Trump's closeness to the people is a mediated proximity. Even his favorite channel Twitter is, after all, a medium, and the majority of the electorate does not directly witness his speeches, but instead gets into contact with them through some media channel (be it 'new' or traditional). In view of this, it is not surprising that many of the characteristics of Trump's political rhetoric are eerily reminiscent of the most pervasive (and persuasive) text genre across all media: advertising—a genre relying on short, catchy slogans, persuasion through emotion, simplified reasoning, and frequent repetition—all of these being features of Trump's language discussed throughout this volume. Of course, all politicians need to advertise themselves or their policies to some degree. It just seems that Trump's language is more like plain advertising than other politicians'—more reliance on simple arguments, simple phrasing, more repetition. Considering that before becoming a politician, Trump's latest claim to fame was his role as host of the reality TV show *The Apprentice*, it is worth also comparing the language of this genre to his political rhetoric. While actual reality does not follow a plot or tell a story, reality shows are usually set up and edited to create a narrative. Characters in this narrative are often monodimensional, that is, centered on a single or few characteristics (e.g., clever, cunning, capable), which are pointed out repeatedly. In addition, Trump's show was famous for harsh criticism and blunt slogans. These features—repetition, catchphrases, and dimensional reduction of characters—are also found in Trump's political speeches and tweets (he basically swapped out "You're fired!" for "Make America Great Again"), and several authors confirm that the features they found contribute to a "narrative" or constitute "storytelling" (see Björkenstam and Gringonitė; Degani and Onysko; Egbert and Biber).

12.6 Conclusion

In this chapter, we asked whether the features of Trump's language described throughout this book fit together as a jigsaw, revealing a pattern of populist rhetoric. We saw that previous analyses tended to conflate Trump's rhetoric with his actions and policies, thus following a definition of populism as ideology. By contrast, we opted for a purely linguistic analysis, following Moffitt's (2016) and Hawkins's (2009) discourse-based definitions of populism as a political style. Moffitt's definition hinges on three characteristics, namely a split between 'the people' and 'the elite,' "bad manners," and instilling a sense of crisis. To these he adds two performative elements, namely the leader–performer and the media–stage. Based on these, we derived twelve hypotheses about the constitutive elements of populist rhetoric. Nearly all of these were corroborated by the findings about Trump's language amassed in this volume. Crucially though, the first and possibly most central hypothesis was only partially confirmed. The findings in this volume revealed a dualistic worldview, yet one where 'the virtuous people' versus 'the corrupt elite' seems a minor distinction with the more prominent rift being that between positively connoted 'Team Trump' and a negatively connoted opposition. This distinction did not seem to be predominantly ideological, but aimed at personal gain, additionally giving the leader precedence over the people.

Furthermore, we found economic principles and media strategies that fit in well with the general rubric of populism but are not mandated by it. This raises the question whether we need to step back and ask, once again, what is populism? At this rhetorical level, it appears to be simply a political get-successful-quick strategy. By purporting a sense of urgency and simple solutions, it allows skillful players to rise through the ranks quickly (or in Trump's case, to skip them altogether). Of necessity, this strategy must share features with similar strategies aimed at speedy success—like advertising and reality TV. At this point, the question whether Trump started out with a self-marketing strategy and enriched it with some populist content, or whether he started with populist ideals and shaped them for mediatization purposes, becomes a chicken-and-egg question. Taking into consideration the findings by Lakoff (2017), McCallum-Bayliss (2019), and Hawkins and Littvay (2019), we may conclude that Trump is best described as 'rhetorically populist,' rather than politically populist.

Notes

1 This point is debated, though; see also arguments by, for example, Laclau (2005), Wodak (2017: 555–6) and Bonikowski (2019: 111).
2 This may explain why, in the past, Trump readily participated in discussions about his physical features, taking great care to 'rectify' claims that his hands are small.
3 Of course, we need to keep in mind that not all elements may be a performance in the sense of being somewhat deliberately chosen. For instance, Björkenstam and Grigonitė show that Trump's off-script passages contain more repetition than scripted passages—some of it due to disfluent repetitions. Furthermore, the frequent vague pronouns scratch the "limits of repetition as a cohesive device . . . because none of the participants are mentioned by name." Ronan and Schneider add that Trump's characteristic irrelevant additions and topic shifts do nothing to "transport . . . a simple populist message," rather they are typical for a speaker Trump's age.

References

Beinard, Peter (2019), "The Utter Emptiness of Trump's Populism," *The Atlantic*, November 5. Available online: https://www.theatlantic.com/ideas/archive/2019/11/trumps-populism-has-nothing-to-offer-the-populace/601390/ (accessed February 21, 2020).

Bonikowski, Bart (2019), "Trump's Populism: The Mobilization of Nationalist Cleavages and the Future of U.S. Democracy," in Kurt Weyland and Raúl L. Madrid (eds.), *When Democracy Trumps Populism: Lessons from Europe and Latin America*, 110–31, Cambridge: Cambridge University Press.

Canovan, Margret (1981), *Populism*, London: Junction Books.

Hawkins, Kirk A. (2009), "Is Chávez Populist? Measuring Populist Discourse in Comparative Perspective," *Comparative Political Studies*, 42 (8): 1040–67.
Hawkins, Kirk A. and Levente Littvay (2019), *Contemporary US Populism in Comparative Perspective*, Cambridge: Cambridge University Press.
Krugman, Paul (2019), "Why Isn't Trump a Real Populist?," *The New York Times*, June 17. Available online: https://www.nytimes.com/2019/06/17/opinion/trump-populist.html (February 21, 2020).
Laclau, Ernesto (2005), *On Populist Reason*, London: Verso.
Lakoff, Robin T. (2017), "The Hollow Man. Donald Trump, Populism, and Post-Truth Politics," *Journal of Language and Politics*, 16 (4): 595–606.
McCallum-Bayliss, Heather (2019), "Donald Trump Is a Conqueror: How the Cognitive Analysis of Trump's Discourse Reveals His Worldview," in Encarnación Hidalgo-Tenorio, Miguel-Ángel Benítez-Castro, and Francesca De Cesare (eds.), *Populist Discourse: Critical Approaches to Contemporary Politics*, 242–58, London and New York: Routledge.
Moffitt, Benjamin (2016), *The Global Rise of Populism: Performance, Political Style, and Representation*, Stanford: Stanford University Press.
Mudde, Cas (2007), *Populist Radical Right Parties in Europe*, New York: Cambridge University Press.
Mudde, Cas and Cristóbal Rovira Kaltwasser (2012), "Populism and (Liberal) Democracy: A Framework for Analysis," in Cas Mudde and Cristóbal Rovira Kaltwasser (eds.), *Populism in Europe and the Americas: Threat or Corrective for Democracy?*, 1–26, Cambridge: Cambridge University Press.
Mudde, Cas and Cristóbal Rovira Kaltwasser (2017), *Populism: A Very Short Introduction*, Oxford: Oxford University Press.
Nicolaci da Costa, Pedro (2017), "Trump Is Doing Populism All Wrong," *Business Insider*, May 5. Available online: https://www.businessinsider.com/if-donald-trump-is-a-populist-hes-doing-it-all-wrong-2017-5?r=DE&IR=T (accessed February 21, 2020).
Norris, Pippa and Ronald Inglehart (2019), *Cultural Backlash: Trump, Brexit, and Authoritarian Populism*, Cambridge: Cambridge University Press.
Olsen, Henry (2019), "Trump Is Living up to His Populist Promise," *The Washington Post*, June 25. Available online: https://www.washingtonpost.com/opinions/2019/06/25/trump-is-living-up-his-populist-promise/ (accessed February 21, 2020).
Pérez, Francisco Seoane, Irene Asiaín Román, and Javier Lorenzo Rodríguez (2019), "Seizing the Populist Rhetorical Toolkit: A Comparative Analysis of Trump and Clinton's Discourse on Twitter during the 2016 U.S. Presidential Campaign," in Michele Lockhart (ed.), *President Donald Trump and His Political Discourse: Ramifications of Rhetoric via Twitter*, 13–32. London & New York: Routledge.
Reinfeldt, Sebastian (2000): *Nicht-wir und Die-da. Studien zum rechten Populismus*, Wien: Braumüller.
Truan, Naomi (2019), "Talking about, for and to the People: Populism and Representation in Parliamentary Debates on Europe," *Zeitschrift für Anglistik und Amerikanistik*, 67 (3): 307–37.
Weyland, Kurt and Raúl L. Madrid (2019), "Introduction: Donald Trump's Populism: What Are the Prospects for US Democracy?," in Kurt Weyland and Raúl L. Madrid (eds.), *When Democracy Trumps Populism: European and Latin American Lessons for the United States*, 1–34, Cambridge: Cambridge University Press.
Wodak, Ruth (2017), "The 'Establishment', the 'Élites', and the 'People'. Who's Who?," *Journal of Language and Politics*, 16 (4): 551–65.

Contributors

Douglas Biber is Regents' Professor of English (Applied Linguistics) at Northern Arizona University. His research efforts have focused on corpus linguistics, English grammar, and register variation (in English and cross-linguistic; synchronic and diachronic).

Kristina Nilsson Björkenstam is Director of Studies at the Department of Linguistics, Stockholm University, Sweden. She is a computational linguist, and her main research interests focus on corpus linguistic approaches to the study of language acquisition.

Marta Degani is Associate Professor of English Language and Linguistics at the University of Verona, Italy, and currently holds a position as Senior Scientist of English Linguistics at the University of Klagenfurt, Austria. Her current research focuses on the analysis of political discourse in the frameworks of cognitive semantics and discourse analysis, and the study of language contact and bilingualism in Aotearoa, New Zealand. Her recent books include *Framing the Rhetoric of a Leader. An Analysis of Obama's Election Campaign Speeches* (2015) and *The Languages of Politics. La politique et ses langages*, 2 Volumes (2016, with Frassi and Lorenzetti).

Jesse Egbert is Associate Professor of Applied Linguistics at Northern Arizona University. He specializes in register variation, quantitative research methods in linguistics, and legal interpretation. His most recent book is *Using Corpus Methods to Triangulate Linguistic Analysis* (2019).

Matthias Eitelmann is an assistant professor of English Linguistics at the University of Mainz, Germany. He received his doctorate from the University of Mannheim for a thesis on the Old English heroic poem *Beowulf*. His current research interests include grammatical variation in English and its determining factors, language and media, cultural linguistics as well as theoretical aspects of language change. Published and forthcoming articles are on the role of end-weight in various grammatical variation phenomena, cognate object constructions as well as contrastive and diachronic aspects of the derivational suffix *-ish*. Currently he is working on "End-weight from a Synchronic and Diachronic Perspective."

Irina Frisk is a senior lecturer in English Linguistics at Mid-Sweden University. Her research interests include English syntax, pragmatics, and corpus linguistics.

Gintarė Grigonytė is a machine learning and natural language processing professional with an extensive background in academia.

Jan David Hauck is a British Academy Newton International Fellow in the Department of Anthropology at the London School of Economics and Political Science. His research focuses on language ideologies, language socialization, ethics and morality, and the narrative construction of self. He has worked in the documentation of indigenous languages in Paraguay and has published on purification and hybridization in language policy debates, language emergence in language contact, metalinguistic repairs, and the ontological underpinnings of conceptions of language.

Anthony Koth works at a technology firm in Austin, TX, using his linguistic skills to improve metadata tagging and search relevance. His research interests include cognitive linguistics and discourse analysis and their application to identity formation practices. He recently completed his dissertation *Framing the 2016 Election: Politicians, Parties, and Perspectives* (2019) at Rice University.

Kristene K. McClure is an assistant professor of English at Georgia Gwinnett College, Lawrenceville, GA. Her research interests focus on critical applied and educational linguistics as well as intersections among critical pedagogy, applied linguistics, and writing studies. Past publications include articles in the *Journal of Language, Identity & Education* (2010) and the *European Journal of Applied Linguistics and Teaching English as a Foreign Language* (2017).

Teruko Vida Mitsuhara teaches in the Anthropology department at the University of California, Los Angeles, CA. Her research interests include new religious movements in India and the United States, language socialization, language enchantment, empathy, and feminist theory. She has done long-term research on the everyday life of women and children living in a utopia project in West Bengal, India. She has published on the enregisterment of "Guru English" among white priests in an Indic-inspired movement in the United States as a linguistic vehicle for establishing authenticity.

Alexander Onysko is Full Professor in English Linguistics at the University of Klagenfurt, Austria. His main research interests and publications are in the fields of World Englishes, Language Contact, Bi/Multilingualism, and Cognitive Linguistics. One of his particular interests is on the application of conceptual metaphors in multilingual contexts, in Englishes in New Zealand, and in political discourse. Some of his recent publications include *Language Contact and World Englishes* (2016), *Metaphor Variation in Englishes Around the World* (2017, with Marcus Callies), and *Conceptual Metaphors in Donald Trump's Political Speeches* (2018, with Kateryna Pilyarchuk).

Patricia Ronan is Chair of English Linguistics at the University of Dortmund, Germany. Her main research interests are in the areas of language variation and change, as well as language and cultural contacts and their outcomes, with a particular focus on morpho-syntax and pragmatics. Her current research is focused on new media language, and recent publications include papers on language development, light verb constructions, and expressive markers in media language.

Gerold Schneider is a senior lecturer, researcher, and computing scientist at the departments of Computational Linguistics and English at the University of Zurich, Switzerland. His doctoral degree is on large-scale dependency parsing, his habilitation on using computational models for corpus linguistics. His research interests include corpus linguistics, statistical approaches, digital humanities, text mining, and language modeling. He has published over one hundred articles on these topics. He has just published a book on statistics for linguists (https://dlf.uzh.ch/openbooks/statisticsfor linguists/), and a new book on digital humanities is forthcoming. His Google scholar page is https://scholar.google.com/citations?user=l_8L7NYAAAAJ

Ulrike Schneider is an assistant professor of English Linguistics at the University of Mainz, Germany. Her current research interests include usage-based and functional grammar, cognitive linguistics as well as grammatical variation and change. Currently she is working on a post-doctoral project on the role of transitivity in the diachronic change of verbal constructions. She holds a PhD from the University of Freiburg, Germany. Her publications include "ΔP as a Measure of Collocation Strength" (2018), "Detransitivisation as a Support Strategy for Causative *Bring*" (2016, with Britta Mondorf), and *Frequency, Chunks and Hesitations. A Usage-based Analysis of Chunking in English* (2014).

Christoph Schubert is Full Professor of English Linguistics at the University of Vechta, Germany. He has published mainly in the areas of discourse studies, pragmatics, stylistics, and text linguistics. He is the author of an introduction to English text linguistics (2012), co-editor of a special issue of the *Journal of Language and Politics* entitled *Cognitive Perspectives on Political Discourse* (2014), co-editor of the collective volumes *Variational Text Linguistics: Revisiting Register in English* (2016) and *Pragmatic Perspectives on Postcolonial Discourse: Linguistics and Literature* (2016), and co-author of the new edition of the handbook *Introduction to Discourse Studies* (2018).

Ulrike Stange is a research assistant at the University of Mainz, Germany. Her research currently focuses on the use of pseudo-passives in British English and on innovative uses of the intensifier *so*. She is the author of *Emotive Interjections in British English* (Benjamins, 2016) and holds a PhD in English linguistics from the University of Mainz.

Jukka Tyrkkö is Full Professor of English Linguistics at Linnaeus University, Sweden, previously Professor of English at the University of Tampere, Finland, and Visiting Professor in Digital Humanities at the University of Turku, Finland. He has published widely on corpus linguistics, text annotation, historical linguistics with particular reference to lexis and phraseology, political language, and multilingualism. Tyrkkö has edited nine academic volumes, most recently *Historical Dictionaries in their Paratextual Context* (2018, with Rod McConchie) and *Applications of Pattern-Driven Methods in Corpus Linguistics* (2018, with Joanna Kopaczyk). He is series co-editor of Language, Data Science and Digital Humanities for Bloomsbury Academic.

Index

Access Hollywood tape 6, 26–7, 216, 220, 222, 224, 226–30
  video statement 221, 223, 225–6, 228–9
accomplishments 25, 28
adjective 27, 31, 88, 90–1, 93–105, 115, 188, 205
  absolute 25, 27–8, 89
  comparative 97, 211
  non-gradable 88, 91, 101–2, 105–6, 245
  pre-modification 21, 36–6, 63, 88, 183
  superlative 186, 211
adverb 21, 87, 208, 211
  intensified 90–1, 94, 96, 99, 101, 103–4
  negative 27
  stance 31–3, 245
advertising 2, 201, 248–9
African Americans 131, 134, 138–9, 143, 145–6, 150 n.1, 244
aggrandizement, *see* self-aggrandizing language
aging
  normal 2, 65–6, 72–81
  pathological 67–8, 72 (*see also* dementia)
Al Smith dinner 51–2
alternative facts 200
American exceptionalism 155, 164, 168–70
American Presidency Project 19, 48, 69, 202
American supremacy 155, 164, 170
anaphoric reference 23, 44, 93
anecdote 23, 32, 242
antagonizing 9, 237
antecedent 23, 171 n.4
anti-environmental stance 9, 175–6, 179
anti-establishment 9, 127, 134, 210, 239–45

apology 9, 215–31, 245
  mass-mediatized 215, 230
The Apprentice 1, 7, 38, 56, 114, 120, 199, 248
attack 113, 199, 202, 204, 211–12
  against the media 113, 123, 199, 204–6, 210, 240
  against opponents 24, 26, 37, 125, 199, 224, 226, 229–30
  response to 24, 27, 37, 114, 207, 210
audience 41–2, 46, 81, 96, 115, 157, 199, 202, 223, 243–4
  interaction with 34, 43, 56, 109, 114, 142, 180, 200, 204, 206, 225, 245
  participation 45, 48, 51–2, 227, 241
authenticity 9, 58, 134, 216, 218, 222–4, 227

believe me 17, 44, 164–5, 200
bigly 17, 23
bigrams 95, 96, 99, 101–2, 106
border 133
  open 117, 139, 147, 169
  security 24, 26, 149, 165, 168–9, 206–8, 244
branding 1, 7, 110, 134, 179, 196, 245, *see also* Trump brand
Bush, George H.W. 4, 19
Bush, George W. 19, 36, 42, 72, 112
Bush, Jeb 120, 126, 202–3, 210–11
businessman 1, 7, 164, 210, 247
business strategies 2–7, 24, 247

campaign speech 42, 46–7, 51–6, 58, 134, 141, 148, 204
candidacy announcement 162–4, 166
casual speech 41–2, 55, 58, 62, 71, 80, 245, *see also* colloquial style; conversational language; informal language
celebrity 1, 216, 242–3, 247
cheating 116, 161–2, 165, 170, 240

Index

child-directed speech   44–6, 49
Christian testimonial   9, 215–16, 218–21, 223, 225, 227, 229–30, 246
clause
   complement   21, 32, 34–5
   coordinated   69, 74–5, 245
   if-clause   75, 222–3
   length   17–18, 36, 64
   relative   142, 144
   subordinated   35, 63, 69, 73–5, 81, 142, 245
climate change   174, 175, 178–9, 184
Clinton, Bill   57, 111, 215, 220–2, 229
Clinton, Hillary
   speaking style   18, 22, 30, 32, 34, 43, 50–2, 239–41
   Trump on   5, 24, 26–7, 37, 48, 55–6, 58, 93, 111, 114, 120–2, 125–6, 168–9, 226, 229
CNN   28, 48, 97, 117, 124, 127, 196, 207–8, 210
coding   222, 224, 228
cognitive linguistics   9, 155, 177
coherence   44–5, 65–6, 80
   existential   218, 222–5, 227, 230
cohesion   45, 57–8
collocation   91–2, 95–8, 102, 104–6, 110, 183, 192
colloquial style   4, 23, 28, 36–8, 63, 81, 87, 245, *see also* casual speech; conversational language; informal language
commentary   1, 173
competition   1, 9, 151 n.7, 155–6, 158–68, 170, 247
complexity   3, 5, 18, 64, 66 n.3, 67, 69, 73, 76, 80–1
   reduction in   155, 160–1, 163, 165, 167, 169, 186
conceptualization   9, 159–63, 166, 168–70, 177, 190, 192, 237, 241
conceptual metaphor   4, 9, 120, 155–62, 174, 177, 181, 183, 189, 240, 243
   BUSINESS IS COMPETITION   151 n.7, 156, 158–63, 165–8, 170, 247
   describing the Paris Accord   190–2
   FAIRNESS IS A FLAT SURFACE   190

Great Chain of Being   167, 247
   THE HUMAN IS AN ANIMAL   128 n.4
   IDEAS ARE FOOD   157–8
   IDEAS ARE LOCATIONS   158
   IMMIGRANTS ARE POLLUTANTS   166–7, 169, 244
   THE LEADER IS A CONQUEROR   240
   THE NATION IS A HOUSE   166
   PEOPLE ARE MACHINES   169
conflict   41, 166, 243, 247
Congress   5–6, 36, 119, 122, 144, 147, 176
conjunction   21, 68, 74
conservative
   language   95, 97, 102
   thinking   95, 176–8, 183, 192
contempt   133, 155–6, 160–2, 167–70, 246
contraction   4, 23–4, 63, 245
conversational language   4, 42–3, 55–6, 58–192, 245–6, *see also* casual speech; colloquial style; informal language
conversational maxims
   flouting   198
   maxim of quality   198–9, 203, 205, 212
   maxim of quantity   198–9, 203, 207, 209, 212
   maxim of relevance   225
   violating   198–9, 203, 212
Conway, Kellyanne   200
Cooper, Anderson   48, 227–8
cooperative principle   198, 203, *see also* conversational maxims
corpus   18, 20, 114
cost–benefit analysis   178–9, 217
crime   18, 55, 104, 113, 117, 119, 139, 147–8, 166, 169, 206–8, 222
crisis   147, 238, 242–3, 247–8
Crooked Hillary   5, 55, 57–8, 93, 97, 99, 102, 109, 111, 118–27, 136, 164, 166, 244
Cruz, Ted   5, 114, 123, 125, 164, 166–7, 169–70, 171 n.5, 202–3, 206–7, 210–11

debate   140–1, 162–3, 200, 239
  presidential   6, 8, 17–20, 27–30, 32–4, 36, 38, 43, 47–8, 50–1, 199, 224, 227–9
  primary   72–3, 169, 197, 199, 201–8, 210, 212
deception   197–8, 208–9, 212
decompetition   159–61, 171 n.2
definite article   9, 90, 131–4, 136–8, 141, 144, 148, 237
deflection   149–50, 215, 224, 228–9
dehumanization   166–7, 169
delegitimization   19, 197, 200–1, 203–12, 240
delexicalization   91
dementia   2, 62, 65, 72
  Alzheimer's dementia   65, 67
denial   185–7, 217, 222, 228, 246
  of climate change   173, 175
  of expert knowledge   242
  of factual evidence   173
denotational content   223, 228, 231 n.9
derogation   122, 133, 146–7, 223
devaluation   211–12, 247
discourse   1, 5, 9, 19, 23, 28, 30–3, 42, 45, 54, 56–7, 115, 130, 145, 171 n.3, 173–4, 177–9, 181, 185–90, 192, 193 n.2, 196–7, 200, 212, 216, 219, 229, 238–9, 241–4
  of dualities   2, 4
  political   4, 7, 38, 77, 103, 105–6, 110, 117, 126–7, 156, 162, 178, 200
  of theater   224
  of truth   224, 228, 230
discourse analysis   17, 115, 174, 181, 200, 218
discourse marker   4, 44, 63, 67, 74, 242
discursive strategies   8–9, 18, 134, 148, 174, 181, 185–7, 192, 201, 216, 239–40
  avoidance   37, 185
  silencing   9, 178–9, 184–92, 193 n.3, 243
disfluency   63, 66–7, 77, 249 n.3, *see also* hesitation
dishonesty   65, 98, 102, 105, 119, 121, 127, 203, 211–12, 223–4
  of the press   49, 57, 97, 197–201, 204–5, 207–8, 247

distancing effect   130–5, 144, 146–8, 189, 218
distinctiveness   7–8, 18, 20, 22, 28, 30, 37–8, 99, 115, 183, 190, 196, 245
drain the swamp   9, 42, 43, 123, 155, 243–4

email   24, 26, 55, 119
emotional
  impact   41, 46, 87, 160, 187–8, 190
  language   42, 90, 96, 104–5, 187, 242, 246–8
emphasis   21, 25, 27, 31–2, 41, 55, 58, 66, 188, 205, 208, 246
energy
  natural gas   182–3, 188, 192
  nuclear   178, 184
  oil   175, 181–4, 188
  renewable   178, 180, 184–7
  wind power   184, 186–8, 247
environment   9, 93, 94, 161, 173–86, 188
  deregulation of the   174, 179
epistrophe   44–5
establishment   58, 208, 215, 226
ethnic groups   9, 130–1, 133–4, 138, 141, 143–4, 147
euphemism   222
evaluation   8–9, 21, 25, 27, 32–4, 101, 112, 125, 130, 134, 157–60, 164, 167, 186, 201, 204–5, 218, 224, 228, 236, *see also* devaluation
Everyman   216, 219, 221, 223, 225–6
  sinner   216, 223, 230
  victim   216, 229–30
evidentiality   33–4
extraordinariness   2, 99, 182, 242, 245–6

face   199, 204, 206, 212, 217–18, 230 n.3
  face-threatening act   199, 205, 211, 230 n.3
Factba.se   48, 135, 140
fake news   1, 9, 97, 104, 106, 116, 121, 126–7, 139, 196–7, 199201, 203–7, 212, 230 n.3, 247
false claims   9, 183, 196–8, 200, 205
false start   63–4, 67, 77–9, 81, *see also* repair
first-frame interaction   202, 205–6, 211
Flesch-Kincaid Test   3

folk knowledge 156, 167–8, 170, 224, 247
  folk economics 161, 167
  folk immigration 167, 169
  folk linguistics 17, 125
formal language 3–4, 51, 58, 64, 75, 104–5
fourth estate 199, 212
Fox & Friends 68, 70–1, 74–5, 77, 79–80
framing 6, 18, 42, 148, 170, 174, 176–8, 181–3, 185–6, 190, 192, 203, 206, 221–4, 228, 242
frankly 22, 25, 74, 209–10, 227

generally speaking 207–8
gesture 17–18, 67, 134
global warming 5, 173, 178–9, 184, 188, 192, 247
grammar 8, 18, 30, 38, 41, 63, 87, 239
grandiose terms 28, 245

hedging 21, 37, 185
hesitation 45, 67, 82 n.2, 145, 162, 242, *see also* disfluency; repair
highlighting 222–4
Hispanics 74, 130–1, 138–50, 151 n.6, 205–6, 244
homogenizing effect 130–1, 133–4, 144, 146, 148, 150, 237
huge 17, 89
hyperbole 17, 27, 37, 87, 212, 241

ideology 155, 160, 170, 176–9, 183, 201, 219, 244
  Democratic 174, 179
  ideological divides 176–7
  fascist 162
  framing 174
  nationalist 162
  Republican 174, 179, 192
idiolect 7–8, 17, 135, 200, 212
immigration 9, 22, 28, 117, 138–9, 147, 156, 166–70, 179, 196, 207–8, 240–1, 244
impeachment 6, 220
imperative 17, 45, 97
impoliteness 199–200, 204, 206, 212, 230 n.3

incoherence 57, 62, 76, 79–81, 218
indefinite terms 66, 71, 206, 211, *see also* vague language
indexical reference 224–5, 228, 231 n.9
industrialization 186, 188–9, 192
informal language 4–5, 17, 36, 51, 58, 75–6, 105, *see also* casual speech; colloquial style; conversational language
in-group 109, 115, 162, 170, 244
intensifier 88–91, 100–1, 104–6, 245–6
  amplifier 21, 27, 31–2, 89, 94–5, 99, 104–6 (*see also totally*; *very*)
  approximator 89, 103
  booster 88–9, 94, 101–2, 104–5
  compromiser 89, 103
  diminisher 89, 103
  downtoner 88–9, 91, 103–6
  maximizer 88–9, 94, 211
  minimizer 89
interruption 17, 211
  self-interruption 56, 149
interview 10, 62, 68, 71–3, 75, 77, 79–80, 87, 109, 140–1, 143, 146, 173, 183, 200
irrelevance 79, 81, 246
ISIS 6, 22, 26–7, 165, 227–8

Kelly, Megyn 102, 121, 123, 166
key feature analysis 20, 30, 37

LancsBox 93
Lewinsky, Monica 9, 215, 220–1
lexical choices 18, 20, 23, 30, 37, 174, 177, 181, 184–5, 192
lexico-grammatical feature 20–1, 30–1, 33, 37
liberalism 176–8, 237
locker room banter 6, 24, 26, 222, 227–9, 231 n.9, 246
losing 1, 5, 9, 113–14, 120, 155–6, 159–61, 163–4, 167–70, 226, 246, 247
lying 2, 9, 25, 27, 29, 34, 44, 77, 121, 123, 197–8, 201, 203–5, 207, 210–12, 218, 228
Lyin' Ted 5, 119, 121, 123, 125, 127, 166, 244

McCain, John 43
Make America Great Again 30, 36, 53–4, 121, 155, 162, 164, 168, 170, 188–9, 248
Manichean worldview 241
mannerism 41–2, 242
mapping process 156–8, 160–3, 165–6, 224, 230
masculinity 215, 228, 230 n.1
matiness 18, *see also* normal guy ethos; ordinariness
media, *see also* populism
    coverage 2, 8, 10 n.2, 17–18, 41, 57, 127, 165, 173, 197, 224, 238
    mainstream 9, 197, 200, 208, 247
    reaction to 9, 26, 46, 57, 102, 104, 116, 126–7, 196, 199–201, 203–10, 212, 240, 243–4, 247
    social 4, 6, 114, 117, 126–7, 197, 199 (*see also* Twitter)
mediatization 7, 215, 219, 225, 230, 243, 248–9
metaphor *see* conceptual metaphor
Mexicans 113, 130, 134, 138–9, 148–50, 164, 166, 207–8
minoritization 9, 130–1, 133–4, 138–40, 150, 150 n.1
misinformation 183, 197–8, 201, 210, 212
misogyny 9, 216, 222
misrepresentation 197, 200–1, 203–5, 207, 209–10, 212
mitigation 62, 91, 146, 175, 185, 217, 222, 224, 230 n.3
mock names 111–12, *see also* nicknames
moral judgment 110, 116, 121, 124–5, 160, 177, 246
Muslims 130–1, 134, 138–9, 146, 167, 208

name-calling 17, 166
narcissism 2, 240
narrative 57–8, 216, 218–19, 223, 248
    frame 222, 224, 228
    language 23, 30–1, 33, 37, 75
    structure 223, 227
negative language 2, 4, 8–9, 27, 29, 99, 105, 111, 113, 133, 147–50, 170, 190, 192, 196–7, 200

New York Times 9, 52, 68, 71–2, 75, 93, 116–17, 125–6, 173, 196, 200, 204, 235–6
nicknames 7–8, 17, 109–13, 115–27, 245–6
normal guy ethos 3, *see also* matiness; ordinariness
noun 21, 27, 31, 35–6, 69–71, 75–6, 242, 245
    phrase 36, 64, 130
    proper 25, 29
Nurturant Parent model 177

Obama, Barack 19, 26, 29, 36, 41, 43, 45, 50, 57, 68, 71–2, 75–7, 79–80, 93, 102, 113–14, 116, 119, 128 n.4, 139, 143, 166, 173–5, 183, 215, 247
Obamacare 25, 49, 70
offense 112, 128 n.4, n.5, 209, 215, 217–20, 222, 223–6, 228, 230 n.3
opening statements 43, 223
opponents 2, 5, 7–9, 17, 22, 26–8, 32, 36–7, 43, 50, 109, 111, 114, 118, 121, 125–7, 155, 161, 163–8, 170, 184, 187–8, 197, 199, 216, 222, 226–7, 229–30, 240, 242, 244, 246–7
ordinariness 3, 127, 242, 245, *see also* matiness; normal guy ethos
othering 9, 130–31, 134–5, 138, 145, 241
overrepresentation 203, 208–10, 212, 248
oxymoron 148, 183, 192

parallelism 42, 44, 50, 53, 87
paraphrase 43, 45–6, 55, 58, 65
Paris Climate Agreement 6, 9, 174–5, 180–1, 189–90
Pence, Mike 55, 91–3, 95, 104, 106
persuasion 2, 33, 41–2, 90, 130, 177, 186, 199–201, 205, 212, 248
plain language 81, 192, 248, *see also* simple language
Podesta, John 55, 119
polarization 38, 175–6, 241
policymaking 174–5, 180
political correctness 110, 123, 134–5, 208, 212, 238, 242, 245
populism 2, 9, 72, 81, 235–43, 245, 247–9

as ideology   237–8, 241, 248
leader as performer   238, 242, 245, 248–9
media as stage   238, 243, 248 (*see also* under media)
people as audience   238, 243
people *vs.* elite   237–41, 244, 248
as political style   238–9, 241, 248
post-truth approach   200
poverty   36, 122, 143, 148
presidential election   5, 43, 51, 117, 123, 170, 197, 205
press conferences   62, 82 n.1, 127, 141, 196, 213 n.13
pronoun   21–2, 31, 63, 65, 69–70, 75–6, 80–114, *see also* under vague
 first person   2, 17, 22, 24
 indefinite   206, 211
 third person   22, 30–1, 65, 243–5
public self   199, 220
Putin, Vladimir   22, 26, 34, 210

quantifier   28, 210, 246

racial figleaves   135, 146, 150
racialization   130, 138
racism   2, 9, 131, 135, 150, 166, 218, 224, 235, 240
Raddatz, Martha   48, 228–9
rally speeches, *see* campaign speeches
Reagan, Ronald   4, 19, 35–6, 44, 128 n.2, 179
reality TV   1, 199, 202, 225, 248–9
Reform Party   1, 150 n.3
remarks   48, 88, 93–7, 100, 104, 106, 146–7, 174, 180–1, 183–5, 190, 192
repair   55–6, 215
 self-repair   66
repentance   216, 221, 224–7, 229
repetition   18, 23, 28, 41, 43–4, 46, 49–58, 63, 78, 248
 disfluent   66–7
 in old age   65, 77, 81
 rhetorical   42, 45
Republican National Convention   44, 47
resource entitlement belief   161–3, 167–70
rhetoric
 of advertising   2, 248

conservative   178
of denial   186
devices   44–5, 53–5, 58, 66, 77, 177, 188
of fear   30, 187, 247
perverse   216
political   36, 46, 48, 215, 219
populist   9, 62, 72–3, 76, 235–6, 238–41, 244, 249
simple   3, 42
strategy   17, 197, 216, 224
style   4, 54, 71, 155
rhetorical question   34
rhythm   45–6, 48
Rubio, Marco   119–20, 125, 202–3, 210–11
rudeness   2, 199

salience   8, 17–18, 20, 30, 37, 114, 131, 159, 179, 218
Sanders, Bernie   22, 55, 126, 239
scandal   6, 27, 123, 243
scripted speech   7, 36, 42–3, 47–8, 51–8
second-frame interaction   202, 205
self-aggrandizing language   28, 189, 242
self-defense   220, 222, 227
self-marketing strategy   1, 7, 28, 122, 126, 155, 208, 240, 249
semantic bleaching   91, 223, 225, 228, 230
Senate   6, 80, 117, 176
sentence
 complexity   3, 18, 58, 63–4, 66, 69, 73, 75–6, 80–1, 140, 242, 245
 length   3, 18, 23, 41, 63, 66, 68–9, 73–6, 245
 well-formed   62, 64
shared knowledge   57–8, 245
simple
 language   2–3, 8, 18, 41–2, 62–4, 69, 192, 238, 248 (*see also* plain language)
 message   73, 76, 81, 155, 243, 247
simplification   38, 110, 155, 167, 170, 238, 243, 248
sincerity condition   198
slogans   5, 36, 155, 164, 168, 188, 200, 236, 243, 248
speech act   198, 217

speechwriters   7, 43, 48, 54, 62, 68, 239
split self   217, 219, 220, 223, 227–30, 246
spontaneous speech   42–6, 48, 54, 71, 74–5, 245, *see also* unscripted speech
stance
　adverb   21, 31–3, 209–10, 245
　impersonal   30–4, 37–8
　noun   21
stop-and-frisk   23, 26
stream of consciousness   17, 23
Strict Father model   177
stump speeches, *see* campaign speeches

tarmac meeting   57
Telemundo   206
teleprompter script   42–3, 48–9, 52–6, 58, 239
theatricality   220, *see also* discourse of theater
third-person references   21–2, 30–1, 65, 189, 219, 243–5, *see also* under pronoun
Time Magazine   68, 71, 75, 82
totally   6, 25, 27, 32, 87–9, 93–5, 97–8, 102, 104–6, 119, 123, 211, 226, 247
trash-talk   162, 166, 169
tremendous   23, 25, 27, 32, 136, 188, 191, 196, 228
trivialization   161, 187
Trump brand   1, 7, 245, *see also* branding
Trump Twitter Archive   93, 114, 128, 135, 150 n.2, 162
Twitter   4–10, 17, 87–8, 91–106, 107 n.8, 109–17, 120–7, 128 n.5, 131, 135–41, 146–7, 155, 162–3, 168–70, 173, 196–7, 212, 240–1, 248
type–token ratio (TTR)   18, 21, 35–6, 63, 65, 68–9, 71–3

underrepresentation   203, 207–8, 212, 248
unemployment   35, 74, 139, 141, 145–6, 148

unscripted speech   23, 43, 52–8, 62, 76, 78–9, 92–3, 96, *see also* spontaneous speech
us versus *them* mentality   146, 159, 162, 167, 244

vague
　language   23, 25, 28–9, 32, 34, 68–71, 81, 106, 150, 179, 217, 225, 241, 243–4
　pronominal reference   22–3, 57, 69–70, 81, 245–7
verb   28, 31, 34, 36, 69, 75–6, 81, 90, 185–6, 188, 222, 242, 245
　auxiliary   63, 140
　communication   30–2
　contracted (*see* contraction)
　lexical   22–4, 26
　negative   27
　past tense   30–2
　phrase   48
verbosity   65, 79–80
very   8, 25, 27, 32, 66, 87–92, 94–6, 100–2, 104–6, 186–7, 208, 246
vocabulary   3, 8, 18, 36–7, 41–2, 50, 63, 69, 87, 120, 122, 163, 177, 181, 185, 242, 245
　richness   64, 67, 71–3, 81, 245

Wall Street Journal   68, 77, 80
Warren, Elizabeth   120, 125–6
Washington Post   104, 109, 196, 200, 236
white supremacy   135, 216, 235, 240
winning   9, 147, 155–6, 158–65, 170, 190, 221, 246–7
working memory   64–5, 69, 73, 77, 80–1
written language   3–4, 63, 66, 222

xenophobia   240

zero-sum situation   9, 155–6, 159–63, 167–70, 247

www.ingramcontent.com/pod-product-compliance
Lightning Source LLC
Chambersburg PA
CBHW072135290426
44111CB00012B/1879